International Education and Foreign Languages

KEYS TO SECURING AMERICA'S FUTURE

Committee to Review the Title VI and Fulbright-Hays
International Education Programs

Mary Ellen O'Connell and Janet L. Norwood, *Editors*

Center for Education
Division of Behavioral and Social Sciences and Education

NATIONAL RESEARCH COUNCIL
OF THE NATIONAL ACADEMIES

THE NATIONAL ACADEMIES PRESS
Washington, D.C.
www.nap.edu

THE NATIONAL ACADEMIES PRESS   500 Fifth Street, N.W.   Washington, DC 20001

NOTICE: The project that is the subject of this report was approved by the Governing Board of the National Research Council, whose members are drawn from the councils of the National Academy of Sciences, the National Academy of Engineering, and the Institute of Medicine. The members of the committee responsible for the report were chosen for their special competences and with regard for appropriate balance.

This study was supported by Grant No. ED05CO0016 between the National Academy of Sciences and the United States Department of Education. Any opinions, findings, conclusions, or recommendations expressed in this publication are those of the author(s) and do not necessarily reflect the views of the organizations or agencies that provided support for the project.

Library of Congress Cataloging-in-Publication Data

International education and foreign languages : keys to securing America's future / Committee to Review the Title VI and Fulbright-Hays International Education Programs ; Mary Ellen O'Connell and Janet L. Norwood, editors.
    p. cm.
  ISBN-13: 978-0-309-10494-4 (case : alk. paper)
  ISBN-10: 0-309-10494-7 (case : alk. paper) 1. Language and languages—Study and teaching (Higher)—United States. 2. Area studies—United States. I. O'Connell, Mary Ellen, 1960- II. Norwood, Janet Lippe. III. National Research Council (U.S.). Committee to Review the Title VI and Fulbright-Hays International Education Programs.
  P57.U7I58 2007
  418.0071'173—dc22
                            2007014905

Additional copies of this report are available from the National Academies Press, 500 Fifth Street, N.W., Lockbox 285, Washington, DC 20055; (800) 624-6242 or (202) 334-3313 (in the Washington metropolitan area); Internet, http://www.nap.edu.

Printed in the United States of America

Cover: The languages used on the cover are the six official languages used by the United Nations in its meetings and documents: Arabic, Chinese, English, French, Russian, and Spanish.

Suggested citation: National Research Council (2007). *International Education and Foreign Languages: Keys to Securing America's Future*, Committee to Review the Title VI and Fulbright-Hays International Education Programs, M.E. O'Connell and J.L. Norwood, Editors. Center for Education, Division of Behavioral and Social Sciences and Education. Washington, DC: The National Academies Press.

THE NATIONAL ACADEMIES
Advisers to the Nation on Science, Engineering, and Medicine

The **National Academy of Sciences** is a private, nonprofit, self-perpetuating society of distinguished scholars engaged in scientific and engineering research, dedicated to the furtherance of science and technology and to their use for the general welfare. Upon the authority of the charter granted to it by the Congress in 1863, the Academy has a mandate that requires it to advise the federal government on scientific and technical matters. Dr. Ralph J. Cicerone is president of the National Academy of Sciences.

The **National Academy of Engineering** was established in 1964, under the charter of the National Academy of Sciences, as a parallel organization of outstanding engineers. It is autonomous in its administration and in the selection of its members, sharing with the National Academy of Sciences the responsibility for advising the federal government. The National Academy of Engineering also sponsors engineering programs aimed at meeting national needs, encourages education and research, and recognizes the superior achievements of engineers. Dr. Charles M. Vest is president of the National Academy of Engineering.

The **Institute of Medicine** was established in 1970 by the National Academy of Sciences to secure the services of eminent members of appropriate professions in the examination of policy matters pertaining to the health of the public. The Institute acts under the responsibility given to the National Academy of Sciences by its congressional charter to be an adviser to the federal government and, upon its own initiative, to identify issues of medical care, research, and education. Dr. Harvey V. Fineberg is president of the Institute of Medicine.

The **National Research Council** was organized by the National Academy of Sciences in 1916 to associate the broad community of science and technology with the Academy's purposes of furthering knowledge and advising the federal government. Functioning in accordance with general policies determined by the Academy, the Council has become the principal operating agency of both the National Academy of Sciences and the National Academy of Engineering in providing services to the government, the public, and the scientific and engineering communities. The Council is administered jointly by both Academies and the Institute of Medicine. Dr. Ralph J. Cicerone and Dr. Charles M. Vest are chair and vice chair, respectively, of the National Research Council.

www.national-academies.org

v

Acknowledgments

This report is the work of the Committee to Review the Title VI and Fulbright-Hays International Education Programs, a project of the National Research Council (NRC). The expertise and hard work of the committee was advanced by the support of our sponsor, the contributions of able consultants and staff, and the input of outside experts and university officials. The funding for this project was provided by the U.S. Department of Education (ED). ED staff provided valuable insight into the programs and readily responded to numerous and repeated requests for financial and other data and other inquiries. Karla Ver Bryck Block, our project officer, provided continued support throughout the project, provided valuable clarification of multiple issues, and served as a valuable resource for the committee.

Throughout this process, the committee benefited from oral or written input by individuals with a range of perspectives: Susan Beaudoin, U.S. Department of Education; Melissa H. Birch, Center for International Business Education and Research, University of Kansas; Robert Blake, University of California Language Consortium; Christine L. Brown, Glastonbury Public Schools; William Brustein, University Center for International Studies, University of Pittsburgh; Diane Castiglione, U.S. Department of State; Mark Chichester, Institute for International Public Policy, The College Fund/UNCF; Donna Christian, Center for Applied Linguistics; The Honorable David S.C. Chu, Under Secretary of Defense for Personnel and Readiness; Carlotta Cooke Joyner, CCJ Consulting; Dan E. Davidson, American Councils for International Education: ACTR/ACCELS; J. David Edwards, Joint National Committee for Languages and the National Council for Languages and International Studies; Bradley Farnsworth, Center for International Business Education, Stephen M. Ross School of Business, University of Michigan; Albert Fishlow, Columbia University; William Foltz, Department of African Studies and Political Science, Yale University; Uliana Gabara, University of Richmond; Ralph Hines, U.S. Department of Education; Interagency Language Roundtable—Frederick H. Jackson, Scott G. McGinnis, and Glenn Nordin; Catharine Keatley, The National Capital Language Resource Center; Ben L. Kedia, Wang Center for International Business and Research and International MBA Program, University of Memphis; Michael D. Kennedy, Center for Russian and East European Studies and Center for European Studies/European Union Center, University of Michigan; Charles Kolb, Committee for Economic Development; Martin Kramer, The Washington Institute for Near East Policy; Lewis Kraus, InfoUse; Stanley Kurtz, Hudson Institute; Mary Ellen Lane, Council of American Overseas Research Centers; Linda Lim, Stephen M. Ross School of Business and Center for Southeast Asian Studies, University of Michigan; Gilbert Merkx, Center for International Studies, Duke University; Barbara D. Metcalf, Center for South Asian Studies, University of Michigan; Kelly Jett Murphrey, Center for Study of Western Hemispheric Trade, Center for International Business Studies, May Business School, Texas A&M University; James Nye, South Asia Language and Area Center, University of Chicago; Patrick O'Meara, Indiana University; Steven Poulos, South Asia Language Resource Center, University of Chicago; Nancy L. Ruther, MacMillan Center for International and Area Studies and Yale University; Sandra Sanneh, Yale Program in African Languages, Yale University; Ann Imlah Schneider, International Education Consultant, Washington, DC; Tony Stewart, North Carolina State University; Vivien Stewart, Asia Society; Mark Tessler, University of Michigan; Karla Ver Bryck Block, U.S. Department of Education; and David Wiley, African Studies Center, Michigan State University. We thank all of them for their valuable contributions, as well as the many people who attended the committee's open sessions.

We appreciate the contributions of several people who responded to inquiries from the committee between meetings, including Richard Brecht, National Foreign Language Center, University of Maryland; Miriam Kazanjian, Coalition for International Education; Carl Falsgraff, University of Oregon; Dorry Kenyon, Center for Applied Linguistics; Frederick H. Jackson, Interagency Language Roundtable and Foreign Service Institute; Rick A. Ruth and Lauren Marcott, Department of State; Robert O. Slater, National Security Education Program; and staff of the International Education Programs Service office.

The committee also thanks those who wrote papers that were invaluable to the committee's discussions: Carlotta Cooke Joyner, CCJ Consulting; Margaret Malone, Center for Applied Linguistics; Nancy L. Ruther, MacMillan Center for International and Area Studies and Yale University;

and Joanna Slater, independent consultant, New York City. Jeremy Browne, Brigham Young University, worked with the committee throughout the study, providing essential feedback on the EELIAS database and provided multiple analyses that aided the committee's deliberations.

The committee gained tremendous insight through site visits conducted at eight universities throughout the country. The committee met with university administrators, Title VI program directors and staff, and faculty, students, and librarians affiliated with the Title VI programs. We would like to thank all of them for the time they spent preparing materials for and meeting with committee members. In particular, we would like to thank Gilles Bousquet and Cynthia Williams from the University of Wisconsin-Madison; Kathy Bellows, Scott Fleming, and James O'Donnell from Georgetown University; Carol Sigelman from the George Washington University; Amanda Ciccarelli and Patrick O'Meara from Indiana University; Pierre C. Hohenberg, David McLaughlin, and Amber Min-Lee from New York University; Joanna Kukielka-Blaser and Jerry Ladman from Ohio State University; Makayla Branscomb, Nancy A. Marlin, and Alan Sweedler from San Diego State University; and German Esparza and Ronald Rogowski from the University of California, Los Angeles, for their help facilitating the meetings.

This report has been reviewed in draft form by individuals chosen for their diverse perspectives and technical expertise, in accordance with procedures approved by the Report Review Committee of the NRC. The purpose of this independent review is to provide candid and critical comments that will assist the institution in making its published report as sound as possible and to ensure that the report meets institutional standards for objectivity, evidence, and responsiveness to the study charge. The review comments and draft manuscript remain confidential to protect the integrity of the deliberative process.

We thank the following individuals for their review of this report: George Breslauer, Provost's Office, University of California, Berkeley; Donna Christian, President's Office, Center for Applied Linguistics, Washington, DC; Ray T. Clifford, Center for Language Studies, Brigham Young University; A. Lee Fritschler, School of Public Policy, George Mason University; Burkart Holzner, Department of Sociology, University of Pittsburgh; Catherine Ingold, Director's Office, National Foreign Language Center, College Park, MD; Lyle V. Jones, L.L. Thurstone Psychometric Laboratory, University of North Carolina; Alfred Mockett, Office of the Chairman and CEO, Motive, Inc., Austin, TX; Michael Nacht, Goldman School of Public Policy, University of California, Berkeley; Robert Sparks, Senior Associate, California Medical Association Foundation, Sacramento, CA; and G. Richard Tucker, Department of Modern Languages, Carnegie Mellon University.

Although the reviewers listed above have provided many constructive comments and suggestions, they were not asked to endorse the conclusions or recommendations nor did they see the final draft of the report before its release. The review of this report was overseen by Kenji Hakuta, School of Education, Stanford University, and Elena Nightingale, Scholar-in-Residence, Institute of Medicine. Appointed by the NRC, they were responsible for making certain that an independent examination of this report was carried out in accordance with institutional procedures and that all review comments were carefully considered. Responsibility for the final content of this report rests entirely with the authoring committee and the institution.

The committee appreciates the support provided by members of the Center for Education (CFE), under the leadership of Richard Murnane. We are grateful for the leadership and support of Michael Feuer, executive director of the NRC's Division of Behavioral and Social Sciences and Education (DBASSE); Martin Orland, senior program director of the CFE; and Patricia Morison, interim director of the CFE and associate director of DBASSE.

The committee also acknowledges the exceptional contributions of the National Academies staff. Throughout its work, the committee benefited from the talent and knowledge of its study director, Mary Ellen O'Connell, who organized the work of the panel, brought together experts to share their experiences with the programs under review, found experts for commissioned papers, and helped to guide the panel through the large amount of material submitted. Her tact and competence in managing many of the difficult questions that faced the panel were especially useful in bringing the project to a successful conclusion. Naomi Chudowsky and Monica Ulewicz conducted critical background research when the committee was first established, and Naomi's ongoing contributions to the committee's research and synthesis tasks were invaluable. Lori Wright analyzed reams of historical financial data, ensured their accuracy, and translated them into a digestible format for the committee. Margaret Hilton provided important leadership in helping to plan and conduct the committee's site visits and helping to collect and synthesize materials for the committee. A final thanks is due to Mary Ann Kasper, who managed the numerous and often complicated administrative tasks of the committee with grace and competence. The panel feels very fortunate to have had them work with us.

Finally, I especially thank the members of the committee for their willingness and dedication in wrestling with an important and complicated issue.

Janet L. Norwood, *Chair*
Committee to Review the Title VI and Fulbright-Hays
International Education Programs

Contents

Acronyms   xiii

Executive Summary   1

PART I: The Title VI and Fulbright-Hays Programs   13
 1 Introduction   15
 2 Demand for Foreign Language, Area, and International
    Expertise   36
 3 Title VI and Fulbright-Hays Implementation   58

PART II: Key Areas of Concern   83
 4 Infusing a Foreign Language and Area Studies Dimension
    and Conducting Outreach and Dissemination   89
 5 Reducing Shortages of Foreign Language and Area Experts 113
 6 Supporting Research, Education and Training   140
 7 Producing Relevant Instructional Materials   156
 8 Advancing Uses of New Technology   171
 9 Addressing Business Needs   182
10 Increasing the Numbers of Underrepresented Minorities in
    International Service   196

PART III: Important Next Steps   209
11 Monitoring, Evaluation, and Continuous Improvement   211
12 Looking Toward the Future   228

References and Bibliography   249

Appendixes

A   Legislative History*   267
B   The Committee's Approach to Its Review   309
C   Selection Criteria and Priorities in Title VI and Fulbright-Hays
     Programs*   350
D   A Brief History of Foreign Language Assessment in the
     United States   360
E   Summary of Federal Foreign Language and Area Studies
     Programs*   365
F   Biographical Sketches of Committee Members and Staff   372

Index   379

---

*Attachment A-1 (Current Title VI Statute, pp. 284-308) of Appendix A, as well as Appendix C (pp. 350-359) and Appendix E (pp. 365-371), are not printed in this volume but are available online. Go to http://www.nap.edu and search for *International Education and Foreign Languages*.

Acronyms

TITLE VI PROGRAMS

AORC   American Overseas Research Centers
BIE   Business and International Education
CIBER   (also CIBE) Centers for International Business Education and Research
FLAS   Foreign Language and Area Studies Fellowships
IIPP   Institute for International Public Policy
IRS   International Research and Studies
LRC   Language Resource Centers
NRC   National Resource Centers
TICFIA   Technological Innovation and Cooperation for Foreign Information Access
UISFL   Undergraduate International Studies and Foreign Language

FULBRIGHT-HAYS PROGRAMS

DDRA   Doctoral Dissertation Research Abroad
FRA   Faculty Research Abroad
GPA   Group Projects Abroad
SA   Seminars Abroad

OTHER ACRONYMS RELATED TO COMMITTEE WORK

AAU	Association of American Universities
ACE	American Council on Education
ACIE	American Councils for International Education
ACLS	American Council of Learned Societies
ACTFL	American Council on the Teaching of Foreign Languages
ADFL	Association of Department of Foreign Languages
AIBER	Association for International Business Education and Research
CAORC	Council of American Overseas Research Centers
CAST	computer-assisted screening tool
CED	Committee for Economic Development
CIE	Coalition for International Education
CIES	Council for International Exchange of Scholars
CLRC	Civilian Linguist Reserve Corps
COPI	Computerized Oral Proficiency Instrument
CNRC	Council of National Research Centers
CPI	Consumer Price Index
CRS	Congressional Research Service
DARPA	Defense Advanced Research Projects Agency, formerly known as the Advanced Research Project Agency, U.S. Department of Defense
DIA	Defense Intelligence Agency
DLI	Defense Language Institute
DoD	U.S. Department of Defense
ED	U.S. Department of Education
EELIAS	Evaluation of Exchange, Language, International and Area Studies database
FAO	U.S. Army Foreign Area Officer Program
FH	Fulbright-Hays International Education Act (Section 102(b)(6)), formally known as the Mutual Educational and Cultural Exchange Act
FIPSE	Fund for the Improvement of Postsecondary Education
FLAP	Foreign Language Assistance Program
FSI	Foreign Service Institute
GAO	Government Accountability Office, formerly known as General Accounting Office
GPRA	Government Performance and Results Act
HBCUs	historically black colleges and universities
HEA	Higher Education Act
IB	International Business Education (also IBE)
IEPS	International Education Programs Service

ILR	Interagency Language Roundtable
IPS	International Programs and Studies
IRIS	International Resource Information System
JNCL	Joint National Committee for Languages
LCTLs	less commonly taught languages (e.g., Arabic, Chinese, Korean, Pashto)
MLA	Modern Language Association
NCASA	National Council of Area Studies Association
NCOLCTL	National Council of Organizations of Less Commonly Taught Languages
NDEA	National Defense Education Act
NFLP	National Flagship Language Program
NSA	National Security Agency
NSEP	National Security Education Program
NSLI	National Security Language Initiative
OPE	Office of Postsecondary Education, U.S. Department of Education
OPEPD	Office of Planning, Evaluation and Policy Development, U.S. Department of Education
OPI	oral proficiency interview
PART	Program Assessment Rating Tool
PPIA	Public Policy and International Affairs Fellowship Program, formerly known as Woodrow Wilson Fellowships in Public Policy and nternational Affairs
RFA	request for applications
SMART	Science and Mathematics Access to Retain Talent
SOFLO	Special Operations Forces Command Foreign Language Office
SOPI	simulated oral proficiency interview
SSRC	Social Science Research Council
Title VI	Title VI of the Higher Education Act

International Education and Foreign Languages

KEYS TO SECURING AMERICA'S FUTURE

Executive Summary

A pervasive lack of knowledge about foreign cultures and foreign languages threatens the security of the United States as well as its ability to compete in the global marketplace and produce an informed citizenry. The U.S. education system has, in recent years, placed little value on speaking languages other than English or on understanding cultures other than one's own. Although there have been times in the country's history when foreign languages were considered as important as mathematics and science, they have reemerged as a significant concern primarily after major events that presented immediate and direct threats to the country's future. Most recently, the events of September 11, 2001, compelled the federal government to reflect on the expertise of its personnel and to focus attention on the need for more and better language skills, particularly in certain languages considered critical.

It would be shortsighted, however, to limit national attention to the needs of government alone. Language skills and cultural expertise are also urgently needed to address economic challenges and the strength of American businesses in an increasingly global marketplace. Professions such as law, health care, social work, and education call out for an international dimension that reflects the changed world environment and increasingly diverse U.S. population. The U.S. education system—from elementary and secondary school to higher education—needs the capacity to provide the requisite training. Higher education needs the capacity to serve as a resource on the politics, economics, religions, and cultures of countries across the globe, countries whose positions on the world stage change over time, often in unpredictable ways. The Title VI and Fulbright-Hays (Title VI/FH)

1

programs are designed to help to serve these broader societal and educational goals as well as to help respond to specific government needs.

During the most recent reauthorization debates related to the Higher Education Act, questions were raised about one set of programs that are designed to help address these needs—the Title VI programs of the Higher Education Act and the education component of the Fulbright-Hays Act. In response, at the request of Congress, the U.S. Department of Education (ED) asked the National Research Council to review the adequacy and effectiveness of these programs in addressing their statutory missions and in building the nation's international and foreign language expertise—particularly as needed for economic, foreign affairs, and national security purposes—and to provide recommendations to enhance future effectiveness. The committee was asked to consider eight key areas specified by Congress in conducting its review. (Box ES-1 presents a list of the eight.)

The Title VI/FH programs were created nearly 50 years ago in response to concerns raised by the Soviet Union's launch of Sputnik and at the time consisted of three programs: the National Resource Centers (NRC), the Foreign Language and Area Studies (FLAS) Fellowships, and International Research and Studies. As a result of reauthorization every six years, programs were added to Title VI to address business needs for international expertise, to improve the programs' reach to undergraduate education, to

---

BOX ES-1
Key Areas Identified by Congress

1. Infusing a foreign language and area studies dimension throughout the education system and across relevant disciplines, including professional education.
2. Conducting public outreach/dissemination to K-12 and higher education, media, government, business, and the public.
3. Reducing shortages of foreign language and area experts.
4. Supporting research, education, and training in foreign languages and international studies, including opportunities for such research, education, and training overseas.
5. Producing relevant instructional materials that meet accepted scholarly standards.
6. Advancing uses of new technology in foreign language and international studies.
7. Addressing business needs for international knowledge and foreign language skills.
8. Increasing the numbers of underrepresented minorities in international service.

focus on international studies as well as area studies, to create new centers focused on language support overseas research centers, to advance technology use, and to bring individuals from minority groups into international service professions. Today there are 10 programs under Title VI and 4 programs under Fulbright-Hays. The legislative history of Title VI has consistently affirmed the connection between language preparation and area scholarship and has adopted a broad focus on creating globally aware students in a range of disciplines.

The committee's review of the programs was hampered by the paucity of rigorous, reliable information on program performance, particularly related to the impacts or outcomes of the programs. The performance measures used by the ED and aggregate annual data reported by grantees provided insufficient information to judge program performance. Also, there have been few well-designed program evaluations that systematically measure outcomes. In reaching our conclusions, the committee relied on the combined weight of the few program evaluation studies, public testimony, historical funding data, grantee data, select commissioned analyses, and a series of site visits to universities that receive Title VI funding. In many cases, however, the limited evidence available did not support making specific recommendations related to the specified key areas.

The committee concluded that the Title VI/FH programs have served as a foundation for internationalization in higher education. Federal funding, sometimes through the priorities set by the ED for individual competitions, has served as a catalyst for language or area studies initiatives in higher education, with a frequent focus on advanced study of less commonly taught languages. Universities themselves have invested significant resources beyond those provided by the ED. The programs have built substantial capacity in the teaching of less commonly taught languages, with Title VI NRCs across the nation offering instruction in more than 250 less commonly taught languages. The programs have also developed instructional and other materials that are used by academia, K-12 education, and government. Box ES-2 presents the committee's specific conclusions related to future program effectiveness as well as with regard to the eight areas specified by Congress.

Nevertheless, Title VI/FH funding, including staff resources, has not kept pace with the expansion in the mission of the programs. While many new programs and objectives have been added since Title VI began, funding in real dollars has not increased proportionately. Not only is there a need for additional resources to match the growing mission of Title VI/FH programs, but there is also a need to expand support for foreign language, area, and international studies throughout the education system. These relatively small programs cannot be expected on their own to address the wide range of needs throughout the entire K-16 education system, as well

---

BOX ES-2
Conclusions Related to Enhancing
Future Program Effectiveness

- ED has not made foreign language and culture a priority and its several programs appear to be fragmented. There is no apparent department master plan or unifying strategic vision.
- Given the recognized lack of knowledge about foreign cultures and foreign languages, additional resources are needed for an integrated and articulated approach in multiple systems, including K-12, higher education, and business, to help address this critical shortcoming.
- There is currently no systematic, ongoing process for assessing national needs for foreign language, area, and international expertise and developing approaches to address those needs.
- Current efforts to develop language assessments and to effectively apply developments in technology to language assessment and the support of language instruction suffer from a dispersion of resources.
- The current data reporting system for Title VI/FH programs (Evaluation of Exchange, Language, International and Area Studies database [EELIAS]) is inadequate, is difficult to use and has significant consistency problems as well as a lack of transparency in the data collected.
- At the present time, limited information is available to rigorously assess the outcomes and impacts of the Title VI/FH programs, and the nature of the funding (partial funding of a larger set of activities) makes it difficult to assess outcomes and impacts.
- Sharing successful grant applications could improve future competitions and contribute to a continual improvement process.

Conclusions Related to the Eight Key Areas

Infusing a foreign language and area studies dimension and conducting outreach (Key Areas 1 and 2)
- NRC and Language Resource Centers have developed multiple and varied methods for reaching out to the K-12 system, particularly to current K-12 teachers. Within the constraints of limited funds, they also attempt to reach out to other audiences.
- The need for teachers with foreign language and international expertise is great.

---

as those of business, government, and the public. Additional resources are needed to develop an integrated and articulated approach in multiple systems, beginning in K-12, to help address this critical shortcoming.

The current administration recently announced the National Security Language Initiative (NSLI) to increase the nation's capacity to provide experts with critical language skills—in languages such as Arabic, Chinese, Farsi/Dari, Hindi/Urdu and Turkic—determined to be vital to national

Reducing shortages of foreign language and area experts **(Key Area 3)**
- The language proficiency of FLAS Fellowships recipients is not at present being adequately assessed.
- Although overseas study has been shown to increase speaking proficiency, ED's policies discourage full-year overseas study by FLAS recipients.

Supporting research, education, and training **(Key Area 4)**
- The Title VI/FH programs have enhanced the body of knowledge about foreign languages and area studies.
- The Title VI/FH programs make a significant contribution to the teaching of less commonly taught languages in particular.

Producing relevant instructional materials **(Key Area 5)**
- The Title VI/FH programs develop a variety of instructional and assessment materials, with many aimed at developing proficiency in less commonly taught languages.
- Although there are no uniform scholarly standards for instructional materials, there are widely accepted "best practice" approaches to materials development that are disseminated by professional associations and journals.

Advancing uses of new technology **(Key Area 6)**
- Title VI/FH programs are using available technologies, such as the Internet and distance learning, but they could do more to maximize the potential created by current technologies.

Addressing business needs **(Key Area 7)**
- The legal requirement for business involvement in Centers for International Business Education and Research (CIBER) boards provides an appropriate mechanism for business input into the program to enable it to address business needs. The CIBER and Business and International Education (BIE) programs appear to act as resources for the larger business education community, providing resources to business education programs that are interested in developing capacity to support teaching and research on business issues.
- The CIBER has created a network for sharing information and learning from each others' experiences that is a model for the other Title VI/FH programs.

Increasing the numbers of underrepresented minorities **(Key Area 8)**
- The Institute for International Public Policy, designed to increase the representation of minorities in international service, has so far produced few graduates who entered international service and would be likely to benefit from a redesign of its program. However, it should not be the sole Title VI/FH program concerned with increasing the number of minorities.

security and foreign policy. The initiative draws on evidence suggesting that mastery of these less commonly taught languages requires many years of study and that learning should begin at an early age. This initiative would provide resources for programs at the U.S. Department of State, the Department of Defense (DoD), the Office of the Director of National Intelligence, and ED, many of them aimed at increasing the number of teachers of critical languages or increasing the number of young students studying critical languages. Although the initiative has not yet been funded, several federal agencies have refocused the resources of existing programs toward these critical languages.

When ED targeted resources toward critical languages under its Foreign Language Assistance Program (FLAP) (a program complementary to Title VI/FH that provides resources to elementary and secondary schools), outside groups expressed concern that such a narrow focus would be detrimental to the foreign language field. The critical, strategic world areas, and the languages people in those areas speak, are not always predictable. Having the capacity to respond to new and unanticipated challenges requires maintaining capacity in a broad range of languages. The committee concluded that, while greater infusion of foreign languages and cultural instruction is vitally needed in K-12 education, too narrow a focus on a small set of languages in either K-12 or higher education could be detrimental to the country.

Although international education has begun to emerge as a concern in ED, strategic coordination either in the department or with other federal agencies has not. The Title VI/FH programs are not currently administered at the executive level at ED; there is no formal mechanism for coordination across programs; and functions and activities related to foreign languages and international education are scattered throughout the agency. And unlike DoD and the State Department, which place responsibility for the NSLI initiative with a senior executive staff person, ED's efforts have been coordinated by a politically appointed adviser to the assistant secretary for postsecondary education. Finally, ED, as the federal agency with clear responsibility for education issues, should have a more visible presence in directing efforts aimed at education, particularly K-12 education.

> ***Recommendation:*** The Department of Education should consolidate oversight of its international education and foreign language programs under an executive-level person who would also provide strategic direction and consult and coordinate with other federal agencies. The position should be one that requires presidential appointment and Senate confirmation (12.1).

The resources of ED should be coordinated with the resources of other programs. The Title VI/FH programs play a unique role among the array of federal programs by focusing on creating a broad infrastructure in higher education, whereas FLAP provides resources to K-12 education. DoD's Defense Language Institute and the State Department's Foreign Service Institute are designed to address specific governmental needs for particular language skills at specific points in time. DoD's National Security Education Program targets critical languages and includes a government service requirement. All relevant federal agencies should have a formal mechanism to consider the range of national needs for area and international education and foreign languages and the appropriate balance between maintaining capacity in a range of languages and areas of the world and responding to immediate needs. The committee concludes that this is best accomplished through a regular, publicly available report to Congress.

> *Recommendation:* Congress should require the secretary of education, in consultation and coordination with the Departments of State and Defense, the Office of the Director of National Intelligence, and other relevant agencies to submit a biennial report outlining national needs identified in foreign language, area, and international studies, plans for addressing these needs, and progress made. This report should be made available to the public (12.2).

To implement this recommendation most effectively, information on both needs and program accomplishments will need to be improved across government. For example, one of the primary criticisms directed at the Title VI/FH programs was that they do not produce graduates with sufficient levels of language proficiency. ED requires recipients of FLAS Fellowships and Doctoral Dissertation Research Abroad, the primary programs aimed at advanced language study by individual students, to provide, upon completion of their fellowship, self-ratings of their proficiency before and after their fellowship. However, there is no available evidence of the reliability or validity of these ratings, and the way it is implemented limits its use in assessing student's proficiency. If self-assessment is to be maintained, a more reliable and valid approach should be developed.

> *Recommendation:* The Department of Education should stop using its current self-assessment approach and develop an alternative approach to measuring foreign language proficiency with demonstrated reliability and validity (5.2).

At the same time, demand for proficiency assessment has increased and is likely to continue to increase, both to demonstrate the language results of select Title VI/FH programs and to determine the success of a range of new foreign language initiatives in government and in elementary and secondary education. Although ED has encouraged the development of other standardized assessments, these efforts have received limited funding, have been widely dispersed among the Title VI centers, and have not yet addressed many of the less commonly taught languages.

Similarly, information and communication technology has made significant and continual progress; this progress provides unharnessed opportunities to advance foreign language assessment and instruction. Technology provides particular opportunities to advance instruction of less commonly taught languages—languages that are among the strengths of the Title VI/FH programs and a subset of which are of particular current interest in the federal government. Investment in research and development that marries language instruction and assessment efforts with technology would benefit the range of federal agencies concerned with international education and foreign languages. It will also require coordinated effort by individuals with a range of specific areas of expertise.

Recommendation: The federal government should contract for a new National Foreign Language Assessment and Technology Project. The initial focus of the project should be on the research and development needed to design and implement a range of new technology-based methods for (1) assessing language proficiency and (2) supporting language instruction through the development of common platforms (12.3).

In general, meaningful data on program performance is lacking. Grantees must report extensive annual information via a web-based reporting system. However, technical issues with the system design, staffing limitations at ED that affect staff ability to ensure data quality and integrity, and widely held perceptions by grantees that the system is a burden without benefit, limit its use. Although the department recognizes many of these issues and has implemented system improvements to address several technical issues, there is no immediate plan to assess the relevance of performance measures or to make data fully available to grantees or to the public that might improve program transparency.

Recommendation: The Department of Education should ensure that its new data system, the International Resource Information System, provides greater standardization, allows comparison across years and across programs, and provides information to all grantees and to the public (11.1).

In addition, meaningful evaluations of outcomes and impacts are lacking. More rigorous, periodic evaluations are needed to ensure public accountability, inform the process of regular reauthorization, and advance continued departmental efforts to stimulate internationalization.

Recommendation: The Department of Education should commission independent outcome and impact evaluations of all programs every 4 to 5 years (11.2).

Unlike earlier years, when the Department of Education measured performance of all 10 Title VI programs using measures based on just two programs, they now have three measures approved by the Office of Management and Budget for most of the 10 programs (one has only two measures). These measures meet federal reporting requirements but appear to have little buy-in from grantees and capture only isolated aspects of the program. The measures used for the NRC program, for example, do not capture outreach activities emphasized by the department nor advanced language offerings. In general, in the recent past, there has been little effort to collaborate with universities to specify mutual goals, measures that address those goals, and promising approaches to best meet goals. Such collaboration requires the executive-level leadership mentioned earlier and could build on emerging efforts by program staff to take a broader view of the program, the collaborative networks developed by grantees of the largest programs, and the significant expertise that has developed in some universities. Universities must be ready partners willing to refine and direct their programs toward mutual goals.

Recommendation: The Department of Education should work with universities to create a system of continuous improvement for the Title VI and Fulbright-Hays programs. The system would help develop performance indicators and other improvement tools and should include networks of similar centers (National Resource Centers, Language Resource Centers, Centers for International Business Education and Research) and university officials with overall responsibilities in language, area, and international studies (11.3).

The Title VI/FH programs were created nearly 50 years ago, when the country's economic, political, and military challenges were narrower than they are today. The mission of the programs has continually expanded to address national needs for internationalization across multiple systems without a concurrent increase in funding. As the programs face their next 50 years, they must be more closely aligned with other federal resources to ensure that resources operate in a complementary way and maximize achievement of multiple goals. They must implement efforts to achieve specific objectives more effectively (see the full list of recommendations in Box ES-3), must be held more accountable for performance via collaborative mechanisms between universities and ED, and must harness the opportunities and challenges presented by a world increasingly dominated by technology.

BOX ES-3
All Recommendations*

Recommendation 4.1: The Department of Education should increase incentives in the application process for National Resource Centers and Language Resource Centers to collaborate with schools or colleges of education on their campuses in the development of curriculum, the design of instructional materials, and teacher education.

Recommendation 5.1: The Department of Education should modify its policy guidelines to encourage overseas study by Foreign Language and Area Studies fellows.

Recommendation 5.2: The Department of Education should stop using its current self-assessment approach and develop an alternative approach to measuring foreign language proficiency with demonstrated reliability and validity.

Recommendation 10.1: The Institute for International Public Policy should redesign its activities in order to increase graduation rates and facilitate entry in careers in international service.

Recommendation 10.2: The Department of Education should encourage Title VI and Fulbright-Hays grantees to actively recruit minority members.

Recommendation 11.1: The Department of Education should ensure that its new data system, the International Resource Information System, provides greater standardization, allows comparison across years and across programs, and provides information to all grantees and to the public.

---

*The recommendation number refers to the chapter in which the recommendation appears and the number of recommendations in that chapter.

Recommendation 11.2: The Department of Education should commission independent outcome and impact evaluations of all programs every 4 to 5 years.

Recommendation 11.3: The Department of Education should work with universities to create a system of continuous improvement for the Title VI and Fulbright-Hays programs. The system would help develop performance indicators and other improvement tools and should include networks of similar centers (National Resource Centers, Language Resource Centers, Centers for International Business Education and Research) and university officials with overall responsibilities in language, area, and international studies.

Recommendation 11.4: The Department of Education should make its award selection process more transparent, including making successful applications publicly available via the Internet.

Recommendation 12.1: The Department of Education should consolidate oversight of its international education and foreign language programs under an executive-level person who would also provide strategic direction and consult and coordinate with other federal agencies. The position should be one that requires presidential appointment and Senate confirmation.

Recommendation 12.2: Congress should require the secretary of education, in consultation and coordination with the Departments of State and Defense, the Office of the Director of National Intelligence, and other relevant agencies to submit a biennial report outlining national needs identified in foreign language, area, and international studies, plans for addressing these needs, and progress made. This report should be made available to the public.

Recommendation 12.3: The federal government should contract for a new National Foreign Language Assessment and Technology Project. The initial focus of the project should be on the research and development needed to design and implement a range of new technology-based methods for (1) assessing language proficiency and (2) supporting language instruction through the development of common platforms.

Part I

The Title VI and Fulbright-Hays Programs

1

Introduction

A pervasive lack of knowledge about foreign cultures and foreign languages[1] in this country threatens the security of the United States as well as its ability to compete in the global marketplace and produce an informed citizenry. The U.S. education system places little value on speaking languages other than English and on understanding cultures other than one's own. Less than half (43.4 percent) of all U.S. high school students were enrolled in a foreign language class in 2000; even fewer study a language when they move on to college (National Center for Education Statistics, 2005). In 2002, less than 10 percent of all college students were enrolled in foreign language courses (Welles, 2004). Similarly, students in the United States tend to understand less about the beliefs, cultures, and history of other nations than their foreign counterparts.

At the same time, the need for language and area expertise is compelling. The federal government has experienced the lack of foreign language experts with appropriate cultural competence for some time. A particularly prescient research report prepared for the U.S. Department of Education (ED) and published August 2001 stated (Brecht and Rivers, 2000, p. 2):

> The United States today faces a critical shortage of linguistically competent professionals across federal agencies and departments responsible for national security. The inability of intelligence officers, military personnel, disease specialists, law enforcement officers and other federal employees to

---

[1]Although there is debate in this country about the appropriate term for languages other than English, with some supporting use of "world languages," we have adopted the term "foreign languages" since it is used in the committee's charge.

understand information from foreign sources and to interact with foreign nationals in virtually every country on the globe presents a threat to their mission and to the well-being of the nation.

The report went on to point out what it characterized as a severe shortage of foreign language professionals in the 80 federal departments or agencies that have a need for them. But foreign language professionals are needed not only in federal bureaucracies. People with language skills and area expertise also are needed to ensure the nation's ability to compete economically. Increasing foreign competition and declining market shares for U.S. products highlight the need for globally competent business representatives. According to statistics compiled by the U.S. Department of Commerce, U.S. exports as a percentage of world trade have fallen over the past 25 years, even in areas of traditional American strength, such as telecommunications equipment and agricultural products (U.S. Department of Commerce, n.d.). For U.S. businesses to penetrate foreign markets, they need an understanding of foreign cultures and economies and how to best interact with possible customers and trading partners (Kedia and Daniel, 2003; Committee for Economic Development, 2006).

The education system is similarly hampered by a lack of needed teaching personnel. Universities report difficulty in identifying instructors for some less commonly taught languages. Elementary and secondary school administrators who want to offer such languages report difficulty finding trained teachers and needed materials. School curricula are considered inadequate in terms of meaningful international or multicultural content (Roper Public Affairs and Media, 2002; Harding, 2005). In addition, as the world economy becomes more and more integrated, there is more need for a citizenry with a greater understanding of global politics and economics. There is a need not only for people with such skills, but also for more institutions, quality resources, and trained teachers to teach them.

The international education programs that focus on foreign languages and area studies at ED—the Title VI and Fulbright-Hays (Title VI/FH) programs—are designed to "strengthen the capability and performance of American education in foreign languages and in area and international studies" and "improve secondary and postsecondary teaching and research concerning other cultures and languages, training of specialists, and the American public's general understanding of the peoples of other countries" (see U.S. Department of Education International Education Programs Service Office of Postesecondary Education, 2007). The effectiveness of these programs is important for the nation's global competitiveness and national security, as well as for the sake of developing globally competent citizens.

TITLE VI AND FULBRIGHT-HAYS PROGRAMS

Title VI/FH consists of 14 constituent programs administered by the International Education Programs Service, part of the Office of Postsecondary Education at ED. Generally, the 10 Title VI-funded programs are viewed as the domestic component, while the four FH-funded programs provide an overseas complement.

Title VI Programs

Programs under Title VI can be arranged in three broad categories, by general goal. The first group is aimed at increasing the level of expertise in foreign languages, area studies, and other international studies:

1. National Resource Centers (NRC)
2. Foreign Language and Area Studies (FLAS) Fellowships
3. Undergraduate International Studies and Foreign Language (UISFL) Program
4. Language Resource Centers (LRC)
5. American Overseas Research Centers (AORC)
6. Technological Innovation and Cooperation for Foreign Information Access (TICFIA)
7. International Research and Studies (IRS)

The second group of programs is aimed at supporting international business education and enhancing U.S. leadership in the global economy:

8. Centers for International Business Education and Research (CIBER)
9. Business and International Education (BIE)

The third category, which has a unique mission, seeks to increase the number of underrepresented minorities in the diplomatic corps and other types of international service:

10. Institute for International Public Policy (IIPP)

Fulbright-Hays Programs

The four programs under Section 102(b)(6) of Fulbright-Hays provide overseas exchange opportunities. The U.S. Department of State operates separate Fulbright-Hays programs, although ED and the State Department cooperate with one another on the administration of their programs. It is helpful to think of the Fulbright-Hays programs at State as being integral to U.S. diplomacy abroad, and the Fulbright-Hays programs at ED as focused on the improvement of domestic teaching and learning of foreign languages and cultures through overseas study. The component programs of Fulbright-Hays at ED are:

1. Fulbright-Hays Training Grants–Doctoral Dissertation Research Abroad (DDRA)
2. Fulbright-Hays Training Grants–Faculty Research Abroad (FRA)
3. Fulbright-Hays Training Grants–Group Projects Abroad (GPA)
4. Fulbright-Hays Seminars Abroad–Bilateral Projects

Each of these 14 programs has a specific, complementary purpose. The Title VI programs provide resources primarily to institutions of higher education,[2] whereas the Fulbright-Hays programs provide grants to a wide range of entities, including K-12 teachers. Table 1-1 provides a snapshot of the purpose of and eligibility for each of the 14 programs.

MEETING NATIONAL NEEDS

In reviewing Title VI/FH and other federal programs that support language study, it is useful to think of how such programs meet national needs in two ways—immediate and long term. Immediate national needs might be viewed as national security and the need to fill positions in the military, intelligence agencies, law enforcement, and the diplomatic corps with people who have language and area expertise, as discussed by the 9/11 Commission (National Commission on Terrorist Attacks Upon the United States, 2004).

Long-term national needs are more expansive and include the need to develop and maintain competencies to respond to future national security needs, to remain competitive in global markets, to retain a scientific and technological advantage, and to develop analytic competencies and a generally more globally aware citizenry. Long-term national needs serve national security purposes over the long term, going far beyond the narrow focus of a specific point in time.

Title VI programs were created by the National Defense Education Act at the height of the Cold War to build language and area expertise because of national security concerns. However, over time the programs have shifted to emphasize language and area study as a matter of general educational

---

[2]The International Research and Studies Program is a notable exception. While institutions of higher education can apply, eligible applicants include public and private agencies, organizations and institutions, and individuals.

TABLE 1-1 Title VI/FH Programs at the U.S. Department of Education

Program Title	Purpose	Eligibility and Frequency
American Overseas Research Centers (AORC)	To establish or operate overseas research centers that promote postgraduate research, exchanges, and area studies.	Consortia of institutions of higher education that receive more than 50 percent of their funding from public or private U.S. sources; have a permanent presence in the country in which the center is located; and are tax-exempt nonprofit organizations. Competition every 4 years.
Business and International Education (BIE)	To improve the academic teaching of the business curriculum; to conduct outreach activities that expand the capacity of the business community to engage in international economic activities; to promote education and training that will contribute to the ability of U.S. business to prosper in an international economy.	Institutions of higher education that enter into an agreement with a trade association and/or business. Competition every 2 years.
Centers for International Business Education and Research (CIBER)	To be national and regional resources for the teaching of improved business techniques, strategies, and methodologies that emphasize the international context in which business is transacted; provide instruction in critical foreign languages and international fields needed to provide an understanding of the cultures and customs of U.S. trading partners.	Institutions of higher education. Competition every 4 years (previously every 3 years).
Foreign Language and Area Studies (FLAS) Fellowships	To assist in the development of knowledge, resources, and trained personnel for modern foreign language and area/international studies; to stimulate the attainment of foreign language acquisition and fluency; and to develop a pool of international experts to meet national needs.	Institutions of higher education. Eligible students apply to and are selected by grantee institutions; must show potential for high academic achievement. Competition every 4 years (previously every 3 years).
Fulbright-Hays Doctoral Dissertation Research Abroad (DDRA)	To provide opportunities to graduate students to engage in full-time dissertation research abroad in modern foreign languages and area studies.	Institutions of higher education. Eligible graduate students apply through their institutions. Annual competition.

continued

TABLE 1-1 Continued

Program Title	Purpose	Eligibility and Frequency
Fulbright-Hays Training Grants Faculty Research Abroad (FRA)	To provide opportunities to faculty of institutions of higher education to engage in research abroad in modern foreign languages and area studies.	Institutions of higher education. Annual competition.
Fulbright-Hays Training Grants Group Projects Abroad (GPA)	To provide grants to support overseas projects in training, research, and curriculum development in modern foreign languages and area studies by teachers, students, and faculty engaged in a common endeavor.	Institutions of higher education, nonprofit organizations, state departments of education, consortia of institutions, and other organizations and/or agencies. Competitions annually for short-term seminars (currently under way) and every 3 years for advanced overseas intensive language projects.
Fulbright-Hays Seminars Abroad Bilateral Projects (SA)	To provide short-term study and travel seminars abroad for U.S. educators in the social sciences and humanities for the purpose of improving their understanding and knowledge of the peoples and cultures of other countries.	Eligible participants include elementary, middle, and high school educators in the fields of social sciences, humanities, and languages, including administrators, curriculum specialists, librarians, museum educators, media or resource specialists, faculty or administrators from institutions of higher education. Annual competitions. Those who have participated in the SA or GPA must wait three summers before they can be eligible to participate a second time.
Institute for International Public Policy (IIPP)	To increase the representation of minorities in international service, including private international voluntary organizations and the foreign service of the United States.	Consortia consisting of one or more of the following entities: an institution eligible for assistance under Part B of Title III of the Higher Education Act; an institution of higher education serving substantial numbers of black or other underrepresented minority students. Competition every 5 years.

TABLE 1-1 Continued

Program Title	Purpose	Eligibility and Frequency
International Research and Studies (IRS)	To improve and strengthen instruction in modern foreign languages, area studies, and other international fields to provide full understanding of the places in which the foreign languages are commonly used.	Public and private agencies, organizations and institutions, and individuals. Annual competition.
Language Resource Centers (LRC)	To improve the nation's capacity for teaching and learning foreign languages (particularly the less commonly taught languages) through teacher training, research, materials development, and dissemination projects.	Institutions of higher education or consortia of institutions of higher education. Competition every 4 years (previously every 3 years).
National Resource Centers (NRC)	To establish, strengthen, and operate comprehensive and undergraduate language and area/international studies centers that will be national resources for teaching of any modern foreign language; instruction in fields needed to provide full understanding of areas, regions, or countries in which the language is commonly used; research and training in international studies; language aspects of professional and other fields of study; and instruction and research on issues in world affairs.	Institutions of higher education or consortia of institutions of higher education. Competition every 4 years (previously every 3 years).
Technological Innovation and Cooperation for Foreign Information Access (TICFIA)	To develop innovative techniques or programs using new electronic technologies to collect information from foreign sources.	Institutions of higher education, public or nonprofit private libraries, or a consortia of such institutions or libraries. Competition every 3-4 years.
Undergraduate International Studies and Foreign Language (UISFL) Program	To strengthen and improve undergraduate instruction in international studies and foreign languages.	Institutions of higher education; combinations of institutions of higher education; partnerships between nonprofit educational organizations and institutions of higher education; and public and private nonprofit agencies and organizations, including professional and scholarly associations. Annual competition.

SOURCE: Adaptation of program descriptions listed on U.S. Department of Education website: http://www.ed.gov/about/offices/list/ope/iegps/index.html.

importance, as well as for national security reasons. This shift in emphasis has contributed to tension and disagreement on the extent to which the programs should be geared to meet immediate federal needs (particularly in agencies related to national security), or whether the programs should serve long-term interests and be geared toward maintaining capacity to teach and study a wide array of languages and areas, beyond those that may be in demand currently.

Current Controversies

Now that the United States faces a new international threat in the form of terrorism, national security has again become a central impetus for U.S. government-funded area studies and language training, as it was at the inception of Title VI. Immediately after the events of September 11, 2001, funding for Title VI/FH programs increased by 10 percent, as Congress made a connection between the terrorist attacks and the need for more expertise to prevent such attacks in the future.

The reauthorization of the programs, originally scheduled for 2004, set off a controversy over the intent of the programs and their current administration, particularly of Title VI-funded NRC and related FLAS Fellowships. A small group of critics, primarily two fellows at prominent research organizations and a former diplomat and administrator of Title VI/FH, asserted that the programs had strayed from their original intent. In congressional testimony and in print, these critics cited three main problems: (1) the programs do not adequately emphasize language proficiency, and over time they have tended toward funding area studies; (2) there is a lack of diversity of opinion and hostility to U.S. foreign policy in some fields, particularly Middle East studies; and (3) the programs are not responsive to national security needs, particularly the language needs of federal bureaucracies, such as the Departments of State and Defense. They also advocated creation of a new advisory board to oversee the programs (Kramer, n.d, 2006; Whitehead, 2004; Kurtz, 2003).

Supporters of Title VI/FH argue that the programs—which have doubled from 7 in their initial incarnation to 14 today—are meant to bolster national capacity in a variety of modern languages and areas, not to focus solely on languages immediately critical to national security. In any case, the list of critical languages changes over time, so it is wise to maintain a pool of expertise in as many languages as possible. Supporters, including those in Title VI and other organizations active in foreign language and international education, contend that Title VI programs play a vital role in the teaching of less commonly taught languages. In addition, they argue, funding for these programs is spent wisely because it serves to leverage additional spending on the part of universities; Title VI funds cover only a small proportion of the actual cost of operating NRC and other institutions, and universities must provide more to continue to obtain these funds. Finally, supporters of the programs deny charges of political bias against U.S. foreign policy goals at funded institutions and point out the importance of academic freedom in the higher education system in the United States.

After hearings on these issues in 2003, in preparation for the reauthorization of Title VI, House Bill 3077 was introduced, which would have created a permanent advisory board to oversee the programs, as a vehicle to address some of the issues noted above (U.S. House of Representatives Committee on Education and the Workforce, 2003). Although supported by critics, the proposed advisory board generated significant controversy, particularly in regard to the board's authority. The House subsequently passed a reauthorization bill (H.R. 609) and the Senate introduced a bill (S. 1614) that had not been considered at the time of the committee's deliberations; neither bill was considered by the full Congress. Despite differences between the bills, both demonstrate a concern with orienting the programs toward areas of national need, directing recipients into government service, and ensuring a diversity of perspectives on international affairs.

Controversies about the Title VI/FH programs occurred in the context of increasing concerns about unmet needs for language and area expertise in the federal government, particularly in the national security community. In addition, other federal programs, either new or in the proposal stages, have goals that seem to overlap with those of Title VI/FH. These include the National Security Education Program and a new National Security Language Initiative (NSLI) proposed by President Bush. Funding for the National Security Education Program has also been an issue as the fund supporting it was depleted, and its apparent overlap with Title VI/FH has also been noted.

CHARGE TO THE COMMITTEE

In light of these controversies, as well as the fact that the programs have not been reviewed since the early 1980s, and recognizing the importance of international education, the U.S. Congress directed ED to contract with the National Academies to conduct this study. The National Academies was asked to review the effectiveness of ED's foreign language, area, and international studies programs—the Title VI programs of the Higher Education Act and Section 102(b)(6) Fulbright-Hays programs. The review came about as a result of the congressional finding, stated in P.L. 108-447, "that globalization and the war on terrorism have increased America's need for international experts as well as for citizens with foreign language skills and global understanding." To fulfill this request, the National Academies established the Committee to Review the Title VI and Fulbright-Hays International Education Programs in February 2006. The members of the committee, who volunteered their time, include researchers and practitioners widely recognized to have expertise in foreign language acquisition, international studies, international business education, and program evaluation.

As requested by Congress, this study reviews the adequacy and effectiveness of the Title VI/FH programs in addressing their statutory missions and in building the nation's international and foreign language expertise—particularly as needed for economic, foreign affairs, and national security purposes. The review gives particular consideration to eight key areas identified by Congress:

1. Infusing a foreign language and area studies dimension throughout the education system and across relevant disciplines, including professional education.

2. Conducting public outreach/dissemination to K-12 and higher education, media, government, business, and the public.

3. Reducing shortages of foreign language and area experts.

4. Supporting research, education, and training in foreign languages and international studies, including opportunities for such research, education, and training overseas.

5. Producing relevant instructional materials that meet accepted scholarly standards.

6. Advancing uses of new technology in foreign language and international studies.

7. Addressing business needs for international knowledge and foreign language skills.

8. Increasing the numbers of underrepresented minorities in international service.

As part of its charge, the committee was asked to develop a conceptual and methodological framework to guide the study; conduct a review of the existing research literature and sources of evidence; describe its findings and conclusions regarding the impacts and effectiveness of the programs based on the available evidence; and provide recommendations for strategies to enhance the effectiveness of the programs in the future, as well as further research that could address any limitation of the current review.

The committee's charge does not direct it to consider the political issues that surfaced during congressional debates related to Title VI reauthorization. The committee therefore has not considered those issues, except as they serve as a context for questions that do fall under our purview.

The broadest critique held that Title VI/FH programs have strayed from the original intent of Congress because, according to critics, funds have been diverted from language proficiency to area studies. In preparation for its tasks, the committee commissioned a legislative history of Title VI/FH and otherwise acquainted itself with the history of the various programs now subsumed under Title VI. The committee agrees, as reflected in several of its recommendations, that improving the language proficiency of those who might serve the nation in international careers is a key and ongoing responsibility of the programs. We do not, however, think that language preparation is somehow separate from cultural understanding, and our review of the history of Title VI suggests that Congress has consistently affirmed the interconnection between language preparation and area scholarship. This issue is discussed in detail in the report.

A related criticism is that university-based language training is not sufficiently linked with the specific language needs of federal bureaucracies, such as the Departments of State and Defense and the intelligence agencies. As the report makes clear, the committee thinks that there is a productive division of labor between Title VI/FH programs, on one hand, and more targeted federal resources, such as the National Security Education Program, the Defense Language Institute, and the Foreign Service Institute, on the other, which are designated to address specific government personnel needs. Universities are best at taking the long view, which explains why between 2001 and 2003 Title VI centers offered instruction in 276 of the less commonly taught languages, while only 74 of these languages were being offered by the Defense Language Institute or the Foreign Service Institute. Because what languages are deemed critical changes in unpredictable ways, the nation benefits from the large pool of language expertise housed in universities.

Finally, the critics claim, there is a pattern of bias in NRCs, with Middle Eastern studies being singled out for particular attention in this regard. Neither Congress nor ED included this issue in the committee's charge. However, committee members familiar with the history of area studies did note that "bias" is a recurring charge, which has been voiced as vigorously by the left as by the right. It is in the nature of scholarship on America's role in the world that at times research will be viewed as too critical and at other times it will be seen as lacking critical perspective. That said, the committee considers it beyond our charge to arrive at any definitive judgment on the issue.

Finally, the committee's charge was to review Title VI/FH programs at ED only. To minimize confusion, we emphasize that our charge does not include the Fulbright programs administered by the State Department. The report considers these and other federal programs that also are aimed at increasing foreign language and area expertise in terms of their possible overlap and the role each plays in addressing the need for international experts, but the focus of the report is on ED's Title VI/FH programs. Similarly, although there is some discussion of ED's Foreign Language Assistance

Program, which provides resources to K-12, the report focuses on higher education, which is the mandate of the Title VI/FH programs.

This report reviews the available evidence, including extant evaluations, public testimony, funding history, program monitoring data, and other program information, and presents the committee's findings, conclusions, and recommendations in each of the eight areas specified by Congress on the basis of this evidence. It provides recommendations for strategies to enhance the effectiveness of the programs in the future, as well as further research to address the limitations of the current review. However, the limited evidence available in some cases precluded recommendations specific to individual programs or related to the relative contributions of the individual component programs.

BRIEF HISTORY AND FEDERAL CONTEXT

The Title VI/FH programs at ED have evolved over time, as national needs have shifted in response to changes in global politics and economics. The legislative history of Title VI charts the evolution of a temporary international education program into an enduring fixture on the federal stage. Over the past 50 years the national security emphasis of the programs decreased, and new programs were added to address changing national priorities. The international education programs originally created under the National Defense Education Act were incorporated into the Higher Education Act, thus expanding the programs beyond the training of specialists and emphasizing the importance of international studies as a matter of general educational importance. Section 102(b)(6) of the Mutual Educational and Cultural Exchange Act, or Fulbright-Hays, created an overseas component to the otherwise domestically based international education programs under Title VI.

Legislative History

The legislative history of Title VI programs can be viewed as following three rough periods of development: the early years (1958-1972), when the foundation of the programs was established; a middle period (1973-1991) of embedding and revising, during which it became finally established in the Higher Education Act and several programs were added; and the current phase (1992 onward), during which the scope of the programs has been broadened (see Figure 1-1 and Appendix A). Title VI was originally passed as part of the National Defense Education Act of 1958. This was a period of increasing cold war tension and competition for influence in developing nations and the launch of the Sputnik satellite by the Soviet Union. According to ED's history of the act, the purpose of the law was specifically tied

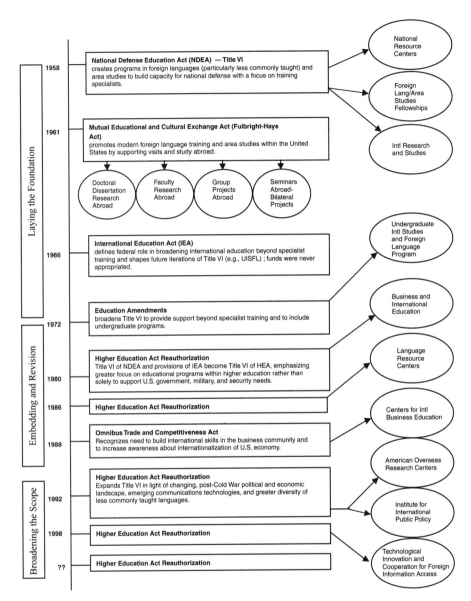

FIGURE 1-1 Legislative time line of current Title VI/FH programs.

to U.S. security interests: "The NDEA aimed to insure trained expertise of sufficient quality and quantity to meet U.S. national security needs" (U.S. Department of Education International Education Programs Service Office of Postsecondary Education, n.d.). The law initially established a range of academic programs and fellowships that supported the development of international expertise. There was a particular focus on the study of languages spoken in nations of strategic value to the United States that were not widely taught at most U.S. universities in the early 1960s, such as Hindi/Urdu, Japanese, Chinese, Arabic, and Russian (Scarfo, 1998).

As time passed, the purpose of Title VI changed slightly as the program expanded. As a result of reauthorization every six years, programs were added to address business needs for international expertise, improve the programs' reach to undergraduate education, create new centers focused on language, support overseas research centers, advance technology use, and bring individuals from minority groups into international service professions.

The programs have been broadened to embrace not only immediate security concerns, but also concerns related to global competitiveness and a more internationally aware citizenry. However, the enterprise retains recognition of the importance of both foreign language learning and an understanding of the cultural context in which the languages are spoken, as well as the political, social, and economic issues in a range of world nations. It also supports the value of internationalization, both in terms of helping to produce experts needed to address national security, government, business, and higher education needs and in terms of enriching the higher education curriculum.

The Fulbright-Hays programs were created separately from Title VI, by the Mutual Educational and Cultural Exchange Act of 1961 (also called the Fulbright-Hays Act). Although the act did not specifically address national security needs, it was passed at a time of increasing public diplomacy efforts on the part of the United States. Its legislative mandate was "to increase mutual understanding between the people of the United States and the people of other countries."[3] Fulbright-Hays programs funded research abroad for professors and graduate students to work on advanced research projects and dissertations. It also provided funds for elementary and high school teachers to make understanding of other cultures a part of the curriculum for younger students. It established a variety of short- and medium-term seminars and research projects abroad for groups of educators. Centers were established in other nations, for example India and Egypt, which

---

[3]See U.S. Department of State, Bureau of Educational and Cultural Affairs, History of International Visitor Leadership Program. Available: http://exchanges.state.gov/education/ivp/history.htm [accessed June 2005].

served as institutes of language and area studies, where American educators could continue to develop their knowledge and skills. After some reshuffling through such agencies as the U.S. Information Agency, part of the Fulbright-Hays programs is now funded through appropriations to the State Department for exchange opportunities integral to public diplomacy, and part is funded through appropriations to ED for various overseas study programs aimed at improving domestic foreign language, international, and area studies expertise.

The evolution of the programs embraces the view that they are designed to serve both immediate and long-term national needs, with an emphasis on the long-term ones. Other federal resources, such as the Foreign Service Institute and the Defense Language Institute, seem to be more suited to meeting the immediate language needs of the federal government. Title VI/FH programs, by current law and by the way the programs are administered, are not ideally or specifically designed to meet the immediate language needs of the federal government. Instead, the programs support the creation of a broad skill base, through research, teaching, and maintaining a long-term national capacity in languages and area studies. They are focused on building a deep pool of area and language expertise nationally, not only in government but also in the K-12 system, academia, and business. By design, the programs cannot necessarily be quickly fine-tuned to meet immediate or short-term needs; they are aimed at creating a broad reservoir of expertise in a wide variety of languages and areas, rather than a direct channel into government positions or areas of need determined by rapidly changing geopolitics.

A specific strength of Title VI/FH programs is that they support research and teaching in a wide variety of areas and languages. Changing geopolitics often causes situations to arise whereby a currently ignored language or area becomes a crucial one. Maintaining a wide pool of expertise would help—and according to supporters has helped—prepare the nation for future crises. For example, after September 11, 2001, U.S. agencies used materials for Central Asian languages that were developed with Title VI funds beginning in the 1960s (Wiley, 2006), and materials and programs at Title VI institutions have been regularly used as a resource by federal agencies (Brustein, 2006). In this way, the programs maintain a base level of expertise and the capacity to teach new languages as needs arise.

The committee notes that the definition of critical languages differs even by agency, based on their particular needs. Although multiple agencies have begun to implement initiatives as part of the president's proposed National Security Language Initiative (NSLI), with a common goal of increasing the nation's capacity in "critical languages," the specific languages identified have differed by agency as well as by program (see Box 1-1).

The list of critical languages used in Title VI/FH programs was report-

---

BOX 1-1
Varying Definitions of Critical Languages

Languages identified by the State Department when announcing the National Security Language Initiative (used for ED's Foreign Language Assistance Program competition):

- Arabic, Chinese, Korean, Japanese, Russian, and
- Indic, Iranian, and Turkic languages

Languages eligible for study (including both languages and literature and, in some cases, linguistics) using Department of Education SMART (Science and Mathematics Access to Retain Talent) grants:

- Chinese, Japanese, Korean, Russian, Hindi, Bengali, Punjabi, Urdu, Portuguese, Arabic, Hebrew, Filipino/Tagalog, Turkish
- African, Iranian/Persian, Bahasa Indonesian/Bahasa Malay, and Turkic, Ural-Altaic, Caucasian, and Central Asian languages

Languages supported under the Department of Defense National Flagship Language Program:

- Current languages: Arabic, Chinese, Korean, Persian, Russian

Languages targeted under expansion:

- Arabic, Chinese, Hindi/Urdu, and Central Asian Languages

SOURCES: Powell and Lowenkron (2006).

---

edly developed with extensive input from the field. The list of 171 languages was left intentionally broad to allow flexibility in response to changing national strategic priorities and emerging requirements. This approach is consistent with the views of at least some experts in the language community, who applaud the NSLI but argue that "there is a critical need for all languages" (Joint National Committee for Languages and the National Council for Languages, 2006). As discussed in the next chapter, the committee concludes that capacity must be maintained in a broad range of languages.

In addition to building foreign language expertise, Title VI/FH programs serve national security needs, in the long term, by developing and sustaining area and international knowledge. There is a need for area studies experts whose skills extend beyond language and who are familiar with the culture, politics, economics, and other characteristics of various regions and countries. It is important that the pool of area studies experts be deep enough to meet changing national needs, because the particular foreign cultures of importance to government, business, humanitarian organizations, and academia have changed over time. Immediately after World War II, area studies were oriented toward European and Soviet studies, because of the cold war, the Marshall Plan, and the development of the North Atlantic Treaty Organisation alliance. When cold war competition shifted to the Third World, interest rose in Latin American and Asian studies. When U.S. businesses began to confront Japanese competition, there was a need for experts on Japan. Currently, attention has moved to the Middle East and Central Asia, because of increasing competition for influence in these regions, their natural resources, and political, religious, and ethnic instability. In addition to these "new areas," there is still need for experts on nations that are important on the world stage because of their size and power, such as Russia, Japan, and China, and emerging regional powers, such as India, South Africa, Brazil, and Nigeria. Again, because it is impossible to predict what future hot spots of attention will emerge, it is important to have a pool of expertise in areas or countries in which interest may increase in the future. For example, Indonesia is the fourth largest nation in the world in terms of population and the largest Muslim nation. Universities may not be prepared to create or sustain programs without sufficient demand to support the faculty positions required to teach about Indonesia. Experts in Indonesian politics or the Indonesian language may have difficulty finding work in academia unless there is an additional federal incentive to universities to fund positions to study and teach about that nation.

Finally, Title VI/FH programs support U.S. competitiveness in both specific and general ways. Title VI funds two programs aimed at internationalizing business school curricula. In general, the programs overall play a role in developing a globally competent citizenry. Such citizens have an understanding of the complexities of global economics, politics, and foreign cultures, in order to be able to compete internationally, interact comfortably with people of other cultures, make informed judgments about international affairs, and supply the federal government with needed expertise. Ideally, the pool of globally competent citizens would serve in a variety of professions of importance to the international standing of the United States, such as diplomacy, law enforcement, the military, health care, business, academia, nongovernmental organizations, and all levels of the education system. This pool should also include people in minority groups, which have been underrepresented in such areas as diplomacy and other areas of international service.

As this report demonstrates, Title VI/FH programs meet many needs. The range of goals and purposes for these programs is quite wide. They are designed not only to help meet national security needs, but also to promote economic competitiveness, to help create an informed citizenry, to support teaching and research on foreign languages and regions, to help minority students enter international fields, to collect and archive foreign language materials, and to generally support university efforts to expand and improve language and area studies programs. At the same time, today's world presents many new challenges and opportunities. ED needs to better position itself and the Title VI/FH programs to incorporate these challenges and opportunities.

Funding History

The current 14 programs that emerged from this legislative process receive 3 appropriations. The IIPP, created in 1992, receives its own appropriation (FY 2006: $1.6 million). The remaining nine programs under Title VI are funded as the domestic component of ED's international education programs (FY 2006: $91.5 million), while the four Fulbright-Hays programs receive an appropriation as the overseas component (FY 2006: $12.6 million). Allocation of funds across the several programs that are part of Title VI or Fulbright-Hays is largely an administrative decision made by ED,[4] although in several instances Congress has directed the department to award new funds in particular ways.

As Figure 1-2 shows, the IIPP appropriation has remained relatively constant since the program was created; it has consistently represented about 2 percent of the combined appropriation for IIPP and the other Title VI programs. The Title VI and Fulbright-Hays appropriations have experienced greater change. The Title VI appropriation,[5] in particular, has experienced periods of significant increase and significant decrease. The fortunes of the programs seemed to be connected in the early years, as the two appropriations generally increased or decreased in unison. In the 1990s, while the Title VI program experienced modest but steady growth, funding for Fulbright-Hays remained relatively constant. Both programs experienced a resurgence in the early 2000s, when they experienced several years of growth. This growth has tapered off slightly in the most recent years.

In the programs' early days, they experienced a peak in funding in fiscal year (FY) 1967. Funding dropped precipitously in FY 1971 as a result of efforts to eliminate Title VI. Despite the addition of multiple programs and

---

[4]The Higher Education Act limits to 10 percent the proportion of funds that can be used for the Undergraduate International Studies and Foreign Language Program. In practice, however, given the limited available funds, its allocation has not reached this amount.

[5]For ease of reference, although IIPP is a Title VI program, the term "Title VI appropriation" refers to the nine programs, excluding IIPP.

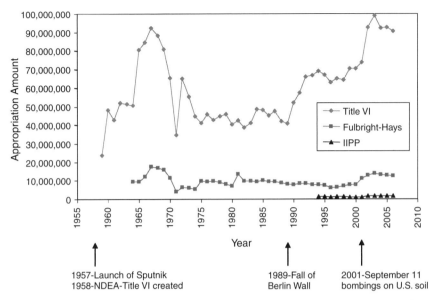

FIGURE 1-2 Appropriations for Title VI/FH programs, 1959-2006 (adjusted to 2006 dollar amounts using the Consumer Price Index for All Urban Consumers). SOURCE: Data provided by U.S. Department of Education. Bureau of Labor Statistics adjustment factors, available: http://www.bls.gov/cpi [accessed March 2007].

an expanded mission, funding did not reach FY 1967 levels until almost four decades later, in FY 2002. This gain was due in large part to significant funding increases in the aftermath of September 11, 2001, when both Title VI and Fulbright-Hays received significant funding increases. Both programs received increases (in absolute terms) in three successive years, as follows:

- FY 2001: Title VI increased by 8 percent and Fulbright-Hays by 50 percent;
- FY 2002: Title VI increased by 27 percent and Fulbright-Hays by 18 percent; and,
- FY 2003: both increased by 10 percent.

In FY 2001, the congressional conference committee acknowledged ED's work on performance indicators but noted that "more work needs to be done in developing specific, numeric goals and baseline data for these programs." The FY 2002 and FY 2003 increases were accompanied by specific language in the Appropriations Committee's conference report providing direction to the department on how to use the additional funds. In general, ED was directed to use Title VI/FH increases to focus on particular world areas and languages, increase the number and amount of FLAS awards, increase the average award for other programs, establish new Language Resource Centers in specific targeted areas, and various efforts to enhance language learning.

Interest in the programs' reaching professional disciplines was also reinforced. Finally, in FY 2002 ED was given the authority to use up to 1 percent for program evaluation, national outreach, and information dissemination, a provision that has continued.

At first glance, it appears that FY 2003 Title VI funding levels rival those of the programs' early days. However, it is important to keep in mind that the recent funding peaks were used to fund nine distinct programs with a broad national agenda, compared with the three programs funded in the FY 1967 heyday. If one considers only the allocations for programs that existed in FY 1967 (NRC, FLAS, and IIRS), the original three programs have actually experienced a significant reduction in funding in constant dollars ($95,368,000 in FY 1967 versus $71,027,844 in FY 2003).[6] Although the appropriation has increased between 2 and 19 percent concurrent with the addition of programs, the increases have been offset by decreases in interim years.

ORGANIZATION OF THE REPORT

Following this introduction, the remainder of Part I provides relevant background for the committee's work. Chapter 2 outlines information on the demand for foreign language, international, and area expertise and the role of the Title VI/FH programs in relation to other federal programs in addressing this demand. Chapter 3 presents information on the implementation and monitoring of Title VI/FH in the higher education system and by the federal government.

Part II, comprised of Chapters 4 through 10, discusses program performance, based on the committee's review of the available evidence, and our conclusions and recommendations for each of the eight key areas identified by Congress. Discussion of the programs' activities related to infusing a foreign language and area studies dimension, and conducting public outreach are discussed in a single chapter, Chapter 4, given the relationship between vertical integration with the K-12 system and outreach by Title VI programs.

Part III outlines the committee's conclusions and recommendations re-

---

[6]Funding was adjusted to 2006 dollars using the Consumer Price Index for All Urban Consumers.

lated to the future effectiveness of the programs and addressing limitations of our review, the two final components of our charge. Chapter 11 discusses program monitoring and evaluation at ED, leading to a discussion of a proposed effort aimed at continuous improvement. Chapter 12 outlines a series of challenges and opportunities that the programs, ED, the education system, and the federal government must address in the decades ahead.

The appendices provide valuable background information. Appendix A provides a legislative history of the programs, with a focus on Title VI, which has experienced the most change. Appendix B provides additional detail on the committee's approach, introduced in Chapter 4. Appendix C provides information on the rating criteria and priorities used in the largest programs. As discussed in Chapter 3, these mechanisms are used to target program applications toward specific priorities. Appendix D provides a brief history of foreign language assessment in the United States. Appendix E presents tabular information on federal programs designed to address international education and foreign language needs. Finally, Appendix F provides biographical sketches of the committee members and staff.

2

Demand for Foreign Language, Area, and International Expertise

Many of the controversies surrounding the Title VI and Fulbright-Hays (Title VI/FH) programs revolve around the extent to which there is unmet need for foreign language and area experts in the federal government and the role that the U.S. Department of Education (ED) programs—particularly the Title VI programs—should play in helping to meet this need. In fact, one of the key areas identified by Congress for the committee's review is the performance of the programs in "reducing shortages of foreign language and area experts." This chapter provides a context for the discussion of that key area in Chapter 6.

We begin with a brief discussion of issues related to defining an occupational "shortage" and reasons why the committee uses the terms "demand" or "shortages" as an alternative. We then present an overview of demand in the context of foreign languages, area studies, and international knowledge, which acknowledges the need for a range of types of expertise and the need not only for "experts" but also for the resources and training needed to develop expertise. We discuss demand both from the long-term perspective of what might be necessary to maintain and even enhance U.S. security and prosperity and from the short-term perspective, taking into account immediate unmet needs for personnel for positions that require language or area expertise. Finally, the chapter presents information from the available studies that define demand for specific sectors with discussion of differences in need across sectors.

DEFINING AN OCCUPATIONAL "SHORTAGE"

To begin to consider the role of Title VI/FH programs in reducing shortages, the committee considered how the term "shortage" should be defined. There have been a number of definitions used to define an occupational labor shortage. The National Research Council (2001, pp. 97-98) described two broad types of definitions: one that refers to market shortages and the other based on "social demand." Economists typically consider a shortage to be a market disequilibrium; an occupational labor shortage is a situation in which the number of workers that employers wish to hire at the prevailing wage exceeds the number available for a sustained period. This is similar to the definition used in previous studies (Blank and Stigler, 1957; Arrow and Capron, 1959; Cohen, 1995; Barnow, 1996) that consider a shortage in terms of a labor market that does not clear for some reason.

An alternative concept of interest is what Arrow and Capron (1959) refer to as a "social demand model." Arrow and Capron observe that what some analysts call a shortage is not a market disequilibrium at all:

> In particular, careful reading of such statements indicates that the speakers have in effect been saying: There are not as many engineers and scientists as this nation should have in order to do all the things that need doing such as maintaining our rapid rate of technological progress, raising our standard of living, keeping us militarily strong, etc. In other words, they are saying that (in the economic sense) demand for technically skilled manpower *ought* to be greater than it is—it is really a shortage of *demand* for scientists and engineers that concerns them.

The market disequilibrium definition requires an investigation of changes in the stock of job vacancies as well as efforts by employers to alleviate the problem while the social demand model requires detailed information on need (Trutko et al., 2003). The committee determined that a thorough examination of the factors that would determine whether a shortage exists and the extent of the shortage, using either model, would be beyond the time and resources available for this review. However, there is clearly a widespread perception that more individuals with expertise in languages and area studies are needed, and there is some evidence that there are vacancies in these areas. With this in mind, the committee endeavors in this chapter to explore the extent to which there is demand for foreign language and area expertise, recognizing that the effectiveness of Title VI/FH programs depends, in part, on the need, or demand, that they are charged with meeting. However, to make clear that we have not conducted a market-based review of shortages, we generally refer to the "demand" or "unmet need" for experts rather than shortages per se.

DEMAND: A LONG-TERM PERSPECTIVE

The long-term perspective of demand is best understood in light of three propositions:

1. Need is difficult to quantify, but, like federal funding for science, federal funding for language and area studies may have future benefits that are difficult to quantify.

2. Maintaining capacity for the teaching of languages and cultures in areas that are not of current strategic importance to the United States but may be in the future is important.

3. The United States needs an informed citizenry with an understanding of global politics and economics and foreign cultures both for long-term national security and prosperity.

Need Is Difficult to Quantify

Need is not static. It is not simply the sum of expected job openings in government, education, and business that require language and area expertise. The broad definition of social demand takes into account the level of expertise required to maintain or even enhance the global position of the United States in terms of security, prosperity, and economic competitiveness. Therefore, need is dynamic; it could be that the more one invests in language and area knowledge, the greater the payoff in terms of security and prosperity. It is difficult to test this proposition, but an analogy can be made to U.S. public investment in scientific research and the development of new technology, as described in the report *Rising Above the Gathering Storm: Energizing and Employing America for a Brighter Future* (National Academy of Sciences, National Academy of Engineering, Institute of Medicine, 2007). Federal funding and incentives for scientific research and greater educational opportunity has had a huge payoff in terms of security, economic competitiveness, longevity, and overall quality of life. This means that federal funding for various types of research (particularly in the area of agriculture) has a high rate of return in terms of subsequent economic activity that occurs as the technology spills over into other areas, and new products and technologies are produced as a result, further increasing productivity. The return on investment for academia as a whole is estimated at 28 percent (National Academy of Sciences, National Academy of Engineering, Institute of Medicine, 2007).

The effect of federal funding in scientific research and development is quite positive, but it is often not known what the end result will be for a specific project. For example, federal funding for basic research on the structure of DNA helped create the field of molecular biology and the tool of gene splicing, which led to the phenomenal growth of the biotechnology industry. Yet those performing the initial groundbreaking research in this area had few clues of its eventual consequences or economic implications. This may also be true of language and area expertise.

Maintaining Capacity Is Important

While it may be difficult to measure the specific payoffs derived from funding for language and area study, we do know that demand and the need for expertise in a variety of languages changes over time, and it is necessary to prepare for these changes. Today's list of critical languages does not match the list of 20 years ago, and it may not match the list of 10 years from now. Even if the nation were theoretically able to meet current needs, the likelihood of unforeseen international crises underscores the prudent requirement for expertise in a broad range of languages and cultures, in order to discern mutually beneficial interactions or outcomes and to better protect, defend, and advance U.S. national interests. One impetus for Title VI was to have available, if necessary, the expertise to meet just such contingences without being able to know in advance exactly what the issues would be and where they would arise.

Demand for greater expertise in foreign language and area studies, in terms of both numbers of individuals and areas of expertise needed, will also create a substantial demand for greater resources—programs, instructors, curricula, teaching materials, facilities—for producing this expertise. In other words, demand should be thought of not only in terms of the people with expertise needed, but also in terms of the capacity to produce people with expertise.

Need for an Informed Citizenry

At the time the Title VI/FH programs were designed, policy makers believed the country needed a relatively small number of deeply trained specialists who would go on to pursue careers principally in academia and government. However, developments over the past 50 years have broadened the need for international expertise. The occupational fields demanding international expertise have expanded dramatically to include business, health, education, law enforcement, the courts, and social services. Language and area knowledge is needed to work with a more culturally diverse domestic population, reflecting growing immigration flows. And the need for international competence has extended to other areas of life beyond work, as expressed in a recent statement of the Committee for Economic Development (2006):

> Full participation in this new global economy will require not just competency in reading, mathematics and science, but also proficiency in foreign languages and deeper knowledge of other countries and cultures. Our efforts in education reform must be harmonized with global realities if we are to confront successfully a multitude of new and growing challenges to America's security and prosperity.

Because the boundaries between international and domestic problems have become increasingly porous, the very demands of government and citizenship now require knowledge of international topics and the ability to communicate with and understand people from other cultures. Elected representatives and voters will be able to make informed decisions about such issues as trade, health epidemics, environmental conservation, energy use, immigration, and especially global stability only if they are educated to understand the global determinants and consequences of those issues and decisions. The exercise of democratic citizenship domestically calls for citizens to understand the connections between local and global affairs and the complex systems of interdependencies that embed the U.S. economy in a globalized world economy.

The demand for international competence has therefore extended to other occupations beyond the area studies specialist, and it has broadened to become necessary for citizenship and for many types of employment. In this regard it is useful to distinguish three necessary and distinct sets of international competencies and skills:

1. Skills and attitudes that reflect an interest in global issues and foreign cultures.
2. Disciplinary knowledge in comparative fields, such as anthropology, political science, economics, and world history.
3. Foreign language expertise.

While the development of competency in each of them may facilitate the acquisition of competencies in the others, these represent sufficiently distinct domains that they can be treated, for purposes of policy and programming, as independent. The mix of these three types of competencies and the level at which they should be developed will vary in different professions, across government, and also at the graduate, undergraduate, and K-12 levels. In graduate schools of business, for example, basic foreign language knowledge combined with knowledge of economics and trade would be more necessary than in some of the other disciplinary areas discussed earlier. In contrast, graduates of schools of public health, nursing, or medicine might be best served with language training. The sections below discuss these in more detail.

Cultural Competencies

The first set of competencies are "soft" skills and attitudes that reflect an openness, interest, and positive disposition to the variation of human cultural expression reflected internationally. In their most basic forms, these skills comprise tolerance toward cultural differences. More advanced are the skills to recognize and negotiate differences in cross-cultural contexts, the cultural flexibility and adaptability necessary to develop empathy, and trust and mutual respect in order to have effective interpersonal interactions in diverse cultural contexts. The value of these skills might be recognized by imagining their absence, the consequences of which might be intolerance, prejudice, bigotry, or a sense of cultural or racial superiority. These are harmful to daily life in a diverse democracy, as well as for the smooth and effective conduct of international relations, including international business.

An example of the importance of these competencies is the recent brochure produced by the nonprofit organization Business for Diplomatic Action, which seeks to use traveling business representatives as a means to improve the image of the United States abroad. The group is distributing its brochure to major international companies, and even wants the U.S. Department of State to distribute it to every U.S. passport holder. According to the *Wall Street Journal*, the brochure advises Americans traveling overseas to avoid "stereotypical American traits such as boastfulness, loudness and speed. The guide urges travelers to eat slower, speak slower, move slower and dress up when abroad since casual dress can be a sign of disrespect. Tone down talk of religion, politics and national pride, as well as your voice. 'Listen as much as you talk,' the guide says, and 'save the lectures for your kids.' 'Anger, impatience and rudeness are universal turnoffs'" (McCartney, 2006).

Openness and cultural awareness can enhance the professional effectiveness of people in a range of occupations, from education, trade and services, law enforcement, and arts to innovation and development in business or science. These skills facilitate not only international transactions, but also domestic ones, as the result of immigration and the growing diversity of the U.S. population.

Disciplines

The second set of global competencies results from disciplinary knowledge in comparative fields: comparative history, anthropology, political science, economics and trade, literature, and world history. These are the competencies that allow knowledge and understanding of problems with an international or global dimension. Recent surveys show young Americans lagging behind youth in other industrialized countries in their knowledge of geography and world affairs. In 2002, only 58 percent of U.S. youth knew that Afghanistan is the base of the Taliban and al-Qaeda, and only 17 percent could find the country on a map. Only 42 percent could locate

Japan on a map of the world, and only 31 percent could locate Great Britain (Roper Public Affairs and Media, 2002). More recently, only 37 percent of young Americans could identify Iraq on a map, 48 percent thought that the majority of the population in India is Muslim, and 60 percent indicated they do not speak a foreign language fluently (Roper Public Affairs and Media, 2006).

These competencies can also be developed at all levels of education, although they should probably be emphasized starting in the middle school curriculum and deepened in high school and higher education. Examples of this kind of skill would be deep knowledge of world history or geography, cultural history or comparative literature, and knowledge of international trade and development economics. There are also global topics of importance to any educated person in the 21st century, which require drawing on different disciplinary fields.

One example is the population paradox. At its core, the population paradox is simply the expression of demographic forces: the increase in health conditions worldwide, reduced birth rates in developed nations, and higher birth rates in developing nations are changing the demographic world balance. The result is an aging and declining population in developed countries and a growing population in developing countries. The population paradox has implications for global patterns of trade and consumption, for energy and resource use, for environmental impact and implications for international relations. Understanding the sources of these demographic trends and of the options to deal with them requires some knowledge of cultural norms in different societies, some knowledge of disparities in resource distribution, some knowledge of development economics, and some knowledge of comparative politics.

Foreign Language

The third set of global competencies, which should be closely aligned with the above cultural competencies, is foreign language expertise. These allow communication through varied forms of language expression, with individuals and groups who communicate principally in languages other than English. The resources to develop these competencies beginning in K-12 education are skilled teachers of foreign languages and adequate instructional materials, as well as space in the curriculum to devote to foreign language instruction. Study abroad can deepen and broaden foreign language competence. Foreign language instruction is most in need of explicit time in the K-12 curriculum and as such will be the most difficult to negotiate, given current pressures to focus instruction in a select range of academic subjects, including English, mathematics, and science.

DEMAND: A SHORT-TERM PERSPECTIVE

It is difficult to quantify the demand for globally competent citizens, those with the aforementioned skills, other than to say that the need is always great, perhaps limitless. The more such citizens the United States can produce, the healthier the outlook for the nation's long-term security and prosperity. However, there are studies that quantify current and near-term needs, in light of current trends. This section reviews recent studies of the short-term demand for people with foreign language and area expertise in government, business, and education. Overall, the studies indicate that:

- The need for people with foreign language and area expertise is growing.
- The most acute unmet need appears to be in government, particularly for people with competency in critical languages (Arabic, Farsi, Chinese, etc.) in the national security agencies—the military, law enforcement, intelligence, and diplomacy.
- In business, the demand is not so much for people with specific foreign language abilities as it is for people with general global awareness and "cross-cultural competence." These are people who can identify business opportunities abroad and are comfortable interacting with people from other nations. Businesses meet some of this demand by recruiting foreign students, either in the United States or abroad.
- In higher education, there is demand for teaching faculty in language and area studies. Student enrollment in foreign languages is increasing, thus increasing the need for qualified instructors. Lack of trained instructors is a special challenge in less commonly taught languages, particularly Arabic.
- Demand appears to be increasing for foreign language teachers at the K-12 level. There is evidence that school districts find it difficult to recruit qualified foreign language teachers. More school districts are starting programs in less commonly taught languages.
- With increasing enrollments in foreign language programs, both in K-12 and in higher education, there will be an increasing need for assessments of language proficiency, for purposes of diagnosis, placement, progress, grading and certification, and program accountability. This need will create a demand for professionals who are trained in language assessment and who can administer assessments of language proficiency that meet current professional standards of reliability, validity, and impact. This demand is likely to be the most critical in elementary school.

Reviewing academic studies and extrapolating from studies conducted in 1979, Merkx (2005) posits that the demand for people with foreign language and area skills across professions will be substantial over the next few decades. Adding demand from government, academia, business, K-12, and state and local government together, Merkx estimates that about 36,000 job openings for people with such skills occur annually.

Placing Demand Estimates in Context

Several other points deserve mention as context for the committee's review of available studies of short-term demand for language and international skills. First, the research literature described below distinguishes between needs in academia and needs in government or public service. Indeed, one criticism of Title VI/FH is that it is of greater benefit to academia than to government, especially the national security community. While the distinction between academia and government is valid for research purposes, it is also somewhat blurred or artificial, in that it may cause one to overlook the revolving door that exists between government and academia, as people shuttle back and forth between the two. Many academics consult for or volunteer their services to the federal government, and military officers, for example, often attend Title VI-funded universities for advanced study.

Second, as noted earlier, demand for expertise in specific languages changes over time. Therefore, it is prudent to maintain capacity across a broad range of languages in order to respond to emerging needs for expertise.

Third, language and area needs vary across government, academia, K-12, and business. They also vary across federal agencies, and functions, because the use of language is domain specific. In academia, the ability of a Ph.D. holder to get a job in a South Asian language department may require a very deep knowledge of regional literature, and not merely language proficiency. In the business community, the emphasis may be on cultural knowledge and colloquial language skills to communicate with a range of people in other countries. At the National Security Agency, the emphasis may be on comprehension, for the sake of translating intercepted communications. The Department of Defense (DoD) or the Federal Bureau of Investigation (FBI) may have such needs as well, but they also need to train soldiers or agents to communicate with foreign citizens or with allies in stressful situations, such as searches or roadblocks. In short, demand is not for one specific skill set but for a wide variety of language skills at different levels that are useful in different domains.

Fourth, the research literature in second language acquisition clearly indicates that (1) acquiring a foreign language requires extensive time, effort, and adequate opportunity to learn and (2) unlike first language acquisition, second language acquisition is extremely variable.

Time Required to Develop Language Proficiency

A virtually unanimous finding in the research is that attaining functional proficiency in a second language requires a great deal of time and exposure to input in the target language through communicative language use (e.g., Kroll and DeGroot, in press). The federal Interagency Language Roundtable (ILR) scale, widely used to measure the language skills of federal employees,[1] includes five levels of proficiency: 0 (none), 1 (survival), 2 (limited working), 3 (professional working), 4 (distinguished) and 5 (native or bilingual). Most federal training programs increasingly aim at ILR level 3 which is "to use the language with sufficient ability to participate in most formal and informal discussions on practical, social and professional topics" (U.S. General Accounting Office, 2002, p. 5). And there is increasing recognition of the need for "beyond 3" level skills.

Several sources illuminate how much time is required to reach the higher levels on the ILR scale. For example, using a highly intensive approach to language instruction (25 classroom hours weekly and 3-4 hours of homework daily), the Foreign Service Institute (FSI) estimates that students take an average of 23-24 weeks (575-600 hours of class time) to reach ILR level 3 if the language studied is close to English (e.g., Romance languages, Swedish, Dutch, Norwegian). If the language is more different from English (e.g., Albanian, Bulgarian, Finnish, Greek, Hindi, Khmer, Latvian, Russian, Turkish), most students require 44 weeks (1,100 hours of class) to reach ILR level 3. Languages that are exceptionally difficult for English speakers, such as Arabic, Chinese, Japanese, and Korean, require an average of 88 weeks, or 2,200 hours (with the second year of instruction taking place in the country) to reach level 3 (Malone, 2006).

In secondary and higher education, in which instruction is much less intensive, developing advanced language proficiency requires much more time. Typically, colleges and university language classes meet 3 hours per week, providing a total of 90 hours over an academic year; at this rate, it would take six years of study to reach ILR level 3 in a language similar to English (Malone, 2006). At the high school level, classes often meet for 45-50 minutes daily, yet the level of teaching and learning is such that two years of high school instruction is equivalent to one year at the undergraduate level.

It is important to keep in mind that an individual may require more or less than these average amounts of time to develop language proficiency—or may never develop such proficiency. The literature on language learning is virtually unanimous in demonstrating that the acquisition of a

---

[1]The American Council on the Teaching of Foreign Languages has developed another proficiency scale that is widely used in academia (Malone, 2006; see Appendix D for a comparison of the two scales).

foreign language is extremely variable, depending on a wide range of individual differences and contextual characteristics. Schumann (1997), for example, describes language acquisition as an instance of sustained deep learning, which varies as a function of individual learners' different learning purposes, language use, and personal characteristics. The long-term and variable nature of foreign language learning must be taken into account when designing language programs and selecting individuals. Thus, even though we may be able to ramp up programs for language instruction with massive infusions of resources, it still takes time, effort, and opportunity for individual learners to reach the levels of proficiency that the various demands discussed below require.

The Heritage Community Paradox

At the same time that the United States is experiencing growing demand for foreign language expertise, disciplinary knowledge of world areas and global issues, and broad cultural competency, the education system is implementing policies that thwart a valuable potential resource—heritage language speakers. Reflecting several waves of immigration over the past 50 years, about 28 million individuals speak Spanish at home, another 2 million speak Chinese, and hundreds of thousands speak Tagalog, Vietnamese, Armenian, Korean, Russian, Arabic, Japanese, and Hindi (U.S. Census, 2000).

A heritage language speaker is considered to be someone who is raised in a home in which a language other than English is spoken and who is "to some degree bilingual in that language and in English" (Valdés, 2001). Those who have spoken the language since birth typically have skills in native pronunciation and fluency, command of a wide range of syntactic structures, extensive vocabulary, and familiarity with implicit cultural norms essential to effective language use (Valdés, 2001). By comparison, an English speaker generally requires hundreds of hours of instruction to develop similar levels of proficiency (see below).

Heritage language speakers vary in their level of language proficiency, depending on such factors as the age at which they arrived in the United States, the availability of community language schools, the extent to which their parents and community maintain a bilingual environment, and the extent to which they see fluency in the heritage language as valuable (Kondo-Brown, 2003). Although some ethnic communities have well-developed weekend or evening schools (Chinen, 2005), many do not.

Even when communities have available heritage language resources, the U.S. education system discourages continued use of heritage languages in favor of assimilation and English language acquisition. Most states and school districts aim to quickly move heritage learners out of these languages and into English-only instruction, which often leads to deterioration or even complete loss of the heritage language (Crawford, 1992; Ovando, 1990; Wiley and Lukes, 1996). Few programs are designed to enhance language skills of heritage speakers. A 1997 survey found that only 7 percent of high schools had language classes for native speakers (Rhodes and Branaman, 1999). A 2002 survey found that even classes for heritage Spanish speakers, the most widely spoken heritage language, were acutely lacking: only 18 percent of higher education Spanish programs offered such classes (Ingold et al., 2002). Yet when high school and higher education students who have lost heritage language abilities end up studying the language with monolingual English speakers in a foreign language classroom, the process can be inefficient and frustrating (Crawford, 1992).

As a result of all of these factors, without active intervention, heritage speaking ability typically dies out within three generations (Wiley, 1996), resulting in loss of a valuable potential resource for teachers, future students, and national foreign language capacity. Other barriers also impede the nation's ability to use heritage speakers when they do maintain their language proficiency. For example, inflexible certification policies sometimes prevent heritage speakers from qualifying as teachers. Similarly, onerous security clearance procedures can make it difficult if not impossible for some heritage speakers to obtain the security clearances necessary for some federal government positions.

GOVERNMENT DEMAND

Even before the events of September 11, 2001, some observers recognized the strategic value of language experts in the federal government. For example, Brecht and Rivers (2000) found that there were 80 federal departments or agencies that needed people with language skills, and many of these agencies' needs were not being met. Following the attacks, concern grew. Immediately after the terrorist attacks, the General Accounting Office (GAO, now the Government Accountability Office) stated that the lack of personnel with needed skills had "hindered US military, law enforcement, intelligence, counterterrorism, and diplomatic efforts" (U.S. General Accounting Office, 2002). This report found that, just prior to the attacks, the intelligence community did not have enough translators to handle counterterrorism intelligence. Another study of the pre-9/11 situation pointed to long backlogs of material to be analyzed, an unmet need for specialists, and a readiness level of only 30 percent when it came to ability to translate languages used by terrorists (House Permanent Select Committee on Intelligence, 2002).

The 9/11 Commission identified similar problems, finding that the Central Intelligence Agency (CIA) had insufficient personnel qualified for counterterrorism work, partly because of a lack of proficiency in Arabic. The commission recommended that both the CIA and the FBI bolster their language and translation capabilities, and that the CIA develop a stronger language program with higher standards and pay incentives (National Commission on Terrorist Attacks Upon the United States, 2004). The earlier shortcomings at the FBI were highlighted by a media report to the effect that the FBI, three years after 9/11, had thousands of hours of intercepted communications from suspected terrorists that had yet to be translated (Lichtblau, 2004).

GAO conducted a study of how four agencies—the FBI, the State Department, the Army, and the Foreign Commercial Service (U.S. Department of Commerce)—were meeting their language needs (U.S. General Accounting Office, 2002). The study found that all four agencies had unmet needs for translators and interpreters, as well as other staff, such as intelligence analysts and diplomats with foreign language skills. These issues adversely affected U.S. military, law enforcement, intelligence, counterterrorism, and diplomatic efforts. Yet another study by the Congressional Research Service (Kuenzi, 2004) reiterated that there was a widespread understanding that federal foreign language needs were not being met, and that there was a particularly acute lack of people with higher level skills.

The most recently available estimates put the number of federal employees in positions that require foreign language skills at somewhere between 25,000 and 34,000. The range in estimates of the number of positions requiring area expertise is quite large: from 14,000 up to 44,000. These figures are estimates because agencies vary in their need for different types and levels of foreign language and area expertise, and because positions requiring such skills are scattered over a wide number of bureaucracies. Gauging the exact number of people in government with foreign language and area expertise is also complicated by the fact that intelligence agencies do not disclose much information.

Federal Employment of People with Language and Area Expertise

The first comprehensive study of the language and area studies needs and capabilities of the entire federal government was conducted in 1979 by a State Department employee (as cited in Merkx, 2005; Ruther, 2003). The study found that 25 federal agencies employed between 30,000 and 40,000 people whose jobs required competence in a foreign language, and another 14,000 to 19,000 people whose jobs required area expertise—analyzing events in foreign countries and international issues. A 1995 study of 33 agencies estimates that 34,000 positions require foreign language skills (excluding area expertise), and 60 percent of these are in the defense and intelligence communities (Merkx, 2005).

Ruther's estimate (2003) is that 100 agencies require people with foreign language and area expertise. Of 4.2 million federal employees, about 72,000 require foreign language or area expertise (or both):

- 25,840 jobs require foreign language skills,
- 44,080 jobs require area and international studies expertise, and
- 2,280 foreign language positions are filled by contractors.

GAO indicated that more than 70 government agencies needed people with foreign language expertise (excluding area expertise) (U.S. General Accounting Office, 2002). These positions were concentrated in the Army, the State Department, the CIA, and the FBI. The Army, the State Department, and the FBI alone had close to 20,000 positions that require foreign language skills. Earlier, Christopher K. Mellon, former deputy assistant secretary of defense for intelligence, presented a higher estimate of the number of language experts needed by the federal government, testifying to Congress that the military and intelligence agencies alone had 30,000 positions requiring foreign language expertise (Mellon, 2000).

On the basis of these studies, the committee estimates that 25,000 to 34,000 federal positions require foreign language skills, and these tend to be concentrated in defense, intelligence, and law enforcement. The estimated range of need for people with area or international studies expertise is a little wider, from 19,000 to 44,000 federal positions.

Turnover

Using 30,000 as the estimated number of people in federal positions that require foreign language skills, Merkx (2005) states that there is a replacement need of about 6,000 people per year due simply to turnover. Ruther (2003) includes people with both language and area skills. Given various retirement and turnover rates, she estimates annual hiring needs for people with both language and area expertise to range from 8,400 to 10,500 each year for this decade. She takes into account normal turnover plus the effect of a higher retirement rate in the aging federal workforce.

Ruther expects these needs to be met, but there are problem areas: a dearth of people with highly proficient language skills in nine critical languages, particularly in national security agencies (military, intelligence, law enforcement, diplomacy). Her assessment is backed up by the fact that most studies of unmet needs for language expertise in the federal government have focused on the military, intelligence, law enforcement, and, to a lesser extent, the diplomatic corps.

Demand in Specific Federal Agencies

Studies of demand at specific federal agencies have focused on the need for foreign language skills, rather than area knowledge, so it appears that demand is most acute for people with language expertise, albeit with appropriate cultural context.

Federal Bureau of Investigation

The FBI needs individuals with language skills to work as translators, interpreters, and "special agent linguists," who can interview suspects in a foreign language, including suspects who speak a colloquial language or a dialect. One study found that about half of the special agent linguists were proficient at ILR level 3 or above (U.S. General Accounting Office, 2002).

After 9/11, numerous reports highlighted the dearth of people with foreign language expertise at the FBI, particularly in critical languages. The most dangerous manifestation of this was the large backlog of intercepted voice transmissions, in the form of audio tapes, that had to be translated from Arabic, Arabic dialects, and other languages for counterintelligence and counterterrorism purposes (Committee on Economic Development, 2006; National Commission on Terrorist Attacks Upon the United States, 2004; House Permanent Select Committee on Intelligence, 2002; U.S. General Accounting Office, 2002; U.S. Department of Justice Office of the Inspector General, 2004). The 9/11 Commission stated that "shortages of translators in languages such as Arabic, Urdu, Farsi, and Pashto remain a barrier to the FBI's understanding of the terrorist threat." In its conclusion, the commission recommended that the FBI hire more people with language skills and better integrate people with language expertise into intelligence operations.

Since 9/11, the FBI has employed more people with language skills, including heritage speakers from U.S. immigrant communities.[2] In 2001, the FBI had 415 translator/interpreter positions authorized but filled only 360, a 13 percent shortfall (U.S. General Accounting Office, 2002). However, by 2004, the FBI had about 1,200 translators and interpreters, including 400 employees and 800 contractors. Between 2001 and 2004, the number of Arabic language experts jumped from 60 to over 200; Chinese from 70 to 120; Russian from 80 to 100 (U.S. Department of Justice, Office of the Inspector General, 2004). In addition to these translators and interpreters, the agency employed nearly 1,800 special agent linguists in 2002 (U.S. General Accounting Office, 2002).

---

[2]Some observers think that the FBI has not fully integrated these heritage speakers into the agency's organizational culture. If they are correct, the new employees may not remain with the FBI, and they may discourage others in their community from joining the agency.

One of the primary tasks of the FBI language experts is translating audio intercepts. However, demand continues to outstrip supply, and the FBI has needs in a wide variety of languages, not just those associated with counterterrorism. The average time necessary to hire people with language skills has increased from 13 to 14 months, resulting in the bureau's failure to meet targets for people with skills in about half of 52 languages (Committee on Economic Development, 2006).

U.S. Department of State

The State Department employs two types of individuals with language skills: Foreign Service officers and staff, who need to communicate with professionals and other diplomats abroad, using "educated" language, and Civil Service personnel, including some hired for their advanced language proficiency. Unlike Foreign Service personnel, Civil Service linguists are expected to bring language skills to their jobs and do not receive training at the Foreign Service Institute (FSI).[3]

The department has found that an optimal use of Foreign Service personnel is to post people in a variety of regions at first, and then allow them to specialize by region or area of endeavor later in their careers. Because Foreign Service personnel usually change job locations (and frequently languages) every two to three years, the department has a continual need for language training, which is met primarily by the FSI.

New Foreign Service officers often possess a master's degree and some proficiency in at least one foreign language (Malone, 2006). Although foreign language proficiency is not required, the department awards bonus points in the hiring process to candidates who can demonstrate ILR level 2 speaking skills in certain critical languages. This enables FSI to train them faster to the needed higher proficiency levels.

Although the intensive approach to language training used at FSI speeds language learning, the time required for learning often creates a lag between the posting of a Foreign Service position and the time it is filled and does not fully meet the need for Foreign Service officers with advanced foreign language skills (U.S. General Accounting Office, 2002). Several government reports have identified such unmet needs for Foreign Service officers with foreign language skills (U.S. General Accounting Office, 2002). For example, in 2004, the State Department had only eight employees with level 5 ability in Arabic, and 27 at level 4 (Committee for Economic Development, 2006). According to a language officer for the State Department personnel

---

[3]In addition to directly employing language specialists in the Civil Service, the State Department maintains a pool of contract linguists, estimated to number about 1,800 in 2002 (U.S. General Accounting Office, 2002).

system, Foreign Service employees assigned to language-designated positions normally have either the required language proficiency or the time to take relevant FSI training. In some instances, however, an employee must be assigned without either. Although the intensive approach to language training used at FSI speeds training time, in many instances—especially in critical languages requiring one to two years to reach needed proficiency— the State Department is forced to choose between sending the employee to post without needed proficiency or forcing the post to accept an extended vacancy while the employee takes training. Positions requiring proficiency in critical languages, such as Arabic, Chinese, and Japanese, are sometimes difficult to fill. To cover such vacancies, the department is currently exploring ways to establish "float" positions that would be able to cover such training-based staffing gaps.[4]

GAO updated its study in 2006, finding that the State Department was still having difficulty filling positions that required language expertise and could not show that its recent efforts in this area were succeeding. Agency-wide, 30 percent of its staff in language designated positions did not fully meet the language proficiency requirements; this percentage was even higher (approaching 60 percent) at embassies in strategically important countries, such as China and Yemen (U.S. Government Accountability Office, 2006). In early 2007, a language officer for the State Department personnel system reported that the Foreign Service had over 4,000 positions requiring some language skills, an increase from about 2,500 such positions in 2001. Among the 2007 positions, most required proficiency at ILR level 2 or above, while a small fraction were "language preferred" positions requiring only courtesy-level language.[5]

The recent Iraq Study Group report provides a vivid portrait of the need for additional personnel with more advanced levels of language proficiency. The report pointed out that of 1,000 personnel in the U.S. embassy in Baghdad, only 31 spoke Arabic. Of those, only six spoke fluent Arabic.

U.S. Department of Defense

In public comments to the committee, under secretary of defense for personnel and readiness David Chu outlined the types and levels of language and area skills needed by the military. He said that the Department of Defense (DoD) was moving toward a future in which the large majority of officers would be expected to be able to speak, read, and understand at least one foreign language, at least at an elementary level. In addition, he said, the military would need some number of officers with advanced proficiency

---

[4]Personal communication, Lauren Marcott, State Department, January 2007.
[5]Personal communication, Lauren Marcott, State Department, January 2007.

in foreign languages and all officers going through the services war colleges would be required to develop "cultural competency" (Chu, 2006). His remarks underscored the conclusions of the 2005 Defense Language Transformation Roadmap, designed to address DoD's significant and increasing need for language and cultural expertise.

The most recent detailed estimates of DoD's language needs come from a 2002 GAO report, which focuses solely on the Army. In 2001, the Army had authorization to fill 329 translator/interpreter positions in critical languages: Arabic, Korean, Chinese, Farsi, and Russian. It was able to fill only 183 of these positions, a shortfall of 44 percent. For Arabic specifically, the shortfall was 50 percent; for Farsi it was 68 percent. A more recent report reconfirmed the significant shortfall of Arabic translators for U.S. military forces in Iraq (Committee for Economic Development, 2006).

In general, all branches of the military are facing the need for personnel with language expertise at increasingly higher levels. The Defense Language Institute is endeavoring to help meet this growing need by expanding capacity and increasing its targeted proficiency levels.

DEMAND IN OTHER SECTORS

Business

Business needs are different from those of government agencies, emphasizing cultural competency over advanced language skills. For example, when Kedia and Daniel (2003) surveyed U.S. firms about their needs, about 30 percent said that the main impediment to more sales overseas was lack of internationally competent personnel. This lack of cultural competency had caused the responding firms to miss marketing or business opportunities as they failed to anticipate the needs of international customers. And 80 percent of the firms said their sales would increase if their staff had more international expertise. When asked about different types of international skills, a global perspective, understanding of foreign business practices, and appreciation for cross-cultural differences were seen to be most important for people in professional positions. A total of 31 percent of the respondents said it was difficult to find people with such skills; 69 percent said it was not. Among a list of international skills required by the firms, respondents indicated that knowledge of a foreign language was least important. These results might be partly due to the fact that the surveyed firms tended to rely primarily on foreign nationals to run their overseas operations, along with a few U.S. managers.

Merkx (2005) estimates that the U.S. business community probably has about 200,000 people whose jobs require foreign language and area skills, and there is a replacement need of about 20,000 positions each year.

Most studies of the need for such personnel have found that U.S. firms expect their overseas business to grow more quickly than domestic business (Kedia and Daniel, 2003; Committee for Economic Development, 2006; Bikson and Law, 1994), increasing demand for people with language and area skills. The firms surveyed by Kedia and Daniel (2003) ranked Asia to be the region of greatest importance to current and future business activities. Europe ranked a little lower, followed by Latin America. Africa and the Middle East were areas of less interest, although the importance of all regions was seen as increasing.

A few studies have identified business needs for people proficient in foreign languages. For example, the average number of languages spoken by a U.S. business executive is 1.5; for European executives the figure is 3.9 (Committee for Economic Development, 2006). However, most of the available evidence indicates that U.S. firms' greatest need is for people with a general awareness of global business and foreign culture that could help them identify and exploit business opportunities abroad.

Institutions of Higher Education

Understanding higher education's demand for language and area expertise and developing strategies to meet those demands is critically important, because universities and colleges train the next generation of language, area, and international experts. This section addresses university demand (see Chapter 6 for a discussion of the role of Title VI/FH programs in supporting universities as suppliers of expertise).

Welles (2003) found that, between 1992 and 2002, the number of academic positions open in foreign language instruction ranged from 535 to 675 annually. While half of these were tenure-track positions, many of the nontenure-track positions were those emphasizing language acquisition. The demand was greatest for teaching Spanish. Between 1985 and 2002, the number of faculty job openings in Spanish roughly doubled, while openings for French, German, and Russian faculty stagnated or declined. Although the supply of Ph.D.s met demand for Spanish and other Romance languages, these are not the critical languages most needed today.

The heavy emphasis on Spanish appears to be shifting somewhat, according to the Welles (2004) study of postsecondary enrollments in foreign languages (see Table 2-1). College enrollment in language courses is increasing, both in terms of absolute numbers and as a percentage of college students (from 7.3 percent in 1980 to 8.6 percent in 2002). Students are increasingly interested in Arabic. Over the four years from 1998 to 2002, enrollment in Arabic classes nearly doubled, although overall enrollment is low compared with other languages. Interest in Chinese is also growing significantly.

TABLE 2-1 Foreign Language Enrollments in Selected Languages in U.S. Institutions of Higher Education, 1998 and 2002

Language	1998 Enrollment	2002 Enrollment	Percentage Change, 1998-2002	Percentage of Overall 2002 Language Enrollment
Spanish	656,590	746,267	13.7	53.4
French	199,064	201,979	1.5	14.5
German	89,020	91,100	2.3	6.5
Italian	49,287	63,899	29.6	4.6
Japanese	43,141	52,238	21.1	3.7
Chinese	28,456	34,153	20.0	2.4
Russian	23,791	23,921	.5	1.7
Arabic	5,505	10,584	92.3	.8

SOURCE: Welles (2004).

Universities need more instructors in Arabic, Chinese, and other critical languages to meet growing student interest. Welles (2003) suggests that universities are not producing enough Arabic Ph.D.s (only 6 in 2001) to meet future demands. Betteridge assessed the availability of Arabic language and area studies faculty through a 2003 study of the membership of the Middle East Studies Association (MESA).[6] Between 1991 and 2002, the membership of MESA grew only slightly, from 2,375 to 2,572, and the percentage of members who were full professors declined. MESA faculty were older than average, and there was some indication that retirees were not being replaced. During this period, 20 percent of MESA members were students. The study suggests that student interest in teaching Arabic at the university level was decreasing because of a perceived lack of prestige and rewards for language faculty. Instead, students were more interested in Middle Eastern politics and economics.

These challenges in the field of Arabic and Middle East studies illuminate a second problem that hinders the potential of universities to supply international and language expertise. Although there is robust demand for faculty in foreign languages and area studies, universities are increasingly relying on graduate assistants, part-time instructors, and adjunct faculty to meet this demand, particularly for language teaching. In 1998, the Modern Language Association warned, on the basis of results of job placement surveys, that "if present employment patterns continue fewer than half the

---

[6]There has not been a systematic review of area studies needs across world areas since a study published in 1991 by NCASA (National Council of Area Studies Associations) based on data collected in the 1980s.

seven or eight thousand graduate students likely to earn PhDs in English and foreign languages between 1996 and 2000 can expect to obtain full-time tenure-track positions within a year of receiving their degrees" (Modern Language Association, 1998).

This practice, if it continues, injects a degree of uncertainty into projections of future demand, and may also discourage young people from helping to meet that demand by preparing for faculty careers in language teaching. In any case, according to Merkx (2005), there will be a need for about 1,400 language faculty and 820 area studies faculty annually over the next decade, as an older generation of faculty retires. Merkx states that there are about 1,900 Ph.D.s produced annually in these disciplines, which would indicate a slight shortfall, but he only counts the Ph.D.s produced by Title VI-funded institutions.

Elementary and Secondary Education

Available evidence suggests that demand for K-12 foreign language teachers is increasing. Enrollments in foreign languages are rising slightly, and there is evidence that school districts are finding it difficult to fill job openings for foreign language teachers. School districts are also starting programs in less commonly taught languages, sometimes with the support of the federal government.

The American Council on the Teaching of Foreign Language conducted a study of public school enrollments in foreign languages (Draper and Hicks, 2002). Enrollment in the latter half of the 1990s increased very slightly, from 32.8 percent of all students in public secondary schools in 1996 to 33.8 percent in 2000. As with the postsecondary level, Spanish is the most studied foreign language, and growth in enrollment from 1996 to 2000 was greatest in Spanish—about 3 percent. Enrollments for French and German decreased.

A survey of principals and foreign language teachers by the Center for Applied Linguistics (1999) had findings on enrollments similar to those in the American Council on the Teaching of Foreign Languages study. It also addressed the lack of teachers. At the secondary level, lack of foreign language teachers was identified as a major problem by survey respondents, along with funding, lack of training, and poor academic counseling. The top issues for elementary schools were overall lack of funding for language instruction, lack of in-service training, and inadequate sequencing from elementary to secondary schools. Larger student-teacher ratios were identified as major problems at both the elementary and the secondary levels.

The lack of foreign language teachers was also addressed in a report by the Center on Reinventing Public Education at the University of Washington (Murphy and DeArmond, 2003). The researchers drew on data from the Schools and Staffing Survey of the U.S. Department of Education's National Center for Education Statistics. One of their findings was that job openings for foreign language teachers were most difficult to fill—more so than openings for other hard-to-fill teaching positions in special education, English as a second language, or science. At the same time, administrators were less likely to use cash incentives to lure foreign language teachers to their districts than they were for teachers of other subjects.

There is some evidence that teachers of less commonly taught languages will be in greater demand, because of a recent push for the teaching of such languages, for example Chinese and Arabic. The Portland, Oregon, school district, for example, received a grant under the new National Flagship Language Program (part of the National Security Education Program under the Department of Defense) to teach Chinese, and Dearborn, Michigan, is implementing a similar program in Arabic. Chicago, Houston, and Philadelphia have also announced Chinese language programs (Manzo, 2006b). Such efforts are hampered by a lack of teachers, however (Manzo, 2006a).

CONCLUSION

Although there is a long-standing and continuing significant unmet need for foreign language, area, and international experts in government, demand is not limited to government. There are clear needs in all levels of the education system—elementary, secondary, and higher education—that also must be addressed to ensure that the nation continues to produce graduates interested and able to pursue international careers in government, business, nonprofit organizations, and other arenas. Businesses need workers with knowledge of world markets and an ability to operate in other cultures. Although immediate needs are significant, longer term needs cannot be ignored. A breadth of expertise in a range of languages and topics that are not yet recognized as critical is likely to yield future benefits that enhance the nation's security and prosperity. While Title VI/FH programs help address immediate demands, their purpose extends beyond this to help address more long-term, but substantial, societal needs.

3

Title VI and Fulbright-Hays Implementation

The Title VI and Fulbright-Hays (Title VI/FH) programs at the U.S. Department of Education (ED) are among many federal programs that support the study of foreign languages and cultures. Some of these programs are in-house training programs that prepare federal employees to meet job-related requirements, while others, like the Title VI/FH ones, are more general educational programs designed to create a broad pool of expertise. This chapter begins with an overview of the federal programs supporting language, area, and international studies based on the committee's review of publicly available descriptive information about the programs to illustrate how the Title VI/FH programs fit into the federal government's broader efforts in this area. It then moves to discussion of how the programs are implemented at ED, including historical funding trends, and how they operate in the university context.

TITLE VI/FH PROGRAMS IN RELATION TO OTHER FEDERAL PROGRAMS

Federally funded language and area studies programs can be divided into two categories, reflecting whether their primary role is to address more immediate demands for job-related language, area, and international skills or longer term, more general needs[1] (see Box 3-1; see also Appendix F for

---

[1]The federal government also meets some of its language training needs through the use of private contractors; language training at some agencies is simply contracted out to companies, such as Berlitz. In addition, some agencies maintain pools of translators who work

58

**BOX 3-1
Two Types of Federal Language
and International Education Programs**

General Education Programs

- Title VI, Department of Education
- Fulbright-Hays, Department of Education
- Foreign Language Assistance Program, Department of Education
- International programs under the Fund for Improvement of Postsecondary Education, Department of Education
- National Security Education Program (NSEP), Department of Defense
- Fulbright Program, Department of State
- Title VIII and Gilman Scholarships, Department of State
- Louis Stokes and Pat Roberts Scholarships, various intelligence agencies

Federal Training Programs

- Foreign Service Institute, Department of State
- Defense Language Institute, Department of Defense
- Special Operations Forces Language Office, Department of Defense
- National Cryptologic School, National Security Agency
- Intelligence Language Institute, Central Intelligence Agency

---

a brief description of each program and information on its purpose, eligibility, funding level, and number of participants.)

In the first category are training programs designed to meet more immediate job-related needs that are available exclusively for federal personnel—people employed in the Foreign Service, military, intelligence, law enforcement, and so forth. Training is provided by government institutes, such as the Foreign Service Institute (FSI) and Defense Language Institute (DLI) (as well as contractors), to address immediate language needs of the federal agencies. The level of proficiency is determined by the operational requirements of the job or task and the domain in which the language is to be used.

---

on a contract basis, such as at the U.S. Department of State's Office of Language Services. In response to a congressional mandate, the Federal Bureau of Investigation established the National Virtual Translation Center in 2003 to coordinate and expand the pool of contract translators with advanced language proficiency. Supported by several intelligence and defense agencies, the center develops and maintains a shared database with up-to-date information on available translators, while simultaneously informing translators about a variety of full-time and part-time work opportunities (National Virtual Translation Center, 2007).

In the second category are scholarship, recruitment, and exchange programs that can be accessed by a wide range of students, academics, administrators, and institutions. This group of federal programs, including the Title VI/FH programs, develops a broad pool of bachelor's, master's, and doctoral graduates with language abilities or knowledge of world regions and international issues (or both), helping to meet long-term needs. Although there are some similarities between the Title VI/FH programs and the other federal programs in this category, there are also several key differences:

- **Title VI/FH programs at ED have no foreign policy component.** Although the Fulbright programs at the U.S. Department of State are of benefit to the nation's academics and society, their primary purpose is fostering mutual understanding among people of different nations. Fulbright programs at the State Department help build connections between opinion makers and academics in the United States and other nations, for the purpose of improving the image of the United States abroad.
- **Title VI/FH programs at ED are not recruitment programs.** Although the legislation that created the programs at ED stresses the importance of language and area studies knowledge for the purpose of national security, most of the component programs are not primarily aimed at creating a direct pipeline into the foreign affairs, intelligence, and military bureaucracies.[2] That is the major purpose of other programs in the group, such as the National Security Education Program, the Pat Roberts and Pickering Fellowships, and the Stokes Scholarships. Those programs seek to identify talented individuals with critical skills and pay for part of their education, with the possibility of permanent employment in the intelligence and national security communities. They also require federal service, unlike the Title VI/FH programs.
- **Title VI/FH programs at ED do not focus solely on "critical" languages.** Critical languages are identified by the national security community as those in which need for language abilities is greatest, because they are spoken in nations considered critical to U.S. national security. The National Security Education Program focuses on these critical languages. The federal government institutes and other resources specific to government personnel focus on languages demanded by their agency at the time of their training. In contrast, Title VI/FH was created to support the study of any "modern" foreign language deemed to be underrepresented in the

---

[2]One exception is the Institute for International Public Policy Program (IIPP) under ED Title VI/FH, which is focused on preparing minority students for a career in international affairs. This program, which has some similarities with the scholarship programs at the State Department, is discussed in Chapter 11.

United States, with a focus on less commonly taught languages. Less commonly taught languages are languages other than English, German, French, and Spanish.

• **Other ED programs supporting language and area studies share similar purposes with Title VI/FH programs, but the relationship is complementary.** ED's Foreign Language Assistance Program (FLAP) is specifically aimed at improving foreign language instruction at the K-12 level, by funding innovative state and district-level programs that can be replicated in other states. The Title VI programs provide resources primarily to institutions of higher education, with some expected to provide outreach to the K-12 system to help develop expertise. Although teachers are eligible for some of the FH programs, it is to study overseas in order to improve their capacity to teach foreign languages and international and area studies. The Fund for the Improvement of Postsecondary Education (FIPSE) includes several components. One component funds three international programs[3] similar to those funded by the Fulbright Group Projects Abroad (GPA) Program. However, the FIPSE programs grew out of international cooperation agreements with Mexico, Canada, Brazil, and the European Union, and the Office of Postsecondary Education appears to distinguish projects geographically between FIPSE and Fulbright GPA. As part of its grants competition, however, FIPSE does fund some higher education international education programs that appear similar to those funded by Title VI.

The greatest overlap in terms of activities exists between ED Title VI/ FH and two other programs: the Fulbright Program at the State Department, which shares its beginnings with the Fulbright-Hays Program at ED, and the National Security Education Program at the U.S. Department of Defense (DoD). While there is some overlap in funded activities, there are also key differences in the purpose and emphases of the programs.

Fulbright-Hays at the Departments of Education and State

Both the Fulbright program at the State Department and the Fulbright program at the ED were created by the Mutual Educational and Cultural Exchange Act of 1961, for the purpose of "increasing mutual understanding between the people of the U.S. and the people of other countries" (U.S. Department of State, 2003). Although the programs have some activities in common, the two Fulbright programs have different purposes. The

---

[3]These are the U.S.-Brazil Higher Education Consortia Program; European Union-United States of America Cooperation Program in Higher Education and Vocational Education and Training; and the Program for North American Mobility in Higher Education.

programs at the State Department are focused abroad in order to make connections and increase understanding among U.S. and foreign students, academics, and opinion makers. The programs at ED have the goal of improving U.S. domestic education in foreign languages and area studies. Although the State Department's Fulbright programs have the residual effect of increasing area and language knowledge, they are designed primarily to serve a foreign policy goal—to counter the sometimes negative image of the United States in foreign universities and among opinion makers. In that sense, there is no overlap in terms of the purposes of both programs.

Despite their different missions, both programs support U.S. citizens in their study abroad, in somewhat similar ways. For example:

• Both fund graduate-level research abroad (ED's Training Grants for Doctoral Dissertation Research Abroad [DDRA] and the State Department's Fulbright-Hays Student Program).
• Both fund faculty travel and research abroad (ED's Fulbright-Hays Faculty Research Abroad [FRA] Fellowship Program and the State Department's Fulbright Scholar Program).
• Both fund travel for K-12 educators abroad (ED's Fulbright-Hays Seminars Abroad [SA] and the State Department's Fulbright Teacher and Administrator Exchange Program).
• With the Fulbright-Hays SA/Bilateral Projects, ED works in tandem with the State Department to provide funding for U.S. citizens to take part in binational projects.

However, the different missions of the two programs are reflected in the quite different topics that are investigated during these study abroad activities. Many participants in the Fulbright program at the State Department are not traveling abroad specifically to improve language and area studies but to lecture and to do research, primarily on social and political issues. The K-12 programs are also different. Unlike the State Department Fulbright programs, the ED Fulbright-Hays programs do not invite foreign teachers to the United States.

Title VI and the National Security Education Program

The National Security Education Program (NSEP) at DoD was created by the David L. Boren National Security Education Act of 1991 (Title VIII of the Intelligence Authorization Act). The primary impetus was post-Desert Storm analyses and congressional hearings. The National Security Education Act mandated that the secretary of defense create a program to award scholarships and fellowships to undergraduate and graduate students to study languages and regions critical to U.S. national security, including the opportunity to study abroad in those regions. It also mandated that DoD provide support to U.S. institutions to develop programs in and about countries and languages critical to U.S. national security. The aim was to create a direct link between identifying the federal government's current and future language needs, supporting individuals studying those languages, and then recruiting those same individuals for careers in national security or to meet other language needs (National Security Education Program, n.d.).

The program surveys federal agencies for their broadly defined area and language needs and then allocates portable scholarship funds to U.S. undergraduate and graduate students. NSEP includes a service requirement that mandates a good faith effort by scholarship recipients to gain employment in a national security-related position in the federal government. The terms of the service agreement have been modified by Congress on three separate occasions, most recently in 2006. The current service provision requires NSEP award recipients to first seek employment in one of four federal organizations (Departments of Defense, Homeland Security, State, and the intelligence community) and, if no position is available, in any federal agency in a position related to national security. In a given year, there are about 350 recipients in the pipeline to fulfill their obligation to work in a federal agency. The largest number of recipients finds positions in the Departments of State and Defense, and the intelligence community.

NSEP receives direction from the Office of the Under Secretary of Defense for Personnel and Readiness and administrative support from the National Defense University. The program currently has three major component parts: (1) undergraduate scholarships, (2) graduate fellowships, and (3) grants to institutions. Since 2003, NSEP has reoriented its institutional grants to the National Flagship Language Program (NFLP). NFLP programs are at major U.S. universities and are designed to develop and implement curriculum to graduate students with Interagency Language Roundable (ILR) level 3 proficiency in "critical" languages (Arabic, Central Asian Chinese, Farsi, Hindi, Urdu, Korean, and Russian) to level 3 proficiency on the ILR scale.

NSEP is different from the ED Title VI/FH programs in a few significant ways. First, it is focused on current language needs in the area of national security, the critical foreign languages spoken in nations that are important allies or actual or potential adversaries of the United States. Second, there is a government service requirement for NSEP individual grantees. Third, fellows typically spend extended periods of time studying overseas.

However, according to a Congressional Research Service report (Kuenzi and Riddle, 2005a) there is some potential overlap between the activities of NSEP and ED Title VI/FH programs. It is in NSEP's grants to institutions of higher education under the National Flagship Language Program, which may overlap with the Title VI grants to National and Language

Resource Centers. Another Congressional Research Service report (Kuenzi and Riddle, 2005b) also raises the issue of an overlap and discusses the possibility of saving administrative costs by consolidating the two programs, focusing Title VI at ED more on critical languages or moving the NSEP to ED or the Central Intelligence Agency.[4] Congress discussed the possibility of moving the NSEP to ED but rejected it in order to retain the connection with defense-related interests. Figure 3-1 illustrates the general overlap between Title VI/FH programs at ED, the Fulbright program at the State Department, and NSEP at DoD, as well as some of the areas in which each program is distinct.

Unique Components of Title VI Programs

There are also several components of the Title VI programs that fund activities unique to the array of federal programs; in some cases, the resources and materials produced by these programs serve as resources to the other federal programs. They include

- Funding U.S. institutions of higher education to provide education and training in international business (Centers for International Business Education and Research [CIBER], Business and International Education [BIE]).
- Supporting international studies programs (as opposed to students) at the undergraduate level (Undergraduate International Studies and Foreign Language [UISFL]).
- Developing instructional and assessment materials related to foreign language teaching (Language Resource Centers [LRC]).
- Supporting overseas research centers that promote postgraduate research (American Overseas Research Centers).
- Developing materials for foreign language instruction (International Research and Studies [IRS]).
- Conducting surveys and evaluations of foreign language instruction (IRS).
- Using technology to collect and archive foreign language instructional materials (Technological Innovation and Cooperation for Foreign Information Access [TICFIA]).

---

[4]The president's proposed National Security Language Initiative would move the pilot K-16 initiatives funded under NSEP into an expanded program at ED.

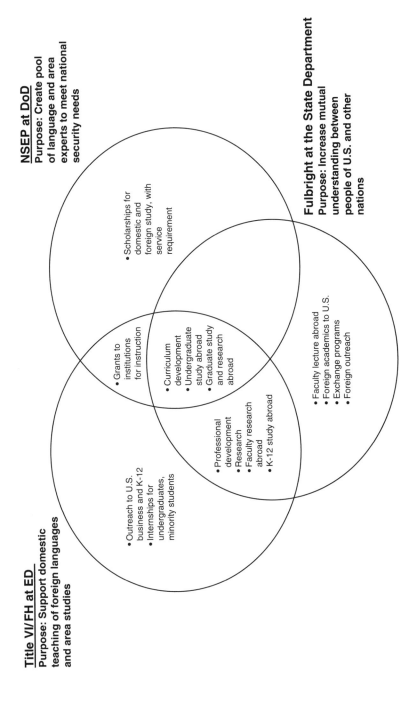

FIGURE 3-1 Overlap in activities of three federal foreign language and area studies programs.
NOTE: The size of the circles or the area of overlap should not be interpreted to indicate an exact level of overlap.

TITLE VI AND FULBRIGHT-HAYS
IN THE DEPARTMENT OF EDUCATION

During 2006, international education began to reemerge as a priority in ED. Early in the year, the secretaries of education and state convened a meeting of university leaders to discuss the Bush administration's proposed National Security Language Initiative, designed to increase the number of Americans learning critical foreign languages, with an emphasis on the K-12 system (see Chapter 13). The American Competitiveness Initiative was also launched, which included SMART (Science and Mathematics Access to Retain Talent) grants awarded by ED for undergraduates and graduates studying critical foreign languages[5] or science, mathematics, or technology.

In September 2006, the secretary of education's Commission on Higher Education released its final report, calling for increased federal investment in higher education to support international education, including study abroad and foreign language training (U.S. Department of Education, 2006a). In October of that year, ED released new grants to school districts for language instruction, including many in the critical foreign languages targeted by the National Security Language Initiative. And in a November speech welcoming participants to the annual International Education Week conference, Secretary Spellings said that globalization highlighted "the importance of foreign languages in communicating and forming partnerships with citizens from other cultures and countries" (Spellings, 2006). At the same time, the committee was unable to identify meaningful reference to foreign language study or international education in ED's current strategic plan.

The ED has several offices with a role in international and foreign language issues: the Office of International Affairs in the Office of the Secretary; the Office of English Language Acquisition, which reports to the deputy secretary of education and houses the Foreign Language Assistance Program; and the Office of Postsecondary Education, which houses the International Education Programs Service and the Fund for the Improvement of Postsecondary Education. According to the Office of Management and Budget, ED at one point had an International Activities Coordinating Group, which was formed to improve the coordination of international programs and activities throughout ED (U.S. Office of Management and Budget, 2004). According to ED staff, the group met periodically for about a year between 2002 and 2003 but is no longer active.

---

[5]Although, as discussed in Chapter 1, it included a broader list of critical languages.

International Education Programs Service

The Title VI/FH programs are administered by the International Education Programs Service (IEPS) in the Office of Postsecondary Education. The director of the office is currently a career civil servant who reports to the deputy assistant secretary for education, who in turn reports to the assistant secretary for postsecondary education. At one point in the past, under the Carter administration, the office was headed by a political appointee who reported to an assistant secretary for international education.[6] The current organizational position of the programs may reflect the relatively low priority that foreign languages, area, and international issues have been given in the recent past.

There appear to be few formal mechanisms for coordination either across programs in the department or across the full range of federal government programs. However, various IEPS staff represent the department on interagency coordinating groups, including a group at the State Department related to the Fulbright-Hays programs and the ILR (Ruther, 2006). The ILR is a loosely knit network of language specialists from across the federal government, academia, and nongovernmental organizations. It organizes monthly plenary meetings with presentations and meetings of three standing committees on language testing, language training, and translation and interpretation (Interagency Language Roundtable, 2006a).

The IEPS office implements each of the 14 programs as a separate competition, although universities applying for both the National Resource Centers (NRC) and the Foreign Language and Area Studies (FLAS) Fellowship Programs do so with a single application. For some of the smaller programs, a single project officer oversees all grants made for that program. For the larger programs, multiple project officers are involved. Project officers appear to operate with significant autonomy, creating both opportunities for creativity (see, for example, Chapter 10) and the risk of stagnation. As mentioned in Chapter 1, the IEPS staff manage funds from three appropriations: one for the Institute of International Public Policy, a second for the remaining Title VI programs, and a third for the Fulbright-Hays programs. Allocation of resources across the Title VI or Fulbright-Hays programs is an administrative decision made by the department; in general, the previous year's amount appears to determine subsequent year funding.

---

[6]President Carter also created a high-level Commission on Foreign Language and International Studies to raise the visibility of international education, assess national needs, and recommend funding and resources to meet those needs.

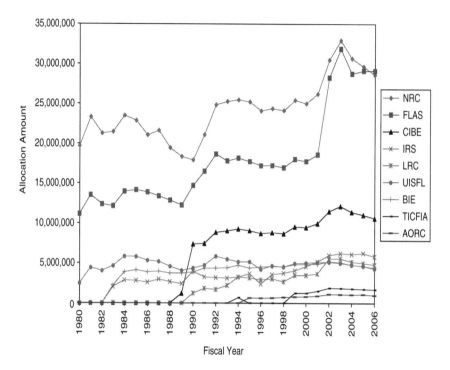

FIGURE 3-2 Allocation history for the Title VI programs, 1997-2006 (adjusted to 2006 dollar amounts.
SOURCE: Data provided by U.S. Department of Education. IIPP is not included since it receives a separate appropriation.

Funding Allocations

Since 1980, the oldest year for which the committee was able to obtain these data,[7] most programs have received more or less the same proportion of the total Title VI or FH appropriation. Although ED is generally given discretion to allocate funds among the component programs, allocations in any given year are guided by the proportional allocations in previous years.[8] Congress has also provided direction on how increases in funding should be used (see Chapter 1). The NRC and FLAS Programs have consistently received the largest share of total Title VI funding, followed by the CIBER

---

[7]ED was not able to provide information on the allocation of funds across programs any earlier than 1980.

[8]As reported by IEPS Program staff at June 19, 2006 meeting, Washington, D.C.

Program. The other programs have received relatively constant shares of overall spending although the LRC Program received an increase in funding in the early 2000s, consistent with a congressional directive (see Figure 3-2). The FLAS Program, the only one that has experienced a sustained increase in the proportion of total funds allocated, is a notable exception. Total FLAS funding increased from 25 percent in 1997 to 32 percent in 2006. Consistent with the intent expressed in appropriations language, both the average per fellowship award and the number of fellowships increased. The average award for an academic year fellowship increased from $20,000 in FY 1997 to $27,000 in FY 2006.

TABLE 3-1 Foreign Language and Area Studies Awards

Year	FLAS Annual	FLAS Summer	FLAS Overall
1980	—	—	$42,680
1981	$50,827	—	—
1982	41,582	—	—
1983	—	—	43,586
1984	—	—	41,520
1985	—	—	38,057
1986	—	—	28,128
1987	—	—	25,459
1988	—	—	27,175
1989	37,579	$ 9,395	25,053
1990	—	—	—
1991	—	—	—
1992	—	—	28,496
1993	36,912	8,685	25,315
1994	—	—	—
1995	38,261	9,604	27,286
1996	36,209	9,091	25,823
1997	34,478	10,357	25,107
1998	33,083	9,938	24,091
1999	31,817	9,545	22,814
2000	32,079	9,165	22,684
2001	30,525	8,721	21,441
2002	34,018	8,164	24,116
2003	31,382	7,532	22,213
2004	28,670	6,881	19,806
2005	27,746	6,936	19,281
2006	27,000	6,500	18,661

— Data not available.
SOURCE: Data provided by U.S. Department of Education. Data were adjusted to 2006 values using the College Tuition subindex of the Consumer Price Index for All Urban Consumers (CPI-U). Available: http://www.bls.gov/cpi.[accessed March 2007].

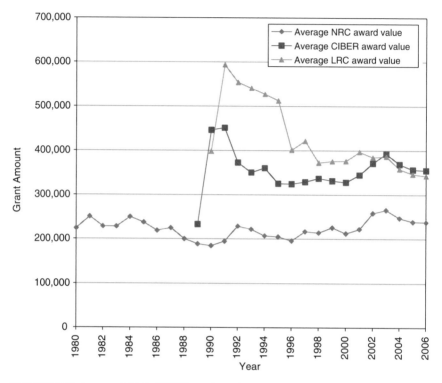

FIGURE 3-3 Average NRC, CIBER, and LRC grant amounts, 1980-2006 (adjusted to 2006 dollar values using the CPI-U).

Although appropriations have sometimes occurred in conjunction with the addition of new Title VI programs, funding overall has not kept pace with the expanded mission of the programs and the expectations (e.g., data collection, outreach) placed on grantees, or with inflation. For example, although FLAS awards have increased since 1980, when adjusted to account for rising tuition costs, their value has decreased (see Table 3-1). Similarly, although the main Title VI appropriation in recent years is near what it was in the program's heyday (see Figure 1-1), it is now used to fund nine programs rather than three. Given the increased number of programs and program objectives, this could be interpreted as a decrease in funding. Finally, although the average NRC grant remained relatively constant between 1980 and 2006 (see Figure 3-3), program expectations have increased. NRCs are required to conduct teacher training activities, expected to reach out to a range of professional disciplines, and required to collect extensive data on courses offered, placement of program graduates, publications, outreach, and related activities. Although LRCs and CIBERs

TABLE 3-2 2003-2006 Competition Results for NRC, CIBER, and LRC Programs, in Real and Adjusted Dollars

Program	FY 2003			FY 2006		Percentage Change		
	Number of Grants	Average Award: Real Value (2003 dollars)	Average Award: Adjusted Value (2006 dollars using CPI-U)	Number of Grants	Average Award: Real Value (2006 dollars)	Number of Grants	Average Award: (FY 2003 Real Value to FY 2006 Real Value)	Average Award: (FY 2003 Adjusted Value to FY 2006 Real Value)
NRC	120	250,250	274,187	124	230,806	3	(8)	(16)
CIBER	30	370,000	405,391	31	343,548	3	(7)	(15)
LRC	14	364,286	399,130	15	320,000	7	(7)	(20)

SOURCE: Data provided by U.S. Department of Education.

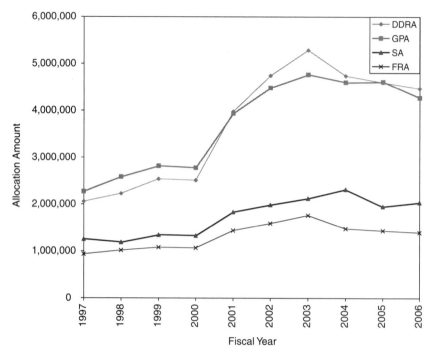

FIGURE 3-4 Allocation history for the Fulbright-Hays programs, 1997-2006 (adjusted to 2006 dollar values using the CPI-U).
SOURCE: Data provided by U.S. Department of Education.

have also experienced fluctuations in their average grant award, the average award for those programs has generally been around $100,000 per year higher than NRC average awards. Over the past three years, the average grant award for the NRCs, CIBERs, and LRCs have all decreased, even without accounting for inflation (see Table 3-2). It appears that this is due in part to the increase in the number of grants.

Like Title VI, Fulbright-Hays received a funding increase in the early 2000s, although the total amount for these programs remains very small in comparison to Title VI. Most of the increased funding was allocated to the DDRA Program, which funds research by individual graduate students, and GPA (see Figure 3-4).

The proliferation of programs has also increased management challenges, while Title VI/FH staffing levels have either decreased or remained stable. At the same time, staff are now required to perform both financial and project monitoring functions, tasks that were performed by two different people in the past. Staff operate separate competitions for each of the 14 programs, with different rating criteria and priorities for each.

Application Process

A separate request for applications (RFA) is published in the *Federal Register* and on the ED website, along with the form, the criteria that will be used to evaluate and rank the applications and priorities that will apply to that competition. Most competitions are held every 3-4 years (see Table 1-1). Awards under the CIBER, NRC, and LRC Programs were recently extended from 3 to 4 years, both to decrease staff burden and to enable more stability for the funded centers.

ED uses application rating criteria and three types of priorities to influence grant applications and direct funds toward perceived federal needs (see Appendix C). An applicant must propose activities responsive to an *absolute priority* to be considered for funding. Applicants who respond to *competitive priorities* may receive extra points in the review process, affecting the likelihood of success in the grant competition. Finally, applicants who respond to an *invitational priority*—a priority that signals IEPS interest in a topic—may receive additional funding for doing so, but they do not receive any competitive preference over other applicants.

During site visits and other meetings with grantees, staff indicated that priorities influence their applications significantly. ED also uses rating criteria to steer applicants in particular directions. For example, in the most recent RFA for NRC grant proposals, IEPS allocated 25 points for "impact and evaluation," encouraging applicants to propose strong self-evaluation plans.

Applications may be submitted online or in paper form. IEPS staff conduct a technical assistance meeting prior to each competition to inform potential grantees about the process and the relevant criteria and priorities for each competition. Once applications are received, IEPS convenes panels of experts to review them according to the detailed rating criteria published in the RFA. This process takes place electronically; reviewers do not meet for face-to-face discussion. To review NRC and FLAS applications, IEPS convenes separate panels for each world area made up of two area experts and one language expert. The expert review panels rank all applications. Panels reviewing NRC and FLAS applications compare and rank them against other applications in that world area, while other panels review and rank all applications in a program (e.g., all CIBER applications, all IRS applications). ED awards grants to applicants ranked above a certain cutoff point established for each program or world area. The committee was told by ED officials that separate panels are used to ensure that there is some capacity retained in each of the world areas and that this process is currently being reconsidered. After a competition, applicants may request from IEPS their rankings for each of the criteria and any specific comments provided by the reviewers. This is typically sent in hard copy and may take several days to receive. Applicants receive information about their own application only.

Grant Monitoring Process

For the several programs that award multiyear grants, IEPS staff conduct annual grant reviews based on the information submitted via the Evaluation of Exchange, Language, International and Area Studies (EELIAS) database.[9] Individual project officers are expected to review the reports to determine that the grantee has made reasonable progress. According to both ED officials and grantee staff, site visits by IEPS project officers have been severely curtailed in recent years, given staff and other resource limitations. In addition, current departmental procedures require senior-level approval of individual travel requests. The committee was told by ED officials that the increased focus on evaluation in the application process, which now includes a requirement to include an outside evaluator, was implemented in part to address the limitations faced by staff to conduct on-site reviews.

Center Grants

As mentioned above, the NRC competition is run by world area, with the targeted world area defined by the grantee. ED has directed applicants toward particular world areas using application priorities. In some cases, this has been in response to specific congressional directives included in appropriations language and may be a factor in the distribution of grants. The preference extended in the application process to applicants with existing capacity may also be a factor in the relative constancy of centers focused on any given world area. NRC awards have maintained three overall tiers with the largest number of centers consistently being in areas of strategic importance (see Figure 3-5):

• Largest number of centers: East Asia, Latin America, Middle East, Russia/Eastern Europe
• Middle number of centers: Africa, International, South Asia, Southeast Asia, Western Europe

---

[9]In February 2007, IEPS launched a redesigned system which was renamed International Resource Information System. However, we refer to the system as EELIAS throughout this report since that was the system in place during the committee's analysis.

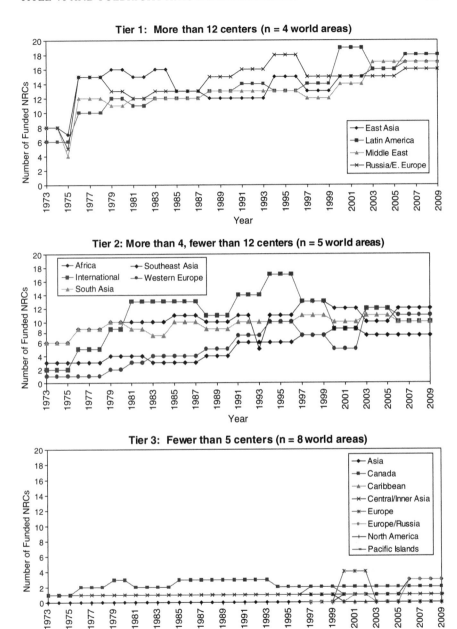

FIGURE 3-5 Number of NRCs by world area and tier, 1973-2009.

• Lowest number of centers: Asia, Canada, Central/Inner Asia, Europe, Europe/Russia.

The committee notes, however, that since the world area focus is defined by the applicant university, grantees focus on various configurations of European and Asian areas. The groupings above are based on how the grantees defined their world area.

Unlike the NRC Program, which has experienced fluctuation in grantees over time, the number of LRC and CIBER grantees has been relatively unchanged. The LRC Program has increased the number of grantees in each competition, typically by adding an LRC with a particular language or topical focus (e.g., K-12, heritage speakers) but only one funded LRC was unsuccessful in a subsequent competition. Similarly, although CIBERs have been added, only one CIBER did not receive funding in a subsequent competition.

Overall Demand

Demand for Title VI grants is substantial. Although more than half of the NRC, FLAS, CIBER, and LRC applicants have received funding in the past several competitions, a much smaller proportion of applicants has been funded for the BIE, IRS, TICFIA, and UISFL Programs. In the most recent competition, only about one-quarter of the applicants for these programs were awarded grants. The number of applications for nearly all programs has steadily increased over the past decade (see Table 3-3).

TITLE VI AND FULBRIGHT-HAYS AND THE UNIVERSITY CONTEXT

The large research-intensive universities, which receive the bulk of Title VI/FH funding, are typically organized into multiple levels. At the bottom of the organizational hierarchy are the basic building blocks of the university (Ruther, 2006), the departments, which are organized by academic discipline. Departments play the central role in key employment decisions, including recruiting, hiring, promoting, retaining, and dismissing faculty and staff. These departmental building blocks are assembled into largely autonomous schools and colleges, which form a higher level of internal organization. At the top of the organizational hierarchy is the university leadership, which typically includes the provost and the president. An understanding of this university context is important as it affects the ability of Title VI/FH to accomplish objectives, such as supporting research, education, and training, infusing a foreign language and area studies dimension across disciplines, and conducting K-12 outreach.

TABLE 3-3 Proportion of Title VI/FH Applications Funded and Applications Received 1997-2006

Program	Percentage of Applications Funded (number of applications received)									
	1997	1998	1999	2000	2001	2002	2003	2004	2005	2006
AORC	53 (15)	30 (10)		65 (17)			80 (15)			
BIE	28 (86)	30 (90)	33 (78)	30 (92)	29 (100)	38 (88)	30 (97)	31 (93)	25 (105)	33 (85)
CIBE		37 (35)	65 (23)			75 (40)				79 (39)
FLAS	82 (157)			73 (163)			71 (175)			73 (171)
IRS	37 (57)	17 (52)	33 (40)	36 (53)	29 (42)	34 (59)	26 (104)	10 (93)	22 (89)	25 (83)
LRC			56 (16)			56 (25)				65 (23)
NRC	68 (161)			68 (167)		71[a] (167)	65 (184)			70 (178)
TICFIA			32 (25)			43 (23)			29 (34)	
UISFL	33 (88)	28 (95)	48 (64)	38 (77)	33 (85)	28 (106)	22 (132)	27 (103)	31 (94)	24 (92)

[a]During this time period, NRC competitions occurred every three years (e.g., 2000, 2003). However, in 2002, to address a legislative mandate, four new NRCs were awarded from the pool of applications received in 2000.
SOURCE: Data provided by U.S. Department of Education.

Knowledge of a world area or global issue requires a range of departments, disciplines, and methods that may range from political science to religious studies to law to language. To be effective, international research and training may require participation of faculty not only from different departments, but also from different schools or colleges. Yet because departments typically reward faculty based on specialized research using deep discipline-specific research methods and knowledge, participating in interdisciplinary international education may hurt a young faculty member's career. As a National Academies report on interdisciplinary research concluded (Committee on Science, Engineering, and Public Policy, 2004, p. 3): "In attempting to balance the strengthening of disciplines and the pursuit of interdisciplinary research, education, and training, many institutions are impeded by traditions and policies that govern hiring, promotion, tenure, and resource allocation."

To counteract such impediments and bring multiple disciplines together around international issues, universities have created area studies centers and other new organizational units. However, because these centers lie outside the mainstream structures and reward systems of the university, they have always depended on external funding. Wealthy donors who had lived or traveled abroad provided support for the earliest area study centers at American universities in the late 19th century. During World War II, the federal government funded additional centers for language and area training. In the postwar era, the Carnegie, Rockefeller, and Ford foundations provided continuing support for some area centers, but the federal government emerged as the most important supporter of research and training in foreign languages and area studies (Biddle, 2003). Although institutional support for such centers has grown, their multidisciplinary approach continues to make them "an alternative axis of organization" (Trubek, 1999, p. 142) in the university.

Challenges for International Education in the University Environment

Several trends over the past three decades have increased the pressures on universities, exacerbating tensions between the mainstream departmental building blocks and the alternative axis of international education structures (Trubek, 1999).

First, with the end of the cold war, some scholars and policy makers questioned the need for in-depth study of world cultures and languages. At the same time, some social science faculty, steeped in disciplinary traditions, challenged the rigor of interdisciplinary area studies and opposed hiring new faculty with area expertise. In language departments, faculty who had won tenure based on scholarship in literature saw little reason to have to teach modern foreign languages themselves, and foreign language instruction was often left to nontenure-track instructors. These critiques were muted somewhat in the wake of the events of September 11, 2001. In early 2007, a Modern Language Association panel recommended restructuring the traditional model of language instruction to discontinue reliance on lecturers and better incorporate study of history, culture, economics, and society (Jaschik, 2007). However, international education faculty continue to face financial and logistical challenges in carrying out their research and teaching, particularly teaching of the less commonly taught languages (Biddle, 2002). By the end of the 1990s, foundation funding that had supported international and area studies had substantially decreased.

Second, since the end of the 1970s, growing enrollments and declining state support have forced public colleges and universities to raise tuitions, becoming competitors in the higher education marketplace rather than providers of a shared public good (Pusser, 2002). Private universities may also face budget constraints, depending on the size of their endowments and the fluctuations of the job market. Today, all universities compete vigorously, nationally and internationally, to recruit the strongest students and faculty, raise external funds, and secure tuitions. Recruiting students, especially the best and brightest, is critically important for economic viability and to win prestige. In a reinforcing cycle, prestige helps a university win external support, and winning external support, in turn, enhances prestige. External funding demonstrates to potential new faculty hires that the university is dynamic and worth devoting a career to. Prestige helps a university place doctoral graduates at top universities, increasing revenues and operating flexibility (Ruther, 2006).

To compete successfully in this marketplace, universities must meet high professional and academic standards. A young faculty member must teach, do research, and publish in well-regarded journals in order to win tenure. Tenure decisions may be reviewed at several levels before becoming final. The quality of faculty publications is enhanced by the peer review process for journal articles, and the quality of faculty teaching is reviewed by students and peers. Some universities have adopted merit pay systems, under which faculty member pay scales are based in part on student reviews of faculty teaching.

Third, as competition for the best students has grown, student interest in international education and foreign languages has been mixed. Between academic years 1989-1990 and 2003-2004, the total number of B.A. degrees awarded in all fields grew by 33 percent, reflecting demographic trends. Within this total, however, the number of social science and history B.A.s grew only 27.3 percent. The number of B.A.s in foreign languages and linguistics grew somewhat more rapidly, at 35.2 percent. However, both of these growth rates were modest compared with the most rapidly growing fields of study, including parks/recreation/leisure/fitness, at 383 percent, computers and information sciences at 117 percent, visual and performing arts at 93 percent, and security and protective services at 83.5 percent (National Center for Education Statistics, 2006).

Benefits and Complexities of Title VI Funding

In this environment of heightened competition for students, faculty, and resources, Title VI funding is even more essential. Title VI funding can help to overcome faculty resistance to new interdisciplinary approaches and can also help to win institutional support. However, Title VI and other external support cannot substitute over the long term for the tuition and institutional resources that reflect success in the competitive higher education marketplace. A key to success of any externally funded innovation is buy-in from the colleges and schools, departments, and centers that make up the building blocks of the university. Because Title VI grants require universities to provide matching funding and other sources of support, they help to generate buy-in and longer term support for international education and foreign language training (Ruther, 2006).

While Title VI programs bring clear benefits to universities, the funding is relatively modest and brings new complexities. Applying for an NRC grant is complex and time-consuming, requiring negotiations with administrators and faculty to ensure that required university commitments of faculty time, funding, and resources are in place. Success is not guaranteed in the highly competitive process. Collaboration across universities or across programs is complicated by the fact that they are in competition with one another for very limited funds. If funds are received, they require further rounds of negotiations to obtain the multidisciplinary expertise needed to develop deep expertise in a region or world area and its languages. The NRC director must have excellent skills in negotiation and persuasion to succeed, and there is frequent turnover in these positions.

In recent years, the job of NRC director has become even more complex and challenging, with reduced funding and expanding missions. The most recent (2006) NRC grant awards average only $230,806, a decline of 8 percent from the previous grant cycle. Less money is available for core activities, such as "buying out" a professor's course load, so that he or she has more time to conduct international research, or paying salaries for instructors of the less commonly taught languages. At the same time, however, the NRC grant must support outreach to K-12 education and other activities. As noted above, the most recent NRC grant awards included an absolute priority for teacher training activities, a competitive priority for activities to measure language proficiency, and five other invitational priorities (Ruther, 2006).

The typical CIBER director faces other challenges. Although the average CIBER award in 2006 was also 7 percent less than in the previous cycle, at $343,548, it was higher than the average NRC grant. By law and through the award process described above, CIBER programs focus on a narrower set of goals than do NRCs. However, the law requires that each CIBER establish an advisory board of key stakeholders on campus, in business, and in government. It also requires a contractual commitment from the university for matching funds equal to the CIBER grant. As a result, the CIBER director has a dedicated budget for the grant cycle, while the NRC director has only the written commitments for matching funds included in the grant application. The law also mandates that the CIBER must focus half of its efforts on internationalizing the business school and the other half on the larger business world and business educators, in order to enhance the global competitiveness of U.S. businesses. This means that the CIBER director can focus program activities on two major audiences—the business education community, including a small, closely knit community on campus and national business faculty associations—and the business community (Ruther, 2006). By comparison, the NRC director must serve a much larger and more diffuse audience with differing needs.

CONCLUSION

The Title VI/FH international education programs at the U.S. Department of Education are among several federal programs that support the study of foreign languages and cultures. Although there are some similarities between the Title VI/FH programs at ED and other foreign language and area studies programs in terms of the types of activities funded, the missions, focus, and purposes of the various programs differ. There are also important differences in the emphases and content of the projects. Some programs, such as the National Security Education Program and the Stokes Scholarships, are specifically aimed at developing a pipeline of individuals with specific talents into jobs at federal bureaucracies. They focus on a narrow set of critical languages. The Fulbright program at the State Department is a key component of U.S. public diplomacy efforts. The proposed NSLI would add capacity in critical languages and move language training to elementary and secondary education. In contrast, the Title VI/FH programs are designed to build capacity and expertise in the U.S. higher education system in the broadly defined areas of modern foreign languages and international and area studies. The Title VI/FH programs play a unique role in the array of federally funded international education programs by stimulating universities to create a broad infrastructure of faculty, courses, and other academic activities focused on modern foreign languages, area studies, and international training.

Although the Title VI/FH programs have a common objective in higher education, they are administered as 14 separate programs. Overall funding has not kept pace with expansion in the number and objectives of the programs, or with the demand for funds. In the case of the FLAS Program, although average awards have increased as requested by Congress, the purchasing power of those grants in relation to tuition costs has declined. The ability of Title VI/FH to accomplish its broad mandate is hampered by the limited availability of funds. For example, NRCs charged with expanded objectives and expectations are expected to do so with little or no increase in funds.

Part II

Key Areas of Concern

In the preceding chapters, the committee briefly reviewed the legislative and funding history of the Title VI and Fulbright-Hays (Title VI/FH) programs and information about the demand for foreign language and area expertise. We also considered the role that the Title VI/FH programs play in relation to other federal programs with a foreign language or area studies emphasis. On the basis of these reviews, we came to the conclusion that the Title VI/FH programs play a unique and vital role in the array of federal programs aimed at addressing foreign language and area knowledge needs. Specifically, their role is to address a broad set of needs for foreign language, international, and area expertise, rather than to respond to the current demand for government expertise. That conclusion forms the context for our discussion of several of the key areas identified in our charge.

This part provides an overview of the evidence that pertains to the effectiveness of the Title VI/FH programs in addressing each of the eight key area specified in the congressional request. In conducting our review, the committee first developed a conceptual model. Before discussing the types of information used by the committee in conducting its review, a word about the committee's model and the available evidence is warranted (see Appendix B for further detail, including schematics of the conceptual model). Our conceptual model clearly illustrates the complexity of the interactions among programs and that multiple programs—directly or indirectly—contribute to most of the areas specified in the committee's charge. In general, therefore, the committee's analysis of the programs' performance related to each of the eight key areas addresses the programs as a whole. Although some of the chapters highlight specific programs given their particular relevance to the key area being discussed, we do not compare the performance of specific programs to one another or specify the relative contribution of individual programs to the overall Title VI/FH goals. Indeed, this would not have been possible with the evidence available.

The conceptual model also articulates the differences among impacts, outcomes, outputs, activities, and inputs. In determining the effectiveness of a program, one should aim to assess impacts and outcomes or the accomplishment of program or social objectives that can be attributed to the program. However, in the case of the committee's review, and indeed in the case of much program decision making, very little evidence that would enable an assessment of outcomes is available. In addition, because the eight key areas identified in the committee's charge include both outcomes (e.g., increasing the numbers of underrepresented minorities in international service, reducing shortages of foreign language and area experts) and outputs (e.g., conducting outreach), in some cases the program's performance in one area might affect its performance in another. For example, effective outreach to K-12 could contribute to increased infusion of a foreign language and area studies dimension throughout the education system. The report is organized to present the available evidence—largely evidence related to outputs and activities—for each of the key areas in turn. The committee recognizes, however, that just as the programs interrelate to one another to achieve the specific objectives reflected in the key areas, the key areas themselves are interrelated and one might contribute to another.

In conducting our review, the committee utilized information from a variety of sources. Although no single source provided sufficient evidence to draw reliable conclusions and the combined evidence is not optimal, the combined sources allow some conclusions to be drawn about the programs. Specifically, the committee

- reviewed all extant evaluations;
- reviewed program monitoring data, selected grant applications, historical financial data, and written comments from experts and officials;
- commissioned papers and targeted analyses;
- conducted public meetings to get input from subject matter experts, officials, and others and met with grantees in Washington and officials from the U.S. Department of Education (ED) with responsibilities for these programs; and
- conducted site visits to eight universities: Georgetown University, George Washington University, Indiana University, New York University, Ohio State University, San Diego State University, the University of California, Los Angeles, and the University of Wisconsin-Madison.

The committee reviewed 11 studies that provide relatively current information about the Title VI/FH programs. Two other important studies were not considered by the committee because they examined the programs almost 30 years ago.[1] In addition to the completed evaluations, a couple of ongoing activities will eventually provide information about some programs.[2] About half of the evaluation studies of the various Title VI/FH programs were performed by people or entities that were themselves receiving funds under Title VI/FH. In a few cases, studies relied on self-reporting on the success of the programs; in other words, administrators were asked to rank the effectiveness of their own efforts, which may produce biased results. Several studies had various methodological issues, including lack of a comparison group (control groups would be infeasible) or low response rates. Descriptions of these studies, with their shortcomings, are provided in Appendix B. Given the reality that these are the only studies available, the committee reports their results with specific needed caveats when appropriate. In some cases, a study is relevant to more than one key area, and specific findings are discussed in different chapters. Recognizing the limitations of the available evaluation evidence, however, the committee recommends in the final chapter that ED invest in more rigorously designed program evaluations.

The committee also reviewed program monitoring data and historical funding data. ED provided direct access to complete the Evaluation of Exchange, Language, International and Area Studies (EELIAS) database as of March 2006. The database is used for grant monitoring purposes; for example, reports are used to decide on continuation awards for multiyear grants. ED has also used the database to collect data needed for its national performance measures. The committee hoped that the database, which includes multiyear data for some programs, would also be a readily available program evaluation tool. We found, however, that while the database has the potential to collect comprehensive information, methodological issues with how it was structured and implemented limit its usefulness beyond individual grant monitoring; in fact, the database itself became a focus for our review. Whenever possible, we have presented relevant information from the database with necessary caveats. The final chapter also discusses in more detail the limitations of the system and the committee's observations about its limitations.

---

[1]Studies by McDonnell, Berryman, and Scott and published by the Rand Corporation in 1981 and 1983 are cited in the references. The study addressed the four programs that had been established at the time: National Resource Centers (NRC), Foreign Language and Area Studies Fellowships, International Research and Studies, and the Undergraduate International Studies and Foreign Language Program.

[2]This includes a study of Middle East Studies Centers by the Social Science Research Council. ED is also in the planning stages of awarding a contract to evaluate the International Research and Studies Program.

The committee also invited individuals and organizations working, participating in, or otherwise affected by or interested in Title VI/FH programs to present information to the committee about the programs' strengths and weaknesses. The committee also solicited input through several public meetings that included comments by people expert in the field and met with Language Resource Centers and NRC directors in Washington, DC. Some of the information presented was based on evidence, whereas some of it was based on their opinion or anecdotes. Over the course of the study, the committee received written comments from 17 individuals representing numerous organizations and grantees and heard from numerous others.[3] The line between evaluation studies and public input may be blurred in some places. The same studies mentioned above were often cited by the individuals who made presentations or submitted information to the committee.

The committee commissioned targeted analyses for areas not addressed at all in existing evaluations: producing relevant instructional materials, advancing uses of new technology, and increasing efforts aimed at participation of minorities in international programs.[4] Although the review provided insights into what is being produced by Title VI grantees in these areas, it did not include necessary information to assess the quality of the materials produced or the extent to which the materials are being used; this would have required a more systematic evaluation.

Finally, the committee gathered qualitative evidence through eight site visits to universities with center programs. The site visits were designed in part to address the shortcomings of other available sources in terms of providing an understanding of how the major programs in this complex array of programs operate in practice. All of the universities had at least one NRC; several also had Language Resource Center grants, Centers for International Business Education and Research grants, or both. Although not a representative sample, the universities chosen provide a general picture of the diversity of grantees and provide qualitative examples of how the center programs are implemented. In some cases, there was unanimity across the universities visited on particular points; these points are highlighted in the text of relevant chapters. In other cases, the committee felt that an example from the site visits illustrates a conclusion drawn from the combined evidence; in these cases, an illustration is provided in the form of a text box in the chapter.

In addition to drawing on all of the sources of evidence listed above,

---

[3]See Appendix B for a list of the individuals who submitted written comments as well as agendas for the committee's public meetings. Written comments are available at http://www7. nationalacademies.org/cfe/International_Education_Programs.html.

[4]During the course of the committee's review, an evaluation of the Institute for International Public Policy Program commissioned by the United Negro College Fund Special Programs Corporation was completed and included in the committee's commissioned analysis.

the committee drew on its own expertise and lessons from relevant related literature to establish findings and draw conclusions. Although no single type of evidence provides a sufficient basis on which to draw conclusions about the program, the committee thinks that the combined weight of the various sources provides sufficient basis to support the conclusions drawn. In many cases, however, the evidence was too limited to support recommendations about specific programs or particular key areas. Clearly additional rigorously designed program evaluations and a better designed program monitoring system would improve future reviews. This issue is discussed in Chapter 11. The chapters that follow provide the committee's discussion of each of the eight key areas specified in the congressional request for this study.

4

Infusing a Foreign Language and Area Studies Dimension and Conducting Outreach and Dissemination

The previous chapters have outlined new needs for foreign language and area expertise among federal personnel, professionals, teachers, and the public—needs created by dramatic changes in the world since the creation of Title VI in 1958. This chapter is the first of several reviewing the performance of the Title VI and Fulbright-Hays (Title VI/FH) in helping to address these needs based on the eight areas specified by Congress. The chapter considers two of these areas in a single chapter given the integral relationship between them: (1) infusing a foreign language and area studies dimension throughout the education system and across relevant disciplines, including professional education, and (2) conducting public outreach/dissemination to K-12 and higher education, media, government, business, and the public.[1]

The Title VI/FH programs are aimed primarily at infusion of foreign language, area, and international studies ("internationalization") horizontally in higher education—across university type, across disciplines, and across the country, and the chapter begins with a review of this activity. The programs have also been charged with helping to internationalize vertically into the K-12 system. Outreach by National Resource Centers (NRC) and Language Resource Centers (LRC) is a major component of internationalization in K-12 and is discussed in this context. The chapter also briefly outlines broader internationalization efforts, in the form of outreach to the

---

[1]Outreach to business is mentioned briefly in this chapter and discussed in more detail in Chapter 10.

media, government, business, and the public as well as outreach activities by the U.S. Department of Education (ED).

INTERNATIONALIZING HIGHER EDUCATION

One measure of progress toward internationalizing higher education is the degree to which the Title VI/FH programs reach various components of higher education (e.g., community colleges, undergraduate institutions, professional schools). Different Title VI/FH programs reach these different components. Both historically and today, NRC program grants have been awarded primarily to the nation's leading research universities in order to provide advanced training and research in foreign languages and area studies. The Undergraduate International Studies and Foreign Language (UISFL) Program, as its name implies, reaches smaller undergraduate colleges and universities to a much greater extent, although not exclusively. In addition, the Business and International Education (BIE) Program reaches smaller colleges and universities (see Chapter 10). Table 4-1 demonstrates, based on the Carnegie classifications (the Carnegie Commission on Higher Education uses empirical university data to classify colleges and universities by type), the distribution of Title VI/FH grants by type of institution.

While institutions classified as predominantly research or that award doctoral or masters degrees receive the bulk of grants across programs, a significant proportion of UISFL and BIE grants—grants viewed as seed money to begin internationalizing the undergraduate curriculum—have been provided to baccalaureate and associate degree-granting institutions. The Faculty Research Abroad (FRA) Program also provides a substantial portion of grants to baccalaureate-awarding institutions.

TABLE 4-1 Percentage of FY 2004 Grants by Type of Institution, Based on Carnegie Classification

Program	Percentage					
	Research	Doctoral	Masters	Baccalaureate	Associates	Other
NRC	88.0	1.8	5.0	5.0		
FLAS	98.0	2.0				
LRC	100.0					
UISFL	43.0	5.0	26.0	13.2	11.8	
CIBER	96.7					3.3
BIE	26.4	8.3	44.4	6 .0	15.0	
DDRA	94.7	3.0				2.6
FRA	69.0	7.7	4.0	19.2		
GPA	73.0	3.8	11.5	3.8	4.0	

SOURCE: Data provided by U.S. Department of Education [EELIAS].

The Title VI/FH programs also reach broadly to higher education institutions across the United States.[2] The programs support higher education institutions in all nine census regions, although both the East North Central and Pacific regions receive a greater share of total funding than all other regions. In addition, all states but Nevada and Wyoming received at least one grant at some point over the past 10 years. It is unclear if applications were received from those states.

It is of course important to look at not only who receives grants but also the effect that they have on the institutions that receive them. Several evaluations have assessed the internalization effect of specific Title VI programs. At the undergraduate level, Schneider and Burn (1999) found that UISFL grants had a positive impact on internationalization. Institutions that received a UISFL grant reported that the program had a positive effect on many elements deemed critical to developing and strengthening international education, such as requiring an international course for graduation and having a formally designated adviser for students doing international or area studies. UISFL grantees reported adding new courses and languages, and nearly all of these courses were still being offered with solid enrollments after the grant ended. Most institutions continued to support the UISFL-funded program for five or more years after the grant ended. Directors of UISFL projects had a high degree of satisfaction with their projects' impacts.

There is evidence that funding from BIE and Centers for International Business Education and Research (CIBER) for business school programs has had a similar effect, adding an international component to the business curriculum. In comparison with non-CIBER schools, business schools with CIBER status were likely to have more international business courses in their core program, to integrate language instruction into the curriculum, and to offer a greater variety of languages, especially less commonly taught languages (Folks, 2002). CIBERs offered language training in several languages of high priority to economic competitiveness (Brecht and Rivers, 2000). BIE grant recipients reported enhancement of faculty expertise in international business as a result of the grant, and 30 percent of the programs continued to fund research on international business topics after the end of the grant period. Courses and curricular programs developed with BIE funds also continued after the initial BIE grant ended[3] (Gerber, 2002).

A report from the national Title VI conference held at the University of California, Los Angeles, in 1997 indicated that NRCs, LRCs, and CIBERs

---

[2] The committee notes that the statute includes a provision that, as practicable and consistent with the selection criteria, grants should be awarded "in such a manner as to achieve an equitable distribution of funds throughout the United States."

[3] Many of the universities surveyed in this study received subsequent BIE and CIBER grants that may have helped support continuation of the new international courses and programs.

were engaged in a variety of efforts to internationalize higher education. The centers were collaborating with departments and schools across the university to develop curricula, host visiting international scholars, sponsor international film festivals, and support programs that bring international students to smaller colleges with few international students (Metzler, 1997). Committee site visits in fall 2006 indicated that, at least at the site visit universities, efforts to internationalize higher education are continuing. At all eight site visit universities, faculty and administrators affiliated with Title VI centers had created or were in the process of creating new undergraduate majors and minors with a global, international, or area studies focus. Several were in the process of increasing the number and level of language or international courses required of all students for graduation. New York University was engaged in efforts to tap the strengths of NRC-funded area studies centers and its network of study abroad sites to develop new, more rigorous area studies undergraduate majors. In addition to these more general curriculum development efforts, some site visit universities were using Title VI funds to create and disseminate specific courses and instructional materials for use beyond the home university. One example is San Diego State University's Digital Media Archive (see Box 4-1).

Experts from the Title VI community who addressed the committee stressed their efforts to internationalize the campus. They argued that Title VI programs help infuse international components into a wide variety of university programs and disciplines. Gabara (2006) provided an example of a university that used USIFL funds for a multidisciplinary Language Across the Curriculum program, which infused linguistic fluency into various disciplinary courses across the undergraduate curriculum. In addition, the committee was told (Merkx, 2006) that many universities now expect graduate students in a broad array of fields to gain proficiency in a foreign language and that the language and area studies courses offered through NRCs lead to a variety of undergraduate and graduate degree options with an international focus. Many NRCs also provide degree options for students in professional programs, such as business, law, medicine, and engineering. In addition, some professional programs now provide the opportunity to integrate an area studies focus into other fields, such as public policy, law, public health, journalism, business, and information and library science (Newhall, 2006). Birch (2006) reported that CIBERs also encourage cooperation between business schools and other academic departments; they leverage the expertise of faculty in language and international studies to help prepare business graduates who may then go on to work for companies competing globally.

This collaborative approach of reaching across disciplines in research and teaching is often difficult in academia, which tends to be compartmentalized by discipline (National Research Council, 2004; Merkx, 2005). According to a National Research Council report (2004), "Despite the

---

BOX 4-1
Developing and Disseminating Curriculum
at San Diego State University

The San Diego State University LRC, in collaboration with the university's Latin America NRC, is developing and disseminating online curriculum materials that can be freely used by higher education faculty and students anywhere in the nation or the world. The LRC has created a Digital Media Archive with authentic (materials created for use by native speakers) Spanish language materials for use by teachers, students, and curriculum designers involved in advanced Spanish and Latin American culture classes.

In September 2006, the archive was populated with two large sets of materials. The first encompassed literature from Baja California linked to Spanish instructional support materials, such as vocabulary lists and grammar examples. These materials are designed to supplement college and university courses on the Spanish language, border culture, economics, history, and sociology, whether those courses are taught in classrooms or online. Preliminary tests of these materials with San Diego State University students indicate that they are effective in enhancing learning (San Diego State University, 2006a). The second set of materials focuses on understanding human rights issues in Latin America by examining authentic Spanish language multinational communications and discourse. Its goal is to combine regional political studies of Latin America and development of advanced Spanish reading and writing skills (San Diego State University, 2006b).

The archive also houses materials for both commonly taught and less commonly taught languages, including Arabic, Persian, Iraqi dialect, Filipino, Korean, French, Italian, Portuguese, Mixtec, German, and others. These materials are either teacher-created or authentic and may contain lesson plans and suggestions for classroom use.

NOTE: Information contained in this box came from a committee site visit (2006) and university project websites (San Diego State University, 2006a, 2006b).

---

apparent benefits of [interdisciplinary research], researchers interested in pursuing it often face daunting obstacles and disincentives." In some cases, this is "related to the tradition in academic institutions of organizing research and teaching activities by discipline based departments" (p. 1). NRC grants support campus centers that are by definition interdisciplinary, and they may be the most successful, long-term, and far-reaching effort that brings social science and humanities together. This achievement is a side benefit of NRCs and area studies generally. Gilbert Merkx (2006), an NRC director and co-chair of the Council of National Resource Center Directors, emphasized to the committee:

It is important to understand that the NRCs are interdisciplinary in nature, but not non-disciplinary. In other words, the area studies faculty affiliated with an NRC have their primary appointments in a disciplinary department such as history or political science. The courses taught are disciplinary courses that may be cross-listed with the area center. Without the presence of the center, these faculty members from different departments would have little contact. The center brings the faculty together to form an intellectual community.

The NRCs and the Foreign Language and Area Studies (FLAS) Fellowship Program also appear to be reaching students from a range of disciplines. University reports on the primary discipline of their NRC master's "graduates" (those who had taken 15 or more area studies or foreign language credit hours) indicate that the NRCs are reaching a diverse set of students (see Table 4-2). While the greatest number of students is studying foreign languages or literature, area studies, or international studies, the universities report that they are reaching students from numerous other disciplines.

The reported discipline of FLAS fellows is similarly diverse, although to a somewhat lesser extent than NRC master's graduates (see Table 4-3). The diversity of disciplines among FLAS recipients reflects the reality that these fellowships are designed primarily to support disciplinary research. FLAS Fellowships for intensive language study, either in the United States or abroad, are designed to provide enough language proficiency to carry

TABLE 4-2 NRC Master's "Graduates" by Discipline, 2002-2004

Discipline	Graduates	Percentage
Foreign languages and literature	1,159	9.07
Area studies	1,077	8.43
Global/international relations and studies	884	6.92
International/area studies	830	6.50
Education	792	6.20
Health sciences	774	6.06
Business administration and management	671	5.25
History	559	4.38
Political science	461	3.61
Law	344	2.69
Anthropology	341	2.67
English	286	2.24
Economics	253	1.98
Public policy	252	1.97
International business	235	1.84
Art/art history	229	1.79
155 other disciplines	3,626	28.39

SOURCE: Data provided by U.S. Department of Education [EELIAS].

TABLE 4-3 Disciplines of FLAS Fellows, 2001-2005

Discipline	Number	Percentage
Area studies	2,638	16
History	2,126	13
Anthropology	1,964	12
Foreign languages and literature	1,950	12
Political science	1,047	6
International/area studies	688	4
Law	466	3
Linguistics	454	3
Religious studies	437	3
43 other disciplines	0	0

SOURCE: Data provided by U.S. Department of Education [EELIAS].

out masters' or doctoral research. The fellowship program is not focused on advanced language study for its own sake.

Committee site visits provided some support for the contention that NRCs provide opportunities for interdisciplinary work that would probably not occur otherwise. Staff reported that Title VI helps fund such activities as seminars that bring students and faculty together from multiple disciplines who might not otherwise interact, grant funds for faculty from a diverse range of disciplines to conduct research on international topics, and leverage the incorporation of international material into the curriculum of a range of courses. Some faculty reported that they would be unlikely to be involved in international work without the involvement of the NRC, given that the disciplinary emphasis of their home departments is elsewhere and does not intrinsically encourage their international interest. The committee also heard from students who had received FLAS awards in which a foreign language was integral to their degree in music, political science, or business. One NRC that offers an area studies master's degree uses half of its FLAS awards for its own master's students and reserves the other half for students from other disciplines. Box 4-2 illustrates the centralized approach used at Ohio State University, a university with multiple NRCs, to infuse a foreign language and area studies dimension throughout the university. Although this model will not be appropriate for all universities, it is an example of an approach that was reported to positively impact internationalization of the campus.

BOX 4-2
Infusion of Foreign Languages and Area Studies
at Ohio State University

Ohio State University's administrative structure facilitates infusion of foreign language and area studies across the disciplines and divisions of the campus. All of the Title VI-funded area studies centers report directly to the Associate Provost of International Affairs. They are all housed together in the International Affairs building, along with the Office of International Education (which operates study abroad and international student programs), which encourages the centers to work with each other. The center directors meet monthly.

Administrators and NRC directors described a highly interdisciplinary approach to foreign language and area studies. Title VI supports this approach by providing seed money that is often used to pay a percentage of the salary of a new hire with a regional focus, in such disciplines as history, anthropology, or political science. Title IV provides funds to develop and initially teach new courses that a department will take on subsequently as its own. The university's coordinated structure for international education also facilitates collaboration between the area studies centers and the professional schools. Although each center has its own outreach coordinator, there is also a coordinator in the Office of International Affairs who facilitates the work of them all. This centralized structure streamlines the NRCs' collaboration with the School of Education, which in turn helps to internationalize the school's curriculum and prepare future teachers to become knowledgeable about world areas and languages. The Slavic NRC helped the School of Agriculture establish a research and study site at Tomsk State University in Siberia. Similarly, the Center for African Studies (CAS) was instrumental in engaging the School of Public Health (SPH) in activities in Africa. Specifically, CAS has worked with SPH to offer global health courses with a focus on Africa. SPH is not (yet) engaged in any tangible projects in Africa.

NOTE: Information contained in this box came from a committee site visit (2006).

INTERNATIONALIZING K-12 EDUCATION

Educational Needs and Teaching Gaps

Early language learning in elementary and secondary school is key to establishing a pipeline of students who can eventually reach a high enough level of proficiency in foreign language and culture to meet national needs. Young children are good language learners and, if permitted to follow well-articulated sequences, can acquire a very solid base for more complex linguistic knowledge or starting another language in high school or college. Investing early in the foreign language skills of students would therefore allow a greater number of them to acquire these competencies and also allow those who would pursue advanced study at the college and graduate level deeper levels of proficiency. Exposure to international content in the K-12 curriculum is also needed to help students understand different world regions (geography, culture, and history) and to inspire students to further this knowledge.

Current efforts to develop language skills and knowledge of world regions at an early age are clearly inadequate to prepare high school graduates with the skills necessary for productivity and citizenship in an integrated global economy (Committee for Economic Development, 2006). According to an American Council on the Teaching of Foreign Languages study of public school enrollments in foreign languages, only 34 percent of U.S. K-12 students were enrolled in foreign language classes in 2000 (Draper and Hicks, 2002). Almost 70 percent of these students were studying Spanish, and another 18 percent were studying French. Next were German (4.8 percent) and Latin (2.7 percent). Very small percentages of students were studying more difficult languages, such as Russian (0.2 percent) and Japanese (0.8 percent). The percentage of students studying Arabic and Chinese was minuscule; only four states even reported teaching Arabic, with 426 students enrolled in grades 7 through 12. Chinese fared a little better, with about 5,000 students taking courses in eight states in grades 7 through 12. In addition, the report states that the length of time students spent studying languages at school had stagnated, so many students reached only introductory levels of proficiency.

Students' knowledge of international issues, aside from language, is also inadequate. The National Commission on Asia in the Schools found that 25 percent of college-bound high school students did not know the name of the Pacific Ocean and that 80 percent of adults and students could not identify India, the world's largest democracy with a rapidly growing economy, on a world map (National Commission on Asia in the Schools, 2005). A 2006 National Geographic/Roper Survey of young Americans ages 18 to 24 found that only 37 percent could locate Iraq on a map and 20 percent thought Sudan was located in Asia (Roper Public Affairs and Media, 2006). These and many other examples illustrate that knowledge of languages and world regions is essential in a wide variety of disciplines, including geography, social studies, history, and perhaps even science and literature.

One of the key deterrents to developing a pipeline of young people prepared to develop advanced language proficiency and deep knowledge of countries and cultures is a lack of trained teachers. The U.S. K-12 system needs foreign language teachers as well as teachers trained on topics in the geography, cultures, and history of various world regions and, therefore, the college programs that will produce them. A survey of secondary school principals and foreign language teachers by the Center for Applied Linguistics (1999) identified a shortage of foreign language teachers as a major impediment to greater foreign language learning, along with funding, lack of training, and poor academic counseling. The top issues for elementary schools were overall lack of funding for language instruction, lack of in-service training, and inadequate sequencing from elementary to secondary schools. Large student-teacher ratios were identified as major barriers to effective language instruction at both the elementary and secondary levels.

The shortage of foreign language teachers was also addressed in a report by the Center on Reinventing Public Education at the University of Washington (Murphy and DeArmond, 2003). The researchers drew on data from the Schools and Staffing Survey of the ED's National Center for Education Statistics. One of their findings was that job openings for foreign language teachers were most difficult to fill—more so than openings for other hard-to-fill teaching positions in special education, English as a second language, and science. At the same time, administrators were less likely to use cash incentives to lure foreign language teachers to their districts than when trying to attract teachers of other subjects.

Role of Title VI/FH Programs in K-12 Education

Clearly, there are many gaps in students' and teachers' knowledge of world regions and languages. Although never intended to fill these large educational gaps, the Title VI/FH programs do assist K-12 education, both directly and indirectly. Two Fulbright-Hays programs provide professional development and travel opportunities for current and future teachers, and the NRC and LRC programs have supported teachers and students in international and language education.

Group Projects Abroad

The Group Projects Abroad (GPA) Program supports groups of students, faculty, and teachers (including K-12 teachers) in overseas travel for training, research, and curriculum development in modern foreign languages and area studies. Each year, ED invites K-12 teachers and administrators to apply for two different types of activities: (1) short-term (5- to 6-week) seminars focusing on an aspect of area studies and designed to help internationalize a school's or higher education institution's curriculum and (2) a curriculum development team. A team composed of several faculty members or teachers or administrators spends four to six weeks abroad, acquiring resource materials for curriculum development in the modern foreign language spoken or the area in which they travel. Participants are required to plan for systematic use and dissemination of these materials.

In addition to these activities, every three years ED holds a competition for another GPA activity—the Advanced Overseas Intensive Language Projects. Not only graduate students but also future teachers—juniors or seniors planning to teach modern foreign languages or area studies—are eligible for advanced language training abroad, lasting at least one summer and up to three years (U.S. Department of Education, 2007b).

Seminars Abroad

The Seminars Abroad Program sends groups of 14 to 16 social science and humanities teachers to countries outside Western Europe for an introduction to the culture. ED funds 7 to 10 seminars each year, involving no more than 160 teachers (U.S. Department of Education, 2007c).

Outreach Priorities

In recent years, ED has used grant competitions both to encourage NRC outreach activities and to target those activities toward K-12 education. The number of potential points for outreach increased from 15 in FY 2003 to 20 in FY 2006. Similarly, as explained earlier, in the four most recent NRC grant competitions, dating to 1996, ED announced an absolute priority for projects that include teacher training activities on the language, languages, area studies, or the thematic focus of the center (see Appendix C). In addition, the two most recent NRC competitions have included invitational priorities encouraging applicants to develop linkages with schools of education to improve teacher training. Finally, the most recent (FY 2006) competition included an invitational priority for "activities that expand and enhance outreach to K-12 constituencies," further reinforcing the department's interest in outreach to elementary and secondary education.

Perhaps because the legislative mandate of the LRC program clearly emphasizes wide dissemination of language instructional materials, the application process has not specifically emphasized outreach. By statute, LRC grants are provided in order to improve language teaching at all levels of education, including the K-12 level. In its most recent (FY 2006) LRC request for applications (U.S. Department of Education, 2005e), ED announced an invitational priority calling for research into new and improved methods of teaching foreign languages and dissemination of the research results.

Examples of NRC and LRC Outreach to K-12

NRC and LRC grantees have carried out an array of projects designed to share expertise in world regions and languages with teachers, schools, and students.

Teacher Training

NRC faculty and staff provide many in-service seminars and workshops, some at school and university sites during the school year and others offered as summer institutes. Often, teachers create instructional units or lesson plans as part of these seminars and workshops. In site visits, the committee learned about two-week intensive summer institutes sponsored by the University of California, Los Angeles (UCLA) Center for Near Eastern Studies and the Ohio State University Middle East Center. To encourage teacher participation, both universities have ensured that the institutes meet school district and state requirements for teacher continuing education. At UCLA, participants may receive either academic credit or salary points from the Los Angeles Unified School District. Participants in the Ohio State program may receive six undergraduate, continuing education, or graduate credits (University of California, Los Angeles, 2006c). Representatives of the UCLA center emphasized that the institute included many opportunities to mix with and learn from Middle East heritage communities. At the same time, the Ohio State institute devotes a full day to a tour of local Middle East religious and community organizations.

Many LRC grantees are also engaged in teacher training. The National Capital LRC, sponsored by Georgetown University, George Washington University, and the Center for Applied Linguistics, offered a three-day intensive Spanish immersion institute for teachers of Spanish in 2005 and 2006, and a two-day institute on teaching Chinese in May 2006. Following the Chinese institute, articles and presentations used by the two instructors were posted to the LRC website for ready access by attendees and other teachers of Chinese (National Capital Language Resource Center, 2006a).

The National K-12 Foreign Language Resource Center

In 1996, Title VI funded the National K-12 Foreign Language Resource Center at Iowa State University. Although other LRCs also conduct activities relevant to the K-12 system, this LRC has a specific focus on K-12. In keeping with its mandate, it is engaged in an array of local, regional, and national outreach activities, including summer teacher training institutes, supporting certification of foreign language teachers, and research on teaching strategies, language proficiency assessment, and new technologies for foreign language teaching (Iowa State University, 2006).

School Site Programs

Many NRC centers provide faculty, staff, and graduate students as speakers to school classrooms and assemblies. Following the World Trade

Center attacks on September 11, 2001, the Harvard Center for Middle East Studies was particularly active, offering over 40 school site programs (Friedlander, McGinley, and Metzler, 2003).

Electronic Outreach

Ohio State University's College of Education and five Title VI-funded area studies centers have developed a course for teachers, with modules for each of the five world areas. All modules focus on the shared themes of women and family, environment, foreign media, and coming of age. The School of Education engaged 45 teachers from 6 states and 3 countries in developing the project (Ohio State University, 2006). The Africa NRC at the University of Pennsylvania developed a comprehensive Internet database of Africana materials for K-12 teachers and students, and the African Studies Center at Michigan State University has created a curriculum on Africa for middle and high school students (Friedlander, McGinley, and Metzler, 2003). The National Capital LRC hosts an online column for language teachers, with advice on classroom solutions and world languages provided by two experts. All questions and answers are posted and organized by topic, providing information not only to the questioner but also to a larger audience of teachers (National Capital Language Resource Center, 2006b).

Review, Development, and Dissemination of Instructional Materials[4]

The Council of Middle East Outreach Directors conducted a comprehensive review of social studies textbooks, compiled recommended K-12 textbooks and websites, and developed new curriculum units (Friedlander, McGinley, and Metzler, 2003). Another national activity that was mentioned frequently during the committee's site visit is Outreach World, a website developed by the UCLA Middle East NRC with funding from the International Research and Studies (IRS) program that supports collaboration and outreach to K-12 education nationally (see Box 4-3). Outreach World provides access to many instructional materials, including materials created by teachers participating in the Fulbright-Hays Group Projects Abroad and Seminars Abroad Programs.

---

[4]See Chapter 8 for further discussion of the role of Title VI/FH programs in producing instructional materials.

BOX 4-3
Outreach World

Outreach World is an Internet portal that serves as a shared website for 120 federally funded NRCs based at 146 universities, along with 42 LRCs and CIBERs based at 44 universities. Launched in September 2003, the portal organizes, catalogues, and disseminates a range of instructional materials produced by teachers and scholars affiliated with these three programs and with the Fulbright-Hays GPA Program. Outreach World also provides information to teachers about opportunities for professional development and overseas study and information on award-winning books about Africa, Asia, and other world regions. Users can search for materials by world region, country, school subject, resource type, time period, instructional strategy, or grade level.

In late 2006, the home page of the website (http://www.outreachworld.org) presented three major groups of information: (1) three searchable databases including the instructional materials described above, contact information on all NRC-funded area studies centers, and a national calendar of professional development events; (2) images and articles about the winners of the 2006 African Studies Association Africana book awards, the Americas award titles for 2005, and the Middle East Outreach Council book award; and (3) links to overseas travel reports and overseas travel opportunities (the GPA Program) along with a listing of top resources for classroom use. According to the developer, more than 100,000 items were downloaded by teachers and educators in 2006.

NOTE: Information contained in this box came from a committee site visit (2006) and university project websites (University of California, Los Angeles, 2006c).

Evaluating K-12 Outreach Activities

Title VI centers do not typically have adequate financial resources to evaluate the long-term outcomes of their outreach activities, including activities targeted to K-12 education. However, in one example, the University of Iowa National K-12 LRC conducted a study of a teacher training institute (see Box 4-4). More recently, an IRS grant has enabled the University of North Carolina School of Education, in collaboration with the university's Center for International Studies and NRC outreach programs at other universities, to create a K-12 international outreach program evaluation "toolkit" (University of North Carolina, 2006). The web-based system is designed to help NRC staff, teachers, administrators, and others assess the extent to which K-12 outreach programs meet goals and expectations. These and other evaluation studies may provide improved information in the future about the effectiveness of NRC outreach activities.

Preparing Teachers for International Education

Clearly, the nation needs more teachers with advanced knowledge of world languages and regions. Addressing this problem will require major changes at the colleges of education that prepare future teachers. A recent study funded by ED (Schneider, 2003) found that teacher education programs typically include little international or foreign language training. However, the Title VI/FH activities for teachers outlined above focus primarily on professional development of the current teaching workforce, rather than on teacher education. The recent study found further evidence

---

BOX 4-4
An Evaluation of a Foreign Language Institute

The University of Iowa National K-12 LRC designed a 10-day summer institute to strengthen the skills and knowledge of teacher educators at schools of education with responsibility for preparing K-6 foreign language teachers for licensure. Based on a needs assessment, they invited two groups to participate in the institute: (1) teacher educators with responsibility for preparing future elementary school foreign language teachers and (2) experienced, knowledgeable K-6 foreign language teachers. Staff at the LRC conducted a study of both short-term and longer term outcomes of the institute. A preinstitute survey indicated that the teacher educators had significantly less understanding than the practicing teachers of topics addressed in the institute, such as program planning, integrating foreign language with the elementary school curriculum, and teaching strategies for young children. A postinstitute survey showed that this gap had disappeared and the teacher educators had gained significant increases in their understanding of most topics.

To assess longer term outcomes, the investigators contacted 27 teacher educators two years after their participation in the institute. They found that 23 of the 26 teacher educators had added or were in the process of adding elementary language teaching methods courses to the curriculum, and most of the new methods courses incorporated topics addressed at the institute. In addition, about half of the teacher educators reported other activities to strengthen preparation of future K-6 foreign language teachers, such as developing a Spanish minor for elementary education majors, planning for a formal K-6 language teacher preparation program, and launching a foreign language practicum and student teaching at the elementary school level. Finally, 19 of the teacher educators said they had developed or taught new courses, workshops, or in-service teacher training sessions related to K-6 foreign language instruction. The authors conclude that the institute was a catalyst for organizational change at most of the colleges and universities represented by the teacher educators who participated in the institute.

NOTE: Information in this box came from Rosenbusch, Kemis, and Moran (2000).

of this limited approach. Schneider (2003) examined NRC websites and found that NRCs offered workshops and seminars for current teachers, but few programs for prospective teachers. It appears that Title VI/FH K-12 outreach programs have reached relatively few teachers to date.

It is important to keep in mind that the Title VI/FH programs are not targeted to schools of education to boost the international component of the teacher education curriculum, but rather to area study centers. Nor do the programs provide funding directly to schools or school districts to support language and social studies teaching. Instead, the programs currently support K-12 language and area instruction indirectly, focusing on capacity-building (production of curricula, research on improving teaching strategies, etc.) and providing supplemental learning and travel opportunities to a small group of current and future teachers. In 2003, the NRC outreach coordinators put it this way (Friedlander, Marshall, and Metzler, 2003): "We are 114 NRCs and 14 LRCs attempting to serve approximately 3.8 million teachers nationwide in diverse geographical locales and settings—from the inner city to the rural schools."

Meeting the diverse international education and foreign language needs of teachers and schools across the nation will require a strategic approach that coordinates and expands Title VI/FH programs with other federal programs and financial resources, as the committee recommends in Chapter 12.

CONDUCTING OUTREACH

Outreach Challenges

Outreach is not a natural fit for most universities, and Title VI funding seems to have served as a catalyst for them to conduct outreach. Universities have developed collaboration and other mechanisms to support their efforts. Outreach activities do not fit naturally in the academic structure of the research university. In a 1997 report on outreach, one NRC outreach coordinator asserted that academia views its primary tasks as research, training the next generation of scholars, and dissemination of knowledge through the traditional means of undergraduate and graduate instruction (Wiley, 1997). The author warned that, because the academic reward structure tends to devalue outreach, few NRC directors "perceive great value in doing outreach" (Wiley, 1997, p. 119). At that time, most NRCs lacked full-time outreach staff, assigning these responsibilities either to an assistant or associate director with many other responsibilities or to a part-time graduate student. At sites visited by the committee in 2006, some NRCs continued to assign outreach activities to associate directors, while other centers had at least one full-time outreach coordinator.

A 2003 report by three NRC outreach coordinators highlighted the same disconnect between the academic area studies center and outreach activities (Friedlander, Marshall, and Metzler, 2003). The authors argued that, although most university mission statements mention service (i.e., outreach), in reality, universities do not view outreach as central to their core missions of knowledge generation and dissemination. Echoing the earlier outreach report, the authors noted that outreach activities are not rewarded by tenure and promotions, and they may even be viewed negatively, as barriers to scholarly research and publication.

Federal Funding as a Catalyst for Outreach Activities

Because the academic environment does not tend to support outreach activities, outreach may be more influenced by federal funding than other Title VI activities. In site visits, faculty and staff associated with NRC-funded centers reported that outreach activities declined in the absence of federal funding. For example, the associate director of an NRC that lost funding between 2003 and 2005 reported that the center's collaboration with the university's school of education in K-12 outreach had stopped during that period. Representatives of many other NRCs indicated that, if their center received reduced funding in the future, outreach would be one of the first activities to be dropped or reduced (the other most common victim was the teaching of less commonly taught languages). NRC representatives also provided detailed financial information showing that outreach activities receive the majority of their total funding from Title VI, in contrast to area studies and language training, which rely primarily on university funds supplemented by Title VI funding.

Outreach Activities

As evidenced by the information available to the committee, NRC outreach activities tend to focus on the culture, politics, and geography of a world region, whereas LRC outreach focuses on languages. The Council of Directors of National Foreign Language Resource Centers reported that the LRCs conducted 299 training activities between May 1998 and September 1999 and were attended by slightly more participants from K-12 (5,550) than higher education (4,232). During that same time period, they reported three types of outreach activities: conferences sponsored (24), newsletters published (28), and websites (18 sites with 973,540 hits) (http://nflrc.msu.edu/performance_indicators.html, accessed February 11, 2006).

The NRCs are required to report outreach activities via the Evaluation of Exchange, Language, International and Area Studies (EELIAS) database, but these reports are not easily aggregated since the "type of activity" (e.g., outreach) is a narrative field. The NRCs reported 30,155 outreach activities from the beginning of 2001 to mid-2006. Attendance at these quite different types of activities was reported as ranging from zero (reported for 459 activities) to 999,999 (which includes estimated viewing/readership numbers for television appearances and editorial columns by faculty and website hits among the 15 activities reported). The audiences identified in these reports suggest that NRCs are targeting outreach to a range of audiences.

Collaborative Approaches

One way in which NRC faculty and staff have addressed the challenge of providing outreach in an inhospitable academic environment is by banding together. In 1981, outreach directors of Middle East centers created the Middle East Outreach Council, an affiliate of the Middle East Studies Association. Similarly, faculty and staff from Africa centers have joined together in the Outreach Council of the African Studies Centers, an affiliate of the African Studies Association. Outreach professionals employed by Latin American centers have created the Consortium in Latin American Studies, which sponsors meetings and promotes collaboration. The Committee About Teaching on Asia engages faculty and staff from Asia centers funded under the NRC program (Friedlander, Marshall, and Metzler, 2003).

By working together through these organizations, outreach coordinators have been able to carry out some activities at a national level. For example, the Outreach Council of the African Studies Center has established a program of book awards to recognize the best books on Africa for elementary school students and for adolescents, and it engages with major publishers, encouraging them to use NRC faculty with Africa expertise as authors and consultants. Similarly, since 1994, the Consortium in Latin American Studies has offered annual Americas Awards, recognizing the best English and Spanish literature and nonfiction works that accurately portray Latin America, the Caribbean, or Latinos in the United States. The award winners are well publicized, providing a focus used by Latin American NRCs to develop lending libraries and curriculum materials (Friedlander, Marshall, and Metzler, 2003). The Committee on Teaching About Asia has sponsored a series of annual symposia on Asia in the curriculum, most recently at UCLA on October 12-15, 2006.

In addition to these region-specific collaborations, in 2006 the Wisconsin International Outreach Consortium convened a national conference focused on international outreach.

OUTREACH TO OTHER AUDIENCES

During the committee's site visits, university staff cited multiple examples of outreach to other audiences, including the media, government, and the public, although there appeared to be a particular emphasis on K-12.

Heritage Communities

Some Title VI centers in urban areas where there are large heritage language communities are working to preserve and develop the language skills of those communities. For example, the San Diego State University (SDSU) LRC worked with the local Arabic heritage community to establish after-school programs in Arabic language and culture (Leonard, 2004). By early in 2007, about 50 learners were participating in twice-weekly Arabic instruction at three sites in the San Diego region. Building on this success, the LRC has collaborated with other heritage language communities to establish after-school language programs in Kurdish, Mixtec (a native Mexican language spoken by large and growing heritage language populations in California and Mexico), Punjabi, and Turkish.

The SDSU LRC is also helping to train more teachers to meet the unique needs of heritage language learners. For example, the center developed an online assessment to evaluate the Spanish skills of applicants to the university's Bilingual Cross-Cultural Language and Academic Development Certificate Program. The assessment, which uses authentic reading and audio texts selected specifically for appropriateness to the bilingual educator's context, has proven a reliable predictor of future teachers' readiness for a summer immersion experience in Queretaro, Mexico (San Diego State University, 2007). The LRC is also working to influence larger state policies affecting language teaching. The California Commission on Teacher Credentialing has established a new system of assessment and certification for teachers of Tagalog/Filipino, and the LRC is working with the commission to establish certification in other heritage languages. State assessment and certification systems are essential to guide colleges of education in creating specialized teacher preparation programs and preparing the next generation of heritage teachers.

In another example, the SDSU Center for Latin American Studies (an NRC) has collaborated with the LRC and local heritage speakers to develop instruction in Mixtec. Local heritage speakers helped SDSU to develop Mixtec instruction through both a summer immersion program and on campus during the academic year. The summer immersion program employs teachers in Mexico who are native Mixtec speakers and have been trained in language acquisition and pedagogy.

In addition, as discussed in the next chapter, Title VI recently funded an LRC focused on heritage speakers with the goal of establishing a field of heritage language acquisition.

Media

In site visits, the committee learned about several efforts to share international and area expertise with the media. At New York University, the associate director of the Middle East NRC (a center that offers a master's degree with a concentration in journalism) demonstrated a website for journalists that was created in 2006 to expand the center's role in providing support to the media. The website (http://www.middleeastdesk.org) highlights current events in the Middle East and links to experts knowledgeable about those recent events and related topics. Some 950 journalists have subscribed to daily emails with alerts on middleeastdesk.org updates.

At UCLA, federally funded area centers have reached out to Hollywood. For example, the Africa Center, which conducts an array of outreach activities targeted to K-12 education and the public, initially ignored requests for help from film and television producers. Later, however, the center decided to respond. Africa center experts helped the producers of *ER* create an episode set in Africa, provided information for a story line about Nigeria in *Lost*, and provided information used in both the film *Hotel Rwanda* and in a series of related documentaries about Rwanda.

The UCLA International Institute (an NRC grantee) has created two online publications of interest to journalists as well as the public. *AsiaMedia* is a daily online publication with news about and from all varieties of news media in Asia. Journalists and scholars from across Asia, as well as from UCLA and other U.S. institutions, contribute material and make use of the site. The staff writers are UCLA students and recent graduates, who learn about journalism through a three-month internship program (University of California, Los Angeles, 2006a). Staff of the UCLA International Institute provided web traffic data indicating that the number of visitors to *AsiaMedia* more than doubled over two years, growing from 591,245 in 2005 to 927,982 in the first 9 months of 2006. The average number of daily website visits grew from 4,542 in 2005 to 12,420 over the first 9 months of 2006.

Asia Pacific Arts is a biweekly online magazine (http://www.asiaarts. ucla.edu) that looks at Asian arts and culture from a global perspective, including reporting on the intersection between Asian and Asian American entertainment. The magazine covers new film releases from a range of larger (e.g., China, India, Japan) and smaller (e.g., Thailand, the Philippines, Taiwan) Asian nations. The magazine also reviews popular and classical music, art and photography, and television and news media from and about Asia. Data from the UCLA International Institute indicate the site had 699,460 visitors in 2005, the vast majority of whom (621,006) visited more than once. The average number of daily visits to the website grew from 3,044 in 2005 to 3,886 in 2006.

Government

Title VI centers share their expertise on world languages and regions with federal, state, and local governments primarily by training future and current government employees (see Chapter 6). In addition, some outreach activities are designed to engage and inform government officials. For example, the UCLA Center for European and Eurasian Studies (an NRC) convened a conference on human trafficking in April 2006. Among other speakers, a Hungarian brigadier general who oversees the Southeast European Cooperative Initiative (SECI) Regional Center for Combating Transborder Crime discussed new approaches to combating human trafficking and other regional crimes. Representatives of the Los Angeles Police Department participated in the conference, gaining new information to help combat trafficking and forging relationships with their overseas counterparts. The UCLA Latin America NRC participates in the Governor's Economic Council and the California State Senate's California-Brazil partnership initiative.

Georgetown University's Center for Contemporary Arab Studies (part of the NRC-Middle East that also includes the Project for Jewish Civilization, the Center for Christian-Muslim Understanding, Department of Arabic and Islamic Studies, and the Laungier Library) offers public seminars on current political topics of interest to U.S. and foreign officials and policy makers. For example, some of the most recent NRC-funded events include a January 2006 Arabic Teacher Training Workshop (cosponsored by the Department of Arabic Language); the Media/IT in the Arab World: A Workshop in January 2006 (cosponsored by the Center for Contemporary Arab Studies); and A Conversation with Cynthia Ozick (cosponsored by the Program for Jewish Civilization) held on February 18, 2006.

Business

While most outreach to business is conducted by business schools with support from CIBER or BIE grants (see Chapter 10), some NRC grantees also conduct outreach to business. For example, the Latin America Center at UCLA operates an "associates" program which links faculty members and students with business partners. The program focuses on identifying business questions and locating experts with the answers. During a site visit, center staff members said that most of the companies they approach had never thought of working with a Latin America Center, but now they agreed it is a good idea. A company in Sao Paulo has expressed interest in sponsoring a symposium with this NRC, and the NRC also works with IBM in Argentina. The UCLA Asia Institute, in a joint project with the university CIBER, has created a three-year program for graduate students. The students will spend time conducting business research in Asia, followed by writing and publication on the UCLA campus.

The Public

In addition to this array of outreach activities targeted to specific audiences, LRC and NRC grantees support outreach for the public. For example, many NRC-funded area studies centers at Indiana University collaborate to support the city of Bloomington's annual Bloomington Multicultural Festival, with foods, entertainment, and art from their respective world regions.

DEPARTMENT OF EDUCATION OUTREACH

ED also engages in outreach to grantees, the larger international education community, and the public. The committee was told that staff of the International Education Programs Service (IEPS) office are planning a national meeting focused on outreach in fall 2007. However, public comments to the committee indicate a need for improved dissemination of information about the IEPS office and particularly about materials produced by grantees. For example, some individuals told the committee that they would like easier access to the research and studies supported by the IRS program. Indeed, the committee encountered some difficulty in locating and obtaining some research reports and studies produced with IRS funding.

In interviews conducted during the committee's eight site visits, some grantees also reported difficulty in understanding the goals and requirements of IEPS program officers. Faculty at one university reported that IEPS program officers had communicated different and conflicting messages about the degree of importance of evaluation in applications for the NRC and CIBER programs. In public discussions with the committee, IEPS program officers acknowledged that they lacked time for adequate communication with grantees, including on-site visits, given the limited staff available.

CONCLUSIONS AND RECOMMENDATIONS

Although the Title VI/FH programs have a role in helping to address the need for both horizontal and vertical internationalization, the programs were not designed to—and, given their limited funding, cannot be expected to—meet all of these needs. In Chapter 12, the committee recommends that ED develop a comprehensive strategy for international and foreign language education from kindergarten through graduate school—a strategy that would integrate Title VI/FH programs with other federal programs targeted to K-12 education.

The Title VI/FH programs are targeted primarily to higher education, and something that the U.S. higher education system should be expected to do best is to prepare future teachers. The committee found much less evidence of collaboration with schools of education to prepare future teachers than of professional development for current K-12 teachers.

Conclusion: The need for teachers with foreign language and international expertise is great.

Recommendation 4.1: **The Department of Education should increase incentives in the application process for National Resource Centers and Language Resource Centers to collaborate with schools or colleges of education on their campuses in the development of curriculum, the design of instructional materials, and teacher education.**

By collaborating with schools of education, NRCs and LRCs could enhance the content of the curriculum used to train teachers and directly impact the international knowledge that teachers bring to their classrooms. However, as discussed below, to make this effective, ED must support these efforts by working with state and local education authorities, helping them to recognize the importance of developing future teachers' knowledge of foreign languages and world regions and to create demand for teachers with appropriate education and training.

Incentives that ED might use to encourage these collaborations include adding a competitive priority that awards additional points to NRC or LRC applications that can demonstrate a formal collaboration agreement recognized by both the applicant and a school(s) or college(s) of education with a positive teacher-training record. Although linkages might be most easily forged at universities that include a school of education, NRCs and LRCs at other universities could establish collaborations with nearby education schools. Another option would be to award separate grants to NRCs specifically for conducting collaborative outreach to colleges of education in the competitive grant process.[5] Or ED may encourage proposals that include such collaborations with larger grant awards. This might, however, place institutions without a school of education at a disadvantage.

---

[5]The committee thinks that this would be possible under the "outreach grants and summer institutes" provision in the current statute.

To best learn from its own experience, ED should systematically identify existing collaborations between Title VI-funded programs and schools of education and share information about these approaches with the rest of the Title VI community.

In addition to supporting existing collaborations, ED should pursue other opportunities to encourage schools of education to prioritize language training and the development of international expertise. Because curriculum decisions are made largely by state and local education agencies, which drives demand for teachers, ED might undertake additional activities that would assist or encourage them to incorporate foreign language learning, geography, and area studies into their educational standards, including:

- Making language and area studies a substantive priority for one of the new national comprehensive centers, or fund a new center with that mission. Comprehensive technical assistance centers help low-performing schools and districts close achievement gaps and meet the goals of the No Child Left Behind Act of 2001. In addition to regional centers, ED supports five content-focused centers focusing on key issues related to the goals of the act (U.S. Department of Education, 2007a).

- Charging one or more of ED's regional education laboratories with research and development of approaches to linking schools of education with Title VI centers. ED funds 10 regional education laboratories across the nation, whose primary mission is "to serve the educational needs of designated regions, using applied research, development, dissemination, and training and technical assistance and to bring the latest and best research and proven practices into school improvement efforts" (U.S. Department of Education, 2007d). With this general mission, the laboratories conduct applied research and development projects on a variety of topics, such as raising achievement in mathematics and science and improving elementary schools.

- Creating a clearinghouse for information on best practices in the field or incorporating foreign language learning as a topic area of ED's What Works Clearinghouse.

- Convening a national conference to showcase positive examples of integrating foreign language and area studies into the K-12 curriculum, including the results of language immersion schools.

Each of these efforts would highlight the importance of foreign language and international knowledge that has been embraced by the secretary of education, while also providing models of promising practices to the field. Ultimately, however, infusion of foreign language and cultural instruction in the K-12 classroom may depend on establishing a national priority

5

Reducing Shortages
of Foreign Language
and Area Experts

As this report describes, the Title VI and Fulbright-Hays (Title VI/FH) programs, under current law and by virtue of the way the programs are administered, support the creation and maintenance of a broad skill base and a long-term national capacity in languages and area studies about every region of the world. They seek to create a pool of language and area expertise for use not only in government, but also across the education system, academia, nongovernmental organizations, and business. Although they are aimed at creating a broad reservoir of expertise in a wide variety of languages and areas, they can also help provide a modest pipeline into the government to help address more immediate needs brought about by rapidly changing geopolitics. This is not, however, the programs' primary statutory purpose.

The committee's charge called for us to review the extent to which Title VI/FH helps to reduce "shortages" of foreign language and area experts. As outlined in Chapter 2, we have not conducted a systematic assessment of the extent to which shortages exist,[1] but instead acknowledge that the significant demand for people with foreign language, area, and international skills for government service, academia, K-12 education, and business suggests that there is a significant unmet need.

The Title VI/FH programs can help to address this unmet need in at least three ways: (1) producing graduates with language, area, and international skills who find employment in relevant fields, (2) serving as a

---

[1]For this reason the committee does not use the term "shortage," referring instead to "demand" or "unmet need."

resource to government and other organizations to address unmet needs more indirectly, and (3) producing graduates with increased levels of foreign language proficiency. It is extremely difficult, however, for the committee to answer the questions that Congress and critics of Title VI/FH are asking about the effectiveness of these programs in meeting the unmet needs in these areas, because of the lack of good data. This chapter reviews the limited available evidence of the programs' effectiveness in these areas, but much of the discussion focuses on data limitations.

JOB PLACEMENTS

The Title VI/FH programs overall play a role in internationalizing the educational experience of undergraduates and graduates in the U.S. higher education system. The programs promote international coursework, foreign language study, and overseas experiences as important parts of education in their own right. Consistent with several other recent national reports (Committee for Economic Development, 2006; Commission on the Abraham Lincoln Study Abroad Fellowship Program, 2005; U.S. Department of Education, 2006a), the committee embraces the value of an understanding of foreign languages and cultures as part of students' general education.

Among the portfolio of Title VI/FH programs, the National Resource Centers (NRC), Foreign Language and Area Studies (FLAS) Fellowships, and Centers for International Business Education and Research (CIBER) programs have a particular emphasis on producing graduates with language, area, and international expertise, although as reported in the previous chapter, this expertise is distributed among students from a wide range of disciplines.[2] The NRCs are required to report via the Evaluation of Exchange, Language, International and Area Studies (EELIAS) database system the aggregate number of job placements of its "graduates"—defined as students with 15 or more area studies or language credit hours—and of FLAS recipients who have graduated, in multiple sector categories, including higher education, elementary or secondary education, federal government, military, state or local government, nonprofit international organization, for-profit international organization, nonprofit business, and for-profit business. A graduate school category is included to capture those who continue their education. Finally, a category for unemployed or out of the labor market and one for unknown are also included. During grant competitions, NRC applicants generally report similar placement data in their applications to demonstrate their past performance. NRCs often conduct surveys of graduates so that the information includes job placements

---

[2]Placement information for CIBER graduates is discussed in Chapter 9 on addressing business needs.

not only of graduates in any given year (as required in EELIAS) but also of all graduates and the jobs they obtain later in their careers.

The U.S. Department of Education (ED) has included job placement of NRC and certain FLAS graduates, as well as language proficiency of FLAS fellows (see the section on proficiency) as national performance measures under the Government Performance and Results Act (GPRA). The NRC measures have been in place since 1991 and, for the FLAS Program, since 1994. In reporting under GPRA, ED measures the performance of the NRC and FLAS Programs based in part on the combined percentage of graduates in each program who find employment in higher education, government, or the military.[3] Although data are reported on bachelor's, master's, and Ph.D. recipients, ED has in the past reported on Ph.D. graduates only. ED's new performance measure, recently approved by the Office of Management and Budget, will include master's graduates. Graduates with bachelor's degrees are excluded because of the high likelihood that they will continue with their education rather than seek employment, and because of greater difficulty identifying the job placement for these graduates. ED measures performance based on a combined category that includes higher education, government, and the military, given their view that the programs are designed to provide experts for both academia and government. ED has reported an increase from 48.5 percent in 2001 to 71.8 percent in 2004 among Ph.D. students, as well as 16 percent of FLAS Ph.D. graduates in 2004, but the committee was unable to duplicate the numbers and ED was unable to clarify the methodology used prior to 2004. In 2004, the NRC graduate percentage was based on employed students only; it excluded students for whom placement was not known, students who continued with graduate study, and students who were not employed. For FLAS recipients, the percentage is based on only the FLAS Ph.D. students who graduated in the year in which they received a FLAS award.

At least three problems arise from the approach of reporting a single percentage for the combined category. First, we do not know the specific percentage of those going into each of the subcategories of government, military, and higher education. Second, it adopts a narrow definition of success. For example, those going into the private sector or the nonprofit arena are not counted as a "success" (e.g., a Ph.D. who finds employment with a defense contractor or a nonprofit contractor to the U.S. Department of State would not be counted as a success, even though each may be performing a task of value to the conduct of U.S. foreign policy.) Similarly, someone who works for a nonprofit organization on international issues would not be considered a success. Third, it is difficult to make judgments about

---

[3]ED has performance targets that increase slightly each year for each of these two measures.

TABLE 5-1 Cumulative Placements of Slavic and Middle Eastern Studies Students from Title VI-Funded Institutions, 2001 to 2003, N and (%)

Area and Degree Granted	Elementary and Secondary Education	Federal Government	U.S. Military	State and Local Government	Foreign Government	Graduate Study
Russian and East European Studies (2,452 records of student placement)[a]						
B.A.	100	74	40	32	1	398
(n = 1,852)	(5.3)	(3.9)	(2.1)	(1.7)	(0)	(21.4)
M.A.	4	25	34	3	6	137
(n = 365)	(1.0)	(6.8)	(9.3)	(.8)	(1.6)	(37.5)
Ph.D.	2	9	0	0	3	8
(n = 233)	(.8)	(3.8)	(0)	(0)	(.8)	(3.4)
Middle East Studies (788 records of student placement)[b]						
B.A.	47	32	7	24	0	186
(n = 715)	(6.5)	(4.4)	(.1)	(3.3)	(0)	(26)
M.A.	7	12	1	0	3	93
(n = 182)	(.5)	(6.6)	(.5)	(0)	(1.6)	(51.1)
Ph.D.	1	3	0	0	0	6
(n = 87)	(1.1)	(3.4)	(0)	(0)	(0)	(6.9)

[a]Data were available for 2,452 of 3,414 students.
[b]Data were available for 788 of 2,094 students.
SOURCE: Adapted from Brecht et al. (2007).

whether the above placement rates are good, bad, or indifferent without some data from comparable groups, such as graduates with similar degrees who did not receive an FLAS Fellowship or attended an institution without an NRC. Placement rates for a similar comparison group would shed light on whether the Title VI/FH programs add value in terms of employment.

Universities have raised legitimate concerns about whether they are being held accountable for the wrong measure. These problems are further aggravated by the fact that, although ED collects data that would enable more detailed reporting, except for special requests, placement information other than what is submitted for GPRA is generally not made available outside of ED.

Where Graduates Are Going

A recent evaluation by Brecht et al. (2007) examines, in more detail than does ED, the career paths of graduates from Title VI-funded Slavic and

Higher Education	International Organizations, U.S.-based	International Organizations, Outside U.S.	Private Sector, For-Profit	Private Sector, Nonprofit	Unemployed	Other
64	31	37	773	127	175	0
(3.4)	(1.6)	(1.9)	(41.7)	(6.8)	(9.4)	(0)
47	9	18	47	25	10	0
(12.8)	(2.4)	(4.9)	(12.8)	(6.8)	(2.7)	(0)
157	2	9	19	8	14	2
(67.4)	(.8)	(3.9)	(8.1)	(3.4)	(6.0)	(0)
73	20	6	231	50	39	0
(10.2)	(2.8)	(.8)	(32.3)	(6.9)	(5.4)	(0)
20	1	3	29	8	5	0
(11.0)	(.5)	(1.6)	(16.0)	(4.4)	(2.7)	(0)
57	1	2	7	7	3	0
(65.5)	(1.1)	(2.3)	(8.5)	(8.5)	(3.4)	(0)

Middle Eastern language and area studies programs, based on a more detailed analysis of EELIAS data.[4] These are summarized in Table 5-1. Placements were not known for roughly a third of the Slavic studies students and more than half of the Middle East studies students. The data do not include graduates of other world area centers. Nonetheless, some patterns are discernible from the table for graduates in these two fields:

• Most undergraduates tend to go on either to work in the private sector or to continue with graduate study.
• The placements of students with master's degrees are more dispersed, with the highest number continuing with graduate study.
• About two-thirds of students with Ph.D.s find employment at institutions of higher education.

---

[4]As the developers of the EELIAS system, Brecht and colleagues had direct access to the underlying data.

TABLE 5-2 Job Placements of NRC Graduates in 2000, as Reported by ED

Field	Percentage of Graduates			
	Bachelor's	Master's	Ph.D.	Total
Elementary/secondary education	3.6	4.5	1.7	3.6
Federal government	2.1	4.4	2.8	2.3
U.S. military	0.9	1.2	0.3	0.9
State and local government	1.4	2.0	1.2	1.4
Foreign government	0.1	1.0	1.3	0.3
Graduate study	15.1	17.7	2.9	14.9
Higher education	3.0	8.9	45.3	5.3
International organization	2.2	6.5	5.9	2.7
Private sector (for profit)	29.3	21.6	12.2	27.9
Nonprofit	4.4	6.7	3.4	4.6
Unemployed	4.5	3.6	3.8	4.4
Unknown	33.4	22.0	19.2	31.8

SOURCE: Spreadsheet based on data downloaded from EELIAS and provided in response to separate requests from Heydemann (2004) and Kramer (2003) to ED. Available: http://www.geocities.com/martinkramerorg/2004_03_17.htm [accessed June 2006].

• Between about 4 and 7 percent find employment with the federal government, with the highest percentage among graduates with master's degrees. The numbers who go on to the U.S. military are negligible, with the exception of those receiving master's degrees in Slavic studies.

Heydemann (2004) and Kramer (2003) both obtained placement data from ED on 43,615 NRC graduates (all levels) in 2000. The job placements for all NRC graduates—those who receive bachelor's, master's, and Ph.D. degrees—from the data provided by ED, are shown in Table 5-2. Heydemann and Kramer highlight different points about the data and come to different conclusions. Heydemann (2004) points out that "more graduates of Middle East Centers go into some form of government service than those who study any other world region except East Asia" (the data include a world area code for individual university reports) and that "more than a third of students who graduate[5] from Middle East centers go into the private sector." He concludes that the criticisms directed at Middle East centers in particular are misguided and that the idea that "Middle East centers

---

[5]The committee notes that "graduate" in this context means a student who took 15 credit hours or more of center courses. The student's degree is very often from another department in the university.

TABLE 5-3 FY 2003 NRC Master's and Ph.D. Graduates

Field	Number of Graduates		Percentage by Sector	
	Master's	Ph.D.	Master's	Ph.D.
Elementary or secondary education	390	31	4.11	2.01
Federal government	273	40	2.88	2.59
Foreign government	38	22	0.40	1.43
Graduate study	806	36	8.49	2.33
Higher education	607	715	6.39	46.37
International organization (in U.S.)	124	30	1.31	1.95
International organization (outside U.S.)	80	44	0.84	2.85
Private sector (for profit)	1,366	181	14.39	11.74
Private sector (nonprofit)	588	61	6.19	3.96
State or local government	50	35	0.53	2.27
U.S. military	1,453	8	15.30	0.52
Unemployed or out of job market	219	53	2.31	3.44
Unknown	3,501	286	36.87	18.55
Total	9,495	1,542		

SOURCE: Data provided by U.S. Department of Education [EELIAS].

are not training students for careers in business and government is false." Kramer (2003) focuses on the percentage of all graduates entering federal government or military service and concludes that there is an "astonishingly low rate of job placement in the federal government and the U.S. military for grads who've taken foreign languages in Title VI centers."[6] In his view, placements should be closer to at least 10 percent, the percentage he reports that Title VI contributes to the university area studies programs. These different conclusions drawn from the same data highlight the difficulties in interpreting these sorts of placement figures without a comparison group or a definition and rationale by ED of what would constitute success.

As with the analysis conducted by Brecht et al., placement information was unknown for almost one-third (31.8 percent) of the graduates. Of those for whom data were available, the majority of Ph.D. graduates found jobs in higher education (45.3); significant numbers of bachelor's and master's students either entered graduate study (15.1 and 17.7 percent, respectively) or found employment in the private sector (29.3 and 21.6 percent, respectively); and relatively few obtained federal government positions, with the largest percentage among graduates with master's degrees (4.4 percent).

The committee conducted its own analysis of FY 2003 job placement data in EELIAS, since that was the most complete year available in the

---

[6]While language courses can be included as part of the 15 credit hours required to be considered an NRC graduate, courses are not exclusively language courses.

database (see Table 5-3). Data for undergraduates were excluded given the widespread sentiment that they are unreliable. This analysis identified the same overall trends as earlier analyses. ED, through its Office of Planning, Evaluation and Policy Development, recently contracted with InfoUse to conduct a survey of fellowship recipients of four ED graduate fellowship programs between 1997 and 1999, including FLAS Fellowships and Doctoral Dissertation Research Abroad (DDRA) recipients. According to the survey data collected by InfoUse, about one-quarter of DDRA recipients worked within a year of completing the fellowship, while another one-half worked within 2-3 years of their fellowship. For FLAS recipients, about 40 percent worked within a year of completing the fellowship, while another 29 percent did so within 2-3 years. Among those who reported that they had at least one job related to the field they had studied with FLAS support, three-quarters had worked in education, one-fifth in a private-sector job, and one-fifth in foreign or international jobs. About 10 percent worked for the military or other government positions.

Fellows in doctoral programs were far more likely than master's fellows to have worked in education (87 versus 53 percent) and master's fellows were more likely than doctoral fellows to work for the military or in another government position, a private-sector position, or a foreign or international position. For DDRA recipients who reported they had held at least one job related to the field they studied with DDRA support, 88 percent worked in education and 11 percent in foreign or international jobs. About 7 percent worked for the military or other government positions.

These results reinforce the general trends identified using EELIAS data for NRC graduates, although the number reporting government or military positions is higher than in the NRC data. This may be due to the longer time period covered. It also highlights a limitation of the reporting requirement for placement data on FLAS recipients. Although the EELIAS placement data are reported when FLAS recipients complete their fellowship, most are not yet employed—only 40 percent reported working within a year. The performance measure related to placement based on these data is in fact based on an extremely small number of recipients.

Tracking Problems

The process of collecting data on student placements upon graduation is difficult and expensive. During our site visits, the committee heard that although NRCs try to track where students go after they leave the university, it can be difficult. Both ED and university staffs with whom the committee met reported that it is most difficult to track bachelor's degree graduates. They may feel less of an allegiance to their undergraduate institution, and their location may be more fluid between graduation and employment. Similarly, FLAS recipients, who often receive fellowships in the early years of their graduate study, are often still in school several years after the fellowship ends, yet placement data are collected when the fellowship is completed. Some NRCs offer area studies degrees. NRCs reported that these students, who have a direct relationship with the NRC, are often easier to track. Other "graduates," those who take 15 or more credit hours associated with the NRC but whose degree is in another department, are more difficult to track. For many students, there may be a significant time lag between graduation and finding employment. Another challenge is that the employment sector alone may not capture the extent to which language, area, or international skills are used on the job. The international content of a given position or career may also evolve over time.

NRC staff visited by the committee uniformly expressed concern about the burden of the extensive data collected, particularly given the decreasing grant resources provided, and emphasized the significant staff resources required. In some cases, NRCs are able to use university alumni offices to get information on placements, but such information is often not known for a large number of graduates. In other cases, NRCs conduct their own surveys to determine placement outcomes. Some NRCs reported that their government service numbers are undercounted because students who obtain sensitive government positions are reluctant to report their status.

Some NRCs also conduct follow-up activities to track their graduates over time. One NRC, which follows all its graduates over time (see Box 5-1), believed that its follow-up activities would probably be curtailed as the alumni office's efforts are adapted to better track the center's graduates.

Addressing Unmet Needs in Government

As discussed in Chapter 2, according to presentations to the committee by representatives of different government agencies and government conference reports (U.S. Department of Defense, 2005; U.S. General Accounting Office, 2002; U.S. Government Accountability Office, 2006) the federal government is faced with significant and immediate unmet language needs, especially for people with skills in critical languages. Although the committee views the Title VI/FH mandate as legitimately calling for it to address a larger set of needs than just those of the federal government, in this section we review issues related to meeting demand at the federal level, because of the attention it has received.

Although the current data available from ED suggest that few NRC graduates obtain government positions, these data have numerous limitations, as discussed above, and may not accurately reflect the number of graduates whose jobs include an international component. Merkx (2006)

BOX 5-1
Tracking Russia and East Europe Specialists
at Indiana University

The Russian and East European Institute (REEI) at Indiana University reports a long history of producing experts for government service. In its most recent application for federal funding, REEI provides a list of 111 graduates who have entered federal jobs over the past 15 years, with the largest groups going into the Army and the State Department. The application also identifies REEI-affiliated graduates who have entered high-level government positions, including former Central Intelligence Agency director Robert Gates; former U.S. ambassador to Russia James Collins; and Victor Jackovich, who was formerly U.S. ambassador to Bosnia and Herzegovina, U.S. ambassador to Slovenia, and senior political advisor to the commander of U.S. forces in Afghanistan.

The institute director acknowledged the difficulty of tracking REEI graduates to obtain information on student placements required by ED. During the 1990s, the center explored the university alumni association data records, but the database included only information on students' major field of study, and it was not possible for the alumni association to complete the necessary coding to identify all students about whom the institute was required to report. Instead, REEI created its own database of all university graduates who enrolled in Russia and East European courses from 1958 to the present, with contact and employment information on 2,500 students. In the last year, the alumni association has made software upgrades that will allow more flexibility in tracking.

The institute sends an e-mail each summer to all those listed, asking about changes in address, new jobs, and any accomplishments to be noted in the newsletter. It explains that the information is needed both to report to ED on graduates' success and also to provide networking opportunities for current students moving into the job market. The response rates vary, depending on what the graduates are doing. Those in academia usually respond promptly, and retirees respond occasionally. However, graduates working in government and public service are often too busy to reply. As one way of maintaining contact with this group, the institute hosts an annual reception or dinner in the Washington, DC, area for all university alumni who are interested in Russian and East European studies. More than 100 university graduates attended the November 2006 event.

NOTE: Information contained in this box came from a committee site visit (2006) and review of the university's NRC application (provided by the U.S. Department of Education).

---

suggests that a better way of assessing whether NRCs are producing graduates to meet government needs would be to conduct a survey of current language or area experts already in government, a tack that would show a different result. He and others point to anecdotal evidence that many experts in government attend or have attended NRC institutions (Interagency Language Roundtable, 2006b; Heydemann, 2004; Merkx, 2006). Staff at universities visited also cited numerous cases of graduates who now work for the federal government.

Government downsizing, with traditional government jobs increasingly being done by contractors, may also mean that the available statistics do not fully capture all NRC graduates who help to address federal needs. According to the Congressional Budget Office, from 1985 to 2000, the size of the federal workforce (excluding the U.S. Postal Service) decreased by 19 percent, largely but not solely due to cuts in military personnel (U.S. Congressional Budget Office, 2001). This has been offset by increased reliance by the federal government on contractors—private companies, nonprofits, consultants, temporary employees, etc., that some analysts call a "shadow government" (Light, 1999). An example from the international context is the U.S. Freedom Support Act, which funded projects to help the transition to democracy and market-oriented economies in the former Soviet Union in the 1990s. Much of this funding went to universities, in particular Harvard University, and to a wide variety of nonprofit and for-profit organizations and consultants. Presumably, many Slavic studies graduates went to work at these organizations, which helped carry out U.S. foreign policy toward former communist nations. These graduates would be reported as being placed in higher education or private organizations, yet they were responding to a government need.

Other considerations, such as a lack of awareness of government needs, recruitment issues, problematic security clearance processes, and the difficulty of matching skills with job openings are also possible reasons that the percentages of students pursing careers in the government and military are not higher. Noteworthy are the challenges that graduates of the National Security Education Program (NSEP) in the Department of Defense (DoD) often face in obtaining a federal government position to fulfill their service requirement. In short, there are many barriers to placement in a government position—these are barriers that Title VI/FH cannot be expected to solve.

Inadequate Communication of Government Needs to the Field

Although reports of unmet needs in government have surfaced for years, there have been relatively limited efforts to specify the skills or quantify particular needs and then communicate them to universities, which might help build the necessary skills. According to Ruther (2003), there is "not much reliable information about the global competences of the government's current workforce or its strategic needs for globally competent talent" (p. 1). A recent Government Accountability Office report on progress made by the State Department in meeting its language needs calls on it to produce a prioritized assessment of language skills and then act to meet these needs, particularly in countries of strategic importance

(U.S. Government Accountability Office, 2006). The Partnership for Public Service (2006) points to a similar issue and, while recognizing efforts to improve recruitment and retention, calls for a "government-wide assessment of needed language skills."

Recruitment Issues

The federal government has in general faced recruiting problems, and there is no reason to think that recruiting students who have participated in Title VI/FH programs is easier. Indeed, one of the most significant problems has been the clearance process and the difficulty of students who have studied critical languages in countries of concern to then get timely clearances or get cleared at all, given the challenges involved in conducting background checks. A 2006 study conducted by the Partnership for Public Service on federal efforts to recruit students on college campuses highlighted the following problems:

- Overall, the federal workforce is middle-aged or older. Only 3 percent of the current federal workforce is under 25.
- Downsizing of the federal workforce and budget cuts have reduced the effectiveness of recruiting efforts, particularly at universities. In 1996 recruiting and hiring was decentralized, from the Office of Personnel Management to individual agencies, each of which adopted varying strategies for recruitment.
- Hiring "from within" is preferable to hiring graduate students. Many federal agencies do not even bother looking for ideal candidates at universities for many positions. In 2003, only 43 percent of mid-level (GS12 to GS15) federal job openings were open to the public, and only 15 percent were filled by people outside the government. The Federal Bureau of Investigation (FBI) was singled out by the 9/11 Commission for this practice: "The FBI's tradition of hiring analysts from within instead of recruiting individuals with relevant education background and experience" was cited as a factor in the failure to thwart the 9/11 terrorist attacks.
- It is difficult for the federal government to compete with the private sector. Business and other sectors of the economy are competing in the same applicant pool, and competition is fierce for people with advanced skills. College juniors and seniors are most interested in working at large companies (49 percent), small companies (45 percent), the federal government (42 percent), and the military (10 percent). However, 53 percent of students indicated that, despite a certain level of interest, they would not want to work for the federal government because they felt it was too bureaucratic.

The Partnership for Public Service study also surveyed another group of students with special skills that are in demand by the federal government: engineering students. Their situation may be somewhat analogous to people with language skills entering (or not entering) the federal workforce, and it is a reminder that the federal government has problems recruiting in a number of fields. First, the needs are great. The federal government employs 91,000 engineers, many of whom will soon retire. DoD alone seeks to hire 6,000 engineers annually. As with people with language skills, the pool of students available to the federal government is small: 57 percent of engineering Ph.D.s go to foreign students studying in the United States, and the federal government cannot hire them for many positions because they are not U.S. citizens. In addition, the survey found that engineering students had a more negative view of federal employment than students overall, and they were much more interested in more remunerative opportunities in the private sector (Partnership for Public Service, 2006).

In the case of graduate students in languages and area studies, the federal government's main competitor for talent is not the corporate world (as with engineering students), but academia.

Matching Skills with Openings

An additional barrier is matching skills to the specific needs of any given agency. As discussed in Chapter 2, the State Department and the FBI both have unmet needs for people with critical language capabilities, but language ability is not a formal criteria for hiring people at these agencies. The State Department, for example, hires not on the basis of foreign language competency, but rather on the basis of a wide range of skills that are required of diplomats, to do a range of jobs and be competitive to progress to senior levels. However, bonus points are given for demonstrated speaking skills once a candidate passes written and oral examinations. The same is true of the FBI. A person with excellent language skills may still find it difficult to get a job with a federal agency because of the multiple criteria to be met in order to gain employment. Similarly, the needs of government agencies are quite variable. The National Security Agency may need people with good listening skills, the FBI may need people with good translating skills, and the State Department may need people with listening, speaking, and reading skills.

Experience in the National Security Education Program

Even DoD's National Security Education Program (see Chapter 3), which has a government service requirement as a condition of participation in the program, has faced challenges placing its graduates in government jobs (NSEP report to Congress, n.d.). These students are highly motivated to get jobs in federal national security-related bureaucracies, and as of 2006, the program had placed over 500 graduates into federal positions. However, in any given year, there are about 350 students still seeking federal employment. Challenges in the federal hiring process include lack of responsiveness of federal agencies and lengthy security clearance processes in some federal agencies.

Consistent with the goals of the legislation, a large percentage of placements are with the DoD, the State Department, and intelligence agencies, although some graduates went on to work at the Departments of Agriculture, Commerce, Energy, or Treasury as well as other organizations such as the Center for Disease Control and Prevention, the Food and Drug Administration, and the Peace Corps. The NSEP Report to Congress (n.d.) states that federal hiring practices and security clearance processes constitute something of a barrier, despite legislative and regulatory adjustments that were made to specifically accommodate NSEP fellows. Both the NSEP Report to Congress and remarks to the committee by a senior DoD official indicate that a top priority for NSEP is to get more federal agencies to hire fellows.

SERVING AS A NATIONAL RESOURCE

Title VI/FH programs assist in providing needed services and resources to the nation, in ways other than directly providing federal government employees. The programs teach a large number of less commonly taught languages (LCTLs), they reach a large number of students, they maintain the capacity to teach less commonly taught languages and other languages that may be crucial in the future, and they produce resources that can be drawn on by the entire nation. Some evaluation studies provide data on how Title VI/FH programs help to meet the need for language and area experts, by emphasizing the numbers of people with language and area skills produced by the funded institutions. A study by a group of Title VI-funded NRCs (e-LCTL, 2005) concludes that Title VI/FH institutions help respond to the need for foreign language instruction based on descriptive information on LCTL enrollments:

• During the 2001-2002 academic year, the 55 NRC/FLAS institutions taught 128 less commonly taught languages, with the capacity to teach 98 more if needed.
• More than 30,000 students per semester received instruction in less commonly taught languages at these institutions, accounting for 80 percent of all instruction in these languages nationwide, and 60 percent of enrollment in critical languages as defined by NSEP.

- In 2002-2003, FLAS Fellowships were awarded to graduate students in 107 less commonly taught languages.

In 2004, the e-LCTL study found that Title VI institutions could teach 226 less commonly taught languages, compared with the 75 taught at the Defense Language Institute and the Foreign Service Institute combined. The Defense Language Institute and the Foreign Service Institute train to high levels, but they lack capacity to teach additional less commonly taught languages, and the training is often for a specific professional purpose (Brecht and Rivers, 2001). In comments to the committee, Wiley (2006) stated that 80 percent of graduate students in languages that the national security community deems critical are at Title VI centers.

While these data do not address the issue of what levels of language proficiency are achieved by students in these programs, it is clear that Title VI institutions support training in a significant number of less commonly taught languages, and they have an ongoing capacity (in contrast to the "on demand" capacity of the Defense Language Institute and the Foreign Service Institute) to teach more languages than institutions designed specifically to train government personnel.

Public comments from grantee organizations stress that the programs also provide indirect services to the federal government, such as creation of a pool of expertise for training needs, production of language materials, and consultation. The committee heard similar sentiments expressed during several site visits, with examples provided, such as government personnel obtaining degrees and NRC staff providing consultation services. Examples cited during public comment include

- Experts in academia often brief military, diplomatic, and intelligence agencies; this was particularly true regarding the conflicts in both Afghanistan and Iraq (Brustein, 2006).
- The U.S. Army Foreign Area Officer Program sends its officers to Title VI centers for training in language and area studies. For example, at the Latin American Institute at the University of New Mexico, 44 active-duty Army officers and four active-duty Air Force officers recently received master's degrees in Latin American studies (Merkx, 2006).
- The U.S. Air Force relies on Title VI centers for course materials, most recently about Turkmen (Brustein, 2006).
- Title VI centers have developed language training materials for Vietnamese, Tagalog, Indonesia, Mandarin, and Korean for the National Security Agency and DoD (Brustein, 2006).
- The State Department recently asked American Overseas Research Centers to help with additional training in critical languages (Brustein, 2006).

- Federal agencies have used materials developed through International Research and Studies (IRS) grants to meet current language training needs in Pashto and Cebuano (Wiley, 2006).

In addition, the large numbers of Ph.D.s produced by these institutions fan out and teach at universities across the country, at both Title VI and non-Title VI institutions. As would be expected, the largest number of NRC Ph.D. graduates move on to positions in higher education. This helps to maintain capacity in language and area education across the U.S. postsecondary education system.

LANGUAGE PROFICIENCY

The Title VI/FH mandate includes area studies, international studies, and language study. The vast majority of the Title VI/FH programs support the study of language by increasing or enhancing language course offerings, developing language materials, supporting study aboard, or providing financial aid for students to study languages. The committee heard remarks from academic leaders who stressed that area and international knowledge is as important as language in order to be able to interpret events in various regions of the world. The committee concurs that an integrated approach that enhances both language acquisition and the attainment of international and area knowledge is desirable. Several programs, including NRCs, Language Resource Centers (LRCs), and IRS, provide indirect support to increase students' language proficiency by maintaining the capacity and infrastructure to teach languages, particularly less commonly taught languages.

The FLAS Program is unique in its focus on language study, although such study is often undertaken to support research in another discipline rather than as an end in itself. Despite its focus on language study, few data are available on the language achievement of FLAS recipients. ED has recognized the need to assess language proficiency more systematically than the current self-rating process (see below), and a number of alternative assessment approaches have emerged. Concern about the approach may have been heightened by recent criticisms that the program does not produce graduates with adequate language proficiency.

Critics of Title VI/FH programs charge that a major shortcoming of them is that they do not educate enough people to high levels of language proficiency. This was also cited as a shortcoming by representatives of the federal government's Interagency Language Roundtable (ILR) in presentations made to the committee, although the ILR also pointed to the lack of adequate assessment of language proficiency. One critic is Kenneth Whitehead, a former administrator of the Title VI/FH programs during the 1980s, who credited the problem of low language proficiency to a drift in the mission of the programs. When Title VI was created as part of the National Defense Education Act, one of its main purposes was to address shortfalls in language expertise for national security purposes. When the program was rolled into the Higher Education Act, he asserts, the emphasis on language proficiency was lost, and more funding went into projects with an area studies rather than a language emphasis.

Brecht and Rivers (2000) also make the case that the reason language proficiency is not as high as it should be among graduates of Title VI/FH-funded programs is because too much funding has shifted toward area studies, rather than languages. In their updated study, Brecht et al. (2007) argue for a periodic review and rebalancing of resources directed toward languages versus area studies. Table 5-4, drawn from the updated study, shows that Title VI institutions produce a much higher number of dissertations in Slavic and Middle Eastern *studies* as opposed to Slavic and Middle Eastern *languages*.

However, the table also shows a similar imbalance between area studies and language dissertations at non-Title VI institutions. Similarly, a survey of the membership of the Middle East Studies Association (Betteridge, 2003) shows a decline in the numbers of students studying Middle Eastern languages, but an increase in those studying Middle Eastern politics and economics. Presumably most, if not all, of those pursuing these advanced degrees have acquired some language competency, but the focus of their professional interest is not foreign languages or linguistics.

The committee can suggest a number of possible reasons, other than a shift in federal funding, for the preponderance of dissertations being completed in area studies rather than languages. In general, a language degree may not be as marketable as that in another discipline. Some academics have observed that there is less prestige in teaching languages at universities than other subjects. A person with a Ph.D. in a language might be forced into teaching many sections of introductory Arabic, for example, but might

TABLE 5-4 Dissertations in Slavic and Middle Eastern Studies, Title VI and Non-Title VI Institutions, 1997-2004

Dissertation area	Number and % of Dissertations Completed at Title VI Institutions	Number and % of Dissertations Completed at Non-Title VI Institutions
Slavic area studies	578 (50)	580 (50)
Slavic language	81 (57)	60 (43)
Middle East area studies	462 (44)	565 (56)
Middle East language	25 (31)	55 (69)

SOURCE: Adapted from Brecht et al. (2007).

TABLE 5-5 Total Graduate and Undergraduate Enrollments in the Most Popular Language Courses at Title VI-funded Institutions, by Region, 2001-2002

Language	Elementary	Intermediate	Advanced	Specialized Advanced[a]
Swahili	483	192	59	16
Uzbek	32	16	0	0
Japanese	5,602	2,973	1,350	977
Russian	1,604	898	724	778
Arabic	1,895	770	279	326
Hindi-Urdu	538	167	16	128
Tagalog	597	242	45	38
Chinese	4,714	2,174	1,350	1,151
Korean	1,259	635	563	302
Spanish	49,054	37,017	6,989	11,800
French	7,149	6,218	1,580	2,546

[a]These are advanced courses for a specific purpose or for a specific aspect of a language or culture; examples are commercial or medical Chinese or Chinese poetry.
SOURCE: Adapted from data on enrollments by world region at http://elctl.msu.edu/summaries [accessed April 2007].

have more interest in teaching some aspect of Arabic literature or culture. Given these circumstances, the imbalance is not surprising.

At the same time, NRCs seem to have significant enrollments in language study, particularly less commonly taught languages, and offer graduated courses from elementary to advanced language study. Although course level cannot be equated to any standard measure of language proficiency, advanced language courses offered by NRCs, as reported by the e-LCTL initiative, have had significant enrollments (see Table 5-5). During site visits, NRCs regularly reported increased enrollments in less commonly taught languages and using funds to seed new, advanced-level language courses. (See Box 5-2 for examples of Title VI/FH funds being used to expand instruction in Arabic language and culture.)

Heritage Language Speakers

Heritage language speakers represent a valuable national resource for developing and strengthening proficiency in less commonly taught languages, including languages currently defined as critical languages. A recent national gathering of experts from government agencies, academia, industry, and the language community recommended (National Language Conference, 2005, p. 9):

BOX 5-2
Expanding Arabic Instruction at Select Title VI Universities

During site visits, the committee found a number of examples of Title VI/FH funds being used to expand the teaching and learning of Arabic language and culture. Some highlights:

- At New York University (NYU), Title VI funding has supported a growing program of Arabic instruction. Between academic years 1995-1996 and 2005-2006, average annual enrollment in all levels of Arabic nearly tripled, increasing from 112 to 302 as more students became interested in Arabic. Enrollment in elementary Arabic I quadrupled, growing from 23 in 2000-2001 to 93 in fall 2006, while enrollment in advanced Arabic I surged from 2 to 26, an increase of over 8 times.

- In 1990, NYU had just one full-time Arabic instructor. By the end of 2006, NYU had four full-time language instructors and one part-time language instructor. Because NYU had already made a commitment to expanding its Arabic language program, it was well positioned to respond to increased student enrollments after 9/11 by leveraging Title VI funds to create a new full-time Arabic faculty position in 2002-2003. By the end of 2006, NYU had four full-time Arabic language instructors and one part-time Arabic instructor. In the past decade, NYU has hired 12 tenure/tenure-track faculty positions in Middle Eastern studies.

- The Center for Near Eastern Studies at the University of California, Los Angeles, also used Title VI funding to respond to growing demand for Arabic. Funds were used to hire additional lecturers and teaching assistants, to develop new courses in Iraqi Arabic and media Arabic, to provide workshops for language instructors, and to purchase film and multimedia materials to support language learning.

- At San Diego State University, LRC grants to the Language Acquisition Resource Center since 1990 have focused on "distinguished-level" (advanced professional proficiency or ILR level 4) language learning. Building on this expertise and with support from the university, the LRC grant, and an NSEP institutional grant, the university created the Center for the Advancement of Distinguished Language Proficiency (ADLP) in 2002, which has been institutionalized as a program offered by the Language Acquisition Resource Center. That program focuses on moving students from ILR level 3 to level 4 in two strategically critical languages—Persian-Farsi and Arabic—while simultaneously training a cadre of teachers to teach at this level. The center offered professional Arabic summer intensive courses for federal employees in 2004 and 2005. Currently, it is developing an intensive course in Iraqi Arabic for the military. Recently, the LRC received a special appropriation from Congress to develop curricula and courses in critical languages, with a focus on language and culture for military and civilian personnel needing in-depth intensive formatted courses. Federal funding to the university also helps to train Reserve Officers' Training Corps students in Arabic. To meet growing demand from these students, the university offered extra sections of Arabic in fall 2006.

NOTE: Information contained in this box came from a 2006 committee site visit.

Government agencies, academic institutions, and private enterprises should develop plans, reinvigorate existing programs, and provide incentives to build upon the foreign language skills and cultural understanding of America's heritage communities. Such incentive programs should increase our national capability in foreign languages—especially in the less commonly taught languages.

Recognizing this potential, federal intelligence agencies and the military have increased their recruitment of heritage speakers (Chu, 2006), although investigators have sometimes had problems in conducting the required background checks in countries in which first-generation speakers learned the language (Kuenzi, 2004). ED and DoD have undertaken targeted efforts involving heritage communities. For example, the ED Foreign Language Assistance Program and the DoD National Flagship Language Program have provided funding to the Dearborn Public Schools and Michigan State University (also an LRC), to collaborate with one another and the local Arabic heritage community to expand and strengthen Arabic instruction in elementary and middle schools. The partners will develop curriculum and aligned assessments and establish a professional development and Arabic teacher certification program that meets Michigan Department of Education requirements. The program will also provide scholarships for 40 Dearborn students with advanced Arabic skills for further study at the university level (Michigan State University, 2007).

In addition, ED recently awarded LRC funding to the UCLA Center for World Languages and the University of California Consortium for Language Learning and Teaching to establish a new National Heritage Language Center. The center's overall mission is to develop the new field of heritage language education. The proportion of individuals who speak a language other than English at home—17.8 percent nationally—is higher in California (39.4 percent) and still higher in Los Angeles Center (54.4) (Kagan, 2006), well positioning the center for this task. The new center will build on previous research on the different learning needs of heritage language and foreign language learners (Kagan and Dillon, 2001; Valdés, 2000). Research suggests that heritage speakers attain high proficiency best if they are taught in separate classes that meet their specific needs.

The center has launched a variety of research, development, and dissemination projects. These include gathering baseline data on demographics and patterns of intergenerational language transmission in selected heritage language communities, building a framework for developing heritage language materials, and researching the grammar of heritage language speakers. Another focus of the center is teacher education to reduce the shortage of heritage language instructors. As discussed in Chapter 4, some NRCs and LRCs have also undertaken targeted outreach efforts to preserve and develop the proficiency of heritage language speakers. However, while utilizing heritage speakers has clear potential to help address shortages in foreign language and area experts, and various Title VI-funded efforts to support development of their expertise is underway, the available evidence did not enable conclusive resolution of this complex area. Further exploration of effective ways to develop and utilize heritage language competences is warranted.

Study Abroad and Foreign Language and Area Studies Fellowships

Davidson and Lehmann (2005) found that oral language proficiency scores of U.S. alumni of the overseas Russian language programs funded by the Group Projects Abroad Program were higher after the experience. The majority of alumni identified the experience as among the top three "most significant learning experiences" of their lives. The program had its greatest impact in increased language proficiency, followed by increases in cultural knowledge and interest. Linton and VandeBerg (2006) similarly found that study abroad students had significantly greater language gains and greater improvement in intercultural sensitivity than control group students. They also found an association between length of time abroad and greater improvement in language proficiency.

Other than the DDRA Program that funds doctoral research abroad, FLAS Fellowships are the main vehicle through which Title VI/FH programs fund foreign language and area study by individual graduate students. The statute currently restricts eligibility to graduate students. Grants have been evenly distributed among commonly and less commonly taught languages and, as discussed earlier in the chapter, are distributed among students from a range of disciplines. In 2003, the number of fellowships jumped from 196 to 420, with the increase focusing on less commonly taught languages.

Although the FLAS Fellowships are not specifically designed to subsidize study abroad, a minority of students do go abroad. ED policies related to FLAS fellowships make it difficult for grantees to use their award for overseas study. The ED requires prior approval of individual requests to use funds for overseas travel, a requirement that is viewed by NRC faculty and staff, as well as by students, as a barrier to achieving higher levels of language proficiency. Federal government regulations require travel on U.S. air carriers, which is frequently more costly than non-U.S. carriers and presents a particular concern, since travel funds are not included in the stipend for academic year fellowships. In addition, from the committee's conversations with NRC staffs, there is a clear lack of understanding about ED policies. One NRC thought that overseas travel for academic year fellowships was prohibited. ED staff acknowledged that a series of myths about the program has evolved, which they have worked to dispel.

Despite the benefits of study abroad, between 2003 and 2005, almost three-quarters (73 percent) of FLAS recipients studied in the United States only, 23 percent spent a summer overseas, and only 3 percent spent a year overseas. Of those who studied overseas in 2005, the top 10 host countries, in descending order, were Brazil, India, China, Mexico, Russia, Egypt, Turkey, Poland, Japan, and Ecuador.

Many of these countries are allies or are of strategic concern to the United States, and several of the languages spoken in them are currently considered critical: Arabic, Chinese, Japanese, Russian, and Turkish. It is unclear if requests for study in these countries are more readily approved by ED. However, since Latin America is the most common destination, study there could also be due to the relative proximity (and low travel cost) and safety of the host country, the ability of the home university to subsidize travel, or both. In the case of Brazil, five NRCs (of 40 Latin America NRCs included in the analysis) account for the vast majority of FLAS recipients studying there. These five centers sent an average of 25 FLAS fellows, compared with the average of 5 students for the other 35 centers. Information is not available related to why these five centers have been so much more successful than others.

Assessing Language Proficiency of FLAS Recipients

The only assessment of FLAS recipients' language proficiency that ED requires is a self-rating. Recipients are required to rate their speaking, reading, and writing proficiency based on six language levels in each of these three areas, ranging from no ability to that of a native speaker. The language levels are intended to approximate an approach to proficiency assessment that has been used by the American Council on the Teaching of Foreign Languages (ACTFL), but without the necessary detail. There is no available evidence of the reliability or validity of these self-ratings, with interpretation of the meaning of language levels left to individual students. FLAS recipients report both their pre- and post-FLAS ratings at the same time (upon completion of their fellowship), which raises concerns about the reliability and validity of the ratings. The ED uses the average change across the three areas (speaking, reading, and reading) as a performance measure for the FLAS Program and is planning to use it for the DDRA, Faculty Research Abroad (FRA), and GPA programs.

In 2005, ED added an item to the EELIAS database asking if the fellow was tested using a standardized instrument and, if so, the name of the instrument and the pre and post scores. This requirement happened about the same time that ED started encouraging proficiency assessment through the priorities applied in its competitions (see Appendix C), sending the message to grantees that proficiency measurement is a priority. On the basis of the data submitted to ED as of March 2006, only 4 percent of students (157 of

3,835) reported having been tested using a standardized approach; an oral proficiency interview was the most commonly reported tool (28.9 percent), with a variety of other instruments making up the balance.

During the committee's site visits, while all NRCs reported assessment as an important objective, they reported a variety of approaches to doing so. University staff indicated that, in many cases, students are assessed on the basis of a short conversation with a linguist or language teacher, or with an oral interview. These interviews may range from a brief conversation with a language teacher to a structured interview along the lines of an ACTFL oral proficiency interview (OPI) but not conducted or rated by an ACTFL-certified examiner. Many NRCs and LRCs were exploring or interested in alternative approaches to assessing language proficiency. This wide variety and inconsistency of methods for assessing language proficiency and the concerns about ED's self-rating method made it difficult to assess the language proficiency component of Title VI/FH success in "reducing shortages of foreign language and area experts." It also underscores the need to develop consistent and valid assessments of language proficiency, as discussed in Chapter 12.

Given the considerable interest in assessing the language proficiency of FLAS students, one might well ask why these assessments are being done so inconsistently. The short answer to this question is that, for many languages, particularly many of the less commonly taught ones, there simply are no assessments, so faculty must rely on their own resources to assess their students. For languages for which assessments are available, some do not meet professional standards for educational measurement (e.g., American Educational Research Association et al., 1999), are too costly to administer, or both.

The dominant approach to language proficiency assessment in Title VI/FH programs is a face-to-face interview. There is considerable variation across languages and programs in how this interview is administered and scored. Some of these are "unofficial" interviews based generally on the ACTFL standards. Others are "official" oral proficiency interviews conducted by examiners who have been certified by ACTFL, whose scale has been developed for use in academic settings. To be implemented properly, the ACTFL approach requires trained testers based on the ACTFL proficiency guidelines. (See Appendix D for a brief history of the OPI, the ACTFL scale, and the ILR scale, which is used mostly in government settings.)

Proponents of the ACTFL scale assert that it has provided a common framework for foreign language educators to describe student achievement, and the proficiency guidelines have become ingrained in the teaching, testing, programmatic, and research activities of a significant segment of the foreign language profession (Liskin-Gasparro, 2003). In a commissioned paper prepared for the committee, Malone (2006) argues that the OPI's greatest strengths are twofold: (1) it provides professional development of the testers who participate in the training sessions and (2) testing oral proficiency positively impacts instruction by emphasizing the importance of speaking. However, researchers and measurement specialists have raised concerns about the OPI's validity and other technical qualities, highlighting the need for additional research and development to identify alternative approaches for measuring language proficiency levels (see Chapter 12).

LRCs have been prompted by ED to develop new approaches to foreign language assessment, in part to address the expense and limited availability of the OPI. A range of them have consequently been developed or are currently under development at multiple organizations, including the Center for Applied Linguistics (2006), a collaborative partner with the National Capital Language Resource Center and the National K-12 Foreign Language Resource Center. In addition, a consortium of two LRCs (Brigham Young University and San Diego State University) and three other institutions (the American Council on the Teaching of Foreign Languages, the Center for Applied Linguistics, and the Defense Language Institute) is developing the computer-assisted screening tool (CAST), with IRS funding. In the fall of 2006, the consortium had developed and was beginning to pilot test web-delivered oral proficiency test modules in Modern Standard Arabic and Spanish. It is hoped that these low-stakes tests will encourage instructors to conduct periodic assessments of students' progress, punctuated by semi-annual or annual OPIs. The Center for Applied Second Language Studies (CASLS), University of Oregon, is developing the standards-based measurement of writing and listening proficiency for the high school grades in French, German, Spanish and Turkish (Center for Applied Second Language Studies, 2006c), the National Online Early Language Learning Assessment (2006b), and the CASLS pilot assessments (2006a). However, the extent to which these efforts are coordinated or address the other underlying concerns outlined here is unclear.

CONCLUSIONS AND RECOMMENDATIONS

The Title VI/FH programs, particularly the NRCs and the FLAS Program, play an important role in addressing unmet needs for individuals with foreign language, area, and international knowledge. This includes producing graduates for academia, government, and business as well as exposing a wide range of students to international and foreign language content.

Job Placement

Title VI/FH programs aim to produce a broad range of language and area experts needed to enhance U.S. security and prosperity over the long term. Given this broad goal, job placements in government, academia, and nongovernmental organizations are all reasonable outcomes that serve broad national needs. Available reporting categories, and the use of those categories by ED, do not provide an adequate measure of success. At a minimum, ED should report on placements in a range of areas, monitor trends, and facilitate transparency of data that will enable public discourse (see Chapter 12).

Although the available data are limited at best, they suggest that undergraduates from Title VI-funded programs are most likely to find employment in the private sector. Among graduate students, those whose placements are known tend to go into academia. Thus, relatively small numbers of undergraduates and graduates appear to go on to employment with the federal government or the military. However, the reporting categories used may not accurately capture job responsibilities.

More importantly, for an NRC graduate or recipient of a Title VI/FH fellowship, choices about career are still best understood as a matter of individual choice and timing. These programs do not have service requirements, so there is no obligation or expectation for students to pursue careers in government. Relatively low percentages employed in the federal government can also be partially attributable to insufficient communication of government needs and career opportunities, negative perceptions of government service, difficulty matching graduate skills with specific jobs, and a cumbersome security clearance process. Even DoD's NSEP, which has a government service requirement, faces challenges in placing its graduates in government jobs, although there has been recent progress. Government efforts have improved in the past several years, with more information provided on specific language needs and government career opportunities.

National Resources

Title VI/FH programs assist in providing needed services and resources to the nation in other ways that cannot be measured by job placements or language proficiency. The programs teach a large number of less commonly taught languages, reach a large number of students, maintain the capacity to teach less commonly taught and other languages that may be crucial in the future, and produce resources that can be drawn on by the nation as a whole. Although there is no systematic evidence, the committee heard many anecdotal reports and examples reported during site visits of the NRCs acting as a resource or training ground for current government personnel.

Language Proficiency

FLAS Fellowships include the study of language as their objective, but despite evidence that overseas study is an effective way to achieve greater oral proficiency, very few FLAS recipients study overseas, and ED policies tend to discourage such study for academic year fellowships. Some grantees have figured out ways to work with these policies to enable fellows to study abroad, but this experience does not appear to be widely practiced.

Conclusion: Although overseas study has been shown to increase speaking proficiency, the Department of Education's policies discourage full-year overseas study by FLAS recipients.

Recommendation 5.1: **The Department of Education should modify its policy guidelines to encourage overseas study by Foreign Language and Area Studies fellows.**

ED should consider ways to encourage FLAS fellows to study abroad in well-designed experiences that are targeted toward gains in language and cultural competency. This might include clarifying policies, continuing to streamline the approval process, and including a travel stipend in academic year awards. The committee acknowledges, however, that such policies will not be able to address situations in which students' safety might be in jeopardy and that travel to some countries where language expertise is most needed will not be practicable.

Assessment of Language Ability

Even though Title VI/FH programs are being encouraged to assess the language proficiency of their students in standardized ways, at present this is not being done in ways that permit ED to monitor them for accountability purposes or that enable universities to evaluate their own effectiveness. The ED has for several years relied on self-ratings to assess the proficiency of FLAS recipients, even though there is no available evidence of the reliability or validity of their approach. ED has also encouraged the development and use of other standardized instruments, partly by including as a competitive priority in its last competition "activities designed to demonstrate the quality of the center's or program's language instruction through the measurement of student proficiency in the less and least commonly taught languages." The oral proficiency interview is the most widely used standardized approach in the United States and, among the few who use such an approach, appears to be the most commonly used standardized approach with FLAS recipients. However, concerns have been raised about the validity and the meaningfulness of OPI ratings, and many have argued that further research and development on assessment approaches is needed. Some universities have turned to language-specific tests or other assessment approaches. In a majority of cases, however, universities restrict their assessment to the self-rating required by ED. Several of the LRCs have developed new approaches based on the OPI, and NRCs have begun to adopt these instruments for reporting the language proficiency of their FLAS recipients.

Conclusion: The language proficiency of FLAS students is not at present being adequately assessed.

Recommendation 5.2: **The Department of Education should stop using its current self-assessment approach and develop an alternative approach to measuring foreign language proficiency with demonstrated reliability and validity.**

If ED determines that continued use of a self-assessment mechanism is necessary to measure performance at a national level, research to establish the validity and reliability of its current approach, or of an alternative approach, should be conducted to ensure that the approach used meets professional testing standards (American Educational Research Association et al., 1999) and produces meaningful results. Research suggests that the usefulness of self-assessment varies from one setting to another and is dependent on having a well-developed and well-implemented instrument (see Ross, 1998; Sasaki, 2003).

In the long term, focused attention on language assessment is needed. The primary reasons for the current lack of adequate standardized assessment appear to be (1) the lack of a single standardized measure of language proficiency that could be used with all languages, and for all programs, for accountability purposes, and (2) inadequate capacity for ongoing research and development of language assessments. In Chapter 12, the committee urges the federal government to support targeted research and development on language assessment to address this shortcoming and develop new approaches to foreign language assessment (Recommendation 12.3).

The committee specifically recommends that the language proficiency of FLAS recipients be assessed. However, we note that NRCs may want to assess the language proficiency of all students, particularly students receiving an area studies degree, to improve their own accountability. Universities should rely on the best available methods in conducting these assessments.

6

Supporting Research, Education, and Training

Each of the individual Title VI and Fulbright-Hays (Title VI/FH) programs plays a role in addressing the key area of supporting research, education, and training in foreign languages and international studies, including opportunities for such research, education, and training overseas. These areas are integral to the statutes guiding the programs and a fundamental part of the activities provided, although the emphases may vary from program to program.

Most of the Title VI/FH programs are designed to support education and training, either directly or indirectly. For example, the Foreign Language and Area Studies (FLAS) Fellowship Program directly supports graduate students by subsidizing their tuition costs, whereas the National Resource Centers (NRC), the Undergraduate International Studies and Foreign Language (UISFL), the Centers for International Business Education and Research (CIBER), and the Business and International Education (BIE) grants support education and training by influencing the curriculum offered to students. Language Resource Centers (LRC), International Research and Studies (IRS), UISFL, and Technological Innovation and Cooperation for Foreign Information Access (TICFIA) grants support education by developing instructional materials and other resources designed to enhance student learning. The Group Projects Abroad (GPA) and Seminars Abroad (SA) Programs support education both directly, in the form of study abroad for teachers, and indirectly, as the teachers' new knowledge translates into improved teaching and learning in K-12 classrooms.

Many of the Title VI programs also support research in a variety of

TABLE 6-1 International Research and Studies Projects Classified as Research and Evaluation (percentage)

	Projects	Funds
FY 2004	25 (2 of 8)	26 ($691,825)
FY 2005	41 (7 of 17)	40 ($2,190,000)
FY 2006	43 (9 of 21)	49 ($4,072,000)

SOURCE: Data provided by U.S. Department of Education [Annual project list, Office of International Education Programs Service].

ways.[1] For example, the FLAS and Doctoral Dissertation Research Abroad (DDRA) Programs directly support graduate student research; in the case of DDRA, research conducted overseas. The Faculty Research Abroad (FRA) Program supports faculty research abroad. The American Overseas Research Centers (AORC) Program helps maintain a capacity for research overseas, while the NRC and CIBER programs support faculty research with an international or area studies component. The LRC Program supports research on language teaching and learning. And the IRS Program funds research, surveys, and studies related to language, international, and area studies in addition to development of instructional materials (see Chapter 8 for discussion of instructional materials).

It appears that, over the past several years, the U.S. Department of Education (ED) has increasingly emphasized research projects in its IRS program. In the most recent grant competition, it awarded about half of the total available funds to projects focused on research and evaluation, an increase from about one quarter in FY2004 (see Table 6-1). However, no evidence is available on the quality of the funded research projects, nor on dissemination or impact of the research results. Although the committee obtained several final reports of IRS-funded projects, it is unclear whether the results also appeared in peer-reviewed publications. In addition, it is unclear whether the department itself or the Title VI/FH community generally is benefiting from the research, as staff was unable to provide final reports for several IRS-funded projects and they are not publicly available in any systematic way.

As the overseas component of ED's international education portfolio, the four Fulbright-Hays programs by definition support overseas study.

---

[1]Several of these programs and their research activities are discussed in more detail in other chapters. See Chapter 9 for additional discussion of TICFIA, Chapter 10 for more details on CIBER and BIE, and Chapter 11 for discussion of the Institute for International Public Policy.

The Institute for International Public Policy (IIPP) Program also includes a semester of study abroad for participating fellows (see Chapter 11). Several of the other programs may include overseas study, although the Title VI programs are generally considered to be the domestic component of ED's international education portfolio. The Title VI/FH programs are required to report extensive information on the number and type of language and international and area studies courses taught, as well as the number of publications and research presentations "developed or written." Although it is clear that individual programs have been prolific in this area, it was not possible to use this information to provide an aggregate picture of the programs' performance.

This chapter explores the role of Title VI/FH programs in supporting research, education, and training and in turn enhancing the body of knowledge in foreign languages and area studies. Because the NRC Program is the oldest and largest (in terms of total funding) of the programs and also the program most clearly targeted to combined objectives of research, education, and training, discussion of this area focuses on the NRCs. Other component programs are also discussed when relevant evidence allows. The chapter then outlines the role of Title VI/FH programs in supporting the teaching of less commonly taught languages, an area that emerged during the committee's review as a specific important contribution to supporting research, education, and training in foreign languages. Finally, the chapter describes the limited information available about the Title VI/FH programs and overseas study.

ENHANCING THE BODY OF KNOWLEDGE IN FOREIGN LANGUAGES AND AREA STUDIES

The Title VI/FH programs enhance the body of knowledge in foreign languages and area studies by increasing grantee institutions' capacity for teaching and research. Title VI/FH grants do this through the prestige they confer, the opportunity they provide funded institutions to leverage additional university funds, and the amount of research conducted.

Research Capacity and Prestige

Title VI/FH funds go to many of the largest research institutions that are recognized as conducting significant amounts of research and producing high numbers of dissertations and Ph.D.s. The grantees include many top private and state universities. The committee conducted an analysis of the grantees included in the Evaluation of Exchange, Language, International and Area Studies (EELIAS) database based on their Carnegie classification. Approximately one-third (35.5 percent) of the universities that received at least one Title VI or Fulbright-Hays grant between 1991 and 2006 were classified as research or doctorate-granting universities, slightly less than one-third (30.3 percent) were predominately master's degree-granting universities, and about 16 percent each were bachelor's or associate's degree-awarding institutions. Although universities classified as research institutions account for a small percentage (4.5 percent) of all schools, the majority (84.9 percent) have had a grant from at least one Title VI program, suggesting that the program is reaching into the core research universities with significant demonstrated research capacity. Similarly, FLAS awards, designed to support graduate study, have gone almost exclusively (98 percent) to institutions considered to be research institutions, and NRC awards have gone predominantly (84.2 percent) to these institutions.

NRC status seems to be viewed, even by the already well-known universities that tend to receive the grants, as a "gold standard" that confers prestige. During the committee's site visits and in meetings with new NRC directors, university faculty consistently reported that NRC status serves as a proxy for the ratings that are available in other fields. They reported that NRC status helps them to attract the best students. Some of the students interviewed independently reported that this was a factor in their decision about which school to attend. The availability of FLAS funds appeared to play a similar role.

Directors of area studies centers also reported that the potential for NRC status helped them to obtain university funds that they felt were necessary to be competitive (see the discussion of leveraging below). In fact, competition for NRC grants is fairly intense. Over the past 30 years, on average, about 30 percent of applicants were not funded. At the same time, continuation of a grant from one competition to the next is not guaranteed. On average, about 18 percent of NRC awards have gone to centers that did not have a grant in the previous period, and an average of 13 percent of NRC grantees lost their funding (see Table 6-2).[2] In many cases, universities that lose funding continue to apply for it in future cycles. The committee also noted that the NRCs that lost funding included some prestigious or elite universities. Among the universities visited, there were multiple examples of area studies programs that had lost and regained NRC status one or more times. In almost all cases, the universities reported that when they lost funding, they spent time investigating their program and exploring ways to make it more competitive in the next round of funding.

---

[2]This assumes that the NRC applied in the subsequent competition. "Lost" indicates that they were funded in one competition but not in the next.

TABLE 6-2 National Resource Center Competition Results, 1976 to 2006

Year of Grant Cycle Competition	% of Funded NRC Applications	Number (%) of NRCs Not Funded in Previous Cycle	Number (%) of NRCs for Which Funding Was Discontinued	Number (%) of NRCs Receiving Funds in Previous Cycle
1976	65	24 (28)	7 (8)	56 (64)
1979	74	20 (20)	12 (12)	68 (68)
1981	72	20 (19)	18 (17)	69 (64)
1983	74	12 (12)	11 (11)	77 (77)
1985	68	18 (17)	16 (15)	73 (68)
1988	66	15 (14)	13 (12)	78 (74)
1991	70	27 (23)	11 (9)	82 (68)
1994	77	19 (15)	10 (8)	100 (78)
1997	68	17 (12)	28 (20)	92 (67)
2000	71*	29 (21)	24 (17)	85 (62)
2003	65	24 (17)	21 (15)	93 (67)
2006	70	21 (15)	17 (13)	103 (69)
Average %	70	17.75	13	69

*In 2000, 114 of 167 applications were funded. In 2002, an additional four NRCs were funded from this application pool, and are included in this percentage.
SOURCE: Data provided by U.S. Department of Education.

Leverage

At institutions with NRCs, substantial university resources are devoted to international and foreign language study, in addition to Title VI funds. Grant competition is structured in such a way that universities must demonstrate significant existing capacity—including in their course offerings, opportunities for study abroad, and library holdings—to support research and training in foreign languages and international studies.

A major theme of public input to the committee and the site visits was the value of Title VI/FH funds in leveraging funds from other sources. The grants give impetus for universities and other funding sources to match and exceed funds received from ED. For example, NRC funding to area studies centers at Ohio State University catalyzed university support for a cross-university program of Interdisciplinary Research on International Themes. This program includes an interdisciplinary project on climate change supported by departments and schools across the university, industrial partners, and overseas universities (Ohio State University, 2007). As mentioned earlier, NRC funding to the university's Slavic Center led the School of Agriculture to conduct research at Tomsk University in Siberia.

Universities therefore bear most of the cost of language and area instruction at NRCs. Some stakeholders say that Title VI funding actually accounts for only about 5 percent of the cost of NRCs and LRCs (Merkx and Schneider, 1999), thus creating a multiplier effect, whereby a substantial impact is made for a small investment of taxpayer dollars (Brustein, 2006). Another estimate is that universities spend $12-20 for every federal dollar (Wiley, 2006).

The proportion of NRC and FLAS funds in relation to university funds for language and area studies appears to vary substantially by university and even by NRC within a university. The committee requested budget information from four private universities and five public universities, including the percentage of NRC funds that came from ED compared with the universities themselves. Federal funding (NRC plus FLAS funds) as a percentage of an NRC budget ranged from 2 percent at one NRC to 82 percent at another; many were in the 30 to 65 percent range. Much of this, of course, depends on the size of the NRC as well as the amount of money requested in grant applications and ultimately received. The differing levels of reliance on federal funding also reflect differences in private endowment funding for language and area studies across universities.

Reliance on federal funding decreases further when viewed as a percentage of the total university resources that are relevant to the world area but not specifically devoted to the NRC. These total resources include university support for language training related to the world area. For most of the area centers, the share supported by Title VI/FH funding drops to less than 10 percent, although the share still varies widely, from 1 to 70 percent.

The committee also analyzed budget information submitted for FY 2002 through FY 2004 via the EELIAS database. Based on these data, significant university ("institutional") funds are provided to match Title VI NRC funds, particularly resources to support area studies. Title VI funds represent only 3 percent of the total reported resources for all NRC activities. Ninety-three percent is provided from institutional funds, with more than half (56.3 percent) reported as supporting area studies. Table 6-3 illustrates the sources of funds by type of activity. Title VI funds represent a larger proportion (9.4 percent) of the total funds available for less

TABLE 6-3 Sources of NRC Funds, Fiscal Years 2002-2004 (percentage)

Category	Title VI Funds	Institutional Funds	Other Funds
Area studies instruction	0.8	98.4	0.8
Commonly taught languages	2.4	96.2	1.4
Less commonly taught languages	9.4	87.7	2.9
Other	6.5	79.6	13.9
Outreach	21.6	46.4	32.0

SOURCE: Data provided by U.S. Department of Education [EELIAS].

commonly taught languages than area studies (0.8 percent). Title VI funds account for the largest percentage of available funds (21.6 percent) for outreach.

Based on these data, it is clear that universities invest additional funds in foreign language and area studies beyond what they receive from Title VI, but this occurs at a variable rate and may not be quite as significant as some stakeholders report.

Universities report that NRC funding serves as a catalyst or as seed money to innovate, providing the funds necessary to introduce courses, particularly courses in the less commonly taught languages, that would not otherwise be offered. Once enrollments in these new courses are established, the universities tend to pick up the cost of the programs, enabling the NRC to move on to new priorities. Another common assertion is that without the seed money and prestige that goes along with a Title VI/FH grant, many language and area studies programs would not exist. For example, some argue that leveraging of Title VI funds was the main factor that led to the growth of South Asian studies, which barely existed in the 1970s (Stewart, 2006). Newhall (2006) reported that NRC seed money has led to 19 tenure-track positions in the field and 33 contract positions. One center reported doubling the number of Arabic instructors from two to four and that it would not have been possible without Title VI funding. During the site visits, university faculty consistently reported that if Title VI funding were eliminated, the teaching of less commonly taught languages would be one of the first things affected.

In another instance of a leveraging effect, undergraduate programs created with Title VI support have continued after funding ended. One study found that UISFL grants had a strong and lasting impact on the research and teaching capacity of higher education institutions, positively affecting many elements deemed critical to the development and strengthening of international education, such as requiring an international course for graduation and having a formally designated adviser for students doing international or area studies (Schneider, 1999). UISFL grantees reported adding new courses and languages as a result of the grants, and nearly all of these courses were still offered, with solid enrollments, even five years after the grants ended. For example, a UISFL grant to the University of Richmond supported development of new undergraduate classes in Portuguese and Swahili and helped launch Latin American and African studies programs (Brustein, 2006).

Dissemination of Knowledge

Evaluation studies identify several ways in which Title VI/FH grantee institutions generate and disseminate new research knowledge about foreign languages, world areas, and international issues. Brecht et al. (2007) compared the education, research, and publication activities of Title VI-funded institutions in Slavic and Middle East studies with the activities of a comparison group drawn from the 100 best American universities, as ranked by *U.S. News & World Report.* The authors found that the Title VI-funded institutions produced more dissertations,[3] more articles in major journals, and more professional awards from peer organizations related to these two world areas than did the comparison universities. These findings reflect the fact that NRC awards are given to institutions with established, prestigious area studies programs, in which faculty conduct significant amounts of research and award large numbers of Ph.D.s.

Brecht et al. (2007) also used a slightly different method to examine the role of Title VI/FH funding in research and publication. They examined the contents of Slavic and Middle East studies academic journals and found that Title VI-funded institutions accounted for a disproportionately large number of articles. For example, between 1997 and 2004, the Title VI institutions contributed, on average, 4.2 articles to the journal *Slavic Review*, while non-Title VI institutions contributed only 1.3. The study also examined the number of dissertations in Slavic and Middle East studies awarded from Title VI and non-Title VI institutions. As in the case of scholarly articles, education and scholarship were again concentrated at Title VI institutions. The number of dissertations produced in Slavic area studies was nearly identical for Title VI and non-Title VI institutions, but individual Title VI institutions produced significantly more dissertations than their counterparts. On average, Title VI institutions produced 30 dissertations compared with 4 dissertations per non-Title VI institution.

The authors note that in most categories, a disproportionate number of dissertations are completed at Title VI universities, particularly Slavic languages. The exception is Middle East language dissertations—non-Title VI institutions produce more than twice as many as Title VI-funded institutions and the difference in the "per institution" measure is not as large as in other areas.

Finally, the study asserts that Title VI-funded institutions have been responsive to world events, as measured by numbers of courses and enrollments in currently critical languages. For example, in fall 2000 there were 18 courses in both Arabic and Persian taught at Title VI-funded universities. By spring 2003 this had increased to 44 courses in Arabic and 26 in Persian. Enrollments almost doubled in Arabic and went up by over 50 percent in Persian in that same time period (Brecht et al., 2007).

---

[3]Production of dissertations represents both a form of education and training of doctoral students and also generation of new knowledge.

SUPPORT FOR LESS COMMONLY TAUGHT LANGUAGES

Evaluation studies, the committee's analysis of Modern Language Association enrollment data, public input, and consistent comments during site visits indicate that Title VI/FH programs play an especially vital role in seeding and sustaining research, education, and training in less commonly taught languages (LCTLs) (see Box 6-1 for illustrations). The National Council of Organizations of Less Commonly Taught Languages defines an LCTL as "all languages not typically part of most U.S. college and high school curricula." As mentioned earlier in this report, the committee concludes that it is important to have an infrastructure for a wide variety of languages, particularly LCTLs, rather than just those deemed critical at a specific point in time.

Brecht et al. (2007) concluded that Title VI-funded institutions are crucial to research related to LCTLs. Between 1996 and 2004, Title VI NRCs

---

BOX 6-1
Catalyzing Instruction in Less Commonly Taught Languages

Administrators and faculty at all eight site visit universities indicated that Title VI funding acts as a vital catalyst for developing instruction in less commonly taught languages. For example, Title VI funding supported five years of expansion in the teaching of Portuguese at Ohio State University. When the Center for Latin American Studies developed individualized instruction for first-year Portuguese, students responded very favorably. Enrollment in first-year language classes jumped from 20 students in 2003-2004, to 58 in 2004-2005 (spring 2005 was the first quarter individualized instruction was offered), and to 115 the following academic year (AY, 2005-2006). By fall 2006, the university offered 14 Portuguese classes, 3 courses on the culture of Brazil and Portugal, and an intensive language study abroad program in Brazil. Total enrollment in all Portuguese courses had nearly doubled, from 161 students in AY 2003-2004 to 317 in AY 2005-2006.

At Georgetown University, Title VI funds allowed the university to offer Turkish to two or three students at beginning through advanced levels; now many more students are enrolled. At the time of the newest grant cycle, Georgetown has absorbed all costs associated with the growing Turkish program. In AY 2006-2007, the university is using Title VI money to underwrite a full-time Persian language instructor, with the intent that the increased student demand for the language and additional area and culture classes will convince the university to absorb the faculty member's salary costs into its regular budget, as was the case with the Turkish language and culture program.

NOTE: Information contained in this box came from 2006 committee site visits.

and LRCs produced almost half (49 percent) of all published research on less commonly taught languages, and 58 percent of all published research on the least taught languages—those with enrollments of fewer than 1,000 students.

In an earlier study, Brecht and Rivers (2000) reported a similar finding: 64 Title VI/FH-funded programs account for 22.5 percent of the U.S. undergraduate language enrollments in languages other than French, German, Italian, and Spanish and 51 percent of the undergraduate enrollments in the least commonly taught languages. This is highly disproportionate because Title VI/FH-funded institutions represent less than 3 percent of the 2,399 colleges and universities in the United States.

The committee's analysis of Modern Language Association enrollment data also suggests that NRCs and their institutions account for a significant proportion of enrollments in less commonly taught languages, particularly those with the smallest enrollments and particularly among graduate students[4] (see Table 6-4). In the "extremely small" enrollment category of 48 languages, 36 are taught at NRC institutions, and advanced graduate classes in 21 of these languages are offered only at NRC institutions. Without these institutions, these languages would probably not be taught in the United States at all. During the site visits, center staff consistently reinforced this point, reporting that their university would not support low-enrollment language courses if not for Title VI support. Languages offered only at NRC institutions include such significant languages as Kazakh, Bengali, Bulgarian, Malay, Slovak, and Uzbek. Bengali, for example, is spoken by 270 million people and is an official language in both Bangladesh and India.

NRCs help sustain the capacity to teach a wide variety of languages, far beyond those deemed critical at a given moment. Table 6-5 compares languages taught at NRCs versus those taught at federal language institutions: the Foreign Service Institute (FSI) and the Defense Language Institute (DLI). NRCs offered 226 less commonly taught languages in 2001-2004, while DLI and FSI offered 75. It's important to note, however, that DLI and FSI are designed to provide on-demand language courses, and that the numbers reported here are the courses that were actually being offered at a specific point in time.

It should be noted that Title VI/FH-funded institutions, DLI, and FSI should not be viewed as in competition with one another; they simply serve different "markets." DLI and FSI are crucial in meeting the short-term needs of the federal government, whereas the role of Title VI is to build long-term capacity in a wide variety of languages. The committee heard a

---

[4]The languages with larger enrollments above 11,000 (Spanish, French, German, Italian, Japanese, Chinese, and Russian) were excluded from the review because so many colleges and universities offer those courses.

TABLE 6-4 Undergraduate and Graduate Students in Less Commonly Taught Languages Enrolled at NRC Institutions, 2002 (percentage)

Languages with Enrollments (total # of students for all languages in category)	Total Undergraduate Enrollment	Total Graduate Enrollment
Extremely small (0-98)	1,138	146
Very small (99-199)	1,399	90
Small (200-499)	2,562	191
Medium (500-775)	3,574	245
Large (900-1,999)	4,795	205
Very large (5,000-9,000)	28,867	1,545

NOTE: An NRC institution was defined as a university with an NRC in the world area in which the language is spoken.
SOURCES: Committee analysis of 2002 Modern Language Association enrollment data, Welles (2004).

great deal of anecdotal evidence and observations to the effect that personnel in government often have degrees from Title VI-funded institutions, and that the institutions are used as a resource by government agencies (Interagency Language Roundtable, 2006b; Merkx, 2006; Wiley, 2006). The infrastructure created by Title VI/FH is also drawn on by other institutions. For example, the Naitonal Security Education Program (NSEP) draws on Title VI-funded institutions to help produce experts in critical languages. FSI and DLI also utilize resources and instructional materials from Title VI-funded institutions (Brustein, 2006).

Representatives of the federal government's Interagency Language Roundtable (ILR) praised the overall performance of Title VI/FH programs in teaching less commonly taught languages, but also offered the caveat that "improvements in them are required and should be implemented to ensure greater accountability."

OVERSEAS STUDY

The four Fulbright-Hays programs all support overseas study for a range of purposes ranging from dissertation and faculty research to enhancing teacher training. The available funding has historically been a very small percentage compared with Title VI funding. In FY 2005, the SA Program supported study tours for K-12 educators in China, Mexico, and South Africa and Botswana. Between FY 1964 and FY 2004, the DDRA

Undergraduate Enrollment at NRC Institution	% Undergraduates Enrolled at an NRC Institution	Graduate Enrollment at NRC Institution	% Graduates Enrolled at an NRC Institution
633	56	132	90
762	54	74	82
1,421	55	171	90
1,596	45	150	61
1,983	41	142	69
7,688	27	666	43

Program provided fellowships for doctoral research projects in seven major world regions (see Table 6-6).[5] Similarly, the FRA (see Table 6-7) and GPA programs have supported study and research projects in each major world region (U.S. Department of Education, 2007).

As mentioned earlier, all Title VI/FH grantees are required to obtain prior ED approval to use funds for overseas travel. This process is automated for Fulbright-Hays programs. For Title VI programs, the approval process has varied with the project officer and is based on whether the overseas travel is considered appropriate and necessary. During our site visits, committee members were told that NRCs often use other non-Title VI resources to support student overseas study. The degree to which overseas study was emphasized or encouraged and the availability of funding sources for overseas study varied among the universities. The committee was told that the revised grantee reporting system under development will include an electronic method for submitting travel requests, which should help streamline the process.

A common concern expressed during the site visits was the difficulty graduate students encounter in using annual FLAS awards to support overseas study, particularly in light of its recognized benefit to language study (discussed in Chapter 6).

---

[5] As defined by ED, the seven world regions are Africa, Western Hemisphere, Central/Eastern Europe/Eurasia, Near East, East Asia, South Asia, and Southeast Asia.

TABLE 6-5 Less Commonly Taught Languages Offered by Title VI
National Resource Centers and by the Defense Language Institute and the
Foreign Service Institute, 2001-2004

World Region	Title VI NRC LCTLs Taught in 2001-2002	Title VI NRC LCTLs Available 2001-2004[d]	FSI[b] & DLI[c] LCTLs Available 2004	Title VI NRC Semester Enrollments in LCTLs 2001-2002	Title VI FLAS Fellowships Awarded 2002-2003
Africa	25	56	10	2,972	141
Middle East	30	52	19	8,028	260
Inner Asia	13	24	12	237	28
South Asia	15	31	11	3,284	180
East Asia	11	14	10	24,790	200
Southeast Asia	11	18	13	2,864	67
Pacific Islands	3	6	0	322	3
Eastern Europe/Russia	26	47	28	6,981	306
Western Europe	23	27	17	8,767	84
Latin America	15	16	2	5,501	255
TOTAL	128[d]	226[d]	75[d]	61,124[e]	1,632[f]

NOTE: Data for these tables are drawn from the applications of the 119 university centers to be designated as Title VI NRCs and FLAS centers submitted to ED in November 2002. (We have not included enrollments from the 11 International Studies NRCs not specialized to a world region and the 2 Canadian NRCs.)

[a]LCTLs available are those that Title VI NRCs state in their 2002 Title VI applications that they have the capacity to teach: 38 of these languages are historical languages, which are ancient or extinct according to Ethnologue (http://www.ethnologue.com) or are used only for reading ancient texts.

[b]FSI data on language offerings available are derived from the FSI pamphlet, "Language Training, School of Language Studies, NFATC, Foreign Service Institute, US Department of State" (distributed June 24, 2004) and from a supplementary list provided by the FSI on June 25, 2005.

[c]DLI data about languages available are derived from the DLI website at http://www.dliflc. edu/Academics/schools/index.html [accessed June 14, 2004], with additional information provided by Scott McGinnis, DLI, Washington, June 24, 2004 and February 2, 2005.

[d]Languages that overlap world regions are counted only once in the "Total" row.

[e]There was some overlap of reported language enrollments at a few universities that host NRCs for more than one world region (e.g., Arabic for African and Middle East centers);those enrollments are counted only once in the "Total" row of the table. We have accounted for a total of 2,622 overlapping LCTL enrollments by subtracting them from the subtotal of all world region enrollments: 63,746 − 2,622 = 61,124.

[f]Total FLAS Fellowships include 11 awarded by Canadian Studies NRCs (all in French) and 97 awarded by international NRCs. These have been added to the 1,523 FLAS Fellowships awarded in the world regions listed above (11 + 97 + 1,523 = 1,632).

SOURCE: Based on data from the e-LCTL Project. Available: http://elctl.msu.edu/summaries/ viewtable2.php?region=world&table=sheet015 [accessed May 2007].

TABLE 6-6 Doctoral Dissertation Research Abroad Fellowships Awarded, FY 1964-2004

Country	Fellowships Awarded
Africa	588
Western Hemisphere	761
Central/Eastern Europe and Eurasia	734
East Asia	661
Near East	497
South Asia	519
Southeast Asia	435
Western Europe	70
Multicountry	186
TOTAL	4,451

SOURCE: Data provided by U.S. Department of Education. Available: http://www.ed.gov/programs/iegpsddrap/awards.html [accessed Jan. 2007].

TABLE 6-7 Faculty Research Abroad Program Summary, FY 2005

World Area	Individual Applications Received	Individual Applications Funded	Totals by World Area
Africa	12	7	$ 534,113
Western Hemisphere	19	6	281,084
Central/Eastern Europe/Eurasia	8	4	214,330
East Asia	10	4	195,462
Near East	2	1	18,559
South Asia	2	1	37,580
Southeast Asia	3	3	109,595
TOTAL	56	26	1,390,723

SOURCE: Data provided by U.S. Department of Education. Available: http://www.ed.gov/pro-grams/iegpsfra/awards.html [accessed Jan. 2007].

CONCLUSIONS

In general, Title VI/FH funding enhances the capacity of grantee institutions for teaching and research. It raises the prestige level of institutions receiving the grants and has an important leveraging effect: universities often end up providing a majority of the funding for the programs. The idea of Title VI funds as leverage or seed money was a consistent theme in public meetings and discussions with university officials; they report often using Title VI funds to seed a course in a new language or a more advanced course in an existing language. Title VI/FH funding also serves to validate the programs and proliferate knowledge through articles published, dissertations granted, and resources produced, which supports foreign language, area, and international studies education. Finally, the programs play a significant role in the teaching of the less commonly taught languages; some important languages might not be taught at all in the United States if not for Title VI funds.

Conclusion: The Title VI/FH programs have enhanced the body of knowledge about foreign languages and area studies.

Conclusion: The Title VI program makes a significant contribution to the teaching of less commonly taught languages in particular.

A common theme that arose from the committee's discussions with university and program representatives is the idea of synergy, meaning that the programs fit together and build on one another to create an infrastructure for the production of language and area knowledge. Multiple supporters of the programs assert that they complement each other in a way that serves to create a pipeline to higher levels of language proficiency and area knowledge, particularly for difficult languages (Wiley, 2006; Lane, 2006; Edwards, 2006; Gabara, 2006; Merkx, 2006).

In theory, the programs do complement each other, as LRC K-12 outreach strengthens language teaching in schools, UISFL grants internationalize the undergraduate curriculum, NRCs support area studies programs that attract and engage students, and FLAS and DDRA awards act as the "intake valve" to prepare the next generation of language and area studies expertise. In theory, FRA grants to support faculty research and IRS and LRC funding of research on how to best teach languages supplement and complement this synergistic system. However, the committee did not find sufficient evidence to conclude that this potential synergy has been fully realized.

We also note that Title VI is the sole source of funds for high-level language research; without federal money, much of this research would not take place. For example, language materials developed by the IRS program have been praised by some in the language community (Christian, 2006; Interagency Language Roundtable, 2006b). ILR representatives told the committee (Interagency Language Roundtable, 2006b):

> This year, when the list of new IRS grants was posted, senior language experts across the government remarked very positively on the value of the topics to be researched and of the anticipated usefulness of the materials and tools to be developed. In addition, this year's grants also include funding for the Modern Language Association's survey of post-secondary

foreign language education [enrollments] in all institutions throughout the United States and for comparable surveys of foreign language education [enrollments] in American primary and secondary schools. Without the data provided by these crucial surveys funded by IRS, there would be no solid objective national information on the state of foreign language education in this country.

ILR representatives also lamented the fact that only 14 LRC proposals were able to be funded during the last grant cycle, as LRCs also play a crucial role in research on languages. They noted that the LRCs have "conducted important research into the learning" of less commonly taught languages (Interagency Language Roundtable, 2006b).

Thus, while there is at least a conceptual synergy to the way the programs are designed, which supports production of language and area knowledge, from K-12 to university faculty and research levels, the Title VI/FH programs were not designed to—and are not adequately funded to— carry out a comprehensive international education and language strategy beginning in kindergarten and continuing through faculty research. Such a strategy would require funding and support from other federal language and international education programs in addition to Title VI/FH, as we discuss in Chapter 12.

7

Producing Relevant
Instructional Materials

The Title VI and Fulbright-Hays (Title VI/FH) programs support creation of a variety of instructional materials, ranging from databases of authentic language materials to textbooks to curriculum guides focusing on world regions. Title VI specifically authorizes creation of instructional materials for four programs—International Research and Studies (IRS), Language Resource Centers (LRC), National Resource Centers (NRC), and Technological Innovation and Cooperation for Foreign Information Access (TICFIA). In addition, the U.S. Department of Education (ED) has used priorities in the grant application process to encourage Title VI programs to support development of instructional materials or to direct instructional materials development toward specific priorities (see Appendix C). For example, in 2002, IRS applicants were invited to submit proposals to develop specialized materials for the languages of the Islamic nations of the Middle East and Central Asia.[1] Similarly, in every NRC grant competition since 1996,[2] applicants have been required to include teacher training activities—activities that often involve creation of instructional materials. Applications for the Seminars Abroad (SA) Program are evaluated based in part on their plans to develop curriculum and instructional materials related to the study tour.

In order to gain understanding about the instructional materials produced by Title VI/FH programs, the committee commissioned a descriptive

---

[1]The invitational priority also included materials for use in teaching the languages of South Asia.

[2]The committee did not have information on priorities available before this time.

analysis of available narrative information for (1) all FY 2000-2005 IRS projects[3] and (2) all projects that were coded in the Evaluation of Exchange, Language, International and Area Studies (EELIAS) database (which includes information on projects funded between FY 2000 and FY 2005) as producing instructional materials or assessment tools. After eliminating many projects that lacked abstracts or other explanatory materials or did not describe the development of instructional materials or assessment tools, the authors identified 95 projects for further analysis (Joyner and Suarez, 2006). Given the particular focus of the IRS Program on instructional materials (in addition to research), IRS projects were analyzed separately from those funded by other Title VI/FH programs.

As a result of the study design, the majority of the projects identified (60 of 95) were IRS-funded, providing a useful, though incomplete, portrait of the IRS projects funded between FY 2002 and FY 2005 that produced instructional materials during this period. (Only 2 of the 60 projects identified were funded in FY 2000 or FY 2001). The committee notes that the other Title VI/FH programs probably funded numerous other projects involving instructional materials development beyond those identified for the analysis (35 of 95). The coding used to identify projects as producing instructional materials was done by a contractor rather than the grantees[4] and was based on an abstract only. In general, the analysis should be viewed as providing descriptive information only; it does not shed light on the quality, dissemination, or use of the materials described.

This chapter describes some of the types of instructional materials produced by Title VI/FH grantees. The description is based primarily on the commissioned analysis, supplemented by information obtained in site visits and from websites of select instructional materials development projects. The chapter also discusses the challenge of determining whether instructional materials are "relevant" and "meet accepted scholarly standards," and provides examples of recent efforts to ensure the relevance and quality of language instructional materials.

Although the review included projects identified as producing both instructional materials and assessments, it identified far fewer to develop assessments. Of those identified, the majority were produced by LRCs and were related to language acquisition rather than to other international areas. Language assessment is discussed in more detail in Chapter 6.

---

[3]The committee chose to review all projects from the IRS Program because ED program office leaders describe the program as funding two types of projects: (1) materials development and (2) research surveys and studies.

[4]The committee was told that, in the redesigned system, grantees will be required to enter the subject area codes that were used to identify projects.

INSTRUCTIONAL MATERIALS PRODUCED

The descriptive analysis identified 95 projects supported by 8 of the 14 Title VI/FH programs. The analysis of information from these 95 projects yielded descriptions of 297 kinds of instructional materials, most of which incorporated technology.

Intended Uses

The instructional materials were classified based on their intended use. While recognizing that many of the materials could serve a variety of purposes, the authors identified three primary intended uses:

BOX 7-1
Instructional Material Examples

Materials for Instruction:

- An IRS grant was awarded to UCLA to develop interactive web-based materials for teaching Zulu language and culture.
- An IRS grant was awarded to the University of Arizona to create language teaching materials in Ukrainian, Turkish, Cantonese, and Kazak, available on DVD and on the Internet (University of Arizona, 2007).
- The LRC at Michigan State University (2007) supported development of the language component for African digital libraries. The project created a pronunciation guide, a grammar course, content-based units, and an instruction guide.
- Georgetown University used an LRC grant to develop professional development materials for the instruction of teachers, including a monthly e-newsletter, *The Language Resource*, and development of the National Capital Language Resource Center's learning standards for Arabic K-16 in collaboration with the American Association of Teachers of Arabic, the Middle East LRC, and the National Learning Standards Collaborative.
- An NRC grant to Ohio State University's Center for Latin American Studies led to development of two quite different types of instructional materials. First, the center created two traveling exhibits: "Mexico Past and Present Through the Art of Diego Rivera" and "Brazil and the Amazon." The center also engaged teachers and the Spanish-speaking heritage community in development of a set of web-based instructional materials, "Latinamerica in Cyberspace" (Ohio State University, 2007).

Materials for Instructors:

- Cornell University received an IRS grant to develop area studies materials focusing on several different countries. One set of web-based teaching materials, "Water and

---

- Materials for instruction: This group of materials included instructional modules, lessons, and curriculum units; courses/full programs; professional development/teacher training materials; and supplemental or support materials.
- Materials for instructors: These materials included teacher resources and curriculum guides/frameworks.
- Materials for students: These materials included texts, study guides/workbooks, grammars, dictionaries, and resource databases.

Most of the types of materials developed were designed for use in instruction or by students. Fewer, although a notable number, were materials for instructors. Box 7-1 presents illustrations of each type.

Development in Nepal," includes extensive background material on Nepal, development, and water, as well as a basic Nepali glossary, student handouts, homework assignments, quizzes and keys, and links to other sources of information. Instructors can use the materials to engage elementary and middle school students in addressing problems of water availability and safety from the perspective of different ethnic and caste groups in Nepal (Cornell University, 2007).

Materials for Students:

- An IRS grant to the University of Wisconsin supported development of student language materials in Indonesian. This project created a set of interactive, multimedia, listening comprehension lessons designed to teach listening strategies, develop cultural and linguistic knowledge, and move students from the intermediate-low to the advanced level on the American Council on the Teaching of Foreign Languages (ACTFL) listening proficiency scale (University of Wisconsin, 2007).
- The LRC at Pennsylvania State University created a Korean grammar workbook and a book-length Russian textbook and workbook, *Narrative and Conceptual Proficiency in Russian*, for students (Pennsylvania State University, 2007).
- The University of Wisconsin used a TICFIA grant to create web-based, searchable digital bilingual dictionaries in several Southeast Asian languages, including Burmese, Lao, Thai, Khmer, and Vietnamese and the ethnic minority languages Mon, Karen, and Shan. The dictionaries were supplemented by historical dictionaries in cases of significant orthographic change and extended by lexicons of newly minted words.

SOURCES: Joyner and Suarez (2006); Cornell University (2007); Michigan State University (2007); Ohio State University (2007); Pennsylvania State University (2007); University of Arizona (2007); University of Wisconsin (2007).

Formats

The instructional materials were classified into one of five types of formats: (1) computer software, (2) web-based programs, (3) computer-based programs and resources (e.g., CD-ROMs), (4) print format (e.g., textbooks), and (5) multimedia resources that sometimes contained the other four formats. Most of the projects that produced instructional materials incorporated technology. Furthermore, among the projects in which the format was discernible from the information reviewed, there were almost twice as many types of materials in web-based format as in any other format.

Language Focus

The instructional materials produced by the IRS Program and the other programs most frequently focus on language instruction. Specifically, of the 155 kinds of materials produced by IRS projects 90 of them (58 percent) were materials or resources to support language teaching and learning. Of the 137 kinds of materials produced by other programs 69 of them (50 percent) were materials or resources to support language teaching and learning. The next largest groups of materials produced by the IRS and the other projects were assessments and area studies materials, followed by cultural materials (Joyner and Suarez, 2006).

Language instructional materials addressed a variety of languages, including many less commonly taught languages. Perhaps in response to ED's 2002 priority that included development of materials in languages of the Islamic nations of the Middle East, Arabic was the language most frequently supported by IRS-funded projects, with 13 such materials. The next most common languages were Russian (7), Spanish (7), Chinese (5) and Japanese (4). The IRS-funded instructional materials focused on 70 different languages (see Box 7-2), while the materials funded by other Title VI/FH programs focused on 69 different languages.[5]

In public comments to the committee, one expert stated that IRS grants dating back to the 1960s had yielded 740 sets of instructional materials. Among these, about 80 were in Chinese, 65 in various forms of Arabic, and 40 in Japanese, with much smaller numbers of materials in the least commonly taught languages, such as Pashto (about 16), Vietnamese (about 7), and Yoruba (about 4) (Wiley, 2006).

---

[5]Projects supported by other Title VI/FH programs most frequently produced Japanese instructional materials and assessments (13), followed by Spanish (13), Chinese (8), Russian (6), Mandarin (5), and Zulu (5). However, as noted above, the small sample considered in the commissioned analysis may not accurately reflect the universe of these projects.

BOX 7-2
Language Focus (as listed by project)
of IRS-Funded Projects, FY 2000-2005

African	Indonesian	Sesotho
Albanian	Kazak	Shan
Amharic	Khmer	Shona
Arabic	Kikuyu	Slavic and Eastern
Aymara	Kinyarwanda	European
Azerbaijani	Korean	Somali
Bosnian/Croatian/	Kriol	Southeast Asian
Serbian	Lao	Spanish
Burmese	Latin	Swahili
Cantonese	Less Commonly	Tagalog
Chichewa	Taught Languages	Tajik
Chinese	(unspecified)	Tamil
Czech	Lingala	Thai
Dardarsha	Macedonian	Tibetan
Egyptian	Mandarin	Turkish
English	Middle Eastern	Ukrainian
Filipino	Mon	Urdu
French	Mopan Maya	Uyghur
Georgian	Pashto	Uzbek
German	Persian	Vietnamese
Gikuku	Polish	Wolof
Greek	Punjabi	Yoruba
Hebrew	Romanian	Zulu
Hindi	Russian	

SOURCE: Joyner and Suarez (2006).

RELEVANCE AND SCHOLARLY STANDARDS

A more challenging aspect of this component of the committee's charge is assessing the degree to which materials are relevant and meet accepted scholarly standards.

Relevance

The relevance of instructional materials may be measured by the extent to which the materials are obtained by intended users, the users actually apply and make use of the materials, and the materials prove to be useful for teaching and student learning.

Some elements of the application process for Title VI/FH grants encourage grantees to develop materials that are relevant. First, as discussed in Chapter 3, ED convenes panels of experts to review grant applications. In recent years, ED has established criteria for ranking and review of applications that may encourage creation of relevant materials. For example, in 2003 and again in 2005, the IRS application review criteria included points for "need for the project," "potential for use in other programs," "account of related materials," and "provisions for pre-testing and revision." Similarly, the criteria for review of NRC applications increased the total number of points possible for "impact and evaluation" from 20 points in 2003 to 25 points in 2005. In both 2003 and 2005, the criteria for review of LRC applications allowed up to 20 points for the "evaluation plan" (see Appendix C).

The ED provides an additional incentive to grantees to demonstrate that their activities—including materials development—are relevant by requiring annual progress reports that address "impact" as well as other aspects of the project. These annual progress reports are the primary information that ED program officers use each year when deciding whether or not to continue the grant (see Chapter 3).

No systematic, comprehensive information is available about the extent to which IRS, NRC, or LRC grantees may be responding to ED's directives by conducting needs assessments, reviewing existing materials, carrying out evaluations, or conducting impact assessments of the instructional materials they create. However, during site visits, the committee learned about many efforts to evaluate materials or assess the extent to which they are used. For example, the faculty and staff at the University of California, Los Angeles (UCLA) provided estimates of the number of hits and downloads from the Outreach World website of teaching materials (see Chapter 5). In addition, many grantees reported conducting pretests, posttests, and surveys to obtain user feedback on the relevance and usefulness of instructional materials. For example, staff at the Indiana University Center for the Languages of the Central Asian Region (an LRC) said that they had pilot-tested a new introductory Uzbek textbook, in both a book and a web-based version, over two summers. The textbook authors taught Uzbek in the university's Summer Workshop of Slavic East European and Central Asian Languages, and students used the new text. Near the end of the workshop, the authors surveyed students and also conducted informal interviews with them to obtain feedback and identify needed revisions.

During the committee's site visit to Indiana University, staff at the university's Center for Evaluation and Education Policy said that, in response to ED's 2005 criteria for review of NRC applications placing greater weight on evaluation, several university NRCs had asked for help in writing the evaluation sections of their applications. For example, the center helped the Russian and East European Institute prepare an application that included plans to evaluate the relevance of teacher training materials through several measures, including workshop attendance, surveys conducted at the end of each workshop, and surveys conducted 6 to 12 months later, to determine the extent to which workshop content had been incorporated into classroom practices.

In public comments to the committee, experts in foreign languages, area studies, and international education stressed the value of the instructional materials developed, particularly those developed by the IRS Program (Wiley, 2006; Edwards, 2006). They commented on the value of a field-driven system that provides grants and creates materials in response to ideas generated from those in the field (Keatley, 2006; Christian, 2006).

Scholarly Standards

In the United States today, there is no single, uniform process for ensuring the quality of instructional materials. In major research universities, individuals, departments, and area centers typically gain prestige based on the quality of their scholarly publications. Research published in peer-reviewed journals is a requisite for tenure and promotion, and the peer review process is intended to provide assurance that publications meet scholarly standards. In general, instructional materials are given less weight than research, so young scholars tend to devote more time to research than creating new instructional materials. Furthermore, standards for assessing the quality of instructional materials are not well defined.

Nevertheless, there are widely used procedures that materials developers can follow to help ensure that the materials they develop will be of high quality. For example, the author of a textbook usually submits the draft to a commercial publisher, who engages outside experts to review its quality and content. On the basis of these reviews, the author may be asked to make extensive revisions prior to publication. Although a commercial publisher may not be involved in the development of textbooks or other instructional materials for the less commonly taught languages, the author may nevertheless engage outside experts in review and pilot-test of the materials to identify needed improvements. Approaches to developing high-quality instructional materials are available from professional journals and from guidelines for good practice developed by professional associations.

APPROACHES TO ENSURING RELEVANCE AND QUALITY

A rigorous process for developing relevant, high-quality instructional materials was reported in a study of federally funded middle school and high school science and mathematics materials (Tushnet et al., 2000). The generous funding provided by the National Science Foundation allowed curriculum developers to assemble large cross-disciplinary teams of scholars, who carried out the following steps:

1. Identify the important content to be covered within the larger area (e.g., in the geometry segment).
2. Brainstorm about types of stories or powerful concepts that could be featured.
3. Meet with writers and review the content with them. Generate a first draft.
4. Send the draft out multiple times to the advisory board for feedback regarding content, dialogue, cultural sensitivity, and gender equity.
5. Conduct focus groups of teachers, scholars, and community groups to review the treatments.
6. Pilot an early version of the module in local classrooms.
7. Revise module, if necessary, based on the pilots.
8. Field test the final version of the module in national sites, revising as necessary.

Often, however, curriculum developers are constrained by much more limited funding, using less sophisticated approaches to create materials that may be highly focused (e.g., vocabulary lists, collections of pictures related to an area culture) or intended only for local classroom use. An individual teacher or faculty member may engage other experts in developing courseware, workbooks, or syllabi or may rely entirely on his or her personal expertise. He or she may or may not conduct pilot tests or field tests to determine how useful the materials are in supporting the learning process.

Current Efforts to Ensure the Quality of Language Instructional Materials

Associations of language educators and other groups are now engaged in two types of efforts to enhance the quality of instructional materials. One type aims to strengthen the process of developing materials, and the other type emphasizes review and evaluation of existing materials with the goal of identifying or selecting only those that meet certain scholarly standards. Because many of the instructional materials developed with Title VI/FH funding are language materials, the following discussion focuses on foreign language materials.

Strengthening Development of Foreign Language Materials

Colleges and universities are currently working to strengthen the development of instructional materials as part of a larger movement to reform and improve undergraduate education. The Boyer Commission on Educating Undergraduates in the Research University (1998) called for a research-based approach to teaching. It encouraged faculty members to collaborate in ongoing research and improvement of their own teaching practices, drawing on the most recent research on teaching and learning. Today, many faculty and administrators across the country are revising course designs and instructional materials in science and other disciplines in order to better support student learning (e.g., Allen, 2000).

Reflecting this larger reform movement, the Association of Departments of Foreign Languages (ADFL), a division of the Modern Language Association, has launched several efforts to strengthen undergraduate foreign language teaching, including instructional materials. The ADFL's 2001 statement of good practice emphasizes ongoing improvement of teaching practices, calling on language departments to value scholarship on teaching methods and assessment procedures equally with traditional forms of scholarship. Its definition of good teaching calls for a more scholarly approach to developing curriculum and instructional materials, including collaboration to engage more scholars in the process (Association of Departments of Foreign Languages, 2001, p. 2, italics added):

> Good teaching begins with *imaginative, conscientious course design* and ongoing efforts to maintain and develop subject-area and methodological expertise. . . . A good teacher recognizes that students learn by hearing the foreign language spoken well and by reading authentic texts, as well as by communicating with others in the foreign language, both orally and in writing. *Practice in using the productive and receptive skills should be an integral part of every course taught in a foreign language, including those that focus on literature or culture.* . . . Good teaching is enhanced when faculty members *work cooperatively* to ensure that instruction in every classroom is related to that in other classes in the department, in the humanities, or across the university.

The ADFL also publishes a quarterly journal, *ADFL Bulletin*, with articles on designing language courses and materials. One recent issue included the articles "Goals, Strategies, and Curricula in Advanced Arabic Learning" (McLarney, 2005) and "Integrating Media into Arabic Instruction: Advantages and Challenges" (Rammuny, 2005). In addition to ADFL, other academic and professional associations publish research and newsletters and offer advice on design of curriculum and selection of instructional materials. For example, the American Association of Teachers of Spanish and Portuguese publishes *Hispania* (American Association of Teachers of Spanish and Portuguese, 2006) and the National Council of Less Commonly Taught Languages (2006) publishes the *Journal of the National Council of Less Commonly Taught Languages.*

With ED funding, the ACTFL created national standards for foreign language learning organized around five goals of communication, cultures, connections, comparisons, and communities. Although the introduction clearly states that "the standards are not a curriculum guide" (American Council on the Teaching of Foreign Languages, 2006a, p. 2), ACTFL has used these standards as a focus in workshops for language teachers on the design of curriculum, instructional materials, and assessments (American Council on the Teaching of Foreign Languages, 2006b). In addition, some states have used the standards as a template to create criteria for evaluation of foreign language textbooks and curriculum materials (see discussion below).

The National Science Foundation and the Hewlett Foundation have also funded a range of activities, some utilizing advances in technology, aimed at advancing foreign language instruction as well as instruction in other disciplines.

Contribution of Title VI Programs to Strengthening Materials Development

The Department of Education's application review process engages scholars in review of the activities proposed for funding under the various Title VI/FH programs. As noted above, the rating criteria for IRS applicants proposing to develop instructional materials are designed to enhance the quality of those materials by encouraging grantees to take a careful approach to materials development, including a survey of existing materials and pilot-testing of preliminary materials.

The committee identified several examples of Title VI/FH-funded efforts to strengthen materials development. For example, the Center for Advanced Research on Language Acquisition (CARLA), an LRC located at the University of Minnesota, conducted a program of competitive minigrants to teachers of the less commonly taught languages to develop shareable teaching materials (University of Minnesota, 2006b). A committee of experts in languages, linguistics, and curriculum development reviewed the proposals in terms of their likelihood of successful completion, appropriate use of technology, potential audience, and goal of enhancing language proficiency. Since 2000, CARLA has also offered an annual summer institute on developing classroom materials for less commonly taught languages. In summer 2006, the five-day institute covered such topics as (1) providing the latest research on second language acquisition and its implications for development of instructional materials in the less commonly taught languages, (2) creating new materials and revising existing materials, (3) adapting materials from other languages, (4) using technology appropriately, and (5) incorporating authentic resources and visual elements (University of Minnesota, 2006a). However, the institute did not address field-testing or evaluation of materials.[6] The leaders of these summer institutes on development of teaching materials were writing a book on materials development in late 2006. The National K-12 Foreign Language LRC at Iowa State University also offers many institutes designed to help teachers improve teaching approaches, including design of curriculum and teaching materials (Iowa State University, 2003).

Evaluating Foreign Language Materials

State education agencies and professional associations have evaluated language textbooks and other instructional materials. Such studies are often designed to identify the best materials for classroom use. At the same time, they may also encourage a more rigorous process of materials development, as developers seek to create materials that will be accepted and purchased.

State education agencies often engage expert panels in review of language materials in order to identify those most aligned with state language standards. For example, in 2003, the California Department of Education convened a panel of experts to review language instructional materials using a set of criteria that reflect the five elements of the ACTFL Standards for Foreign Language Teaching (California Department of Education, 2006). The Oklahoma State Department of Education has disseminated a language textbook evaluation guide based on the ACTFL standards and developed by an expert at Indiana University (Oklahoma State Department of Education, 2006).

Title VI-funded projects have initiated similar efforts to evaluate and thereby improve language instruction materials. In 1998, the National K-12 Foreign Language LRC at Iowa State University, in collaboration with ACTFL, launched a major effort to strengthen language teaching, New Visions in Action (Iowa State University, 2000-2004). The New Visions project created "action groups" on materials selection and assessment. Among other goals, these two action groups sought to "develop and disseminate an evaluative criteria instrument for print and technology-based materials selection" and to develop a database with reviews of effective instructional materials (Iowa State University, 2000-2004).

The National Foreign Language LRC at the University of Hawaii will offer a summer institute in 2007 on evaluation of foreign language programs for teachers and college faculty. Among other topics, the summer institute will address curriculum development and improvement, course

---

[6]Personal correspondence, Margaret Hilton with Louis Janus, LCTL project coordinator, CARLA, November, 2006.

evaluation, and student learning outcomes assessment (University of Hawaii, 2006).

The Language Materials Project (LMP) at UCLA has created an online bibliographic database of instructional materials for less commonly taught languages (University of California at Los Angeles, 2006d). The Department of Defense originally funded the project at the time of the Persian Gulf war, with the goal of rationalizing the various language training programs in the federal government. During the 1990s, ED provided additional funding through the TICFIA grant, and the project is currently supported with IRS funding. Housed at the UCLA Center for World Languages, the project engages graduate students to review materials and create an abstract for each item, describing its content and features, to aid users in making selections.

The LMP website (http://www.lmp.ucla.edu/index.aspx?menu=001) allows users to enter language portals in order to access two types of materials—pedagogical materials (classroom materials intended for foreign language teaching) and authentic materials (originally intended for use by native speakers, not language learners). Each language portal also provides information about the history, culture, and origins of the language, a map showing where the language is spoken, basic facts about the grammar, writing systems, and a history of the language, with references.

The LMP database is designed to be inclusive, while also establishing minimal standards of quality. An advisory board of nationally known language experts oversees the development and maintenance of the database. For example, the database defines pedagogical materials very widely, including textbooks, computer-aided instruction, videos, audiotapes, games, puzzles, and workbooks. At the same time, however, teaching materials must meet three criteria to be included: (1) must be pedagogically useful or relevant to the teacher, the student, or the curriculum development; (2) must provide at least some information, such as a preface, in English; and (3) must include publication information. Similarly, the project defines authentic materials broadly, encompassing books, periodicals, maps, games, puzzles, currency, and advertisements. Authentic materials must meet five criteria for inclusion: (1) must be pedagogically useful, (2) must be of foreign origin, (3) must come from a sustainable source, (4) must be readily available in the United States, and (5) must be free of copyright restrictions.

In addition, the LMP database links directly to a database of language teaching materials developed and maintained by the University of Minnesota's CARLA. The CARLA database of teaching materials for the less commonly taught languages includes two types of materials: (1) materials created by CARLA graduate assistants, including a Virtual Picture Album, Virtual Audio-Video Archive, and exercises on Irish, Portuguese, Basque, and other less commonly taught languages and (2) materials created by instructors through the mini-grants process described above. Materials are selected based on both need for materials related to a particular language and the coordinator's expert judgment about their quality.[7] Finally, the LMP database hosts an historic database originally developed by the Center for Applied Linguistics, a partner in two Title VI-funded LRCs. Although no longer maintained, the database includes information on textbooks, grammars, readers, and bilingual dictionaries for approximately 900 languages.

CONCLUSIONS

The Title VI/FH programs have developed a variety of language and cultural materials, many of which are designed to address gaps in the availability of curricula and materials to support teaching and learning in the less commonly taught languages. Many of these materials can be easily accessed by instructors via websites developed with support from Title VI/FH programs.

> **Conclusion:** Title VI programs develop a variety of instructional and assessment materials, with many aimed at developing proficiency in the less commonly taught languages.

Systematic, national information on the quality of these materials and the extent to which they are disseminated and used is not currently available. However, surveys, web access data, and site visit interviews provide evidence that at least some of these materials are being used by their intended audiences. Although there are no uniform scholarly standards for instructional materials, site visit interviews indicate that some federally funded teachers, faculty members, and curriculum developers follow approaches to materials development that incorporate efforts to ensure the quality and relevance of materials.

> **Conclusion:** Although there are no uniform scholarly standards for instructional materials, there are widely accepted "best practice" approaches to materials development that are disseminated by professional associations and journals.

Furthermore, the selection criteria used to rate IRS applications encourage grantees to follow aspects of the best practice approaches to development

---

[7]Personal correspondence, Margaret Hilton with Louis Janus, LCTL project coordinator, CARLA, November, 2006.

of instructional materials. Specifically, IRS grant applications are awarded points for review of existing materials and for pilot-testing and revision, two aspects of the widely accepted approaches to developing quality curricula and materials. If use of these criteria has actually resulted in pilot-testing of materials and improved the quality of the resulting materials, ED may want to consider ways of incorporating these criteria in the review process for applicants who propose to produce instructional materials through other programs.

8

Advancing Uses of
New Technology

During the past half century, since the passage of the National Defense
Education Act (NDEA), which created the now-Title VI programs,
there have been significant changes in information and communication technologies (ICT). These changes have tremendous implications for
reconsidering how best to realize the goals of the Title VI and Fulbright-
Hays (Title VI/FH) programs. This chapter briefly reviews changes in these
technologies themselves and then examines the ways in which Title VI/FH
programs have used technology up to the present, in order to address the
question of how well the programs are advancing the use of new technology
in foreign language and area studies.

Briefly, almost all areas of human endeavor have been deeply affected
by changes in ICT. The ability to communicate in multiple media with
people around the world at low cost, as well as the ability to look for and
publish any information on a distributed global information network,
have profound implications for research, education, and outreach activities
that have an international focus, such as those included in the Title VI/FH
programs. These new technologies have created a new context and a new
set of tools for conducting research, teaching, and outreach activities in
area studies and foreign language education. Below we discuss some of the
more prominent changes in information and communication technologies,
their implications for Title VI/FH programs, and the extent to which, based
on the limited available evidence, the programs have adapted to or taken
advantage of these developments.

ADVANCES IN INFORMATION AND
COMMUNICATION TECHNOLOGIES

ICT have affected mass communication, the use of digital media, and the ease of publications, with implications for the Title VI/FH programs.

Mass Communication

Over the past 50 years, ICT have made person-to-person communication across geographical and political borders a mass phenomenon, available and affordable to people in almost every corner of the world. The first transatlantic telephone cable was built in 1956, two years before the NDEA, which drastically expanded telephone communication capacities between Europe and North America. Prior to that, telephone calls between England and the United States cost more than $200 per minute,[1] and only about 2,000 phone calls could be placed each year. Today, with fiber optic lines and satellites, phone calls anywhere cost only cents, and the capacity is virtually unlimited. In 2006, there are over 2 billion mobile phone subscribers worldwide, which means over one-third of the world's population had access to a mobile phone. Telephone is of course not the only means of communication across distances. The Internet has made available extremely low cost computer-to-computer and computer-to-phone communication capabilities to over 1 billion Internet users in the world.[2]

Not only has communication technology become more available and affordable, but also it has become more powerful in terms of the quantity and quality of information it can transmit. Today, audio, video, text, and images can be easily transmitted over the Internet between computers. The upcoming third generation (3G) mobile phone technology enables multimedia communications on cell phones worldwide. It is no exaggeration to say that with today's technology one can communicate with people in any place in the world through video, images, text, and voice.

Digital Revolution

Another major change is the digital revolution brought about by computers. In the 1950s, the computer was still what its name suggested, a machine that did mathematical calculations. But today, the computer is a television, a telephone, a telegram machine, a piano, a typewriter, a music box, a library, a community center, and much more. Thanks to digitization,

---

[1]Based on a 3-minute phone call which cost £9 in 1927, which would be around £360 in 2005 using the inflation calculator at http://eh.net/hmit/ppowerbp/.

[2]The number of Internet users is based on information obtained at http://www.internet-worldstats.com/stats.htm.

the computer has integrated many media into one—enabling the mixing of contents that were once not mixable.

While digitization enables the mixing of information, rapid development in storage technology has made it possible to distribute massive amounts of multimedia information to individuals at low cost. In 1956, the world's first random access hard disk was created. It weighed a full ton and would cost about $250,000 to lease it for a year, but it would hold only 5 megabytes of information. Today, the 1.8-inch drive inside a $299 iPod has a 40 gigabyte storage space.

High-speed computer networks, low-cost massive storage, increasingly sophisticated search engines, and the digital format together enable the accumulation and sharing of an unprecedented amount of information among institutions and individuals. Google's attempt to digitize and make available millions of books to worldwide users is yet another example of global information gathering and sharing.

Personalized Publishing and Broadcasting

Perhaps the most fundamental change in ICT is the capability they afford individuals and organizations to publish and broadcast their ideas to a broader audience. Thanks to low-cost digital tools and easy access to the Internet, publishing and broadcasting are no longer controlled solely by corporations or governments; practically any individual or organization that wishes to publicize its ideas, images, or any other personal information can do so.

Implications for Title VI/FH Programs

The changes in ICT briefly described above have significant implications for Title VI/FH programs. The first change, which has already affected Title VI/FH quite a bit, is the potential for expanded access to primary sources of information. For example, in the 1950s, it was almost impossible for most people in the United States to have access to a Chinese newspaper published in China on a regular basis. Today, hundreds of newspapers published in China are available on the Internet. Also on the Internet, anyone can watch the Nile TV live from Egypt, listen to CapitalFM broadcast live from Nairobi, Kenya,[3] or follow online conversations among youth in India. Many organizations have made available on the Internet documents that may otherwise be difficult or expensive to obtain, such as historical documents, literary works, museum items, and library collections.

---

[3]For a list of foreign radio and TV stations on the Internet, visit http://www.multilingual-books.com/online-radio.html.

As a result, information that used to require extensive international travel to obtain is now available at the fingertips of the ordinary citizen; documents that may have been accessible to few are now accessible to many; and data that would have required extensive observation and participation in foreign settings are now collectable from one's own computer. Perhaps even more significant is that these materials and documents can be represented, rearranged, and easily incorporated into education materials for students and the public.

Another important implication of the technology revolution for Title VI/FH programs is expanded access to expertise and enhanced capacity for dissemination and education. In the 1950s, it would have been difficult if not impossible for the ordinary college student interested in studying Russian to have daily conversations with a Russian college student. It would have been similarly difficult to conduct interviews with people in villages in Thailand without being physically present. Communications with colleagues in foreign universities were conducted mostly by postal mail—which could be costly and even with the fastest airmail, could take days, if not weeks.

Fifty years ago, when Title VI was put into place, the primary means of disseminating information was paper and physical meetings. But today, emailing, audio chatting, text messaging, and videoconferencing have become commonplace for cross-national communications. With inexpensive and easily set-up videoconferencing equipment, one can more easily bring experts in other countries into classrooms and offices without traveling. Online collaboration among researchers, international virtual conferences, and virtual courses from foreign universities have become increasingly common practices in business and academia. Today, researchers and organizations can instantly disseminate information and distribute documents to a broad audience located anywhere on the globe. This not only dramatically reduces costs but also reaches a broader audience in a much shorter time. Institutions can use this enhanced capacity to reach more students through online distance courses and seminars.

Technology has also created new opportunities for foreign language instruction. For example, the National Science Foundation has funded a series of learning labs, some of which include foreign language instruction among their areas of focus (see, for example, Pittsburgh Science of Learning Center, visit http://www.learnlab.org/about.php).

TITLE VI/FH PROGRAMS AND TECHNOLOGY

Because limited information and no evaluations addressing the use of new technologies by Title VI/FH programs are available, the committee commissioned a review by Joyner and Suarez (2006). The review included projects aimed at developing new instructional materials, as discussed in Chapter 8, as there was significant overlap between that key area and the use of new technology. The researchers examined 111 projects using technology, including all of those funded under Technological Innovation and Cooperation for Foreign Information Access (TICFIA), which has use of technology as a specific part of its mandate.

The main shortcoming in the committee's analysis is a lack of information about the quality of funded projects that use new technology, in terms of how widely they are being used, or how effective they are in achieving their goals. It is not known, for example, how well some of these projects are actually improving language instruction. One could argue that the use of technology itself is not what is most relevant to the field of international education; the more relevant issue is the appropriateness of the technology for its users and for the way in which it is being used. From that viewpoint, the question of interest would involve relating the technology to its users and use—information that is not available in any systematic way in grant applications and reports. Indeed, a paper on second language acquisition prepared for another recent National Academies study stated that, although use of new technology has made its way into language classrooms, "very little research has been conducted from a cognitive perspective to determine how the method of delivery and context of learning affect the acquisition of [second language] skills" (Kroll, 2006). Therefore, this section focuses more on quantifying and describing technology-related projects funded by Title VI than on judging their effectiveness or how widely they are used.

Kinds of Technology-Related Activities

In the committee's analysis (Joyner and Suarez, 2006), projects' use of technology is described largely by illustration rather than by a strict categorization of projects and a quantitative report on the number in each category. One reason for this approach is that available information about the projects is sparse and sometimes dated. For example, if a project was funded five or six years ago, what was described as new or on the cutting edge at that time may well be commonplace in 2006, given the rate at which technology has been changing. Most if not all National Resource Centers (NRC), Language Resource Centers (LRC), and Centers for International Business Education and Research (CIBER) have web pages with information about their work, often with links to other programs. However, this is now rather routine and would not necessarily count as "advancing new technologies" unless the web pages were being used in a novel way—and indeed many appear to be (an online English-Urdu dictionary is one example; more are described below). But another problem is that, even if the project has evolved into more sophisticated or innovative techniques, the frequent absence from the Evaluation of Exchange, Language, International and Area Studies (EELIAS) database of the grantees' progress reports or final reports deprive the reader of knowledge about how it evolved. Also, while it might be useful to analyze the technology uses in terms of a typology, such as whether projects (1) developed new technological tools, (2) adapted existing tools, or (3) used existing technology, the level of detail for analyses such as that was generally not available.

In broad terms, the examples of technology in Title VI/FH programs fall into two general groups:

1. Technology as a delivery tool, which addresses the problem of geographical distance or helps achieve maximum access to material. In this group, existing content material is brought to a wider audience through the use of technology, such as in the case of language or area courses that can be taken electronically.

2. Technology that serves to create new content or enhance it. This usually means digitization of material that was previously available only in hard copy or the creation of interactive online learning materials.

Technology as a Delivery Tool

One important use of technology as a delivery tool is to support outreach, a required activity of the NRC Program (see Chapter 5). Some examples:

• Outreach World at the University of California, Los Angeles (http://www.outreachworld.org), funded by International Research and Studies (IRS), presents itself as a clearinghouse for outreach activities undertaken by NRCs nationwide, which may be of use to foreign language and social studies teachers at the K-12 level. It helps to break down the distance barrier by making NRC outreach available to an audience that is not confined to the geographic area in which the NRC is located. Teachers can draw on Outreach World for resources on such topics as African geography, human migration, the diversity of cultures in Latin America, the effects of air pollution in Mexico City, and the history of Cairo, Egypt. Teachers can also communicate with one another to share experiences in teaching languages, study abroad, and other topics (see Chapter 5).

• A similar resource for those in business is CIBERWeb, housed at Michigan State University. The web page (http://ciberweb.msu.edu) brings together outreach activities for all CIBERs, organizing them by topic. It includes events that would be of interest to business representatives looking to export products or services, as well as business school faculty and students (see Chapter 10).

• The National Capital Language Resource Center (a consortium consisting of Georgetown University, George Washington University, and the Center for Applied Linguistics) has a web page (http://www.ncrlc.org) that serves as a resource for language teachers at the postsecondary level. It contains large amounts of material related to classroom teaching and assessments, as well as information on professional development and training opportunities. It even houses an "advice" page, on which experienced teachers help novices with specific classroom issues.

In the projects funded by programs other than NRCs, the content delivered by technology was most often courses or other distance learning activities. Box 8-1 illustrates several uses of technology as a delivery tool.

Technology as a Content Enhancer

The largest number of projects in the second category, in which technology is used to create, enhance, and then deliver content, is funded through TICFIA. This is consistent with its mission—to access, collect, preserve, and widely disseminate information from foreign sources. The projects identified seek to develop foreign source materials for research use by scholars or for language instruction. Many projects collect primary documents in foreign languages and other language learning materials, catalog and digitize them, and then make them available to researchers and language teachers through the Internet. Table 8-1 is a summary of recent TICFIA awards.

IRS is the other major program identified that funded projects that use technology to enhance content. These projects often developed language and area instruction content and then used new technologies as a means of delivery and dissemination. Box 8-2 describes some IRS-funded projects that were specifically designed with new technology in mind as a means of delivery.

CONCLUSIONS

Rapid changes in ICT have made it possible for Title VI/FH programs to make great strides in the areas of distance learning, the digitization of foreign source materials, and enhancing the ability of people to communicate, whether between instructors and students, or K-12 teachers sharing information on best practices in their classrooms. New technologies have been put to imaginative use, such as for the creation of online dictionaries, lesson plans for use by teachers, and advice lines for novice language instructors.

Because of a lack of information, the committee could not make judgments about the effectiveness of projects using new technologies, that is,

BOX 8-1
Illustrations of Technology as a Delivery Tool

Florida Network for Global Studies

As part of an NRC grant, the Florida Network for Global Studies at Florida International University will be expanded beyond the International Center of the University of Florida (Gainesville) and the Center for Transnational and Comparative Studies of Florida International University (Miami) to other universities in the state of Florida system and to selected community colleges and secondary schools, employing the latest technology in web-based, virtual connectivity, and distance learning.

Russian, East European, and Eurasian Studies (REEES) Consortium

Using an Undergraduate International Studies and Foreign Language grant, REEES at the University of Iowa, in partnership with the Department of Foreign Languages and Literatures at Iowa State University and the Department of Modern Languages at the University of Northern Iowa, has begun a pilot program of distance learning for REEES students at the three Iowa institutions. The project pools faculty expertise and student populations through a combination of Internet-based instructional delivery platforms, enriching offerings in these areas at all three campuses simultaneously. Based on specific institutional strengths, instructor expertise, and student demand, three languages—Czech, Polish, and Serbian-Croatian—were selected for initial concentration.

Global E-Commerce Training for Business and Educators

Using a Business and International Education grant, an e-commerce project at State Center Community College District in Fresno, California, was designed to train businesses on how to complete export transactions through their websites, establish an e-commerce Internet course, and disseminate project results through websites, listservs, and other means.

Center for Advanced Research on Language Acquisition

The Center for Advanced Research on Language Acquisition, a Language Resource Center (LRC) at the University of Minnesota-Twin Cities, planned to use part of its LRC grant to create a professional development program and a web-based resource center for K-16 language teachers that provides instruction and practical tools for incorporating content-based language instruction into the classroom using technology. Another of the center's projects helps increase communication among teachers of the least commonly taught languages, through databases of where such languages are taught, relevant listservs, and a website of resources for teachers.

SOURCE: Joyner and Suarez (2006).

TABLE 8-1 Summary of Technological Innovation and Cooperation for Foreign Information Access Awards, 2005

Institution	Project Title and Description
Michigan State University	**South African Collaborative Film and Video Project**—create an online searchable database of archival video on the history of South Africa.
Yale University	**OACIS for the Middle East: On-Line Access to Consolidated Information on Serials**—make Middle Eastern language resources widely available by creating a publicly accessible, continuously updated list of Middle East journals and serials, including those available in print, microform, and online.
University of California, Los Angeles	**Sources of Authentic Materials for the Less Commonly Taught Languages**—develop an online tool for bringing authentic materials into the classroom for less commonly taught languages.
University of California, Los Angeles	**Mining Hidden Gems: Building a Latin American Open Archives Portal for Scholars**—address the need for improved control of and access to Latin America's "grey literature," the publications, working documents, and other materials produced by research institutes, nongovernmental organizations, and peripheral agencies produced in print and electronic formats.
University of Chicago	**South Asian Information Access: A Federated Program to Expand the Resources for Understanding the Subcontinent**—online collection of digital resources that will encompass Afghanistan, Bangladesh, Bhutan, India, the Maldive Islands Nepal, Pakistan, and Sri Lanka. Language materials selected from among the 27 modern literary languages of South Asia will be a special focus.
University of Kansas	**Access to Russian Archives**—create a digital database of regional and national guides to the Russian archives. The project will digitize guides to the approximately 270 central and regional archives in Russia.
University of Southern California	**Access Indonesia**—identify, collect, and collate information on Indonesia, with a focus on information that is not yet accessible in the United States.
University of Southern California	**Japan Media Review Website on Developments in Japan in On-Line Journalism**—support *Japan Media Review* (http://www.japanmediareview.com), which monitors and collects relevant data from Japan related to electronic media and broadband, wireless, and Internet communications technology.
University of Virginia and Cornell University consortium	**Tibetan Digital Library Access**—online archive and communication hub for research and documentation in Tibetan and Himalayan studies.
University of Wisconsin	**Portal to Asian Internet Resources**—to support the Portal to Asian Internet Resources, which provides access to Internet resources from Asia in its vernacular languages.

SOURCE: Data provided by U.S. Department of Education.

BOX 8-2
Illustrations of Technology as a Content Enhancer in Projects Funded by International Research and Studies

Darvazah: A Door into Urdu

North Carolina State University in this project will use emerging technologies and pedagogical principles derived from the field of computer-assisted language learning to create a fully interactive elementary Urdu course. The course will employ the full range of multimedia capabilities of the Internet, integrating video, audio, and animation into graded lessons that emphasize performance and proficiency in the target language. Glossaries, grammar units, cultural concepts, and other learning tools will be hyperlinked to lesson movie texts. This project will result in the equivalent of a two-semester university class in Urdu that can serve as the basic text for formal classroom instruction, for supplemental tutorials and drills, or for self-directed learning. For the classroom environment, the materials will be designed to dovetail with course delivery platforms like WebCT.

Uzbek-English/English-Uzbek Dictionary

This Indiana University, Bloomington, project aims to produce a new, comprehensive Uzbek-English/English-Uzbek dictionary that will contain at least 40,000 headwords in each of its Uzbek-English and English-Uzbek parts, making it the most comprehensive and useful Uzbek dictionary designed for English speakers to date. The effort makes extensive use of technology to convert and migrate words from an earlier dictionary to the new one and to conduct web searches to identify new words to be included. The two dictionaries produced by this project will eventually be published in both book and searchable CD-ROM format.

Online Diagnostic Tests and Course Materials for Dialects of Arabic, Chinese, and Persian

This San Diego State University project employs the computer-assisted screening tool (CAST) to create assessments in Iraqi and Egyptian dialects of Arabic, Mandarin Chinese, and Persian Farsi. It builds on a previous IRS project that developed CAST to create online diagnostic speaking assessments in Arabic and Spanish. CAST can assess the language skills of remotely located individuals (practicing and aspiring teachers, interpreters, international business employees, and government workers) and can help organizations evaluate large proficiency-based language programs. The objectives are to (1) elicit, online, a speech sample that establishes a baseline rating for an examinee; (2) serve as a reliable predictor of performance on an official oral proficiency instrument, and (3) provide positive feedback for proficiency-based teaching. Examinees will be directed to authentic text, video, and audio materials for advanced and superior levels, which will model the oral skills expected.

SOURCE: Joyner and Suarez (2006).

how well they are achieving their goals. The committee's analysis could only quantify, categorize, and describe the projects. So, for example, NRCs are making a great deal of outreach material available to K-12 teachers, but how often it is used or its usefulness in the classroom is not known.

There is no doubt that some projects are making good use of new technology in creative ways. However, there is clear opportunity for additional innovation, particularly given the rapid changes in technology. Some avenues to pursue include virtual language or area centers, common technology platforms that can serve as the foundation for the teaching of a wide variety of languages, more online learning, global collaboration, and making better use of original foreign language source materials. These are discussed further in Chapter 12.

Conclusion: Title VI and Fulbright-Hays programs are using available technologies, such as the Internet and distance learning, but they could do more to maximize the potential created by current technologies.

9

Addressing Business Needs

Two Title VI programs focus on meeting business needs for international knowledge and foreign language skills: the Business and International Education (BIE) Program, created in 1980, and the Centers for International Business Education and Research (CIBER) Program, created in 1988. The BIE program aims to encourage innovation, helping a range of higher education institutions, including two-year colleges, to develop international and foreign language capacity in their business programs. To carry this program out, the U.S. Department of Education (ED) provides two-year seed grants. In contrast, the CIBER Program is designed to create and sustain international business curricula and faculty at the nation's top-ranked business schools. To advance this goal, ED provides larger and more sustained CIBER grants (averaging about $340,000 per year), lasting four years rather than two (until the most recent grant competition, CIBER grants were awarded for three years) (Ruther, 2006). CIBER grantees are also charged with being "regional resources to business." This chapter focuses on these two programs, given their particular focus on business needs.

As with other key areas, the available evidence does not allow a rigorous assessment of business-related outcomes, such as the programs' impact on enhancing the international competitiveness of U.S. businesses or improving global understanding in the business community. Similarly, it is not possible to determine the extent to which the two programs may have improved institutional capacity in international business education, given the lack of information about baseline institutional capacity or quality in international business education.

The programs were launched during a time of intense international competition that affected not only U.S. businesses, but also business schools. In the early 1970s, well before Congress created BIE and CIBER, the Assembly of Collegiate Schools of Business recommended that business school accreditation standards be changed to require a more international emphasis (Biddle, 2002). In 1980, this accreditation requirement was added.[1] In a mid-1990s study of internationalization at large research universities, some business school faculty and administrators felt that, because of their need to respond to the needs of prospective employers, they were ahead of the rest of the university in internationalizing (Biddle, 2002). The changing context of U.S. business education makes it difficult to isolate the effects of the BIE and CIBER programs.

Given the nature of the available evidence, this chapter, like others, focuses primarily on the activities and outputs of the BIE and CIBER programs. It begins with a discussion of mechanisms in the CIBER Program to facilitate coordination and collaboration and highlight accomplishments, featuring reported CIBER activities in key areas, such as homeland security, foreign languages in the business curriculum, knowledge about international trade and competitiveness, and institutional capacity. The chapter then moves to the BIE Program and discussion of the available evidence related to its accomplishments in the areas of infusing foreign languages and area studies into the business curriculum and improving outreach and dissemination. Each of these areas is an indirect indicator of the programs' ability to respond to business needs.

CIBER PROGRAM

The vast majority (95.7 percent) of CIBER awards are to institutions classified as primarily research. Most CIBER grants are awarded to top-tier business schools, in keeping with the law's goal of supporting national resources in international business education and foreign languages. In its 2006 rankings of graduate business schools, *U.S. News & World Report* (2006b) identified 51 top schools (with a 3-way tie for 49th place). Among the 30 business schools with CIBER grants in 2006, 20 (66 percent) were included in the top 51 schools. Among the 10 other institutions that received CIBER awards, several offer nationally ranked undergraduate business degrees (*U.S. News & World Report*, 2006a). These institutions include the University of South Carolina, Florida International University, and the University of Hawaii-Manoa.

---

[1]In 2006, accreditation required that the business programs "prepare students for careers in the global context" (American Association to Advance Collegiate Schools of Business International, 2006, p. 9).

CIBER Network

A unique feature of the CIBER Program, in comparison to other Title VI and Fulbright-Hays (Title VI/FH) programs, is the extent to which grantees share information and best practices. The 31 centers have created a strong yet flexible network that supports collaboration, communication, and shared learning.

Legislative and Administrative Supports

The legislative mandate in Title VI[2] and ED's administration of the program have encouraged the centers to collaborate through the CIBER network. The first part of the CIBER mandate focuses the center inward, on strengthening its university's capacity as a national resource for international business education, while the second part focuses the center outward, toward businesses and other institutions of higher education. In addition, the law mandates each center to establish an advisory board of business and government stakeholders. These two legal requirements for an outward focus encourage the centers to work together to serve the regional and national business community (Ruther, 2006).

ED program administrators have encouraged collaboration among grantees by developing an essential mechanism underlying the CIBER network—the CIBERweb Internet portal[3]—and suggesting topics to highlight (see below.) The ED provided financial support to the Purdue University CIBER to develop the website portal in 1995. Today, Michigan State University hosts CIBERweb, with funding from the university's CIBER grant, along with contributions from all of the other centers. A committee of ED program administrators and CIBER representatives oversees the website. CIBERweb provides easy access to all past and current CIBER activities, organized into six broad areas: research, foreign language development, business outreach, faculty development, academic program development, and study abroad (University of Connecticut, 2005).

Stable funding and few application priorities may also contribute to the centers' ability to focus outward on the activities of other grantees (Ruther, 2006). Initially, in 1989, there were only six CIBERs. With additional funding from Congress the number of centers steadily grew, reaching the current level of 31 centers in 2006. Although CIBERs have been added in each competition, the universities involved have remained relatively stable. In the most recent grant competition, all but one center successfully competed

---

[2]See Part B of the Title VI statute, included as Attachment A of Appendix A. It can be accessed at http://www.nap.edu by searching for International Education and Foreign Languages.

[3]The portal can be accessed at http://ciberweb.msu.edu.

for a new award, and one new university was added. (By comparison, there are four times as many NRC grantees and more change in grantees from one competition to the next.) In addition, ED has attached fewer priorities to recent requests for CIBER grant applications than it has to requests for other programs (see Appendix C).

Association for International Business Education and Research (AIBER)

In addition to collaborating through CIBERweb, all 31 centers belong to AIBER, a nonprofit organization. The association is supported through dues paid from private resources of the host CIBER institutions and does not receive any federal funding (Ruther, 2006). AIBER surveys the centers annually, compiling data on activities and outputs, such as the numbers of international business courses taught, the number of courses with international emphasis created or revised, and the number of faculty internationalization workshops held. In general, this is the same information submitted by CIBER institutions to ED via the grantee reporting system. However, the data collected by the centers goes back further and is currently more accessible to CIBERs than the data submitted to ED.

Network Activities

The CIBER network shares and compiles information through CIBERweb, AIBER, regular conferences, and written reports. Periodically, the ED program officer asks a given CIBER to survey other centers about a particular issue and prepare a report that is then published on CIBERweb. Some of the reports summarize CIBER activities and accomplishments over time (University of Connecticut, 2006), whereas others focus on ED priorities for the program (Purdue University, 2006). In addition, the network sponsors national conferences on topics of interest to all.

Program Highlights

The CIBER network has produced numerous documents highlighting accomplishments based on data and programmatic information provided by individual grantees. Much of the discussion below is based on two of these documents, one that addresses homeland security and one that outlines the program's accomplishments during its first 15 years. Information from a study that compared CIBER and non-CIBER business degree programs and from the committee's site visits is also included. The program highlights presented relate to homeland security, foreign languages in the business curriculum, an enhanced body of relevant knowledge, and improved institutional capacity.

Homeland Security and U.S. International Competitiveness

The terrorist attacks on September 11, 2001, raised grave concerns throughout the U.S. business community. CIBERs responded with a series of activities designed to investigate and address the challenges of ensuring security for U.S. businesses while maintaining the benefits of international trade. In 2005, as ED announced an invitational priority for grant applications focusing on homeland security and international competitiveness for the 2006-2010 grants,[4] the CIBER network issued a report on homeland security projects carried out from 2003 to 2005 (Grosse, 2006).

The CIBER homeland security report documents a range of activities, from convening conferences to research on the costs and risks that firms face, to development of new business school courses on national security and competitiveness (Grosse, 2006). According to this report, the centers plan a sustained program of research and teaching on homeland security and U.S. international competitiveness. The goal is to help U.S. firms and the U.S. government to develop comprehensive, cost-effective responses to the threat of terrorism.

The presence of the strong CIBER network, which facilitates information sharing, may have played an important role in this rapid response to a new and unexpected national priority.

Foreign Languages in the Business Curriculum

A recent comparative study of CIBER and non-CIBER business degree programs indicates that CIBER grants have contributed to infusing foreign languages into the business school curriculum. CIBER schools offered instruction in more languages (an average of 4.4 languages per school) than non-CIBER schools (an average of 2.1 languages per school). CIBER funding also appeared particularly important for support in teaching the less commonly taught languages: seven of the CIBER schools offered Chinese, compared with one non-CIBER school, and eight CIBER schools offered Japanese, compared with only three non-CIBER schools (Folks, 2003).

The CIBER report on the first 15 years of the program (University of Connecticut, 2005) also highlights the contributions of the CIBER Program, indicating that grantee institutions had conducted 4 types of activities to promote foreign language in the business curriculum:

Teaching foreign languages for business purposes. In 2003-2004, CIBER institutions taught 15 foreign languages, including several languages desig-

---

[4]The most recent competition also included an invitational priority for innovative approaches to teaching languages in the business context.

nated as critical in the proposed National Security Language Initiative, such as Arabic, Chinese, and Russian. Grantees offered 224 business language courses to undergraduates and 571 courses to graduate students. Brigham Young University offered 11 languages, the highest among the CIBERs.

Faculty development in teaching foreign languages for business purposes. Many CIBERs offer workshops preparing foreign language faculty to teach business Chinese, business Portuguese, or other languages. For example, the University of South Carolina's undergraduate business CIBER presents a six-day workshop for Spanish language faculty. Since 1990, over 250 faculty members, including faculty from historically black colleges and universities, have attended the annual workshops. In addition, the CIBER network sponsors an annual conference on teaching business languages that generally draws about 200 attendees each year.

Development of language teaching and testing materials. CIBERs are actively engaged in developing instructional materials and in professional development to enhance the teaching of business languages. Many of the materials support distance learning, such as the University of Texas's free online video clips and materials on business culture, Spanish, and Portuguese. From 1989 to 2004, CIBER universities taught over 7,300 commercial language courses to over 140,000 students, while engaging over 17,800 language faculty in business language workshops. Language materials developed by CIBERs enhanced commercial language courses, affecting an estimated 2.4 million students.

Research on business languages. Two current or former CIBER grantees publish research on business language teaching and learning. The Thunderbird Center for International Business at the Garvin School of International Management, a CIBER at the time of this writing, publishes *The Journal of Language for International Business*, a refereed journal published twice annually. Purdue University annually publishes *Global Business Languages*, with theoretical and practical articles and book reviews.

Enhanced Body of Knowledge

CIBER grants to higher education institutions support research that develops new knowledge about international trade and competitiveness issues. The grants also help universities disseminate this new knowledge to the business community, K-12 education, and the public. In addition, CIBER grants develop the international and foreign language knowledge of students, who bring that knowledge to the business world after graduation.

Research. All of the CIBERs support research on international and area business issues (University of Connecticut, 2005). Often, grantees organize competitions among faculty for minigrants supporting international travel and research. In addition to supporting research based on faculty interests, some CIBER research projects focus on particular themes of national interest. For example, the CIBER network project on homeland security and U.S. international competitiveness discussed above includes research on such questions as the costs of protecting U.S. businesses from terrorist attacks and immigration of skilled foreign nationals. The Duke University CIBER's multiyear offshoring research initiative includes an ongoing survey of hundreds of companies to clarify the extent of offshoring and perceptions of offshoring. In its first 15 years, its CIBER funding supported over 5,200 research projects by international business faculty and Ph.D. candidates. Research results have been disseminated in over 1,000 research conferences.

Dissemination. By law, every CIBER advisory board meets at least annually. The advisory board facilitates two-way communication, allowing business leaders to provide feedback to the business faculty on the quality and usefulness of their program, while also allowing business faculty to brief the business community on important issues. A recent survey found that the five most frequent functions of CIBER advisory boards included (University of Connecticut, 2005):

1. Serve to exchange information between the university, faculty, and business community/government.
2. Provide business advice to the university on new or revised curricula and programs.
3. Identify additional services and activities to be provided by the CIBER.
4. Give feedback from the business community to the university regarding the quality and effectiveness of existing curricula.
5. Develop strategies for obtaining financial support for the CIBER.

CIBER grantees typically focus their dissemination on unique, specialized niches. This may be because their network makes them aware of other CIBER activities as well as because of their mandate to meet the needs of local and regional business. For example, the University of Washington offers the Global Business Breakfast Series for local businesses in partnership with the World Affairs Council, and the University of Hawaii partners with the Pacific Basin Economic Council, the Hawaii World Trade Center, and various government agencies to convene an annual Hawaii Business Forum each spring. The University of Florida CIBER, with only a small local business community, has emphasized translating the university's expertise on international business into programs and publications targeted to state, national, and international business needs. It has worked with the U.S. Department of Agriculture's Agricultural Extension Service to educate Florida and U.S. farmers about overseas markets, and it publishes an annual report on the Latin American Business Environment (University of Connecticut, 2005).

Over the past 15 years, CIBERs offered over 4,000 business seminars, conferences, and workshops attended by an estimated 200,800 participants. In 2003-2004, CIBER schools offered 534 executive master's in business administration programs with an international focus, and 28,488 executives were enrolled in these programs. Among these programs, 70 percent included overseas experience for participating executives. In addition, CIBERs disseminate information by publishing scholarly research and providing newsletters, searchable databases, and other resources to the business community. In 2002-2003, CIBER-furnished websites reported nearly 60 million combined hits, with a median of 1.9 million hits per CIBER (University of Connecticut, 2005).

Graduate placements. CIBERs report that they awarded 11,000 master's degrees with an international focus in 2003-2004 (University of Connecticut, 2005). Reflecting the difficulty of tracking students' activities after graduation (see Chapter 6), CIBERs indicated not knowing where one-third of the graduates had gone. However, they reported that nearly one-half of the master's graduates had been placed in a variety of industries, including consulting, energy/chemicals, autos, and pharmaceutical/biotechnology. CIBERs appear to have greater success in tracking outcomes for doctoral students. They indicated that 300 doctoral students graduated with international business expertise in 2003-2004, and outcomes for 17 percent of these were unknown. The largest group of new doctoral graduates (62 percent) had entered academia, where they will prepare future international business leaders. Others went to work for private firms, nonprofit organizations, state or local government, the federal government, foreign government, and international organizations (University of Connecticut, 2005).

A representative of AIBER illustrated the way in which graduate placements enhance knowledge of international trade and competitiveness issues using Paul Gaspari, a graduate of the Temple University CIBER's international business program, as an example (Birch, 2006). Gaspari is now employed by the U.S. Export Assistance Center in Philadelphia, where he advises small and medium-sized businesses on how to make overseas sales. During site visits, universities also cited numerous examples of former students whose positions made use of their international expertise.

Institutional Capacity

A central goal of the CIBER Program is to create "national resources" for teaching of international business. Since the program's inception, the CIBERs have conducted many activities aimed at increasing their own institutions' capacity in international business education, while also providing resources and support to other business schools. Between 1989 and 2004, the CIBERs reported that they created or enhanced over 4,000 international business courses and created or revised 780 new degrees, majors, and concentrations. In total, over that time period, about 903,000 students took over 28,450 courses with an international business emphasis (University of Connecticut, 2005). To help doctoral students at non-CIBER institutions, seven CIBER schools created the Doctoral Internationalization Consortium, which provides training in the internationalization of seven different academic disciplines. Another consortium of 11 CIBER schools offers an annual seminar for doctoral students in business and other fields that seek to incorporate an international dimension in their research and teaching (University of Connecticut, 2005).

A study by Folks (2003) provides some additional evidence that CIBER funding has contributed to improved institutional capacity and quality in international business education. MBA programs at schools with a CIBER were more likely than those without a CIBER to require international business courses, offer advanced level international business classes, and, as discussed above, offer a greater variety of languages (see also Chapter 5). During site visits, universities reported that CIBER resources played an important role in their international activities, providing support for faculty to conduct international research and the development of international curriculum or programs (see Box 9-1 for illustrations.) Some students said that the presence of the CIBER attracted them to the business program.

BIE PROGRAM

Since 1983, the first year of funding, ED has awarded nearly 600 two-year BIE grants. In comparison to CIBER grants, the BIE grant amounts are smaller, averaging $75,000 per year, and are targeted to a much more diverse group of colleges and universities, including community colleges, technical schools, historically black colleges and universities, and Hispanic-serving institutions as well as four-year research universities (Murphrey, 2006). The BIE Program has the greatest reach of all Title VI programs into institutions classified as master's, baccalaureate, or associate's degree-granting institutions, with two-thirds (65.4 percent) of FY 2004 awards going to these institutions.

BOX 9-1
CIBER Programs for Undergraduate and
Graduate Business Training

Ohio State University

Students in Ohio State University's Fisher College of Business programs are eligible to participate in an emerging markets field study course. They begin by studying a world region, then locate specific companies, and target them as case studies. Then the students and faculty visit the region (for about 12 days) and the companies under study and prepare a case study and strategic plan when they return to campus. In comments to the committee, students who had conducted field studies in Thailand and Brazil said the experience abroad had had a greater impact on their education than any other program. They indicated that simply the opportunity to see the differences in the way a plant in another part of the world operates was eye-opening. Two of the students emphasized that, because of full-time work and family obligations, a longer visit abroad would have been impossible. They were so grateful for the opportunity, they said, that they would always support the Fisher School. The Business School ranked 22nd in the 2007 *U.S. News & World Report* business school rankings (U.S. News & World Report, 2006b).

San Diego State University (SDSU)

At SDSU, the undergraduate business degree is extremely popular. With fewer openings than applicants, students must maintain a high grade point average and meet other requirements to enter and stay in the program. Once enrolled, each student selects a language emphasis, which then pairs with one of six world regions as a focus for his or her study. After completing required coursework in business, 32 units of language study, and area studies related to this region, the student spends one semester at an exchange university near the end of their five-year program. While abroad, the student takes courses in both international business and language, paying their SDSU fees. Equal numbers of business students from these institutions spend a semester at SDSU. Originally created with CIBER funds, the program has grown to the point that it is now self-sustaining, with about 800 students enrolled. According to CIBER administrators, graduates of this program command salaries averaging $10,000 more per year than graduates from the regular business program.

SOURCES: Committee site visits (2006) and review of university websites; U.S. News & World Report (2006b).

Infusion of Foreign Languages and Area Studies
into the Business Curriculum

The assistant director of the Texas A&M University CIBER reported that BIE grantees, like CIBERs, frequently emphasize building institutional capacity and quality in international business education (Murphrey, 2006).

Colleges and universities use BIE funds to develop new international business courses and to incorporate international content into existing courses. Many grantees have established formal international business education programs, including certificate programs, and undergraduate majors and minors. They also use funds for faculty development, sponsoring workshops and seminars for business, foreign language, and area studies faculty.

ED supports a shared web portal for the BIE Program, hosted by Grand Valley State University,[5] which is designed to include information about grantees, courses, and events, among other things. Perhaps because of the shorter time frame for BIE grants, the content of the website is not as complete or as extensive as the CIBER webpage.

The primary source of information about the BIE Program is a 2002 survey by Linda V. Gerber, a faculty member affiliated with the CIBER at Texas A&M University. The survey, which included individuals involved in 152 BIE awards between 1989 and 1997, was designed to demonstrate effectiveness in response to the Government Performance and Results Act. The survey focused on typical BIE activities: faculty development, course development, curriculum development, and outreach to business and academia.

Faculty Development

All survey respondents reported at least some faculty development activities, involving an average of 30 faculty members at each institution. The most frequent activity was faculty workshops, followed by support for faculty members to attend professional conferences and to lead international study trips and internships. Showing the linkages between CIBER and BIE grantees, over 60 percent of respondents reported sending faculty to CIBER-sponsored programs. They also reported that they frequently funded individual faculty research projects, indicating that nearly 45 percent of these projects resulted in publications. In addition, over 60 percent of respondents used BIE funding to support individual faculty research.

Course Development

Over 80 percent of respondents said BIE funds were used to support faculty in revising existing courses or creating new international business courses. Survey respondents reported that nearly 130,000 students were enrolled in courses that had been developed or revised with BIE support, an average of nearly 1,900 per institution.

---

[5]See http://www.gvsu.edu/bie/index.cfm?fuseaction=home.first.

Curriculum Development

Sixty-five percent of respondents reported developing new programs. Most frequently, BIE grantees had developed specialized concentrations in MBA programs, such as international accounting or global technology management. Community colleges developed new associate degree programs in business or trade.

Outreach

Most BIE respondents reported agreements with multiple partners. Most frequently, grantees reported agreements with a trade promotion organization, including both governmental organizations, such as the U.S. Department of Commerce Export Assistance Centers, and quasi-governmental organizations, such as world trade councils. The next most common type of partnership was with state and local economic development organizations.

The respondents indicated that, in collaboration with these partners, their most frequent activity was consulting with individual companies on trade and exporting issues, followed by business internships for students and faculty (Gerber, 2002). In addition, two BIE grantees included in the Gerber survey indicated that their outreach activities included development of trade directories. These two grantees indicated that they had distributed over 30,000 copies of the trade directories.

The survey indicated that, in addition to supporting outreach to business, BIE grants support outreach to business education programs: 68 percent of respondents reported activities aimed at helping other institutions internationalize their business curricula. The most frequent way respondents did so was by organizing seminars, workshops, or conferences attended by faculty and administrators from other colleges and universities. They also indicated that they conducted faculty development programs and shared instructional materials with other institutions.

These types of activities may be facilitated by the definition of an eligible BIE applicant. BIE applicants are restricted to higher education institutions that have developed a formal agreement with a business enterprise, trade association, or association engaged in international business activities. These agreements allow two-way communication between business education programs and the business community, guiding grantees toward research, publications, and events tailored to meet specific business needs.

Institutional Capacity

The Gerber study suggests that BIE grants were effective in catalyzing ongoing, sustained activity related to internationalization of business education. For example, in the area of faculty development, nearly 50 percent of respondents indicated that their institution continued to support faculty in attending CIBER-sponsored international business programs following the end of the grant period, and over 30 percent reported that their institution continued to fund individual faculty research on international topics after the end of the grant period. In the area of curriculum development, over 85 percent indicated that their institution continued to offer newly developed international business courses after the end of the grant period. In terms of collaboration with business, over 80 percent reported that their institution continued to work with at least one of their BIE partners after the end of the grant period, and they also reported increased activity with one or more of these partners after the conclusion of the grant. Finally, over 80 percent of BIE grantees that were involved in outreach to other business education programs indicated that they were continuing such activities after the end of the grant period.

However, the extent to which these activities were truly institutionalized, with ongoing financial commitment from the college or university, was not clear. Nearly 80 percent of survey respondents reported applying for subsequent grants, and, among these, 79 percent reported success. Some reported receiving multiple awards, most often in the form of BIE grants. Others reported receiving CIBER or Undergraduate International Studies and Foreign Language grants. Thus, the sustained activity may have been supported by additional outside money, rather than by the host institution itself. In addition, the respondents (the survey had a 58-percent response rate) may have given a more positive outlook than nonrespondents.

Implementation Challenges

The survey illuminated challenges as well as successes. Survey respondents identified two general types of problems. First, they reported problems in bringing together business representatives and faculty and administrators from a variety of disciplines. These ranged from simple scheduling problems to the greater challenge of bridging the cultural divide between business and academic disciplines. The second type of problem appeared to result from insufficient advance planning to ensure that activities were carefully designed to address specific needs or interests in the business or academic community. As a result of poor planning, some activities were poorly attended, some were canceled, and some required extra marketing to succeed (Gerber, 2002).

CONCLUSIONS

In comparison to other Title VI/FH programs, more information is available about the BIE and CIBER programs. The CIBER network, facilitated by ED, has played a key role in generating information about outputs and accomplishments. Two studies have suggested that the programs have contributed to the infusion of foreign language or international business content into the curriculum. BIE and CIBER grants have generated a great deal of activity aimed at Title VI goals. The grants have been used to create new courses on international business and to infuse existing courses with international content. They have been used to support faculty in conducting international business research, developing international courses, and leading students in studies and internships abroad. Grantees have forged collaborations with businesses, government organizations, and trade associations, helping to ensure that international business research, publications, and conferences are aligned with business needs.

Conclusion: The legal requirement for business involvement on CIBER advisory boards provides an appropriate mechanism for business input into the program to enable it to address business needs. The CIBER and BIE programs appear to act as resources for the larger business education community, assisting business schools and undergraduate business programs that are interested in developing capacity to support teaching and research on international business issues.

ED has supported the CIBER grantees in creating and sustaining a strong, collaborative network facilitated by the shared CIBERweb portal.

Conclusion: The CIBERs have created a network for sharing information and learning from each others' experiences that is a model for the other Title VI programs.

The CIBERs, located primarily at large, nationally ranked business schools, share expertise and resources with BIE grantees and with other, smaller, business schools. The BIE grantees, located in a wide range of four-year and two-year institutions, learn from the CIBERs, at the same time sharing their developing expertise in international business education with other institutions.

10

Increasing the Numbers of Underrepresented Minorities in International Service

It is generally recognized that the upper reaches of the U.S. diplomatic corps do not reflect the diversity of the nation. To address this, former secretary of state Colin Powell made the recruitment of minorities at the U.S. Department of State a top priority, stating that he wanted a foreign service that "looks like America" (Powell, 2003). However, recruitment efforts at the late stages of a student's career might also be augmented by reaching out to them at earlier ages, to encourage interest in international affairs, the study of languages, and study abroad. While minority students make up 30 percent of the population of postsecondary students, they make up only 15 percent of the students who choose to study abroad (Institute of International Education, 2004). The Institute for International Public Policy (IIPP) was created in Title VI by Congress in 1992 with the specific mission of preparing minority students for careers in international service. When the law was passed, the Senate Committee on Labor and Human Resources noted with concern that only 13 percent of those serving in the U.S. foreign service were minorities, and only 6 percent were black (Slater, 2006). Around that time, just below 25 percent of the U.S. labor force consisted of people in minority groups, and 11.1 percent of the workforce was black. In 2004, 30 percent of the U.S. labor force consisted of people in minority groups; this is predicted to rise to about 35 percent in 2014 (Toosi, 2005).

There are two ways Title VI and Fulbright-Hays (Title VI/FH) programs strive toward the goal of increasing representation of minorities in international service. The first and most direct way is through IIPP. The second way that this goal is pursued is through projects that have some focus on underrepresented groups, but are funded under other Title VI/FH programs, such as Business and International Education (BIE), Centers for International Business Education and Research (CIBER), Language Resource Centers (LRC), and National Resource Centers (NRC). Title VI/FH efforts to increase minority representation also differ in the organizational level of their focus. IIPP's Fellowship Program focuses on individual participants by encouraging their interest in possible careers in international affairs, helping them learn a language, providing them with study abroad opportunities, preparing them for and assisting them with graduate studies, and helping them enter employment in an international field. IIPP's Institutional Resource Development Grant Program and the projects funded through other Title VI/FH programs focus at the level of the educational institutions and ways that those institutions can more effectively engage and educate minority students on international issues.

IIPP conducted an internal review in 2006 that provides some of the data for this chapter (United Negro College Fund Special Programs Corporation, 2006). In addition, the committee commissioned an analysis of ongoing IIPP data and award information across programs to identify ways in which Title VI/FH programs are attempting to increase the number of underrepresented minorities in international service (Joyner, 2006a). Most of the material in this chapter is drawn from these two sources. Joyner's analysis included a review of data collected by IIPP as well as its internal review of its activities; a review of narrative information provided to the U.S. Department of Education (ED) by institutions that received grants through Title VI/FH programs; and a search of the Evaluation of Exchange, Language, International and Area Studies (EELIAS) database using the minorities subject area to identify other Title VI/FH programs that included a focus on minorities. Joyner notes that this methodology may not have identified all the projects that are targeting efforts toward underrepresented minorities; the strategy used at the time of the committee's review to code subject areas in EELIAS may not have identified all relevant projects.[1] She identified some projects that were not picked up by the subject area search but did not conduct a systematic search of all projects.

IIPP FELLOWSHIP PROGRAM

IIPP is a fairly new program, created in 1992 when the Higher Education Act was reauthorized. The program officially began in 1994 with a congressional appropriation of approximately $1 million. The first award

---

[1]Subject areas were coded by the ED contractor managing the EELIAS system based on their review of the project abstract. In ED's proposed redesigned system, subject area will be entered by the grantee.

was made to the United Negro College Fund, which established the institute. The grant was later transferred to the United Negro College Fund Special Programs Corporation, which competed for it successfully in the most recent competition in 2004. The current grant (FY 2004 through FY 2008) provides $4,871,428 in total funding for the four years.

ED describes its grant to IIPP as being intended to "establish an institute designed to increase the representation of minorities in international services, including private international voluntary organizations and the U.S. Foreign Service" (see http://www.ed.gov/programs/iegpsiipp/index. html, accessed Nov. 2006). Program administrators identify part of their goal as increasing the numbers of members of racial and ethnic minority groups going into the nation's foreign policy institutions with a broader goal of "enhanc[ing] U.S. national security and global competitiveness by promoting excellence, international service and awareness among a broader, more representative cross-section of the American citizenry" (see http://www.uncfsp.org/iipp/content/objectives.cfm, accessed Feb. 2007).

There are two main projects under IIPP: the Fellowship Program, which reaches individual students, and the Institutional Resource Development Grant Program, which targets institutions. Under the institutional program, only one project is currently in operation, the Globalizing Business Schools project, whereby historically black colleges and universities are paired with CIBERs to internationalize the institutions' business curriculum. Two previous projects, no longer funded, involved creation of an Asian studies program and Chinese language studies through distance learning for predominantly minority-serving institutions. Given that there are no available evaluations of the prior projects and an evaluation of the current project is still under way, the committee was not able to come to any conclusions regarding the Institutional Resource Development Grant Program.

IIPP's primary emphasis is on its Fellowship Program, which offers a comprehensive six-component program to undergraduates who are members of racial and ethnic minority groups aimed at preparing them for careers in international affairs. A total of 20 students enter the program each year. Since the program's inception in 1994, there have been 254 participants. IIPP reports that the racial/ethnic breakdown of participants to date is 48.6 percent black, 24.1 percent Hispanic, and 15.6 percent Asian/Pacific Islander; with the remainder in other categories or not reported (United Negro College Fund Special Programs Corporation, 2006). Participants are predominantly female—almost 75 percent. The figure reflects enrollments nationwide: 65 percent of black undergraduates and 74 percent of black graduate students are female (Toosi, 2005). IIPP cites a study by the Institute for International Education (2002), which reports that 65 percent of participants in study abroad programs are female, to suggest that the gender imbalance is not unusual and to highlight that the percentage of women admitted to IIPP is higher than the national average for students in study abroad programs. Fellowship students are offered the following program components:

- Sophomore Summer Policy Institute—students are introduced to international affairs as a field of study; included is a trip to Washington, DC, for briefings at foreign policy agencies and nonprofits, such as the Council on Foreign Relations.
- Junior Year Study Abroad—students study abroad for a semester during their junior year at an accredited institution, following preparation and orientation sessions. IIPP pays for half of the total cost of the semester abroad, including program fees and personal expenses.
- Junior Summer Policy Institute—preparation for graduate study. Students attend an eight-week Junior Summer Policy Institute at the University of Maryland School of Public Policy during the summer following overseas study. The institute is designed to prepare fellows for the rigor of graduate programs and the graduate school application process.
- Summer Language Institute—intensive language study to prepare students for a career or to facilitate acceptance into graduate school. Most fellows study at the Middlebury College Language Schools in Vermont.
- Internship—usually at one of the 100 federal agencies with area or language needs.
- Graduate Fellowships—students are encouraged to enroll in graduate programs in international relations or a related field.

Joyner (2006b) found that students participating in the program are not required to participate in all components; in fact, according to data provided by IIPP, only 16 percent can be shown to have done so. Almost all (99 percent) of program graduates completed the initial Sophomore Summer Policy Institute, and 82 percent studied abroad. Most (91 percent) also completed the Junior Summer Policy Institute. The completion rate for other components was less impressive—35 percent completed the Summer Language Institute, 56 percent completed internships, and 43 percent went on to graduate school (Joyner, 2006b). However, students can skip the language portion if they feel they have adequate skills, and others may choose to attend graduate school at a later date.

IIPP estimates that the program spends, on average, approximately $70,000 to $80,000 per student for those who participate in the full set of activities. Each of the components listed above costs between $9,000 and $12,000 per student, except for the Graduate Fellowship, which costs IIPP $15,000. The IIPP cost is matched by the graduate institution the student is attending.

Given the Fellowship Program's design (i.e., the number of years required to complete all components and the relatively small number of students in any given year) and its relatively short number of years in operation, one would not expect to see a large number of program graduates in international service careers. The first participants entered as college sophomores in summer 1995, and it takes several years to complete an undergraduate degree and a master's degree and then find employment. By IIPP's own estimate, there are only 141 graduates who would meet these criteria.

IIPP did conduct a survey to collect placement data on the first seven cohorts of the program—those IIPP considers to have had time to complete graduate school and enter the workforce. However, they point out several limitations similar to the ones related to NRC graduate placement data discussed in Chapter 6, including the lack of employment history for 35 percent of the students in these seven cohorts (placement data are also unknown for about one-third of NRC graduates). For participants who did provide employment data, responses are difficult to interpret because the employment categories are not well defined in the survey. Participants' employment choices were business, government, international organization, educational organization, nonprofit organization, and research organization, with no definitions or instructions on how the categories differed (United Negro College Fund Special Programs Corporation, 2006).

Of the 141 participants in the first seven cohorts, employment data were obtained for 93 of them. The program could clearly document only 38 placements (27 percent of all participants and 41 percent of those for whom placement data were available) that they would consider a success: 22 participants employed in government and another 16 employed at an international organization. IIPP considers employment in either government or an international organization to represent employment in a position "congruent with the IIPP program." Given the ambiguity in definitions, however, it is unclear whether this number overstates or understates the number of program alumni in international service. For example, those employed in government could be employed in federal, state, or local government and in any kind of capacity, engaged in activity with no relationship to international affairs. Those who found employment in other categories—educational, nonprofit, or research—might indeed be engaged in international activities. There is also no record of how many program graduates found employment with the State Department, in accord with ED's goals.

The goals of IIPP's internal evaluation also included assessing the program's impact on the participants' personal and professional lives. Of the 212 students who had entered in cohorts 1 through 10, 122 (57.5 percent) completed the web-based survey that elicited self-reports on this aspect of the program. Their responses indicated that the program led to multiple personal benefits, such as an enhanced personal support network, goal focus, and personal insight; increased commitment to work in international service; and provided multiple professional benefits, including expanded career options and improved knowledge of international issues and events.

The internal evaluation also identified several ways in which IIPP could improve its activities, including the collection of better data on employment outcomes and doing more to encourage and facilitate careers in international service. The latter point is an important one. While IIPP participants report that the program has had a positive impact on them, it is not yet getting large numbers of participants into international service. The Fellowship Program produced only 212 students from underrepresented groups in its first 10 years, and only a small number of the graduates who might be expected to be employed can be shown to have gained employment in international service or to be pursuing such employment. Its evaluation states that there is a "gap between the commitment to international service, the percentage of fellows that major in this area in graduate school, and the number of fellows that pursue a career in international service" (United Negro College Fund Special Programs Corporation, 2006, p. 39). Former IIPP fellows have recommended that the program explore service agreements with federal agencies (as with the National Security Education Program); agreements with federal agencies and other organizations to open entry-level positions would have to be negotiated as a means to address this problem. IIPP also concluded that career advising had to be strengthened in order to get more participants employed in international service careers, and that current and former participants could be better used in a networking or mentoring role in order to help other participants with decisions about graduate school or career opportunities.

OTHER TITLE VI-FUNDED PROJECTS
AIMED AT MINORITY STUDENTS

Projects other than IIPP aimed at increasing opportunities for minorities in international careers fall into two categories: outreach to students and faculty and research on barriers to fuller participation of underrepresented minorities in international service.

Table 10-1 summarizes some of the institutional efforts to increase minority representation that have been funded by other programs under Title VI/FH. For example, two CIBER programs have collaborated with IIPP, through its Institutional Resource Development Grant Program, in involving historically black colleges and universities. The University of Washington NRC has introduced Arabic classes in Seattle high schools with high minority enrollments. The University of the Incarnate Word, which serves predominantly Hispanic students, has received a BIE grant to sup-

TABLE 10-1 Title VI-Funded Institutional Projects Related to Increasing Representation of Minorities

Grantee	Grant Cycle	Description
Program: Institute for International Public Policy (IIPP)		
United Negro College Fund Special Programs Corporation	FY 2004- 2008	Administers training, institutional resource development, outreach, and research programs aimed at involving a more representative cross-section of the American citizenry in international affairs.
Program: Business and International Education (BIE)		
University of the Incarnate Word	FY 2005- 2006	The grantee, a Hispanic-serving institution, will expand internships and study abroad and other opportunities for students to acquire international business expertise in the European Union; and strengthen faculty expertise and instructional resources on the European Union.
Program: Center for International Business Education (CIBER)		
Indiana University-Bloomington	FY 2002- 2005	The grantee's CIBER participated in a consortium project that pairs eight business schools with a partner from the community of historically black colleges and universities. This CIBER assisted Norfolk State University with a BIE proposal to ED. A collaboration with IIPP.
Texas A&M University	FY 2002- 2005	One of this CIBER's outreach activities is its membership in the CIBER/United Negro College Fund initiative to promote the internationalization of business education at historically black colleges and universities. A collaboration with IIPP.
Program: Language Resource Centers (LRC)		
University of Hawaii-Manoa	FY 2002- 2005	The grantee, an LRC, has focused on distance learning of less commonly taught languages, particularly Asian languages. One project extended instruction to the beginning and second-year levels via a mix of face-to-face and online instruction. Testing of the beginning-level Mandarin Chinese course was done in cooperation with the United Negro College Fund and Dillard University in New Orleans. A collaboration with IIPP.
Program: National Resource Centers (NRC)		
University of Hawaii-Manoa	FY 2003- 2005	The Center for Southeast Asian Studies has emphasized mentoring faculties from other minority-serving institutions in Southeast Asian studies. A collaboration with IIPP.
University of Washington	FY 2003- 2005	One outreach activity of this NRC was to teach Arabic in four Seattle public high schools, three of which were in economically disadvantaged neighborhoods with a high proportion of minorities enrolled.

TABLE 10-1 Continued

Grantee	Grant Cycle	Description
Program: International Research and Studies (IRS)		
National Association for Equal Opportunity in Higher Education	FY 2005-2007	The National Association for Equal Opportunity in Higher Education, an association of 118 historically and predominantly black colleges and universities, will conduct a survey of these institutions to understand their current status and capacity to provide instruction in common and less commonly taught foreign languages as well as international studies.
United Negro College Fund Special Programs Corporation	FY 2005-2006	This project has four goals: (1) to provide relevant and comprehensive data about the attitudes and participation patterns of minority undergraduates with respect to international education activities and programs; (2) to identify factors that impact their participation; (3) to develop replicable strategies and assessment tools that institutions can use to assess and increase minority participation; and (4) to widely disseminate the results in an effort to broaden the national dialogue among federal, state, and campus leaders on international education issues to include topics of access, diversity, and minority student interests and needs.
University of Pittsburgh	FY 2003-2004	A national study of the effects of institutional factors at public four-year colleges and universities on the participation of undergraduate ethnic and racial minorities in international education opportunities.

SOURCE: Joyner (2006b).

port study of the European Union. In addition to the above efforts, three research projects have been funded by IRS to address barriers to minority participation in international programs and subsequent careers.

These studies may yield useful insights about how to increase minority representation in international education. Joyner (2006b) concludes that the initiatives that are attempting institutional change have the potential to affect a larger number of students than does IIPP's Fellowship Program. Current Title VI/FH programs aside from IIPP might be reworked in such a way as to involve more minority students, even at the high school level. Although there have been no studies of the success of these programs, it appears that adding a component of outreach to minority students under other Title VI programs, such as NRC, LRC, Undergraduate International Studies and Foreign Language, BIE, and CIBER, is worth exploring.

OTHER FEDERAL PROGRAMS WITH SIMILAR GOALS

Other federal programs with similar goals appear to be reaching out to far larger numbers of students in minority groups and getting them to study abroad, attend graduate school, and go into international service careers. These programs appear to have a strong expectation that participants will continue in international service careers. Some State Department programs feature mentors who are currently in the Foreign Service to guide students along in the process. While the committee did not undertake any review of the effectiveness of these programs and makes no judgments about them, we discuss these programs for the purpose of rough comparison and to place Title VI/FH programs such as IIPP in the context of similar programs that also seek to increase minority interest in international careers.

The State Department's Thomas Pickering Foreign Affairs Fellowship Program identifies promising students interested in careers at the State Department. The legislation creating the program states that "special emphasis" should be placed on recruiting minority students. Fellowships are awarded each year on the basis of academic merit and financial need to sophomore or senior students attending a four-year college or university. Participants selected as sophomores are eligible to receive funding for their junior and senior years and first year of graduate school. Participating schools provide financial support for the final year of graduate study, based on need. Students selected as seniors are eligible to receive funding for both years of graduate school.

Participants then attain a master's degree in a field related to international affairs from a leading graduate school. Also, participants complete two required paid internships: a 10-week domestic internship in various offices throughout the State Department, depending on their academic interest, and a 10-week internship at a U.S. embassy or consulate abroad. In addition, all participants partner with a senior Foreign Service officer as a mentor prior to the start of their graduate studies; the mentor keeps in touch with the student to help make decisions about graduate study and to prepare academically for the Foreign Service examination. Administrators of the Pickering Program report that the mentoring component is crucial to its success.

There also is a service requirement for the Pickering Program; that is, fellows are contractually tied to employment as Foreign Service officers. Students completing the undergraduate fellowship serve for a period of at least 4.5 years, and graduate fellows must serve for a period of at least 3 years.

The Pickering Program has a high completion rate: 94.5 percent. Since the program's inception in 1992, it has funded 325 participants, and of these, fewer than 20 fellows have withdrawn or resigned. Again, administrators attribute this in part to the mentoring aspect of the program. A total of 40 new fellows are chosen each year. For an annual budget of $5 million (FY 2007), the program funds 118 students at various stages of their studies (email correspondence with State Department staff, January 3, 2007).

Additional programs that seek to increase minority interest in international careers also exist:

- The *Charles Rangel International Affairs Graduate Fellowship Program* (administered by Howard University), is very similar to the Pickering Program but is even more specifically aimed at getting minority students into graduate international affairs programs and then into the Foreign Service. Like IIPP, it starts with a summer session following the students' junior year to prepare them for graduate school and educate them about career paths. As with the Pickering Program, participants benefit from two internships: one with a member of Congress and another at a U.S. embassy overseas. Participants are required to attend graduate school in a relevant field and then take the State Department's Foreign Service examination. Current Foreign Service officers act as mentors. A total of 10 fellowships of up to $28,000 are awarded annually.

- The *Louis Stokes Educational Scholarship Program* was created by U.S. Representative Louis Stokes (D-OH), whose tenure in Congress included chairmanship of the House Intelligence Committee. The purpose is to bring more women and minorities into employment with the federal law enforcement and intelligence agencies. The program is administered in different ways by participating agencies. At the National Security Agency (NSA), for example, applicants for the Stokes language program must be minority college sophomores majoring in foreign languages, with at least six credits completed in Arabic, Chinese, Farsi, or Korean. They must have a minimum college freshman grade point average of 3.0. Grantees work during the summer at NSA in areas related to their course of study. They receive tuition at the college of their choice, reimbursement for books and fees, housing and travel, a year-round salary, and employment with NSA after graduation for at least 1.5 times the length of study.

- The *Gilman Scholarship*, sponsored by the State Department, aims to broaden the student population that studies abroad by supporting undergraduates who have been traditionally underrepresented and those who might otherwise not participate due to financial constraints. This includes students studying in nontraditional locations, community college students, students of diverse ethnic backgrounds, students representing a diverse range of institutions and institutional types, students with disabilities, and students of nontraditional age. The scholarship program provides awards to students who are receiving federal Pell grant funding at a two-year or four-year college or university; the average award is approximately $4,000. There were 351 recipients in 2004-2005.

• The *Public Policy and International Affairs Fellowship Program*, formerly known as Woodrow Wilson Fellowships in Public Policy and International Affairs, has produced over 2,500 alumni since its inception in 1980. Interestingly, it is not a federal program; instead, it was formed when a number of professional associations for policy analysts and public administrators joined with foundations to address the problem of minority representation in positions of leadership in public service. Increasing minority representation in international service was added as a goal in 1989. The program targets minority students in their junior year of college. Participants are expected to attend a junior summer institute to prepare them for graduate study; to attend graduate school and earn a degree related to public policy, public administration, or international affairs; and then to pursue employment in a public service-related career. The graduate schools that form the consortium of participating institutions represent the nation's major public policy graduate schools. Graduates of the program have gone on to employment with the State Department.

CONCLUSIONS AND RECOMMENDATIONS

International education programs appear to have had little effect so far on the number of underrepresented minorities in international service, but it is possible to make more of an impact in the future. Currently, primary responsibility for encouraging minority involvement in international studies seems concentrated in one program, IIPP. There are two problems with this approach. First, IIPP is not reaching very many students and, second, greater potential may exist under other component parts of Title VI/FH to reach many more minority students. The goal of maximizing interest by minority students in foreign languages, area, and international studies is too important to be left to one corner of Title VI/FH; instead, efforts in this area should be made across a wide variety of the programs.

IIPP has enrolled approximately 250 students over the past 12 years, but the grantees can document only 22 students who have entered any kind of government employment and only 16 who work for an international organization. While this may be an undercount, and collection of data and analysis of job placements of graduates are difficult in general, the IIPP Program has not yet demonstrated significant results and has few graduates to date and significant costs per fellow. The general awareness of what IIPP does is quite low; it might attract more students with a significant interest in international service or the Foreign Service if its profile was raised.

The small number of graduates and significant costs per fellow for all components is influenced by the comprehensive design of the program. Yet few fellows complete all components of the program—particularly the final components. Fewer, more targeted components would enable more students to participate and might result in more fellows completing the program and pursuing international careers. This would require an assessment of the relative contributions of each component and should include exploration of promising models from other similar programs. IIPP has engaged in some institutionally based collaborative efforts with other Title VI-funded projects, but no information is available about how successful those have been.

Recommendation 10-1: **The Institute for International Public Policy should redesign its activities in order to increase graduation rates and facilitate entry in careers in international service.**

In considering how to redesign its programs, IIPP should examine other programs with similar goals, such as PPIA and the Pickering, Rangel, and Stokes fellowship programs. This should include exploring how these programs nurture an interest in international service, encourage completion of the program, and facilitate graduates' employment in the Foreign Service, other federal bureaucracies, and international organizations. IIPP might also do well to partner with institutions, such as those in PPIA's consortium of graduate schools, that already graduate large numbers of students who go on to careers in international affairs. IIPP should also explore opportunities for direct partnerships with potential government employers. In addition, in accord with the recommendations of its internal review, IIPP should also make more use of program alumni as mentors to assist current participants in completing the program and finding relevant employment. Mentors can also be identified at the foreign affairs bureaucracies who could advise participants wishing to pursue a career in international service; the Pickering and Rangel fellowship programs might serve as models.

There is potential in efforts under a wide variety of Title VI/FH programs to reach out to minority students. Greater responsibility for this important goal should be shared among as many of the programs as possible. Because foreign language, area, and international studies programs are already established at a wide variety of college campuses with significant minority enrollments, minority outreach should be emphasized. ED should do more to increase the numbers of minority students who see international service as a viable career track and to indicate their interest in grantees reaching this population. This might include ensuring that new initiatives aimed at K-12 include efforts to recruit minority students. Universities' ability to attract minority students will be dependent in part on the interests students bring with them from high school.

Recommendation 10-2: **The Department of Education should encourage Title VI and Fulbright-Hays grantees to actively recruit minority members.**

The potential reach of other Title VI/FH programs is far greater than IIPP alone and ED should convey its interest in enhanced efforts to recruit minority students. Applicants might be encouraged, for example, to conduct outreach to K-12 school districts with large minority enrollments or heritage and immigrant populations, and ED might facilitate partnerships between Foreign Language Assistance Program grantees with substantial minority enrollments and Title VI grantees. ED could award points for such efforts in the review process. To help raise awareness of interest in recruiting members of minority groups and to collect information on the overall number of minority students who participate in Title VI/FH, ED might also consider requiring grantees to report the number of minority students served via its online grantee monitoring system. The feasibility of this data collection should be discussed as part of the recommended continuous improvement process (see Chapter 11).

Part III

Important Next Steps

In addition to reviewing the performance of the Title VI and Fulbright-Hays programs in the eight key areas, the committee was asked to make recommendations for strategies to enhance the effectiveness of the programs in the future, as well as further research to address the limitations of the current review. This part addresses those aspects of the committee's charge. Chapter 11 discusses issues related to program implementation, monitoring, and evaluation, and Chapter 12 discusses needed strategic actions as the programs look toward future challenges and opportunities.

11

Monitoring, Evaluation, and Continuous Improvement

The extent to which programs can meet their objectives is dependent in part on how they are managed at the national level. The preceding several chapters outlined the evidence available to characterize the performance of the Title VI and Fulbright-Hays (Title VI/FH) programs in each of the eight key areas identified by Congress. However, neither the data available in the Evaluation of Exchange, Language, International and Area Studies (EELIAS) database nor the few available evaluation studies enable an assessment of the relative value of each of the 14 component programs. Program monitoring and performance measurement efforts have largely been conducted as a top-down enterprise accompanied by little consultation with grantees. Yet program performance is also partially dependent on the extent to which universities and other grantees share program goals and work collaboratively to accomplish those goals. Although there are a few examples of mechanisms that facilitate coordination and identification of promising practices across programs (see the description in Chapter 9 of CIBERweb), and the center programs have established an effective process for involvement in national policy making, there is no established process to facilitate continual assessment and improvement.

This chapter discusses the status of program monitoring and program evaluation activities and outlines ways that the U.S. Department of Education (ED) should advance its efforts in these areas. It also presents the limitations of current collaborations with grantees and a recommended approach to continuous improvement that would complement and potentially enhance the department's efforts to ensure the effectiveness of the Title VI/FH programs.

PROGRAM MONITORING

At ED, program monitoring is carried out by program officers in the International Education Programs Service (IEPS) who are assigned to a particular program(s) or, in the case of the National Resource Center (NRC) program, a particular world area. Unlike in the past, when financial and project (programmatic) monitoring was conducted by separate staff, program officers are currently responsible for both functions, although their work focuses primarily on financial monitoring. At the same time, the number of program staff required to administer has increased over time. In recent years, full-time-equivalent staffing levels have decreased, dropping from 23 in FY 2003 to 21 in FY 2006, despite congressional concerns articulated in the FY 2003 budget.[1]

Limited staff combined with limited travel resources and departmental policies related to travel approval have severely limited the ability of staff to visit grantees. ED has an increased emphasis in project-level evaluation in part to address the limits on their ability to conduct on-site reviews. For example, the number of points awarded for evaluation plans has been increased in the past several NRC competitions, and it is now the criterion with the highest number of points (25 of 165). In addition, ED is now requiring NRCs to include a professional evaluator as well as a peer evaluator in their evaluation plans. The effectiveness of this new emphasis on evaluation is as yet unknown.

Like most federal programs, the Title VI/FH programs require their grantees to submit annual reports to review the progress of individual grantees and to assist efforts to evaluate the performance of the programs overall. For most of the programs' history, annual reports were submitted in paper format. In recent years, as discussed below, IEPS shifted from a paper to an electronic, web-based system (EELIAS) for collecting grantee information.[2]

In 1978, the General Accounting Office recommended that Title VI/FH programs share evaluative data with grantees to provide information about accomplishments and guidance for possible improvements. At the request of the President's Commission on Foreign Language and International Studies in 1979, ED staff prepared an analysis on how NRCs use their funds based on reports submitted by grantees (Scheider, 1979). Other staff-generated memos to the NRC and Foreign Language and Area Studies (FLAS) Fellowships directors distributed in the mid-1990s provide analytic syntheses

---

[1]Congress stated: "The conferees are disappointed that the Department has not fully addressed the staffing needs of the Title VI and Fulbright-Hays international education programs" (House Report 108-010).

[2]Shortly before release of the committee's report, the system was revised and released as the International Resource Information System.

BOX 11-1
Categories of Performance Measures

Inputs: Resources used (e.g., amount of funding).

Activities: Types of work performed (e.g., number of publications or workshops, number of students who study abroad).

Outputs: Results from program activities (e.g., number of students enrolled).

Outcomes: An accomplishment attributable to program outputs (e.g., improvement in language proficiency, job placement).

Impact: Achievement of broad social objectives (e.g., increased global understanding).

SOURCES: Adapted from Joyner (2006a).

---

of data from annual reports on such criteria as average number of degrees awarded, career choice, and distribution of degrees by discipline (Schneider, 1995). The committee was told that data had been compiled from reports at the end of every funding cycle since the 1970s. Other reports on program performance, such as those mentioned above, seem to have disappeared with the transition to an electronic system.

Performance Measures

The Government Performance and Results Act (GPRA) requires all federal programs to report measures of program performance, with several types of possible measures (see Box 11-1). Until recently, ED had performance measures for the NRC and FLAS programs only, which were used to report performance on all the Title VI domestic programs. After an Office of Management and Budget (OMB) review under the Program Assessment Rating Tool (PART) process[3] that resulted in a rating of "results not demonstrated," the program developed specific performance measures for each of the 14 programs (see Table 11-1). There are now two performance measures and one efficiency measure for most programs with an emphasis on measures intended to indicate outcomes, as preferred by OMB. The measures were recently approved by OMB.

---

[3]OMB conducts periodic program reviews using PART and assigns one of five ratings as a result of the process: (1) effective, (2) moderately effective, (3) adequate, (4) ineffective, and (5) results not demonstrated.

TABLE 11-1 Planned Title VI/Fulbright-Hays Performance Measures

Program	Performance Measures		Efficiency Measure
NRC	Percentage of critical languages taught, as reflected in the list of critical languages referenced in the Title VI program statute.	Percentage of employed master's and doctoral degree graduates in fields of postsecondary education or government.	Cost per master's or doctoral degree graduate employed in fields of postsecondary education or government.
FLAS	Average language competency score of FLAS fellowship recipients at the end of one full year of instruction will be at least 1.20 levels higher than their average score at the beginning of the year.	Percentage of employed master's and doctoral degree graduates in fields of postsecondary education or government.	Cost per fellow increasing average language competency by at least one level.
CIBE	Percentage of graduates of a Ph.D. or master's, including MBA, program with significant international business concentration at the postsecondary institution who are employed in business-related fields, including teaching at a business school.	Percentage of projects reported and validated as of high quality or successfully completed.	Cost per master's, including MBA, degree recipient or Ph.D. graduate employed in business-related fields, including teaching in a business school.
IRS	Number of outreach activities that result in adoption or further dissemination within a year, divided by the total number of IRS outreach activities conducted in the current reporting period.	Percentage of projects reported and validated as of high quality or successfully completed.	Cost per high-quality, successfully completed project.
LRC	Number of outreach activities that result in adoption or further dissemination within a year, divided by the total number of LRC outreach activities conducted in the current reporting period.	Percentage of projects reported and validated as of high quality or successfully completed.	Cost per high-quality, successfully completed project.
UISFL	Percentage of critical languages addressed/covered by foreign language major, minor, or certificate programs created or enhanced; or by language courses created or enhanced; or by faculty or instructor positions created with UISFL or matching funds in the reporting period.	Percentage of projects reported and validated as of high quality or successfully completed.	Cost per high-quality, successfully completed project.

TABLE 11-1 Continued

Program	Performance Measures		Efficiency Measure
BIE	Number of outreach activities that result in adoption or further dissemination within a year, divided by the total number of BIE outreach activities conducted in the current reporting period.	Percentage of projects reported and validated as of high quality or successfully completed.	Cost per high-quality, successfully completed project.
TICFIA	Percentage of projects reported and validated as of high quality or successfully completed.	N/A	Cost per high-quality, successfully completed project.
AORC	Percentage of projects reported and validated as of high quality or successfully completed.	Percentage of scholars who indicated they were "highly satisfied" with the services the center provided.	Cost per high-quality, successfully completed project.
DDRA	Average fellow increases language competency by at least 0.75 level.	Percentage of projects reported and validated as of high quality or successfully completed.	Cost per grantee increasing language competency by at least one level in one area (or all three).
FRA	Average fellow increases language competency by at least 0.50 level.	Percentage of projects reported and validated as of high quality or successfully completed.	Cost per grantee increasing language competency by at least one level in one area (or all three).
GPA	Average fellow increases language competency by at least 0.50 level.	Percentage of projects reported and validated as of high quality or successfully completed.	Cost per grantee increasing language competency by at least one level in one area (or all three).
SA	Percentage of projects reported and validated as of high quality or successfully completed.	N/A	Cost per high-quality, successfully completed project.
IIPP	Percentage of employed IIPP graduates in government or international service.	Percentage of IIPP participants who complete a master's degree within six years of enrolling in the program.	Cost per IIPP graduate employed in government or international service.

The measures are based on a combination of quantitative (e.g., graduate placements, language courses, self-reported language proficiency) and narrative (e.g., accomplishments) information provided by grantees to ED via its web-based grantee reporting system.

The performance measures identified appear to have been developed with little or no input from the universities or other organizations who receive funding. Although designed to measure outcomes as much as possible, little thought seems to have been given to the goals of the programs or how to best measure performance against those goals. Several universities expressed concern about the measures for which they are being held accountable, pointing to several issues: (1) Monitoring the percentage of languages taught overlooks the level of language taught and might create a disincentive to offer advanced-level language courses. (2) Placements in fields other than academia and government are reasonable outcomes not reflected in the placement measures (see Chapter 6 for further discussion of this issue). (3) The two measures used do not reflect the emphasis placed on outreach.

EELIAS Database

The EELIAS system, reportedly developed with input from the field, appears to have been designed to capture all potentially useful data, using the NRC program as the model (see Box 11-2 for background information). It is not clear, however, whether full consideration was given to how the data would be used for program monitoring—that is, the specific performance measures to be used and how the required data would be used to report those measures. In practice, the system has been used by ED exclusively for two purposes: (1) to enable project officers to review the performance of individual grantees and make decisions about annual continuation grants for multiyear grants[4] and (2) to report performance measures. The project officer review uses primarily narrative information and appears to be a one-way review, with no feedback to the grantee.

The purpose of the extensive quantifiable data collected that are not used for performance measures is also unclear. No information has been given to grantees on how their performance compares with other grantees, and no other aggregate reports have been produced. The system is widely viewed by universities as a burdensome, time-consuming requirement, not a resource. Many universities pointed out that the time required to collect and then enter the required information is significant, particularly in rela-

---

[4]The committee was told that a continuation award has never been denied as a result of this review.

BOX 11-2
Evolution of ED's Grant Monitoring Database

The Evaluation of Exchange, Language, and International Area Studies (EELIAS) database was developed by the National Foreign Language Center under a grant from the Title VI International Research and Studies program. Developed over a period of several years, it was intended to be used as a grant monitoring tool and to provide data for ED to report program performance to the Office of Management and Budget, as required by the Government Performance and Results Act. It was developed as an online grantee reporting system intended to provide information on the language, international, and area studies components of the Title VI/FH programs. National Resource Centers (NRC) and Foreign Language and Area Studies (FLAS) grantees were the first to report information into the system, beginning in the early 2000s. Other programs were phased in over time, and an ED contractor has been entering historical grantee information. Multiyear grantees submit both annual and final reports. According to both ED staff and the committee's own review, the data are most reliable for the NRC and FLAS programs. In fact, there is some thought among other grantees that the system was designed for those programs and imposed onto their programs.

Technical issues with the design of the system, as well as incompleteness of data, make it difficult to use aggregate data for program evaluation purposes. ED worked with a contractor to develop a revised system designed to correct technical issues. The revised and renamed International Resource Information System should address some of the database's technical limitations and make grantee-level information more readily accessible. However, it is unclear whether and if so, how, the new system will result in improved program-level or aggregate information or public access to data used in reporting performance measures, which are necessary to ensure transparency.

---

tion to the relatively small amount of money received and given that they do not get any summary data or other feedback.[5]

The department has grappled with the same technical issues related to lack of internal controls, frequent use of open-ended questions and an "other" category, limited data verification, and missing data encountered by the committee (see Appendix B, Box B-1) that limited our ability to use much of the EELIAS data for program-level review. The committee notes that the system was designed under a grant rather than a contract. Grants do not typically allow significant feedback from the sponsoring agency and are not the ideal mechanism for developing a program monitoring

---

[5]In fact, several universities reported that they were not aware that they could access their own data, and certainly did not know how to do so once it had been submitted.

tool. Nonetheless, ED made the decision to implement the system across all Title VI/FH programs. Perhaps recognizing the limitations posed by the grant mechanism, ED is now managing the system with the assistance of a contractor, which enables substantially greater control over the product. Concurrent with the committee's deliberations, ED was in the midst of a systematic review of the database, with the assistance of its contractor. ED is aware of many of the issues encountered by the committee. In fact, it independently shared observations about the system's limitations and its proposed solutions. Near the end of the committee's deliberations, ED published in the *Federal Register* proposed system changes that will reportedly fix most if not all of the technical issues with the system we have identified (U.S. Department of Education, 2006d). Select grantees were asked to review the navigability of the new system, including a prototype for a new user interface.

However, it appears that use of the redesigned system, which was renamed the International Resource Information System when launched as a "new" system (see http://www.ieps-iris.org) shortly before release of the committee's report, will continue to focus on individual grant monitoring and reporting performance measures. The redesign will make access to select system components more readily available, but it will not make basic data available. It also does not make data used for performance measures readily accessible. In addition, the redesign does not appear to address questions related to the purpose and use of the required data.

Data Transparency

At the time of this writing, although ED reported that it has considered open web-based access to the database, a web-based interface with additional query potential (e.g., languages taught, graduate placements), and production of additional summary reports, a decision had not been made about whether to make data public and, if so, which data. Several universities made the observation that open access to the data would reveal any differences in the way universities are reporting data and highlight missing data, informally encouraging data continuity. Greater system transparency would be likely to facilitate a vested interest on the part of grantees in the timeliness and comparability of data.

The committee is aware of only three efforts (two of which were requests for the same data) by organizations other than the system developer[6] to access the data. The Social Science Research Council planned to undertake an evaluation of Middle East NRCs funded by the International

---

[6]The system developers conducted two related studies that used EELIAS data to review language enrollments: Brecht and Rivers (2000) and Brecht et al. (2007).

Research and Studies Program (IRS) using EELIAS data and was required to submit a Freedom of Information Act request to access the database. However, such issues as the difficulty of analyzing responses to open-ended questions related to languages taught and type of instructor hampered the ability of the research team to use the data to answer their initial questions (Browne, 2006). In addition, Steven Heydemann of Georgetown University and Martin Kramer of the Washington Institute for Near East Policy[7] submitted separate requests to ED and received a spreadsheet with NRC placement data for 2002 (see the discussion in Chapter 6). Although using the same data, they came to very different conclusions about the program's success in producing graduates who enter government service, based on their starting assumptions. Had these data been publicly available, a more informed public discourse might have been possible.

If the planned improvements to the database are well implemented, the system may offer the potential to provide better information to the field. Well-designed grantee data systems can be useful program monitoring tools to help track trends, collect data on outputs, and ensure that funds are used for their intended purposes. When the information collected is viewed as useful to those reporting it, and information is in fact returned to them, it is likely to be of higher quality. It is important to note that the planned improvements to the system are aimed at fixing technical glitches and improving user navigability. Consideration was not given to whether the data collected should be collected and how it would be used for program monitoring or improvement purposes. Basic functionality will not change. That is, data elements are not being increased or decreased. ED might be well served by convening grantees to discuss the current data collected and how it can be modified to address mutual objectives (see below for further discussion). ED should undertake a systematic evaluation involving grantees to ensure that the changes made through the launch of its redesign system have been implemented effectively, that the data are fully usable and understandable, and that the expected value of the data is clear. In comments shared with the committee, Brustein (2006) reinforced this and related points, claiming that there is insufficient dissemination of project outcomes and best practices, as well as a lack of accessible and searchable databases.

PROGRAM EVALUATION

Although well-designed grantee data systems are vital program monitoring tools, they are rarely adequate to assess the effectiveness of programs

---

[7]Martin Kramer requested the data to verify information included in an article published by Steven Heydemann based in part on the placement data.

in terms of outcomes and impacts or to understand why identified trends are occurring. These more detailed and nuanced assessments require well-designed program evaluations that include information on both what is achieved and how it is achieved. Few Title VI/FH program evaluations have been conducted in general; even fewer have focused on program outcomes. Of the evaluations that have been conducted (see Appendix B, Attachment B-1), most have involved surveys of grantees only. Although control groups are infeasible, almost none have had a comparison group. Many have been funded by the IRS Program via grants designed and implemented with little ED input. Although IRS proposals are reviewed by peer review panels, and some of the criteria seem to be aimed at ensuring a quality evaluation project (e.g., 15 of 100 points for an evaluation plan, 10 points for adequacy of method and scope of project, 10 points for knowledge to be gained), grants are initiated and managed by the principal investigator. Grants are typically not the ideal mechanism for federal program evaluation, given the relative independence given to grantees. Contracts, which allow more specification of research questions and methodology and greater involvement in the research design and implementation, would be a preferable mechanism.

Only one recent evaluation—the survey of fellowship recipients that included the FLAS and Doctoral Dissertation Research Abroad (DDRA) programs in addition to two other ED fellowship programs—was conducted under an ED contract that enabled regular, ongoing review and feedback by the department. This survey was funded by the Office of Planning, Evaluation and Policy Development (OPEPD). It is also the only evaluation that included more than one Title VI program. As Gabara (2006) reported to the committee, more research should be done on national needs, and evaluations of programs should look at their accomplishments over the past 15 years. Given that the programs are now firmly established, more periodic, well-designed evaluations with clearly articulated outcomes are warranted—perhaps every four to five years. This would make available up-to-date program evaluation information for PART reviews and for reauthorization deliberations.[8] Christian (2006) reported that there seems to be some dissatisfaction with the way projects are evaluated (regarding the indicators used), as well as some thought that it is difficult to measure success for some of them, or that they cannot all be evaluated in the same way. Program evaluations, ideally with input from the field, will have to carefully consider the expectations of the programs and the use of best practices in achieving those goals.

---

[8]Under PART, each program is to be reviewed at least every five years. The Higher Education Act is supposed to be reauthorized on a six-year cycle.

CONTINUOUS IMPROVEMENT

Modern governance theory suggests that educational programs are more likely to improve if goals are clear, participants have a voice in defining objectives and internalizing the goals in their own systems, quantitative indicators of process are available and made public, and efforts are made to identify and duplicate promising practices (see, for example, Liebman and Sabel, 2003). Neither ED nor the established mechanisms to communicate across grantees have made this a priority. In fact, universities (the primary Title VI/FH grantees) have been little involved in ED's efforts to monitor performance or identify strategic directions, although there have been some recent attempts to improve in this area.

ED has historically convened a meeting in Washington, DC, of all grantees for each program after each competition, but it has not held national meetings in the years between the multiyear award cycles and has met separately with each program. In September 2006, ED convened all NRC and Language Resource Centers (LRC) grantees at the same event, the first such meeting involving leaders of both programs. The agenda included not only presentations by IEPS staff about grant reporting requirements, but also panels of invited experts and grantees, who shared their knowledge of such complex topics as assessing language acquisition and evaluating the impact of study abroad. This event also included an open town hall meeting for feedback from the field to IEPS staff. ED plans to convene more information-sharing and technical assistance meetings in 2007: the first will focus on language acquisition, and the second will be about outreach. This appears to represent a distinct shift from earlier years and an attempt to actively engage the field in relevant issues.

Each of the major programs has established an independent mechanism for communication across projects. Each program has a dues-paying organization of program directors: NRCs have the Council of NRC Directors, LRCs have the Council of Directors of National Foreign Language Resource Centers, and Centers for International Business Education and Research (CIBER) have the Association for International Business and Research. At a minimum, each group gets together (without ED staff present) in conjunction with the ED-sponsored grantee meeting for its program. The Council of NRC Directors organized a major conference at the University of California, Los Angeles, in 1997 prior to renewal of the Higher Education Act. The conference, which included grantees of other Title VI programs as well as NRC directors, was reported to have a major influence on Congress and to have led to creation of the Technological Innovation and Cooperation for Foreign Information Access (TICFIA) program (Ruther, 2003). American Overseas Research Centers (AORC) have created the Council of American Overseas Research Centers.

The LRCs and the CIBERs also have websites (the content of the CIBER web site is significantly greater than the LRC site; see Chapter 9) and collect and synthesize performance data based on the data submitted via EELIAS. IEPS staff have actively encouraged the creation and content of the CIBER web site and have supported a shared web portal for the Business and International Education (BIE) program, hosted by Grand Valley State University (2006). The committee was told that the Council of NRC Directors agreed in September 2006 to establish a web presence, but that it is on hold pending a decision by ED regarding what EELIAS information they might be making available via the web.

The director of each council or association is also a member of the Coalition for International Education (CIE), whose membership includes a range of other national organizations concerned with higher education, foreign language, or international education issues. CIE aims to build consensus within the higher education community on policies affecting the programs and advocates for grantees in the annual federal budgeting and appropriations process. CIE convened a national conference in 2003, with support from ED and the Ford Foundation, for Title VI grantees to discuss demand for global education after the terrorist attacks of September 11, 2001, and to prepare for reauthorization of the Higher Education Act. The upcoming 50th anniversary of Title VI in 2008 is likely to provide another opportunity for a reflective view of the programs.

In addition to sharing information through these national associations, grantees report that they discuss common issues and opportunities for collaboration through informal meetings at professional associations, such as the Asia Studies Association and the Joint National Committee on Languages.

These efforts have an important role to play. However, few of these efforts are aimed at collaborations across programs or between ED and grantees, efforts that would encourage a partnership approach to the programs. They are also not being implemented in a coordinated, systematic manner that would facilitate accomplishment of common goals. ED appears to recognize the value of collaboration, as illustrated in its introduction of an invitational priority related to collaboration in the NRC and LRC 2005 competitions. Curiously, however, the NRC priority included collaboration with LRC, AORC, and CIBER programs but did not mention other NRCs. In addition, the collaborations are aimed at interactions between grantees, with little department involvement and no attention to the way the program is managed at a national level or to the content of collaborations.

Several National Academies reports in the health care arena have called for a collaborative approach to performance measurement that embraces an interactive process involving the public and private sectors in the development of program goals, performance measures consistent with those goals, and evaluation of the measures (see National Academy of Sciences, National Academy of Engineering, Institute of Medicine, 2007; Institute of Medicine, 1997). The recent report of the secretary of education's Commission on Higher Education (U.S. Department of Education, 2006a) reinforced a similar idea when it called for a change to a system based on performance, emphasizing that higher education institutions need to "embrace and implement serious accountability measures."

A collaborative approach in which ED and the universities work together to develop performance measures should increase the programs' effectiveness and encourage continuous improvement. Universities are more likely to internalize performance measures if they have had a voice in their creation. Such measures can also help universities learn from each other.

Once specific performance measures are identified, universities can compare their performance on these measures with those of their peers. This could lead to the identification of promising practices that they may be able to adapt. For example, why is a particular university or program particularly good at increasing language proficiency? How has a given program been able to establish linkages with their college of education or local education authority? Why are graduates of a particular program getting significant numbers of government jobs? If universities find that these results are brought about by practices that are transferable, they are likely to improve their own performance. Systems to encourage and support measurement of performance and sharing of information concerning promising and transferable approaches could improve overall performance of the Title VI/FH programs.

AWARD TRANSPARENCY

At the most basic level, successful grant applications are a source of information about best practice; at a minimum, they represent proposals that expert review panels rated as most responsive to application criteria. During site visits and the committee's meeting with directors of newly awarded NRCs, multiple project staff mentioned the potential usefulness of applications as a source of information about what it takes to put together a successful program. Feedback on applications was also cited as a potentially useful source of information about program strengths and needed program improvements, even for successful applicants.

At the same time, the committee heard repeated concerns about the difficulty of accessing successful grant applications. According to ED staff and grantees, applications can only be viewed (but not removed or copied) in the ED offices in Washington, DC. This limits public access generally and creates a clear disadvantage for anyone not based in the area. Limiting access to successful applications may limit unsuccessful applicants' ability to identify shortcomings and develop more competitive proposals in future competitions, thus limiting competition. In addition, since they are federal programs, the process used to make Title VI/FH awards and the results of the competition should be readily available to the public. Information technology makes this easy to do.

The committee also heard specific criticisms about the grant selection process, which has moved to electronic review. In the past, reviewers met face-to-face to discuss their review and their planned point assignment for each criterion. Ratings are now done electronically, with a teleconference held for reviewers to discuss their ratings. Critics claim that this change has made it difficult to deliberate and has reduced substantive comment on applications. Wiley and Schneider (2006) state that in the case of IRS grants, for example, the effectiveness of the program has been negatively impacted by the grant selection procedure. The committee notes, however, that the electronic review process helps minimize travel costs for reviewers and is designed to increase review efficiency. Curiously, while electronic review should make sharing of review results with applicants a quick process, ED prints and mails paper copies of the review.

CONCLUSIONS AND RECOMMENDATIONS

Monitoring, evaluation, and continuous improvement efforts at ED have been affected by staffing limitations, the availability of data, resources, and program leadership. The committee was told of several initiatives under way that will improve recent efforts, including systematic annual grant review processes, redesigning the data system, and plans for future grantee meetings focused on issues important to the field. The grantees themselves have also implemented mechanisms to improve collaboration within and among programs. Nonetheless, there is much room for continued improvement both within ED and between ED and its grantees.

Program Monitoring

The limitations and burden of the ED data system are widely recognized, including by ED. The recently implemented redesign appears to be aimed at addressing the technical issues encountered by the committee. However, the usefulness of the system will not be fully realized unless the grantees gain some advantage from the demanding data entry required. Universities should be able to compare their performance with that of other similar grantees. The redesigned system should be used more aggressively to report program performance beyond the narrow criteria reflected in the performance indicators, and it should include the monitoring of trends.

Finally, data should be publicly available to facilitate open, public discourse about the program and its accomplishments.

Conclusion: The original online data reporting system for Title VI and Fulbright-Hays programs (EELIAS) is inadequate, is difficult to use, and has significant consistency problems as well as a lack of transparency in the data collected.

Recommendation 11.1: **The Department of Education should ensure that its new data system, the International Resource Information System, provides greater standardization, allows comparison across years and across programs, and provides information to all grantees and to the public.**

Program Evaluation

Few program evaluations have been conducted; those that are available have been generated mainly by interested researchers, conducted as grants, and covered a single program. Even the ED-funded evaluation of FLAS and DDRA recipients did not emanate from the program office.

Conclusion: At the present time, limited information is available to rigorously assess the outcomes and impacts of the Title VI and Fulbright-Hays programs and the nature of the funding (partial funding of a larger set of activities) makes it difficult to assess outcomes and impacts.

Recommendation 11.2: **The Department of Education should commission independent outcome and impact evaluations of all programs every 4 to 5 years.**

Well-designed program evaluations would be a more reliable approach to determine program outcomes and impacts than use of performance measures. There are several options available to fund evaluations. First, IEPS could develop evaluations in collaboration with OPEPD, as it did for the survey of fellowship programs. Another alternative would be to fund evaluations using the 1 percent of the appropriation available for program evaluation, national outreach, and information dissemination. However, these are the same resources currently being used for redesign and maintenance of the IEPS data system, and to date they have not been used for program evaluation. Although program evaluations have been funded through IRS in the past, this mechanism provides little opportunity for national-level direction or guidance.

Continuous Improvement

To date, neither the Title VI/FH programs nor the universities that make up the bulk of its grantees have established a process that facilitates continuous improvement. ED has by and large implemented its reporting system and performance measures using a top-down approach, with little buy-in from grantees or consideration of data collection costs, and no clear rationale for the measures chosen. Networks created by grantees provide a framework for interactions across grantees, but there is large variation in the role of the networks, and they function largely independent of ED. There is little activity that supports interactive governance involving collaborative specification of program goals, development of performance measures, or assessment of the extent to which goals are accomplished.

Recommendation 11.3: **The Department of Education should work with universities to create a system of continuous improvement for Title VI and Fulbright-Hays programs. The system would help develop performance indicators and other improvement tools and should include networks of similar centers (National Resource Centers, Language Resource Centers, Centers for International Business Education and Research) and university officials with overall responsibilities in language, area, and international studies.**

While the system could build on existing networks, the process developed should include senior university officials with university-wide decision-making authority that affects language, area, and international studies. Such officials will have the ability to speak on behalf of the broader pressures and opportunities affecting the programs and reflect on how the discussions regarding the Title VI/FH programs would be affected or would affect the larger university system. The system should also capitalize on existing expertise in universities on given world areas or languages. As part of this process, ED might consider convening individuals with established credentials in foreign languages and cultures in major world areas to build on their successes.

Award Transparency

The most basic example of a successful practice is a successful grant application. Yet unlike some other federal agencies, ED has not made applications readily available. This lack of access hampers competition and thwarts public access to information about a federally funded program. Although a successful application does not necessarily indicate that a project will be successful or well implemented, sharing successful applications provides one public resource on which to build other efforts aimed at continuous improvement.

Conclusion: Sharing successful grant applications could improve future competitions and contribute to a continual improvement process.

Recommendation 11.4: **The Department of Education should make its award selection process more transparent, including making successful applications publicly available via the Internet.**

ED has been moving all of its grant competitions to the web-based http://resource-grants.gov. Although this web-based system is not currently used to make applications publicly available, it has the capacity to do so. It is difficult to imagine an applicant who does not prepare his or her application in electronic form. Submitting it electronically is a logical next step. ED could establish a process for making the applications publicly available, while protecting any necessary financial or other information.

An alternative model for an electronic system, Fastlane, is used by all programs at the National Science Foundation (NSF).[9] Fastlane can be used to conduct virtually all business with NSF, including submitting grant proposals, reviewing grant proposals, and determining the status of one's proposal, including comments from reviewers. It does not make unsuccessful applications or rankings or comments about individual proposals available to the public or to anyone other than the applicant. All successful applications, however, are readily available.

Of course, none of the recommendations in this chapter can be effectively implemented without an institutional structure in the department that supports innovation, recognizes the importance of strong program leadership, and encourages program change. The next chapter turns to discussion of these issues.

---

[9]See https://www.fastlane.nsf.gov/fastlane.jsp.

12

Looking Toward the Future

When the Title VI and Fulbright-Hays (Title VI/FH) programs were created nearly 50 years ago, the international challenges facing the United States were different than they are today. The country's eye was focused primarily at the Soviet bloc nations, perceived as the greatest threat. The end of the cold war and the events of September 11, 2001, created new political and military concerns. Increased globalization and international business competition highlighted inadequacies in the U.S. education system and challenges to continued global competitiveness. The economic and security maps continue to be redrawn as new nations emerge as military, energy, and economic powers.

As outlined in this report, the nation's investment in Title VI/FH programs has been a catalyst in the efforts of many of the country's best universities to focus on teaching the languages and cultural knowledge needed to respond to world conditions. It has also supported needed research and other activities by nonprofit organizations and individual researchers active in foreign language, area, and international issues. The Bush administration's proposed National Security Language Initiative (NSLI) will go a step further by focusing on critical language needs, particularly in K-12 education, and several agencies have taken steps to implement aspects of the proposal. At the same time, a reinvigorated and expanded focus on foreign languages will accentuate current issues and create new demands for foreign language assessment. Similarly, significant advances in information and communication technologies present opportunities to both support assessment and advance instruction.

As the Title VI/FH programs and the U.S. Department of Education

(ED) look toward their next 50 years, they will need to consider how they can best harmonize with other related programs and agencies to achieve multiple goals and how to best address emerging and ever-changing challenges. This chapter begins by discussing current federal efforts to respond to national needs and what the committee views as needed structural changes in ED. It then moves to a discussion of the particular challenges posed by foreign language assessment and advances in new technology. The chapter touches on many of the topics covered in earlier chapters of the report, including language proficiency assessment, use of technology, and program oversight.

NEW FEDERAL DIRECTIONS

The nation's deficiencies in international understanding and language skills cannot be corrected solely at the level of university education. Corrections have to start earlier in the education system. Nevertheless, universities can play key roles regarding 21st-century challenges by extending access to foreign language instruction to more students, by contributing to deepening the level of instruction to more advanced levels, and by collaborating with the K-12 system so that students begin to learn foreign languages much earlier in their education. Title VI/FH programs have been and will continue to be a foundation in the internationalization of higher education. Looking ahead, this internationalization has both a horizontal and a vertical dimension. Horizontal implies even stronger reach into the professional schools, until America's research universities are internationalized across the entire array of careers for which it is the training ground: careers not only in academia itself, but also in elementary and secondary education, public service, business, law, medicine, social work, journalism, engineering, and so on. As university education comes to demand such perspectives and skills, high schools will adjust accordingly. This horizontal internationalization should be one of the next great tasks of the Title VI/FH tradition.

The other great challenge is in the vertical reach, which should be calibrated to what research universities are best suited to do. What universities can do best in public outreach is to prepare undergraduates and professional school enrollees to become new kinds of leaders in whatever career track they choose; what universities can do best for K-12 education is the teaching of teachers, the preparation of curriculum and instructional material, and the establishment of standards. Chapter 4 outlines a specific recommendation that ED should provide incentives for more formal collaborations between Title VI/FH universities and colleges of education. Both the horizontal and vertical broadening of Title VI/FH should involve teaching international subjects—such as history, geography, and the study of globalization itself—as well as language instruction. As federal efforts to infuse foreign languages into the elementary and secondary curriculum gain momentum (such as through NSLI), and high school graduates start to move to college with a higher language base, higher education will respond in turn by providing more advanced language courses.

At present, Title VI/FH programs cannot be expected to play a major role in both horizontal and vertical broadening on their own, given the meager resources available to accomplish these tasks. Significantly more resources are needed for these programs in order to realize the potential of horizontal and vertical integration. In addition, the resources provided to higher education must be coordinated with those available to K-12 and with those of other federal agencies, paying attention to the priorities of each in light of current education, national security, and other needs. In the committee's view, however, the combined current resources of these programs pale in comparison to the task of internationalizing throughout

---

BOX 12-1
Components of the Proposed
National Security Language Initiative

In K-12 education, the National Security Language Initiative (NSLI), as proposed, would

- Provide $24 million to ED for the study of critical languages by refocusing the Foreign Language Assistance Program (FLAP) grants.
- Provide $27 million for a new program at ED to build continuous programs of study of critical languages from kindergarten to university. The program would start with 27 schools and be based on the National Security Education Program's (NSEP) National Flagship Language Initiative K-16 pilot programs.
- Create a new scholarship program at the State Department for summer, academic year/semester study abroad, and short-term opportunities for high school students studying critical languages. The goal is to reach 3,000 high school students by summer 2009.
- Establish a new component in the State Department's Fulbright-Hays program to annually assist 100 U.S. teachers of critical languages to study abroad.
- Establish language study "feeder" programs under the director of national intelligence. These would be grants and initiatives with K-16 educational institutions to provide summer student and teacher immersion experiences, academic courses and curricula, and other resources. The goal is to reach 400 students and 400 teachers in 5 states in 2007 and up to 3,000 students and 3,000 teachers by 2011 in additional states.

To increase the number of foreign language teachers, NSLI would

- Establish a National Language Service Corps for Americans with proficiencies in

the education system and across relevant disciplines, including professional education.

NSLI

The Bush administration, through its National Security Language Initiative, has proposed a set of new programs and activities aimed at increasing national capacity in critical languages, with a focus on the K-12 system. The initiative recognizes the need for more foreign language instruction at the K-12 level, as well as a seamless continuum from K-12 through college. The proposed initiative would scatter new programs throughout ED, the U.S. Department of State, the Department of Defense (DoD), and even the Office of the Director of National Intelligence and also provide targeted funding for existing programs (see Box 12-1 for specific components of the proposal).

critical languages to serve the nation by working for the federal government, teaching at the K-12 level, or serving in a newly created Civilian Linguist Reserve Corps (CLRC). The program would spend $14 million in FY 2007 with the goal of having 1,000 volunteers in the CLRC and 1,000 teachers in schools before the end of the decade.
- Establish a new $1 million nationwide distance e-learning clearinghouse through ED to deliver foreign language education resources to teachers and students across the country.
- Expand teacher-to-teacher seminars and training through a $3 million ED effort to reach thousands of foreign language teachers in 2007.
- Expand the State Department's Fulbright Foreign Language Teaching Assistant Program, to allow 300 native speakers of critical languages to come to the United States to teach in universities and schools in 2006-2007.

Other components of the initiative, aimed at increasing the number of advanced-level speakers of defined critical languages, include

- Expand NSEP's National Flagship Language Initiative to a $13.2 million program aiming to produce 2,000 advanced speakers of Arabic, Chinese, Russian, Persian, Hindi, and Central Asian languages by 2009.
- Increase by 200 the number of annual Gilman Scholarships (State Department) for financially needy undergraduates to study critical languages abroad by the year 2008.
- Create a new State Department summer immersion study program for up to 275 university-level students per year in critical languages.
- Add overseas language study to 150 U.S. Fulbright student scholarships annually.
- Increase support for immersion language study centers abroad.

SOURCE: Powell and Lowenkron (2006).

The Title VI/FH programs have been identified in public presentations as a building block for NSLI, and Title VI grantees are recognized as logically competent potential applicants for some of the new programs. However, of the multiple requested NSLI resources, only the e-learning clearinghouse is proposed to be conducted under Title VI/FH, despite the fact that some of the activities appear to overlap with those conducted via Title VI/FH. If funded as envisioned, NSLI will significantly increase the role of other agencies in language training, particularly at the K-12 level.

Although as of this writing NSLI has not yet received targeted funding, various departments have realigned existing funds to begin to achieve NSLI objectives. For example, DoD has already launched two K-16 critical language programs. As part of the National Security Education Program's (NSEP) National Flagship Language Program, it gave a $700,000 grant to the University of Oregon and the Portland Public Schools for an immersion Chinese program for students starting in elementary school. The language study program follows an articulated curriculum that continues through college. Scholarships are available for those students who want to pursue the study of Chinese at the University of Oregon. A similar program was started at Michigan State University and the Dearborn Public Schools for the creation of a K-16 Arabic curriculum. Again, instruction starts at the elementary school level, with scholarships available for students to continue at Michigan State University. ED is supplementing the Michigan program with a Foreign Language Assistance Program[1] (FLAP) grant to the Lansing and Dearborn public schools to support the teaching of Chinese and Arabic. Both the University of Oregon and Michigan State University also operate Language Resource Centers (LRCs) under Title VI. According to David Chu, undersecretary of defense for personnel and readiness, although DoD will fund the initial K-16 projects, the hope is that NSLI will allow ED to take up the challenge they have begun and fund 90 or so additional K-16 programs.

ED Role

As part of the K-12 component of the NSLI, ED implemented a competitive priority for critical languages in the FY 2006 FLAP[2] competition and awarded 12.9 million in grants to school districts in 22 states to help increase the number of Americans learning foreign languages deemed critical to national security and commerce (October 13, 2006, ED press release).

---

[1]FLAP provides resources to elementary and secondary school districts. Until NSEP's National Flagship Initiative and NSLI, it was the only federal funding that supported elementary and secondary programs.

[2]FLAP provides resources to elementary and secondary school districts for foreign language study. It is not part of Title VI or Fulbright-Hays (see Chapter 2).

It has also begun plans for a summer teacher training seminar. Both DoD and ED are positioning themselves to expand the study of critical languages at the K-12 level. ED's focus on critical languages was controversial, however, because of concern that this would narrow the nation's language competency by reducing existing capacity in other languages over the longer term. Although there are universities with National Resource Centers (NRC) or Language Resource Centers (LRC) funding in all but three of the states receiving FLAP funds, there has been no apparent effort to encourage coordination of their expertise.

As the federal agency with clear responsibility for education issues, ED should have a more visible presence in directing efforts aimed at education, particularly K-12 education. ED's priorities have changed over time, with international education and foreign languages just beginning to reemerge as a national priority. The new NSLI provides an opportunity for ED not only to take the lead among its federal partners but also to improve coordination of the programs within its own department that deal with these issues.

Given its pressing need for people with skills in critical languages, DoD appears to be quite motivated to step into the vacuum and directly support K-12 language programs. Language programs at DoD (and the State Department as well) are overseen at a senior level in the agency and are systematically and clearly integrated in their strategic thinking, as evidenced by their Defense Language Transformation Roadmap (U.S. Department of Defense, 2005). This document reiterates assumptions about the U.S. military's future global reach and their implications for the DoD's language needs, and then lays out a clear series of goals that serve to meet these anticipated needs. Thus, DoD's language plans are connected to future security needs. The DoD official responsible for carrying out these plans is at the undersecretary level.

By contrast, international education programs at ED appear to have a lower priority; they are not integrated into long-term goals, like those of DoD, and are administered at the lowest possible office level in the Office of Postsecondary Education (OPE), with several reporting levels between them and the Executive Office staff. FLAP, which provides resources to elementary and secondary schools, is administered by the Office of English Language Acquisition, a parallel office to OPE. There appears to be little formal opportunity for collaboration or coordination between them, and certainly nothing in the department's strategic plan or other public documents connects the missions of the two offices.

NEW DEMANDS AND OPPORTUNITIES

As ED and other agencies implement new initiatives, issues related to language proficiency assessment will become more pronounced. Similarly, although Title VI universities have used technology to support their internationalization and foreign language goals, advances in this area have taken place at a phenomenal pace. For example, technology provides new opportunities for both conducting instruction and implementing foreign language assessments. Harnessing these issues in ways that will best advance internationalization goals and support the needs of the multiple involved federal agencies will require targeted and strategic direction.

Expanded Foreign Language Assessment Needs

The needs for assessments of foreign language proficiency that meet accepted measurement standards (see American Educational Research Association et al., 1999) have expanded greatly since the 1950s when the Foreign Service Institute (FSI) developed a ratings scale and oral proficiency test and the Title VI/FH programs were launched (see Appendix D for a historical summary). Given the various initiatives in the government to increase national capacity in foreign languages and the numbers of individuals learning a critical foreign language to more advanced levels, existing needs can be expected to increase at an even more rapid rate than in the past 50 years.

There is and is likely to continue to be an increasing need to certify the language proficiency of government personnel, both civilian and military, for different specific contexts and different activities of language use (listening, speaking, reading), in a wide range of languages, from elementary to advanced levels. Businesses will also need assurance that their employees or prospective employees who will be interacting with speakers of languages other than English have the level of language proficiency desired and the appropriate level of cultural sensitivity. Colleges and universities that train language teachers continue to need assessments to certify their professional competence in the language they will be teaching.

With the increasing requirements for government employees, particularly in DoD, to develop proficiency from elementary to more advanced levels in a range of foreign languages, government language schools will face an increasing need for language assessments to diagnose students' strengths and challenges and to make decisions about achievement and progress. As universities seek to train more students to more advanced levels, they will also require more refined and accurate assessment tools. In addition, although much attention has been paid to assessing speaking proficiency, needed language competencies (e.g., reading, writing, speaking) vary greatly both across government agencies and positions and across students. Tools need to be available appropriate to these various purposes.

Finally, given the increased amounts of government resources likely to be going into foreign language instruction in the coming years, there is likely to be a concomitant need for greater accountability. The congressional call for this study is but one indicator of the federal government's requirement for accountability—in this case, for federal funds granted to colleges and universities through the Title VI/FH programs. In K-12 education, the No Child Left Behind Act of 2001 already provides a strong accountability mechanism for the core curriculum; as more federal funds are invested in K-12 language instruction, a similar accountability mechanism will be required. This will necessitate the development of assessments of foreign language proficiency that meet accepted professional standards.

New Approach to Language Assessment Needed

The most common approach to language proficiency assessment in both government and academia is an oral interview. The original oral proficiency interview (OPI) was developed by FSI and was specifically designed to certify the language proficiency of Foreign Service officers. The development of the original FSI scales was informed by expertise in languages and linguistics and by accepted psychometric standards and practice. During the initial years of their use, qualified measurement specialists were directly involved in conducting research to improve and better understand the ratings. As the OPI became more widely used in other government agencies for other purposes, the Interagency Language Roundtable (ILR) assumed primary responsibility for what is now called the ILR oral proficiency rating scale, a uniform scale used across agencies. The committee was told that DoD has efforts under way to develop alternative assessment approaches to address its varied needs.

The American Council on the Teaching of Foreign Languages (ACTFL) adapted the oral proficiency approach to an academic setting, and its ratings came to be widely accepted, although dissemination was limited by the expense and time required to reliably administer the exams using certified examiners. In developing its instrument, ACTFL relied on the credibility of FSI's OPI, initially conducting none of its own research to ensure that the basic measurement qualities of the assessment generalized from a government to an academic context. Healthy debate about use of the OPI has continued even while the ILR and ACTFL approaches have become more widely used in government and academia, respectively. There is general consensus that the OPI has shifted attention in academia toward teaching for oral proficiency.

In addition to the ACTFL and ILR OPI, there are a variety of newer, technology-based approaches to assessing oral proficiency that have been developed to help lower some of the administrative costs of face-to-face interviews, many of which are based on the ACTFL OPI (Malone, 2006). For example, in 1986, the Center for Applied Linguistics (CAL) developed the simulated oral proficiency interview (SOPI), a tape-mediated assessment. Since then, the SOPI has been widely used, and CAL is working to operationalize a CD-ROM-based semidirect test of oral proficiency, the Computerized Oral Proficiency Instrument (COPI) in Spanish and Arabic. While some research has indicated that ratings from SOPIs and standard face-to-face interviews are highly correlated (e.g., Kenyon and Tschirner, 2000; Stansfield and Kenyon, 1992), and that an individual is likely to receive the same rating whether tested face-to-face or over the telephone (Swender, 2003), very little research has been conducted on the effects of other computer- and web-based delivery systems on the performance of test takers. At this point in the field of testing, very little is known about the effects of these technologies on the reliability, validity, or fairness of assessments. One cannot simply assume that delivering these assessments with the latest technology, in different formats, with different tasks and input, rather than in a face-to-face interview, will have no effect on test takers' performance or on raters' ratings (Chapelle, 1997, 2003; Bachman, 2004; Canale, 1986).

In response to the expense and time needed to conduct an OPI, as well as the limited availability of assessment tools for some of the less commonly taught languages, ED prompted LRCs to develop new approaches to foreign language assessment. ED also encouraged NRCs to measure the language proficiency of their Foreign Language and Area Studies (FLAS) students. Multiple efforts have emerged, but it is unclear if these efforts are being conducted with a strategic vision, with the necessary measurement expertise to ensure that their assessments will be reliable and valid, or with adequate funding. In some cases, centers have used collaborations or consultative mechanisms to bring in necessary expertise. In others, given their very limited funding, they may have to rely on faculty and staff who are also busy working on other projects in language teaching or curriculum and materials development, in addition to language assessment.

These recent ED-funded efforts to improve foreign language proficiency assessments have suffered from both a lack of adequate resources and a diffusion of the Title VI/FH resources available. Looking at the current projects aimed at developing new assessments of foreign language proficiency at Title VI centers, a general pattern of expertise is evident: content specialists, who include linguists as well as language teachers with varying degrees of understanding of second language acquisition and language pedagogy, are often well supported in terms of technical (computer/web programming) staff, but typically there are no staff with expertise in measurement or language testing. One exception is the projects involving CAL, which has had a long history of developing foreign language assessments, and which has also always had staff with professional expertise in language testing and measurement—but its reach is limited.

The ILR and ACTFL versions of the OPI and the associated rating scales[3] are regarded by many as a "gold standard" for language assessment in government and academia, respectively, and the interrater reliability of the ACTFL OPI is well established when administered using a certified tester. However, assessment experts concur that issues about comparability across contexts, validity, and feasibility make these instruments difficult to use as a sole common metric across languages and contexts. (Box 12-2 summarizes the major issues with the OPI that suggest the need for new research and development.) There is also consensus that there is no obvious, currently available alternative. Furthermore, despite progress resulting from work by ACTFL and others, including Title VI centers, scales are still not available for many of the less commonly taught languages taught by Title VI programs. Given the diversity of languages, programs, and needs, a common metric presents serious challenges to the field of foreign language assessment.

The nation's needs for expertise in foreign languages have diversified and expanded since the current approaches to assessment were developed. Progress has been made since FSI was first developed, and multiple efforts are under way to attempt to address the limitations of prevailing approaches.[4] However, additional strategic work is vitally needed to develop assessment approaches that are affordable; address multiple contexts and new languages; reflect current knowledge of languages, language pedagogy, and language assessment; and draw on advances in technology.

Technology and Instruction

Over the past 50 years, Title VI has helped build a national human infrastructure for retaining expertise and delivering instruction in foreign languages, particularly less commonly taught languages, and in area and international studies. These instructional programs and expertise, however, are still largely confined to the physical locality of university campuses. Because of the scarcity of instructional resources and personnel in less commonly taught languages and the relatively small number of students interested in a given language, it would be of tremendous benefit both economically and pedagogically to develop ways for programs to extend these resources and personnel to students enrolled in other universities through the use of technology. For example, Title VI/FH programs could make their courses available to other universities via teleconferencing and other

---

[3]See Appendix D for an explanation of the scales used by ACTFL and ILR and an illustrative example of the descriptors used in applying the scale.

[4]The European Union has also undertaken substantial efforts to establish standards for language qualifications through its Common European Framework of Reference for Languages (see http://www.coe.int/t/dg4/linguistic/CADRE_EN.asp). The committee did not fully explore the reliability or validity of this approach.

BOX 12-2
Oral Proficiency Interview Issues

There are several issues with the oral proficiency interview that suggest the need for additional research and development on proficiency measurement approaches:

Validity: A number of concerns have been raised regarding the validity of the ACTFL scale—that is, the extent to which evidence and theory support the interpretation of the ratings (Chaloub-Deville and Fulcher, 2003). For example, it has been objected that the ACTFL guidelines were constructed based on intuitive judgments rather than on any documented collection or analysis of empirical evidence about how competence in a second language actually develops (Fulcher, 1996b). After over 50 years of use, debate about the validity of the ILR and ACTFL scales continues (Chalhoub-Deville and Fulcher, 2003; Arnett and Haglund, 2001; Bachman and Savignon, 1986).

Reliability: Investigations of the quality of the OPI have focused primarily on interrater reliability or consistency (Chalhoub-Deville and Fulcher, 2003). The research generally supports the consistency of ratings across multiple raters when the OPI is administered and scored by certified ILR or ACTFL examiners (Malone, 2003; Surface and Dierdorff, 2003). However, research has also suggested potential sources of inconsistency, or unreliability, based on the questions or prompts used by the examiner. The questions or prompts asked during an OPI are, by design, tailored for different examinees, and little research has investigated the reliability of ratings across different questions or prompts (that is, whether an examinee would earn virtually the same rating had he or she been given an alternative prompt). Research has found that the largest sources of measurement error in performance assessments of speaking are due to inconsistencies across different assessment tasks, interactions between test takers and tasks or between raters and tasks, rather than to inconsistencies among raters (e.g., Lynch and McNamara, 1998; Bachman et al., 1995). Similar issues have been reported in the educational measurement literature with respect to a wide range of performance assessments (e.g., Brennan et al., 1995; Lane et al., 1996; Lynch and McNamara, 1998; Shavelson et al., 1999; Stecher et al., 2000; van Weeren and Theunissen, 1987). This potential reliability issue has not been adequately researched.

Conversational language: The claim that the OPI assesses authentic conversational language was questioned nearly 30 years ago by a former director of the Foreign Service Institute, who stated then that "one of the principal limitations is the inability of this system [the OPI] to make meaningful judgments or to measure the most significant objective of human speech—effective communication" (Sollenberger, 1978, pp. 7-8). The OPI claim has also been seriously challenged more recently by applied linguists working in conversation and discourse analysis (e.g., papers in Young and He, 1998).

---

electronic media. In addition, once less commonly taught language courses are made available online, it is expected that more students will become aware of those languages and the chances of more students learning less commonly taught languages will likely increase.

In fact, our review found that some Title VI/FH programs have al-

Nature of language ability: When the original FSI OPI was developed, oral language ability was viewed, within the then current literature on psychological abilities, as an essentially unitary trait (Lowe, 1988). The dominant view among language testing researchers now is that language, like many other psychological abilities, is multicomponential (e.g., Chapelle et al., 1997; Chalhoub-Deville, 1996; Fulcher, 1996; Hudson et al., 1992; Bachman, 1990; Canale, 1984; Vollmer and Sang, 1983). Because this research rejects the original theoretical basis of the holistic rating for the OPI, questions are raised about the validity of interpretations of language ability based on the ratings.

Developmental scale: Finally, the claim that the oral proficiency rating scales represent a progression of second language acquisition has also been repeatedly challenged by a number of researchers in second language acquisition (e.g., Lantolf and Frawley, 1985, 1988; Pienemann et al., 1988). Indeed, current research and experience in second language acquisition strongly support the idea that second language development is neither purely linear nor uniform but consists of a series of starts, stops, spurts, and plateaus and varies considerably across contexts and from learner to learner (e.g., Bayley and Preston, 1996; Markee, 2006; Tarone, 2000; Young, 2002).

Comparability in ratings: To date, there is virtually no research that demonstrates the comparability of ILR or ACTFL ratings across languages and contexts (see Thompson, 1991, for a discussion of some of the problems of adapting the ACTFL scales across languages). The challenge of ensuring that a level 3 is the same in Russian, Arabic, and Chinese, for example, or that a level 2 in speaking is the same as a level 2 in reading has long been recognized in government agencies but has not yet been adequately addressed.

Expense and limited availability: Although some NRCs reported to the committee that they use certified ACTFL OPI testers to assess their students' language proficiency, among those that do not, the most common reasons given included the expense and resources involved (see Malone, 2006, for more about the financial burden). Faculty and staff reported that the cost of getting certified as an ACTFL OPI examiner in a particular language was prohibitive, given the constraints of their budgets. Furthermore, many of the individuals with whom we spoke said that neither they nor their fellow language instructors had the time to administer and score individual oral interviews to all of their students. The other commonly expressed reason was that an ACTFL OPI is not yet available in many of the languages that are taught, particularly the less commonly taught ones.

ready organized summer cross-campus programs for less commonly taught languages to bring students from multiple universities. Some programs have also been using videoconference facilities to deliver courses to remote campuses or to share resources. For example, Indiana University, which has a Uzbek program, is making it available to other universities, so that more students can take the course. Ohio State University also has an Uzbek instructor, enabling the two instructors to codevelop courses and offer a greater variety of them, instead of each teaching the same course to a very small number of students. However, there is no national infrastructure to support this type of effort systematically, so they have remained fragmented and not institutionalized and thus may easily disappear.

Over the past decade or so, information and communication technologies have advanced dramatically and become widely available. Large quantities of live and archived content in many languages are easily available online. Young people, so-called digital natives, are very accustomed to using technology for entertainment and learning. In addition, research and development efforts in technology and language instruction over the past two decades have accumulated sufficient insights about effective ways to deliver language learning using technology. The opportunity is thus ripe to develop large-scale language learning platforms that can be adapted to support learning and instruction of many languages.

Language Platforms

Despite the uniqueness of different languages and the individuality of different language teaching approaches, there are very basic and universal elements that all language learning activities can use to support the work of language instructors. For example, all language learning must start with exposure to high-quality input in the target language and culture. Language learners must first be able to interact with content in the target language. Such interactions typically start comprehension of the target language content, which can come in different forms—video, audio, text, or a combination of them (multimedia and multimodal).

Digital technology can be used to facilitate comprehension and enhance acquisition at this stage. For example, the ability to control the speed of video and audio can help the learner better comprehend the content, as does the ability to quickly access the meaning of words and grammar. Technological tools that enable the learner to memorize vocabulary, complete grammatical exercises, and practice pronunciation can also be built to assist comprehension and learning. Given the nature of digital content, these tools can be language independent—that is, separate from the language under consideration—because the content is digital and thus can be manipulated with generic tools. These tools can be used differently under different language teaching and learning approaches.

The commonalities of technological functions designed to assist language learning can be observed in many current language teaching software applications. While differences exist among today's different language software, most of it mimics the process of language teaching and shares a set of common functions: modeling the target language (input), offering practicing opportunities (exercises output), providing feedback on student performance (feedback), and keeping track of student progress and the learning process. It is also evident that the large foreign language software makers, such as Rosetta Stone and Auralog, use a similar set of functions to teach a variety of languages.

The benefits of common technology platforms have been demonstrated by the popularity of large online learning management systems, such as WebCT, Blackboard, and Moodle. These systems provide a set of common tools to support instruction in all sorts of subject areas for a variety of instructional settings, enabling instructors to focus on content and teaching instead of technology and thus making it possible for hundreds of thousands of instructors to deliver their own content without being technologically proficient. Moodle, an open source course management system, for example, has over 130,000 registered teachers serving over 1 million students in over 100 countries.[5]

There is a long tradition of developing tools for foreign language teachers to develop computer-based courses.[6] Today, there are many such tools available. For example, the University of Wisconsin's Multimedia Annotator and the Multimedia Lesson Builder[7] can be used to develop video-based language lessons. Hot Potatoes[8] is a popular tool used to develop web-based foreign language quizzes. WordChamp.com is a tool that helps students learn vocabulary, provides instant feedback, and tracks results, allowing teachers to assess progress.[9]

However, a number of problems prevent the effective use of technology in language teaching for Title VI/FH programs. First, in general, commercial software companies pay attention only to languages that have a large market share. While that is an understandable business decision, it means that the less commonly taught languages of most concern to Title VI/FH programs are left out. In addition, very often the proprietary platform of commercial software developers is not publicly available, so the Title VI/FH community cannot take advantage of their systems. Second, the generally available course/learning management systems do not provide language learning functions. Third, the publicly available tools have limited functionality because they typically focus on part of the whole language learning and teaching process. An integration of all available tools might lead to an effective language learning system, but such integration cannot happen

---

[5]See http://moodle.org/stats/.
[6]See http://llt.msu.edu/vol5num2/emerging/default.html.
[7]See http://llt.msu.edu/vol5num2/emerging/default.html.
[8]See http://hotpot.uvic.ca/.
[9]See http://www.wordchamp.com/lingua2/Splash.do.

easily, because it requires smooth data communications and interface synchronization. This is not possible if technical and communications experts are not a part of the team creating the language learning and teaching platform.

CONCLUSIONS AND RECOMMENDATIONS

The Title VI/FH programs have served as a foundation in the internationalization of higher education and should continue to do so. However, since the programs were created more than 50 years ago, demands for foreign language and cultural expertise have expanded both horizontally in the higher education system and vertically with other components of the education system. Although the need for internationalization of business has been apparent for some time, other professional disciplines face similar needs. Given current resources, the Title VI/FH programs alone are ill-equipped to respond to this range of increased needs.

> **Conclusion:** Given the recognized lack of knowledge about foreign cultures and foreign languages, additional resources are needed for an integrated and articulated approach in multiple systems, including K-12, higher education, and business, to help address this critical shortcoming.

The federal government has begun efforts to stimulate introduction of foreign languages at an earlier age, with a particular focus on what are considered critical languages, through NSEP's National Flagship Language Program and the Bush administration's proposed National Security Language Initiative. ED has targeted its Foreign Language Assistance Program toward critical languages. However, international education and foreign languages have only recently emerged as an apparent ED priority, although their role in relation to other ED priorities or the needs of other federal agencies has not yet been clearly defined and articulated. Similarly, ED has not fully considered how it will maximize the infrastructure and knowledge built over the past few years by the Title VI/FH programs. The current organization of international and foreign language programs in the department significantly hampers its ability to effectively and coherently address any of these issues.

> **Conclusion:** The Department of Education has not made foreign language and cultures a clear priority and its several programs appear to be fragmented. There is no apparent Department master plan or unifying strategic vision.

Recommendation 12.1: The Department of Education should consolidate oversight of its international education and foreign language programs under an executive-level person who would also provide strategic direction and consult and coordinate with other federal agencies. The position should be one that requires presidential appointment and Senate confirmation.

The priority of international education programs at ED should be raised and all programs (e.g., Title VI/FH, FLAP, NSLI) with an emphasis on foreign language, area, and international education should be consolidated under an executive-level person who reports directly to the secretary. The person appointed to this new position also should coordinate ED programs with those of other federal agencies, such as the State Department and DoD, and have lead responsibility for developing and implementing a new strategic vision and overseeing the biennial report recommended below. Raising the status of the programs is vital to demonstrate clearly the importance of foreign languages and other area and international education to ED and put direction and oversight of the programs at a level more comparable to the level of oversight at other key agencies. For example, NSLI and other foreign language initiatives are overseen at the DoD by an undersecretary and at the State Department by an assistant secretary, both executive-level positions. In contrast, the programmatic, planning, and strategic functions at ED related to foreign language, area, and international issues are currently dispersed across a range of offices and individuals; the Title VI programs specifically are at the lowest organizational level within ED possible. Consolidation and elevation of these functions is needed to achieve the goals of Title VI and related programs.

The Department of Education Organization Act (P.L. 96-88), which established ED, identified "functions related to encouraging and promoting the study of foreign languages and the study of cultures of other countries at the elementary, secondary, and postsecondary levels" as ones that should be performed by a politically appointed ED officer. To do so effectively, the programs and initiatives currently scattered throughout ED should be consolidated under a single, strategic unit. The person responsible for these programs will need to be supported by adequate staff and resources to accomplish their strategic vision. ED might consider approaches that would enable it to enhance its expertise by hiring subject experts as consultants or temporary personnel in addition to adequate core staff.

In Chapter 11, the committee recommended the formation of a new system to facilitate continuous improvement, involving ED, Title VI center representatives, and senior university staff. The presence of a senior-level decision maker, with the authority to implement mutually agreed-on approaches to program improvement that result from this system, is essential.

In addition, it would also provide a focal point for elementary, secondary, and postsecondary education system, business, foreign language, and area studies communities to share input for consideration by ED in strategic planning and the setting of priorities. Input from these sources would provide the necessary input to enable ED to develop a well-informed strategic master plan aimed at addressing a range of international education and foreign language issues. Implementing such a plan requires the involvement of a leader with the authority to leverage all appropriate departmental resources.

In establishing the duties of this office, particular attention should be paid to support for integrated and articulated approaches that support long-term acquisition of advanced levels of foreign language competency and knowledge about language acquisition and related cultures, consistent with the goals of the proposed NSLI. In short, the holder of this office should be concerned with thinking and working strategically with other agencies about how to raise language competency levels and direct the relevant ED programs toward that goal.

> **Conclusion:** There is currently no systematic, ongoing process for assessing national needs for foreign language, area, and international expertise and developing approaches to address those needs.

> *Recommendation 12.2:* **Congress should require the secretary of education, in consultation and coordination with the Departments of State and Defense, the Office of the Director of National Intelligence, and other relevant agencies to submit a biennial report outlining national needs identified in foreign language, area, and international studies, plans for addressing these needs, and progress made. This report should be made available to the public.**

The production of such a report every two years would be sufficiently frequent to be useful while not overburdening the staff tasked with developing the report. The report would create the opportunity to identify gaps and priorities, share information from different agencies on their respective needs and training efforts, and facilitate strategic planning across agencies, with an emphasis on the role of the elementary, secondary, and postsecondary education systems. It would bring together all of the federal agencies with a significant role in defining national needs for foreign language, area, and international expertise and in developing a system designed to address these needs.

The committee notes, however, that coordination across agencies might be facilitated by a formal consultative mechanism in the White House.

Once needs have been defined, relevant agencies should then consider how to address the needs and gaps more systematically through their own programs as well as through collaboration and coordination across programs. For example, while there appears to be consensus that foreign language learning needs to start in K-12, there is some debate about where resources should be targeted in higher education. FLAS Fellowship awards have in the past been available to undergraduates but are now limited by statute to graduate students. In contrast, NSEP fellow awards were initially targeted at graduate students and are now refocusing on undergraduates. The targeting of investments across all components of the education system is one issue such a report should address. Similarly, it should determine the appropriate balancing of federal resources for the complementary national needs for a broad reservoir of expertise in a wide variety of languages and areas—the need that Title VI/FH programs are well positioned to address—and the need for a pipeline of experts into government positions. Although the committee strongly supports the need for language education beyond a set of critical languages defined at any particular point in time, the federal government may not need to be involved in supporting capacity in all 171 languages on the current list of critical Title VI languages. This task would be one for the agencies to consider in conjunction with experts in foreign languages, area, and international studies, perhaps as part of the continuous improvement process discussed in the previous chapter. This group of experts might be tasked with identifying criteria for widely teaching a language in K-12, ensuring that there is a core of scholarly activity in a range of core languages, and forming international networks of scholars who can respond to emerging needs.

In addition, public release of this report will increase awareness and debate and provide an opportunity to share overall federal needs in area and international studies and foreign languages with the academic, education, and business communities. Communication of needs and available resources to the field has been identified as a need in itself. Its release would better inform Congress about the status of the programs to be used in decisions about funding and reauthorization.

Some critics of the Title VI/FH programs have recommended an advisory board to oversee the program. Both the House and the Senate proposed variations of a board aimed at orienting the programs toward areas of national need, directing recipients into government service, and ensuring a diversity of perspectives in the Title VI NRCs, although this was never taken up by the full Congress. Significant controversy erupted, particularly as a result of early congressional proposals and questions about what specific authorities the board should be granted. In the committee's view, an advisory board is unlikely to accomplish the stated objectives and would just add another bureaucratic drain on the program. The committee contends that elevating the status of the programs in ED, combined with requiring regular reporting to Congress, is more likely to effectively direct the programs. As mentioned above, establishment of a formal consultative mechanism in the White House might reinforce these efforts.

The committee also encourages agencies to continue their support for staff-level efforts to identify and share best practices and solicit input from the field. The ILR, currently administered on an informal basis by the State Department's Foreign Service Institute, is one possible mechanism for this effort.

Foreign Language Assessment, Instruction, and Technology

New demands resulting from increased federal interest in international education and foreign languages as well as new instruction and assessment opportunities provided by advancements in technology should push relevant federal agencies to think about new approaches.

Foreign Language Assessment

Title VI/FH programs have stimulated multiple and varied efforts to address the lack of common measures of language proficiency for use by NRCs, particularly for the less commonly taught languages. Despite these efforts, and given the lack of evidence to support the reliability and validity of ED's current approach to self-assessment as well as the inability to compare with other available scales, there is little conclusive evidence about proficiency levels achieved by FLAS recipients either overall or among the NRCs that teach the same languages. Nevertheless, it is reasonable to expect a program designed to support language study to measure changes in language proficiency. In addition, national trends aimed at both expanding language training in the K-12 system and producing highly proficient language experts for government service suggest that the need for new approaches to language assessment will become even greater.

In order to meet current and future assessment needs, the committee thinks that funding for both the research and development of assessments of foreign language proficiency, including appropriate application of technology to these new assessments, as well as funding for their appropriate dissemination to the field, need to be increased. Tomorrow's students will be even better versed in the use of technology than those of today, and they may fully expect to complete electronic assessments. The administrative efficiency of a well-designed assessment that meets professional standards would probably also be increased if implemented with the use of technology. Furthermore, the field of language assessment has been increasingly using computer and web-based technologies for developing and administering language assessments. A considerable research base has emerged that investigates issues in applying these technologies to language assessment (e.g., Chapelle and Douglas, 2006; Bachman, 2004; Chalhoub-Deville, 1999). The committee also thinks that in order to make available to the field (government agencies, colleges and universities, and K-12 schools) assessments of language proficiency that are appropriate to the varied needs and contexts described in this chapter and that meet accepted professional standards, a critical mass of resources—increased funding, appropriate levels and types of expertise, structural support—must be brought together in a single targeted resource.

Technology and Instruction

Technology has made tremendous advances over the past several decades. It continues to evolve, and new possibilities emerge all the time. The international education and foreign language community, including Title VI/FH programs, needs to take advantage of all the emerging possibilities. For example, concerted efforts must be made to develop comprehensive language learning and teaching platforms that can effectively take advantage of the possibilities of technology to enhance the instruction of foreign languages, especially less commonly taught languages. While not replacing the need for an instructor, these platforms can serve as the primary content development and delivery systems for Title VI/FH language programs. They can enable the development of technology-supported language instruction efficiently by assisting individual efforts resulting from the limited resources available. They can also free individual Title VI/FH programs from unnecessarily devoting time to repetitive development of technology tools and focus their limited resources on content and instruction. A national technology infrastructure could significantly enhance the nation's capacity for education in critical and less commonly taught languages across the federal programs designed to teach them.

> **Conclusion:** Current efforts to develop language assessments and to effectively apply developments in technology to language assessment and the support of language instruction suffer from a dispersion of resources.

> *Recommendation 12.3:* The federal government should contract for a new National Foreign Language Assessment and Technology Project. The initial focus of the project should be research and development needed to design and implement a range of new technology-based methods for (1) assessing language proficiency and (2) supporting language instruction through the development of common platforms.

Strategic development of new approaches to foreign language assessment would benefit multiple federal agencies and the broader education sector. Similarly, seizing the opportunities for foreign language instruction and assessment posed by rapid advances in technology would be broadly beneficial. A project aimed at these opportunities might be advanced by collaboration among a consortium of multiple universities or organizations. Over the longer term, the project might be tasked with coordinated investment in technologies aimed at advancing teacher training, materials development, and language instruction, particularly for languages with low enrollments, as discussed earlier in this report.

To meet its goals, the new project (or its consortium members) would need to involve a range of expertise including second or foreign language acquisition, second or foreign language assessment (including expertise in statistics and measurement theory), language pedagogy, curriculum development, education psychology, education technology, instructional design, information systems, networking and databases, and digital media design and development.

The project should be guided by an advisory group composed of representatives of existing Title VI/FH programs with foreign language instruction and assessment needs, as well as representatives of key programs of other sponsoring federal agencies, to identify needs and provide services to them. The advisory group should also include a member who represents the continuous improvement process discussed in Chapter 11 to ensure that the center's work supports the goals, performance measurement approaches, and other activities endorsed by the continuous improvement effort.

As the Title VI/FH programs face their next 50 years, they must be more closely aligned with other federal resources to ensure they operate in a complementary way that maximizes achievement of multiple goals. To effectively build on the programs' multiple accomplishments, they must be collaboratively implemented with universities and other institutions and strategically structured to harness new opportunities and challenges. Although the programs have demonstrated some success in achieving the objectives articulated in the eight key areas, more meaningful performance measures and well-designed research and evaluation are needed to assess program accomplishments.

References and Bibliography

Alba, D.E. (2000). Statement before the International Security, Proliferation, and Federal Services Subcommittee of the Committee on Government Affairs, U.S. Senate, Sept. 14, 19, Washington, DC.

Allen, D. (2000). *Problem-based learning at Delaware: A faculty-driven initiative.* Prepared for the Workshop on Implementing Change: Involving the Campus Community at the Project Kaleidoscope 2000 Summer Institute, July 26-29, Keystone (CO) Conference Center. Available: http://ws.cc.stonybrook.edu/Reinventioncenter/pkalevent.htm [accessed Nov. 2006].

American Association for the Advancement of Science. (2000). *Big biology books fail to convey big ideas, reports AAAS's Project 2061.* Washington, DC: Author. Available: http://www.project2061.org/press//pr000627.htm [accessed Sept. 2004].

American Association of Teachers of Spanish and Portuguese. (2006). *Hispania.* Available: http://www.aatsp.org/scriptcontent/custom/members/02_resources/publications/publications.cfm [accessed Dec. 2006].

American Council on the Teaching of Foreign Languages. (2006a). *Standards for foreign language learning: Preparing for the 21st century.* Yonkers, NY: Author. Also available: http://www.actfl.org/i4a/pages/index.cfm?pageid=3324 [accessed Dec. 2006].

American Council on the Teaching of Foreign Languages. (2006b). *Strand C: Curriculum design.* Available: http://www.actfl.org/i4a/pages/index.cfm?pageid=3636 [accessed Nov. 2006].

American Educational Research Association, American Psychological Association, and National Council on Measurement in Education. (1999). *Standards for educational and psychological testing.* Washington, DC: Author.

Arnett, K., and Haglund, J. (2001). Review of the ACTFL oral proficiency interview. *Canadian Modern Language Review, 58*(2), Dec.

Arrow, K.J., and Capron, W.M. (1959). Dynamic shortages and price rises: The engineer-scientist case. *The Quarterly Journal of Economics, 73*(May), 292-308.

Association of Departments of Foreign Languages. (2001). *ADFL guidelines on the administration of foreign language departments. ADFL statement of good practice: Teaching, evaluation, and scholarship.* Available: http://www.adfl.org/resources/resources_practice. htm [accessed Nov. 2006].

Association to Advance Collegiate Schools of Business International. (2006). *Eligibility procedures and accreditation standards for business accreditation.* Available: http://www. aacsb.edu/accreditation/standards.asp [accessed Nov. 2006].

Axelrod, J., and Bigelow, D. (1962). *Resources for language and area studies.* Washington, DC: American Council on Education.

Bachman, L.F. (1990). *Fundamental considerations in language testing.* New York: Oxford University Press.

Bachman, L.F. (2004). *Validity issues in web-based language assessment.* Paper presented at the Fourth International Conference on English Language Teaching, May 21-25, Beijing, China.

Bachman, L.F., Lynch, B.K., and Mason, M. (1995). Investigating variability in tasks and rater judgments in a performance test of foreign language speaking. *Language Testing, 12,* 238-257.

Bachman, L.F., and Savignon, S.J. (1986). The evaluation of communicative language proficiency: A critique of the ACTFL oral interview. *The Modern Language Journal, 70*(iv), 380-390.

Barnow, B.S. (1996). The economics of occupational labor shortages. In W. Crown (Ed.), *Handbook on employment and the elderly.* Westport, CT: Greenwood.

Bayley, R., and Preston, D. (Eds.). (1996). *Second language acquisition and linguistic variation.* Amsterdam, Netherlands: John Benjamins.

Betteridge, A. (2003). *A case study in higher education international and foreign area needs: Changes in the Middle East Studies Association membership from 1990 to 2002.* Paper presented at Global Challenges Conference, Jan., Duke University, Durham, NC.

Biddle, S. (2002). *Internationalization: Rhetoric or reality.* (ACLS Occasional Paper No. 56). New York: American Council of Learned Societies.

Bikson, T.K., and Law, S.A. (1994). *Global preparedness and human resources: Corporate and college perspectives.* Santa Monica, CA: RAND.

Birch, M. (2006). Statement for the National Academy of Sciences on The Higher Education Act, Title VI, Part B, Centers for International Business Education, on behalf of the Association for International Business Education and Research. Presentation and written submission, Feb. 14, National Research Council Committee to Review the Title VI and Fulbright-Hays International Education Programs, Washington, DC.

Blank, D.J., and Stigler, G.J. (1957). *The demand and supply of scientific personnel.* New York: National Bureau of Economic Research.

Brecht, R.D., Golonka, E.M., Rivers, W.P., and Hart, M.E. (2007). *Language and critical area studies after September 11: An evaluation of the contributions of Title VI/FH to the national interest.* (Report submitted to the U.S. Department of Education). College Park: The National Foreign Language Center at the University of Maryland.

Brecht, R.D., and Rivers, W. (2000). *Language and national security in the 21st century: The role of Title VI/Fulbright-Hays in supporting national language capacity.* Dubuque, IA: Kendall/Hunt.

Brecht, R.D., and William, P. (2001). *Language and national security: The federal role in building language capacity in the U.S.* Prepared for the National Foreign Language Center, University of Maryland. Available: http://www.internationaled.org/BriefingBook/6. Building/6.e%20Language%20National%20Sec.doc [accessed May 2005].

Brennan, R.L., Gao, X., and Colton, D.A. (1995). Generalizability analyses of work keys listening and writing tests. *Educational and Psychological Measurement, 55,* 157-176.

Browne, J. (2006). *What the government knows about your Title VI national resource center: A look inside EELIA.* Presented at the Middle East Studies Association Annual Meeting, Nov., Boston, MA.

Brustein, W. (2006). Statement for the National Academy of Sciences on The Higher Education Act, Title VI and the Mutual Educational and Cultural Exchange Act, Section 102(b)(6), International and Foreign Language Studies. Presentation and written submission, Feb. 14, National Research Council Committee to Review the Title VI and Fulbright-Hays International Education Programs, Washington, DC.

Burton, J.L. (2005). Language transformation plan to build culturally savvy soldiers. *Special Warfare, 18*(Sept.), 14-17.

California Department of Education. (2006). *Instructional materials: Foreign languages.* Available: http://www.cde.ca/gov/ci/fl/im/ [accessed Nov. 2006].

Canale, M. (1984). A communicative approach to language proficiency assessment in a minority setting. In C. Rivera (Ed.), *Communicative competence approaches to language proficiency assessment: Research and application* (pp. 107-122). North Somerset, England: Multilingual Matters.

Canale, M. (1988). The measurement of communicative competence. *Annual Review of Applied Linguistics, 8,* 67-84.

Canale, M., and Swain, M. (1980). Theoretical bases of communicative approaches to second language teaching and testing. *Applied Linguistics, 1*(1), 1-47.

Carroll, J.B. (1967). Foreign language proficiency levels attained by language majors near graduation from college. *Foreign Language Annals, 1*(2), 131-151.

Center for Advanced Study of Language. (2004). *An introduction to America's language needs and resources.* Paper presented at National Language Conference, June 22-24, University of Maryland, College Park.

Center for Applied Linguistics. (1999). *Foreign language instruction in the United States: A national survey of elementary and secondary schools.* Washington, DC: Author.

Center for Applied Linguistics. (2006). *Testing/assessment: Foreign language assessments.* Available: http://www.cal.org/topics/ta/flassess.html [accessed Feb. 2007].

Center for Applied Second Language Studies. (2006a). *CASLS pilot.* Available: http://caslspilot.uoregon.edu/caslspilot/do/login [accessed Feb. 2007].

Center for Applied Second Language Studies. (2006b). *National online early language learning assessment.* Available: http://noella.uoregon.edu/noella/do/login [accessed Feb. 2007].

Center for Applied Second Language Studies. (2006c). *Standards-based measurement of proficiency.* Available: http://casls.uoregon.edu/stamp2.php [accessed Feb. 2007].

Chalhoub-Deville, M. (1996). Performance assessment and the components of the oral construct across different tests and rater groups. In M. Milanovic and N. Saville (Eds.), *Performance testing, cognition, and assessment* (pp. 55-73). Cambridge, England: Press Syndicate of Cambridge University.

Chalhoub-Deville, M. (1999). *Issues in computer-adaptive testing of reading proficiency.* Cambridge, England: Press Syndicate of Cambridge University.

Chalhoub-Deville, M. (2002). Technology in standardized language assessments. In R. Kaplan (Ed.), *Oxford handbook of applied linguistics* (pp. 471-484). New York: Oxford University Press.

Chalhoub-Deville, M., and Fulcher, G. (2003). The oral proficiency interview: A research agenda. *Foreign Language Annals, 36*(4), 498-506.

Chapelle, C. (1997). Conceptual foundations for the design of computer-assisted language tests. In A. Huhta, V. Kohonen, L. Kurki-Suonio, and S. Luoma (Eds.), *Current developments and alternatives in language assessment. Proceedings of LTRC 96* (pp. 520-525). Jyvaskyla, Finland: University of Jyvaskyla.

Chapelle, C. (2003). *English language learning and technology: Lectures on applied linguistics in the age of information and communication technology.* Amsterdam, Netherlands: John Benjamins.

Chapelle, C., and Douglas, D. (2006). *Assessing language ability through computer technology.* Cambridge, England: Cambridge University Press.

Chapelle, C., Grabe, W., and Berns, M. (1997). *Communicative language proficiency: Definition and implications for TOEFL 2000* (vol. MS-10). Princeton, NJ: Educational Testing Service.

Chichester, M. (2006). Statement for the National Academy of Sciences, Title VI, Part C, The Institute for International Public Policy. Presentation and written submission, Feb. 14, National Research Council Committee to Review the Title VI and Fulbright-Hays International Education Programs, Washington, DC.

Chinen, K., and Tucker, G.R. (2005). Heritage language development: Understanding the roles of ethnic identity and Saturday school participation. *Heritage Language Journal, 3*, 1.

Christian, D. (2006). *Center for Applied Linguistics (CAL): Perspective on the international research and studies program. Title VI-international education programs, Part A: International and foreign language studies.* Written submission, Feb. 14, National Research Council Committee to Review the Title VI and Fulbright-Hays International Education Programs, Washington, DC.

Chu, D. (2006). Remarks to the National Research Council Committee to Review Title VI and Fulbright-Hays International Education Programs, Oct. 10, U.S. Department of Education, Washington, DC.

Clark, J.L.D. (1978). Interview testing research at educational testing service. In J.L.D. Clark (Ed.), *Direct testing of speaking proficiency: Theory and application* (pp. 211-228). Princeton, NJ: Educational Testing Service.

Clark, J.L.D. (1981). Language. Chapter 3 in T.S. Barrows (Ed.), *A survey of global understanding: Final report* (pp. 25-35). New Rochelle, NY: Change Magazine Press.

Clark, J.L.D., and Clifford, R.T. (1988). The FSI/ILR/ACTFL proficiency scales and testing techniques: Development, current status and needed research. *Studies in Second Language Acquisition, 10*(2), 129-147.

Clowse, B. (1981). *Brainpower for the cold war: The Sputnik crisis and National Defense Education Act of 1958.* Westport, CT: Greenwood Press.

Cohen, M.S. (1995). Labor shortages as America approaches dynamic shortages and price rises: The engineer-scientist case. *Quarterly Journal of Economics*, 292-308.

Commission on the Abraham Lincoln Study Abroad Fellowship Program. (2005). *Global competence and national needs: One million Americans studying abroad.* Available: http://www.lincolncommission.org/LincolnReport.pdf [accessed Nov. 2005].

Committee for Economic Development. (2006). *Education for global leadership: The importance of international studies and foreign language education for U.S. economic and national security.* Washington, DC: Author.

Committee on Science, Engineering, and Public Policy. (2004). *Facilitating interdisciplinary research.* Committee on Facilitating Interdisciplinary Research. National Academy of Sciences, National Academy of Engineering, and Institute of Medicine. Washington, DC: The National Academies Press.

Connor-Linton, J., and VandeBerg, M. (in press). The assessment of student learning abroad: Addressing a critical national need. Submitted to *Frontiers: The Interdisciplinary Journal of Study Abroad.*

Cornell University. (2007). *To sustain life: Water and development in Nepal.* Available: http://www.einaudi.cornell.edu/southasia/outreach/pdf/Nepal_water.pdf [accessed Jan. 2007].

Council of American Overseas Research Centers. (1998). *Three decades of excellence 1965-1994: The Fulbright-Hays doctoral dissertation research abroad fellowship program and its impact on the American academy.* Washington, DC: Author.

Crawford, J. (1992). *Hold your tongue: Bilingualism and the politics of "English only."* Boston, MA: Addison-Wesley.

Davidson, D.E. (2006) Statement concerning the performance and effectiveness of the Fulbright-Hays Training Programs, Center for International Education and Programs Service in the U.S. Department of Education for NAS review. Presentation and written submission, Feb. 14, National Research Council Committee to Review the Title VI and Fulbright- Hays International Education Programs, Washington, DC.

de Wit, H. (2002). *Internationalization of higher education in the United States: A historical, comparative, and conceptual analysis.* Westport, CT: Greenwood Press.

Draper, J.B., and Hicks, J.H. (2002). *Foreign language enrollments in public secondary schools, fall 2000.* Alexandria, VA: American Council on the Teaching of Foreign Languages.

Edwards, J.D. (2006). Written comments, Feb. 14, to the National Research Council Committee to Review the Title VI and Fulbright-Hays International Education Programs, Washington, DC.

E-LCTL Initiative. (2005). *National language offerings and enrollments at Title VI centers.* Available http://www.elctl.msu.edu/summaries/ [accessed Feb. 2007].

Folks, W.R., Jr. (2003). *Producing international expertise in MBA programs.* Research paper prepared for the Global Challenges and U.S. Higher Education Conference: National Needs and Policy Implications, Jan. 23-25, Duke University, Durham, NC. Available: http://www.jhfc.duke.edu/ducis/globalchallenges/research_papers.html.

Freed, B.F. (1981). Establishing proficiency-based language requirements. *ADFL Bulletin, 13*(2), 6-12.

Friedlander, J., Marshall, V., and Metzler, J. (2003). *Outreach: Current challenges and future prospects.* Available: http://www.jhfc.duke.edu/ducis/globalchallenges/research_papers. html [accessed Dec. 2006].

Fulcher, G. (1996a). Does thick description lead to smart tests? A data-based approach to rating scale construction. *Language Testing, 13,* 208-238.

Fulcher, G. (1996b). Invalidating validity claims for the ACTFL oral rating scale. *System, 24,* 163-172.

Gabara, U. (2006). Statement for the National Academy of Sciences on The Higher Education Act, Title VI, and the Mutual Educational and Cultural Exchange Act, Section 102(b)(6), International Education and Foreign Language Studies on Title VI, Section 604, Undergraduate International Studies and Foreign Language Program. Presentation and written submission, Feb. 14, National Research Council Committee to Review the Title VI and Fulbright-Hays International Education Programs, Washington, DC.

Georgetown University. (2006). *Event information: Syria, problem or solution in the Middle East?* Available: http://www14.georgetown.edu/explore/calendars/events/index.cfm?Action=View&CalendarID=89&EventID=45676 [accessed Jan. 2007].

Gerber, L. (2002). Title VI-B BIE funding, A survey of success. In R.F. Scherer, S.T. Beaton, M.F. Ainina, and J.F. Meyer (Eds.), *Internationalizing the business curriculum: A field guide.* Euclid, OH: Williams Custom.

Grand Valley State University. (2006). *BIE: Business and international education.* Available: http://www.gvsu.edu/bie/index.cfm?fuseaction=home.first [accessed Nov. 2006].

Grosse, R. (2006). *Homeland security and U.S. international competitiveness: 2003-2005 projects.* Glendale, AZ: Thunderbird, The Gavin School of International Management. Available: http://ciberweb.msu.edu/NationalImpact.asp [accessed Nov. 2006].

Gumperz, E.M. (1970). *Internationalizing American higher education.* Berkeley: University of California.

Harding, H. (2005). Creating curiosity about international affairs. *The State Education Standard*, 6(1), 8-11. Also available: http://www.nasbe.org/Standard/17_March2005/ Creating_Curoisity_Harding_03.05.pdf [accessed Feb. 2007].

Hawkins, J.N., Haro, C.M., Kazanjian, M.A., Merkx, G.W., and Wiley, D. (Eds.). (1998). *International education in the new global era: Proceedings of a national policy conference on the Higher Education Act, Title VI, and Fulbright-Hays programs.* Los Angeles: International Studies and Overseas Programs, University of California. Also available: http://www.isop.ucla.edu/pacrim/title6/T6%20contents.htm [accessed Feb. 2007].

Henke, R., Nevill, S., and Kraus, L. (2007). *Education and employment outcomes of participants in four federal graduate fellowship programs.* Washington, DC: U.S. Department of Education.

Heydemann, S. (2004).Warping mideast judgments. *The Chicago Tribune*, March 14.

Hines, R. (2001). An overview of Title VI. In P. O'Meara, H.D. Mehlinger, and R.M. Newman (Eds.), *Changing perspectives on international education* (pp. 6-10). Bloomington: Indiana University Press.

Honley, S.A. (2005). FSI settles into Arlington Hall. *Foreign Service Journal*, July/August, 17-31. Also available: http://www.afsa.org/fsj/JulAug05/honley.pdf [accessed Feb. 2007].

House Permanent Select Committee on Intelligence, Senate Select Committee on Intelligence. (2002). *Report of the joint inquiry into the terrorist attacks of September 11, 2001.* Washington, DC: Author.

Hudson, T., Detmer, E., and Brown, J.D. (1992). *A framework for testing cross-cultural pragmatics.* Honolulu: Second Language Teaching and Curriculum Center, University of Hawaii at Manoa.

Indiana University. (2002). *Indiana in the world: Themes and lesson plans.* Available: http://www.indianaintheworld.indiana.edu [accessed Dec. 2006].

Ingold, C.W., Rivers, W., Tesser, C.C., and Ashby, E. (2002). Report on the NFLC/AATSP survey of Spanish language programs for native speakers. *Hispania*, 85, 324-329.

Institute for International Education. (2002). *Open doors report on international education exchange.* New York: Author.

Interagency Language Roundtable. (2006a). *About the ILR.* Available: http://www.govtilr. org/IRL%20Add_ons%2006/ILR_History.htm [accessed Nov. 2006].

Interagency Language Roundtable. (2006b). Written comments to the National Research Council Committee to Review the Title VI and Fulbright-Hays International Education Programs, by S.G. McGinnis, and G. Nordin. Written submission, May 9, to the Committee to Review the Title VI and Fulbright-Hays International Education Programs, Washington, DC.

Iowa State University. (2000-2004). *New visions in action.* Available: http://nflrc.iastate. edu/nva/ [accessed Nov. 2006].

Iowa State University. (2003). *2003 summer institutes at Iowa State University: Mentoring, leadership and change.* Available: http://nflrc.iastate.edu/inst/2003/homepage.html [accessed April 2007].

Iowa State University. (2006). *National K-12 foreign language resource center.* Available: http://nclrc.org/about_teaching/inst_highlights.html [accessed Dec. 2006].

Jackson, F.H., and Kaplan, M.A. (n.d.). *Theory and practice in government language training.* Available: http://www.govtilr.org/PapersArchive/TESOL03ReadingFull.htm [accessed Dec. 2005].

Jaschik, S. (2007). Dramatic plan for language programs. *Inside Higher Education*, Jan. 2. Available: http://www.insidehighered.com/news/2007/01/02/languages [accessed March 2007].

Joint Committee for Languages and the National Council for Languages. (2006). *A response to the National Security Language Initiative by the language profession.* Available: http://www.languagepolicy.org/documents/JNCL_Response_to_NSLI08-06.doc [accessed Nov. 2006].

Joyner, C. (2006a). *A framework for considering evaluation of the Title VI and Fulbright-Hays international education programs.* Paper commissioned by the National Research Council Committee to Review the Title VI and Fulbright-Hays International Education Programs, Washington, DC.

Joyner, C. (2006b). *Increasing representation of minorities in international service through international education programs.* Paper commissioned by the National Research Council Committee to Review the Title VI and Fulbright-Hays International Education Programs, Washington, DC.

Joyner, C., and Suarez, T. (2006). *Technology and instructional materials in Title VI and Fulbright-Hays international education programs.* Paper commissioned by the National Research Council Committee to Review the Title VI and Fulbright-Hays International Education Programs, Washington, DC.

Kagan, O. (2006). *UCLA Language Resource Center.* Presentation to site visit team of the National Research Council Committee to Review the Title VI and Fulbright-Hays International Education Programs, Oct. 4, Department of Education, Washington, DC.

Kagan, O., and Dillon, K. (2001). A new perspective on teaching Russian: Focus on the heritage learner. *Slavic and East European Journal, 45*(3), 507-518.

Keatley, C. (2006). *Title VI—Language resource centers.* Prepared by the Council of Directors of the Language Resource Centers. Presentation and written submission, Feb. 14, to the National Research Council Committee to Review the Title VI and Fulbright-Hays International Education Programs, Washington, DC.

Kedia, B.L., and Daniel, S. (2003). *U.S. business needs for employees with international expertise.* Paper presented at Global Challenges Conference, Jan., Duke University, Durham, NC.

Kenyon, D.M., and Tschirner, E. (2000). The rating of direct and semi-direct oral proficiency interviews: Comparing performance at lower proficiency levels. *Modern Language Journal, 84*(1), 85-101.

Kondo-Brown, K. (2003). Heritage language instruction for postsecondary students from immigrant backgrounds. *Heritage Language Journal, 1*(1), Spring. Available: http://www.heritagelanguages.org/ [accessed March 2007].

Kramer, M. (2003). *Can Congress fix Middle East studies?* Presentation to the panel "Can Congress Fix Middle Eastern Studies?" at the Washington Institute for Near East Policy, November 20, Washington, DC. Available: http://www.geocities.com/martinkramerorg/HR3077.htm [accessed June 2006].

Kramer, M. (2001). *Ivory towers on sand: The failure of Middle Eastern studies in America.* Washington, DC: The Washington Institute for Near East Policy.

Kramer, M. (2006). *Title VI: Bring the languages back.* Available: http://www.geocities.com/martinkramerorg/2006_02_15.htm [accessed June 2006].

Kramsch, C. (1986). From language proficiency to interactional competence. *The Modern Language Journal, 70*(4), 366-372.

Kroll, J., and De Groot, A.M.B. (Eds.). (in press). *Handbook of bilingualism: Psycholinguistic approaches.* New York: Oxford University Press.

Kuenzi, J.J. (2004). *Requirements for linguists in government agencies.* Washington, DC: Congressional Research Service.

Kuenzi, J.J., and Riddle, W.C. (2005a). *Foreign language and area studies: Federal aid under Title VI of the Higher Education Act.* Washington, DC: Congressional Research Service.

Kuenzi, J.J., and Riddle, W.C. (2005b). *National security education program: Background and issues.* Washington, DC: Congressional Research Service.

Kurtz, S. (2003). Testimony: International Programs in Higher Education and Questions of Bias. Hearing before the Subcommittee on Select Education of the House Committee on Education and the Workforce, 108th Congress, Washington, DC.

Kurtz, S. (2006). Language @ war: The Middle East-studies front. *National Review Online*, Feb. 14. Available: http://www.nationalreview.com/script/printpage.p?ref=/kurtz/kurtz200602140808.asp [accessed Feb. 2007].

Lane, M.E. (2006). Statement for the National Academy of Sciences, The Higher Education Act, Title VI, Section 609, American Overseas Research Centers. Presentation and written submission, Feb. 14, National Research Council Committee to Review the Title VI and Fulbright-Hays International Education Programs, Washington, DC.

Lane, S., Liu, M., Ankenmann, R.D., and Stone, C.A. (1996). Generalizability and validity of mathematics performance assessments. *Journal of Educational Measurement, 33*(1), 71-92.

Language Acquisition Resource Center. (2006). *Computer assisted screening tool.* Available: http://cast.sdsu.edu/ [accessed Feb. 2007].

Language Testing International. (2006). *The ACTFL language testing office.* Available: http://www.languagetesting.com/index.html [accessed Feb. 2007].

Lantolf, J.P., and Frawley, W. (1985). Oral proficiency testing: A critical analysis. *Modern Language Journal, 69*, 337-345.

Lantolf, J.P., and Frawley, W. (1988). Proficiency: Understanding the construct. *Studies in Second Language Acquisition, 10*(2), 181-195.

Lazaraton, A. (1996). Interlocutor support in oral proficiency interviews: The case of CASE. *Language Testing, 13*(2), 151-172.

Leonard, N. (2004). *After-school Arabic program San Diego.* (LARC update, #13). San Diego, CA: San Diego State University Language Acquisition Resource Center.

Lichtblau, E. (2004). FBI said to lag on translations of terror tapes. *New York Times*, Sept. 28.

Liebman, J.S., and Sabel, C.F. (2003). A public laboratory Dewey barely imagined: The emerging model of school governance and legal reform. *New York University Review of Law and Social Change, 28*(2), 183-304.

Light, P. (1999). *The true size of government.* Washington, DC: Brookings Institution.

Liskin-Gasparro, J.E. (2003). The ACTFL proficiency guidelines and the oral proficiency interview: A brief history and analysis of their survival. *Foreign Language Annals, 36*(4) 483-489.

Lowe, P., Jr. (1986). Proficiency: Panacea, framework, process? A reply to Kramsch, Schulz, and particularly Bachman and Savignon. *Modern Language Journal, 70*(4), 391-397.

Lowe, P., Jr. (1988). The unassimilated history. In P. Lowe, Jr. and C.W. Stansfield (Eds.), *Second language proficiency: Current issues* (pp. 11-51). Englewood Cliffs, NJ: Prentice-Hall Regents.

Lowe, P., Jr., and Stansfield, C.W. (1988). Introduction. In P. Lowe, Jr. and C.W. Stansfield (Eds.), *Second language proficiency assessment: Current issues.* Englewood Cliffs, NJ: Prentice-Hall Regents.

Lynch, B.K., and McNamara, T.F. (1998). Using g-theory and many-facet Rasch measurement in the development of performance assessments of ESL speaking skills of immigrants. *Language Testing, 15*(2), 158-180.

Malone, M. (2003). Research on the oral proficiency interview: Analysis, synthesis and future directions. *Foreign Language Annals, 36*(4), 491-497.

Malone, M. (2006). *The oral proficiency interview approach to foreign language assessment.* Paper commissioned by the National Research Council Committee to Review the Title VI and Fulbright-Hays International Education Programs, Washington, DC.

Manzo, K.K. (2006a). Scarcity of language teachers retards growth. *Education Week,* March 29.

Manzo, K.K. (2006b). Students taking Spanish, French; Leaders pushing Chinese, Arabic. *Education Week,* March 29.

Markee, N. (2006). A conversation analytic perspective on the role of quantification in second language. In M. Chalhoub, C.A. Chapelle, and P.A. Duffs (Eds.), *Inference and generalizability in applied linguistics: Multiple research perspectives* (pp. 135-162). Amsterdam, Netherlands: John Benjamins.

McCarthy, J.A. (1998). Continuing and emerging national needs for the internationalization of undergraduate education. In J.N. Hawkins, C.M. Haro, M.A. Kazanjian, G.W., Merkx, and D. Wiley (Eds.). *International education in the new global era: Proceedings of a national policy conference on the Higher Education Act, Title VI, and Fulbright-Hays programs* (Plenary Paper #2, pp. 65-75). Los Angeles: International Studies and Overseas Programs, University of California. Also available: http://www.isop.ucla.edu/pacrim/ title6/Plen2-McCarthy.pdf [accessed March 2007].

McCartney, S. (2006). Teaching Americans how to behave abroad. *Wall Street Journal Online,* April 13. Available: http://www.careerjournal.com/myc/workabroad/20060413-mccartney.html [accessed Aug. 2006].

McDonnell, L., Berryman, S.E., Scott, D., Pincus, J., and Robyn, A. (1981, May). *Federal support for international studies: The role of NDEA Title VI.* Santa Monica, CA: RAND.

McDonnell, L., Stasz, C., and Madison, R. (1983). *Federal support for training foreign language and area specialists: The education and careers of FLAS fellowship recipients.* Santa Monica, CA: RAND.

McLarney, E. (2005). Goals, strategies, and curricula in advanced Arabic learning. *ADFL Bulletin* (37), 1.

Mellon, C.K. (2000). Statement before the International Security, Proliferation, and Federal Services Subcommittee of the Committee on Government Affairs, U.S. Senate, Sept. 14, 19, Washington, DC.

Merkx, G.W. (2005). *The institutional context of Title VI area and international studies.* Paper prepared for the National Academies, Washington, DC.

Merkx, G.W. (2006). *Four key programs in Title VI and Fulbright-Hays 102(b)(6): NRC's, FLAS Fellowships, DDRA and FRA.* Presentation and written submission, Feb. 14, National Research Council Committee to Review the Title VI and Fulbright-Hays International Education Programs, Washington, DC.

Metzler, J.M. (1997). Challenges for Title VI programs of outreach in foreign language and international studies. In J.M. Hawkins and C.M. Haro (Eds.), *International Education in the New Global Era: Proceedings of a National Policy Conference* (pp. 117-133). Los Angeles: International Studies and Overseas Programs, University of California. Also available: http://www.isop.ucla.edu/pacrim/title6/Break2-P-R-Metzler-Williams.pdf [accessed May 2007].

Michigan State University. (n.d.). *The interagency language roundtable 2006-2007.* Available: http://www.govtilr.org/IRL%20Add_ons%2006/ILR_History.htm [accessed Nov. 2006].

Michigan State University. (2006a). *MSU center for international business education and research, globalEDGE™.* Available: http://ciber.msu.edu/globalEDGE/ [accessed Nov. 2006].

Michigan State University. (2006b). News release: MSU, U.S. Departments of Defense, Education announce major grants to improve teaching of critical foreign languages in Michigan K-12 schools. Available: http://newsroom.msu.edu/site/indexer/2870/content.htm [accessed Feb. 2007].

Michigan State University. (2007). *African online digital library.* Available: http://www.aodl. org/ [accessed Jan. 2007].

Modern Language Association. (1998). Final report of the MLA committee on professional employment. *Association of Department of English Bulletin, 119*(spring), 27-45. Also available: http://www.mla.org/ade/bulletin/n119/119027.htm [accessed Sept. 2006].

Murphrey, K.J. (2006). Statement for the National Academy of Sciences on The Higher Education Act, Title VI, and the Mutual Educational and Cultural Exchange Act, Section 102(b)(6), International Education and Foreign Language Studies on behalf of the Business and International Education (BIE) Program. Presentation and written submission, Feb. 14, National Research Council Committee to Review the Title VI and Fulbright-Hays International Education Programs, Washington, DC.

Murphy, P.J., and DeArmond, M.M. (2003). *From the headlines to the frontlines: The teacher shortage and its implications for recruitment policy.* Seattle: University of Washington, Center on Reinventing Public Education.

National Academy of Sciences, National Academy of Engineering, and Institute of Medicine. (2007). *Rising above the gathering storm: Energizing and employing America for a brighter economic future.* Committee on Prospering in the Global Economy of the 21st Century: An Agenda for American Science and Technology. Committee on Science, Engineering, and Public Policy. Washington, DC: The National Academies Press.

National Bureau of Economic Research, Arrow, K.J., and Capron, W.M. (1959). Dynamic shortages and price rises: The engineer-scientist case. *Quarterly Journal of Economics,* 292-308, May.

National Capital Language Resource Center. (2006a). *About teaching: Institutes highlights.* Available: http://nclrc.org/about_teaching/inst_highlights.html [accessed Dec. 2006].

National Capital Language Resource Center. (2006b). *Teachers' corner. Languages? Ask Dora.* Available: http://www.nclrc.org/teachers_corner/languages_dora.html [accessed Dec. 2006].

National Center for Education Statistics. (2005). *Digest of Education Statistics: 2005. Table 250.* Available: http://nces.ed.gov/programs/digest/d05/tables/dt05_250.asp [accessed Nov. 2006].

National Center for Education Statistics. (2006). *The condition of education: Contexts of postsecondary education.* Washington, DC: Author. Also available: http://nces.ed.gov/programs/coe/2006/section5/table.asp?tableID=521 [accessed Nov. 2006].

National Commission on Terrorist Attacks Upon the United States. (2004). *Reforming law enforcement, counterterrorism, and intelligence collection in the United States.* (Tenth Public Hearing, Staff Statement No. 12). Available: http://www.9-11commission.gov/staff_statements/index.htm. [accessed Feb. 2007].

National Council of Less Commonly Taught Languages. (n.d.). *Frequently asked questions about the council.* Available: http://www.councilnet.org/council/learn_faqs.htm#2 [accessed Jan. 2006].

National Council of Less Commonly Taught Languages. (2006). *Journal of the National Council of Less Commonly Taught Languages.* Available: http://www.councilnet.org/conf/announce.htm [accessed Dec. 2006].

National Commission on Asia in the Schools. (2005). *Asia in the schools: Preparing young Americans for today's interconnected world.* New York: The Asia Society. Also available: http://www.asiasociety.org/pressroom/rel-study.html [accessed Jan. 2007].

National Commission on Terrorist Attacks Upon the United States. (2004). *The 9/11 Commission Report: Final report of the National Commission on Terrorist Attacks Upon the United States.* Washington, DC: Author.

National Language Conference. (2005). *A call to action for national foreign language capabilities white paper.* Proceedings of the National Language Conference sponsored by the Department of Defense and the Center for Advanced Study of Language, June 22-24, 2004, University of Maryland, College Park. Available: http://www.nlconference.org/docs/White_Paper.pdf [accessed March 2007].

National Research Council. (2001). *Building a workforce for the information economy.* Committee on Workforce Needs in Information Technology, Computer Science and Telecommunications Board, Board on Testing and Assessment, Board on Science, Technology, and Economic Policy, Office of Scientific and Engineering Personnel. Washington, DC: National Academy Press.

National Research Council. (2004). *Strengthening peer review in federal agencies that support education research.* Committee on Research in Education. L. Towne, J.M. Fletcher, and L. Wise, Eds. Center for Education, Division of Behavioral and Social Sciences and Education. Washington, DC: The National Academies Press.

National Security Education Program. (n.d.). *National security education program: Report to Congress.* Available: http://www.ndu.edu/nsep/NSEPRpt.pdf [accessed Nov. 2005].

National Virtual Translation Center. (2007). *What we offer.* Available: http://www.nvtc.gov/whatWeOffer.html [accessed Jan. 2007].

Newhall, A.W. (2006). Statement for the National Academy of Sciences on The Higher Education Act, Title VI, and the Mutual Educational and Cultural Exchange Act, Section 102(b)(6), International Education and Foreign Language Studies on behalf of the Middle East Studies Association and the Middle East National Resource Centers. Presentation and written submission, Feb. 14, National Research Council Committee to Review the Title VI and Fulbright-Hays International Education Programs, Washington, DC.

Ohio State University. (2006). *Online modules for global educators.* Available: http://www.coe.ohio-state.edu/mmerryfield/global_resources/default.htm [accessed Dec. 2006].

Ohio State University. (2007). *Center for Latin American studies: Resources for teachers.* Available: http://clas.osu.edu/rescources%20for%20teachers.htm [accessed Jan. 2007].

Oklahoma State Department of Education. (2006). *Standards-based textbook evaluation guide.* Available: http://title2.sde.state.ok.us/languages/textbookevaluation-3.htm [accessed Nov. 2006].

Oller, J.W., Jr. (1976). Evidence of a general language proficiency factor: An expectancy grammar. *Die neuren sprachen, 76,* 165-174.

Oller, J.W., Jr. (1979). *Language tests at school.* London, England: Longman.

Oller, J.W., Jr. (1983). A consensus for the eighties? In J.W. Oller (Ed.), *Issues in language testing research* (pp. 351-356.). Rowley, MA: Newbury House.

Omaggio, A.C. (1983). Methodology in transition: Focus on proficiency. *Modern Language Journal, 67*(4), 330-341.

Omaggio, A.C., and Shinall, S.L. (1987). Foreign language teacher education: Current practices and assessment needs. *Annals of the American Academy of Political and Social Science, 490,* 147-162.

O'Meara, P., Mehlinger, H.D., and Newman, R.M. (Eds.). (2001). *Changing perspectives on international education.* Bloomington: Indiana University Press.

Ovando, C.J. (1990). Essay review: Politics and pedagogy: The case of bilingual education. *Harvard Educational Review, 60,* 350-356.

Paquette, F.A. (1980). The mandate for a national program for assessment of language proficiency. *ADFL Bulletin, 11*(3), 12-15.

Partnership for Public Service. (2006, May). *Back to school: Rethinking federal recruiting on college campuses.* (Issue Brief PPS-06-01). Washington, DC: Author.

Partnership for Public Service. (2006, May). *Foreign language skills.* (Issue Brief PPS-06-02). Washington, DC: Author.

Peace Corps. (2005). *Peace Corps performance and accountability report, fiscal year 2005.* Available: http://www.peacecorps.gov/policies/pdf/annrept2005.pdf [accessed Feb. 2007].

Pennsylvania State University. (2007). *Narrative and conceptual proficiency in Russian: A website for students and teachers.* Available: http://calper.la.psu.edu/russian/index.php [accessed Jan. 2007].

Pienemann, M., Johnson, J., and Brindley, G. (1988). Constructing an acquisition-based procedure for language assessment. *Studies in Second Language Acquisition, 10,* 217-243.

Powell, C. (2003). *The Foreign Service: Taking America's case to the world.* Available: http://www.state.gov/secretary/former/powell/remarks/2003/20589.htm [accessed Nov. 2006].

Powell, D., and Lowenkron, B. (2006). *National security language initiative.* (U.S. Department of State fact sheet, Jan. 5). Available: http://www.state.gov/r/pa/prs/ps/2006/58733.htm [accessed Jan. 2007].

Purcell, E.T. (1983). Models of pronunciation accuracy. In J.W. Oller, Jr. (Ed.), *Issues in language testing research* (pp. 133-151). Rowley, MA: Newbury House.

Purcell, E.T., and Suter, R.W. (1981). Predictors of pronunciation accuracy: A reexamination. *Language Learning, 30,* 271-288.

Purdue University. (2006). *International business education: Outreach initiatives for k-12 education.* West Lafayette, IN: Author. Also available: http://ciberweb.msu.edu/NationalImpact.asp [accessed Nov. 2006].

Rammuny, R.J. (2005). Integrating media into Arabic instruction: Advantages and challenges. *ADFL Bulletin,* (37), 1.

Rhodes, N.D., and Branaman, L.E. (1999). *Foreign language instruction in the United States: A national survey of elementary and secondary schools.* McHenry, IL and Washington, DC: Delta Systems and Center for Applied Linguistics.

Riddle, W.C. (1989). *Foreign language and international education: The federal role.* Washington, DC: Congressional Research Service.

Rieffl, L. (2003). *The Peace Corps in a turbulent world.* Available: http://www.brook.edu/views/papers/rieffel20031015.pdf [accessed Oct. 2005].

Roper Public Affairs and Media. (2002). *Global geographic literacy survey.* Available: http://www.nationalgeographic.com/geosurvey2002/download/RoperSurvey.pdf [accessed March 2007].

Roper Public Affairs and Media. (2006). *2006 National Geographic-Roper survey of geographic literacy.* Available: http://www.nationalgeographic.com/roper2006/findings.html [accessed Jan. 2007].

Rosenbusch, M.H., Kemis, M., and Moran, K.J. (2000). Changing practice: Impact of a national institute on foreign language teacher preparation for the k-6 level of instruction *ACTFL Foreign Language Annals, 33*(3), May/June. Available: http://www.yearoflanguages.org/i4a/pages/Index.cfm?pageid=4137 [accessed Feb. 2007].

Ruther, N.L. (2002). *Barely there, powerfully present: Thirty years of U.S. policy on international higher education.* New York: RoutledgeFalmer.

Ruther, N.L. (2003). *The international and foreign language human capital challenge of the U.S. federal government.* Paper presented at Global Challenges Conference, Jan., Duke University, Durham, NC.

Ruther, N.L. (2006). *Implementation issues and options for the HEA Title VI and Fulbright Hays programs.* Paper written for the National Research Council Committee to Review the Title VI and Fulbright-Hays International Education Programs, Washington, DC.

Salaberry, R. (2000). Revising the revised format of the ACTFL oral proficiency interview. *Language Testing, 17*(3), 289-310.

San Diego State University Language Acquisition Research Center. (2006a). *Baja literature project: Every land is a border land*. Available: http://larcnet.sdsu.edu/tech.php?page=baja [accessed Dec. 2006].

San Diego State University Language Acquisition Research Center. (2006b). *Human rights: Human by any language*. Available: http://larcnet.sdsu.edu/tech.php?page=humanrights [accessed Dec. 2006].

San Diego State University Language Acquisition Research Center. (2007). *Diagnostic testing and materials*. Available: http://larcnet.sdsu.edu/testing.php?page=bclad [accessed Feb. 2007].

Scarfo, R. (1998). The history of Title VI and Fulbright-Hays. In J.N. Hawkins, C.M. Haro, M.A. Kazanjian, G.W. Merkx, and D. Wiley (Eds.), *International education in the new global era: Proceedings of a National Policy Conference on the Higher Education Act, Title VI, and Fulbright-Hays programs* (pp. 23-25). Los Angeles: University of California, International Studies and Overseas Programs.

Schneider, A.I. (2003). *Internationalizing teacher education: What can be done?: A research report on the undergraduate training of secondary school teachers*. Available: http://www.internationaledadvice.org/pdfs/What_Can_Be_Done.pdf [accessed Feb. 2007].

Schneider, A.I. (2006). Comments for Committee for Review of Title VI and Fulbright-Hays Programs. Written submission, Feb. 14, to the National Research Council Committee to Review the Title VI and Fulbright-Hays International Education Programs, Washington, DC.

Schneider, A.I., and Burn, B.B. (1999). *Federal funding for international studies: Does it help? Does it matter? A study of the long-term impacts of federal funding on international studies and foreign language programs*. Amherst: International Programs Office, University of Massachusetts.

Schulz, R.A. (1988). Proficiency-based foreign language requirements: A plan for action. *ADFL Bulletin, 19*(2), 24-28.

Schumann, J. (1978). The acculturation model for second language acquisition. In R. Gingras (Ed.), *Second language acquisition and foreign language teaching*. (pp. 27-50). Arlington, VA: Center for Applied Linguistics.

Schumann, J. (1997). *The neurobiology of affect in language*. Malden, MA: Blackwell.

Shavelson, R.J., Baxter, G., and Gao, X. (1993). Sampling variability of performance assessments. *Journal of Educational Measurement, 30*(3), 215-232.

Shavelson, R.J., Ruiz-Primo, M.A., and Wiley, E.W. (1999). Note on sources of sampling variability in science performance assessments. *Journal of Educational Measurement, 36*(1), 61-71.

Slater, J. (2006). *An analysis of the legislative history of the Title VI and Fulbright-Hays international education programs*. Paper prepared for the National Research Council Committee to Review the Title VI and Fulbright-Hays International Education Programs, Washington, DC.

Sollenberger, H.E. (1978). Development and current use of the FSI oral interview test. In J.L.D. Clark (Ed.), *Direct testing of speaking proficiency: Theory and application*. Princeton, NJ: Educational Testing Service.

Spellings, M. (2006). *Statement on international education week 2006*. Available: http://www.ed.gov/about/inits/ed/internationaled/iew2006-spellings.html [accessed Nov. 2006].

SRI International. (2005a, June). *Outcome assessment of the U.S. Fulbright student program*. Arlington, VA: Author.

SRI International. (2005b, June). *Outcome assessment of the visiting Fulbright scholar program*. Arlington, VA: Author.

Stansfield, C.W., and Kenyon, D.M. (1992). The development and validation of a simulated oral proficiency interview. *Modern Language Journal, 76*, 129-141.

Stecher, B.M., Klein, S.P., Solarno-Flores, G., McCaffrey, D., Robyn, A., and Shavelson, R.J. (2000). The effects of content, format, and inquiry level on science performance assessment scores. *Applied Measurement in Education, 13*(2), 139-160.

Stewart, T.K. (2006). *Complementarity and collaboration: Leveraging the Title VI and Fulbright-Hays international programs.* Presentation and written submission, Feb. 14, National Research Council Committee to Review the Title VI and Fulbright-Hays International Education Programs, Washington, DC.

Stewart, V. (2006). Remarks before the National Research Council Committee to Review Title VI and Fulbright-Hays. Presentation and written submission, Feb. 14, National Research Council Committee to Review the Title VI and Fulbright-Hays International Education Programs, Washington, DC.

Stokes, L. (1991). Cosponsorship of legislation to establish an undergraduate critical skills scholarship program. *Congressional Record, E3562.* Available: http://www.fas.org/irp/congress/1991_cr/h911028-skill.htm [accessed Feb. 2007].

Surface, E.A., and Dierdorff, E.C. (2003). Reliability and the ACTFL oral proficiency interview: Reporting indices of interrater consistency and agreement for 19 languages. *Foreign Language Annals, 36*(4), 507-519.

Swender, E. (2003). Oral proficiency testing in the real world: Answers to frequently asked questions. *Foreign Language Annals, 36*(4), 520-526.

Tarone, E. (2000). Still wrestling with "context" in interlanguage theory. *Annual Review of Applied Linguistics, 20*, 182-198.

Thompson, I. (1991). The proficiency movement: Where do we go from here? *The Slavic and East European Journal, 35*(3), 375-389.

Trubek, D.M. (1999). The future of international studies. In D. Ward and N. Radomski (Eds.), *Proud traditions and future challenges—The University of Wisconsin-Madison celebrates 150 years.* Madison: Office of University Publications, University of Wisconsin. Also available: http://www.law.wisc.edu/facstaff/trubek/publications.html [accessed Nov. 2006].

Trutko, J., Barnow, B.S., Chasanov, A.B., and Pande, A. (2003). *Labor shortage case studies.* (Report Series 93–E). Washington, DC: U.S. Department of Labor, Employment and Training Administration Research and Evaluation.

Tushnet, N.C., Millsap, M.A., Abdullah-Welsh, N., Brigham, N., Cooley, E., Elliott, J., Johnston, K., Martinez, A., Nierenberg, M., and Rosenblum, S. (2000). *Final report on the evaluation of the National Science Foundation's instructional materials development program.* Arlington, VA: National Science Foundation.

United Negro College Fund Special Programs Corporation. (2006, August). *Institute for International Public Policy impact assessment.* Fairfax, VA: Author.

United States Congressional Budget Office. (2001). *Changes in federal civilian employment: An update.* Washington, DC: Author. Also available: http://www.cbo.gov/showdoc.cfm?index=2864&sequence=0 [accessed Oct. 2006].

United States Department of Commerce, International Trade Administration. (n.d.). *U.S. shares of world trade, by type.* Available: http://www.ita.doc.gov/td/industry/otea/usfth/aggregate/h03t54.html [accessed Aug. 2006].

United States Department of Defense. (2005). *Defense language transformation roadmap.* Washington, DC: Author.

United States Department of Education. (n.d.). *The history of Title VI and Fulbright Hays: An impressive international timeline.* Available: http://www.ed.gov/about/offices/list/ope/iegps/history.html [accessed Jan. 2006].

United States Department of Education. (2005a). Centers for international business education and research—Notice inviting applications for new awards for fiscal year (FY) 2006. *Federal Register, (70)*196, 59329-59333. Also available: http://www.ed.gov/legislation/FedRegister/announcements/2005-4/101205b.html [accessed Nov. 2005].

United States Department of Education. (2005b). *ESEA: Foreign language assistance 2005.* Available: http://www.ed.gov/about/reports/annual/2005plan/edlite-esea-foreign.html [accessed Dec. 2005].

United States Department of Education. (2005c). *HEA: Fund for the improvement of postsecondary education.* Available: http://www.ed.gov/about/reports/annual/2005plan/edlite-hea-fund.html [accessed Dec. 2005].

United States Department of Education. (2005d). Higher education programs: Final regulations. *Federal Register, (70)*53, 13371-13377. Also available: http://www.ed.gov/legislation/FedRegister/finrule/2005-1/032105a.html [accessed Nov. 2005].

United States Department of Education. (2005e). Language resource centers—Notice inviting applications for new awards for fiscal year (FY) 2006. *Federal Register, (70)*200, 60505-60508. Also available: http://www.ed.gov/legislation/FedRegister/announcements/2005-4/101805f.html [accessed Nov. 2006].

United States Department of Education. (2005f). National resource centers—Notice inviting applications for new awards for fiscal year (FY) 2006. *Federal Register, (70)*198, 60066-60072. Also available: http://www.ed.gov/legislation/FedRegister/announcements/2005-4/101405b.html [accessed Nov. 2006].

United States Department of Education. (2005g). *Title VI technological innovation and cooperation for foreign information access—Program description and project abstracts for 2002-2005 funding cycle.* Available: http://www.ed.gov/programs/iegpsticfia/ticfia-abstracts2002-05.doc [accessed Jan. 2006].

United States Department of Education. (2006a). *A test of leadership: Charting the future of U.S. higher education.* Washington, DC: Author.

United States Department of Education. (2006b). Business and international education program notice—Inviting applications for new awards for fiscal year (FY) 2006. *Federal Register, (70)*196, 59322-59325. Also available: http://www.ed.gov/legislation/FedRegister/announcements/2005-4/101205a.html [accessed Nov. 2006].

United States Department of Education. (2006c). Foreign language assistance program—Notice of final priority and notice inviting applications for new awards for fiscal year 2006. *Federal Register, (71)*97, May 19. Also available: http://www.ed.gov/legislation/FedRegister/finrule/2006-2/051906d.html [accessed Nov. 2006].

United States Department of Education. (2006d). Submission for OMB review: Comment request. *Federal Register,* 71(241), 75513. Also available: http://www.ed.gov/legislation/FedRegister/other/2006-4/121506c.html [accessed Jan. 2007].

United States Department of Education. (2007a). *Comprehensive centers program.* Available: http://www.ed.gov/programs/newccp/index.html [accessed Jan. 2007].

United States Department of Education. (2007b). *Fulbright-Hays—Group projects abroad program.* Available: http://www.ed.gov/programs/iegpsgpa/index.html [accessed Jan. 2007].

United States Department of Education. (2007c). *Fulbright-Hays—Seminars abroad program.* Available: http://www.ed.gov/programs/iegpssap/index.html [accessed Jan. 2007].

United States Department of Education. (2007d). *IES regional education laboratory program: About us.* Available: http://ies.ed.gov/ncee/edlabs/about/ [accessed Jan. 2007].

United States Department of Education International Education Programs Service Office of Postsecondary Education. (n.d.). *The history of Title VI and Fulbright Hays: An impressive international timeline.* Available: http://www.ed.gov/print/about/offices/list/ope/iegps/history.html [accessed May 2005].

United States Department of Education International Education Programs Service Office of Postsecondary Education. (2007). *International Education Programs Service home page.* Available: http://www.ed.gov/about/offices/list/ope/iegps/index.html [accessed March 2007].

United States Department of Education Office of Postsecondary Education. (1998). *Demonstrating results: An introduction to the Government Performance and Results Act.* Washington, DC: Author.

United States Department of Justice, Office of the Inspector General. (2004, July). *The Federal Bureau of Investigation's foreign language program–Translation of counterterrorism and counterintelligence foreign language material.* Washington, DC: Author.

United States Department of State. (2003). *The Fulbright program: Facts and figures.* Available: http://exchanges.state.gov/education/fulbright/ffsb/annualreport/2003/facts.pdf [acccessed Dec. 2005].

United States Department of State. (2004). *Department of State and international assistance programs PART assessments.* Available: http://www.whitehouse.gov/omb/budget/fy2005/pma/state.pdf [accessed Feb. 2007].

United States Department of State. (2005a). *OMB PART summaries by strategic goal.* Available: http://www.state.gov/s/d/rm/rls/perfrpt/2004/html/c13498.htm [accessed Dec. 2005].

United States Department of State. (2005b). *Performance and accountability report, fiscal year 2005.* Available: http://www.state.gov/s/d/rm/rls/perfrpt/2005/ [accessed Feb. 2007].

United States Department of State. (2006). *Briefing on the national security language initiative.* Available: http://www.state.gov/g/rls/rm/2005/58737.htm [accessed Jan. 2006].

United States General Accounting Office. (1978). *Study of foreign languages and related areas: Federal support, administration, need. Comptroller General's report to the Congress of the United States.* (ID 78-46, Sept. 13). Washington, DC: Author.

United States General Accounting Office. (2002). *Foreign languages: Human capital approach needed to correct staffing and proficiency shortfalls.* Available: http://www.gao.gov/new.items/d02375.pdf [accessed May 2005].

United States General Accounting Office. (2003, Sept.). *Military training: Strategic planning and distributive learning could benefit the Special Operations Forces foreign language program.* Available: http://www.gao.gov/new.items/d031026.pdf [accessed Feb. 2007].

United States Government Accountability Office. (2004a). *Performance budgeting: PART focuses attention on program performance, but more can be done to engage Congress.* Available: http://www.gao.gov/new.items/d0628.pdf [accessed Feb. 2007].

United States Government Accountability Office. (2004b). *Results-oriented government: GPRA has established a solid foundation for achieving results.* (GAO #04-594T). Available: http://www.gao.gov/htext/d04594t.html [accessed Feb. 2007].

United States Government Accountability Office. (2005, October). *Performance budgeting: PART focuses attention on program performance, but more can be done to engage Congress.* (GAO-#06-28). Available: http://www.gao.gov/new.items/d0628.pdf [accessed Jan. 2006.]

United States Government Accountability Office. (2006, August). *Department of State: Staffing and foreign language shortfalls persist despite initiatives to address gaps.* (GAO #06-894). Available: http://www.gao.gov/new.items/d06894.pdf [accessed Sept. 2006].

United States House of Representatives, Committee on Education and Labor. (1992). *Report of the House of Representatives Committee on Education and Labor on the Higher Education Amendments of 1992.* (H.R. 3553, 102nd Congress, 2nd session). Washington, DC: U.S. Government Printing Office.

United States House of Representatives Committee on Education and the Workforce. (2003). *Education subcommittee approves Hoekstra measure to strengthen international studies in higher education, ensure programs fulfill national security needs.* Available: http://edworkforce.house.gov/press/press108/09sep/hr3077psub091703.htm [accessed June 2006].

United States News & World Report. (2006a). America's best colleges 2007, undergraduate business specialties: International business. *U.S. News and World Report, (141)7,* 122.

United States News & World Report. (2006b). *America's best graduate schools 2007, top business schools.* Available: http://www.usnews.com/usnews/edu/grad/rankings/mba/brief/mbarank_brief.php [accessed Nov. 2006].

United States Office of Management and Budget. (2004). *Detailed information on the international education domestic programs assessment.* Available: http://www.whitehouse.gov/omb/expectmore/detail/10002102.2004.html [accessed Feb. 2007].

University of Arizona. (2007). *Computer aided language instruction group.* Available: http://cali.arizona.edu/. [accessed Jan. 2007].

University of California at Los Angeles. (2001). *Heritage language research priorities conference report.* Available: http://www.cal.org/heritage/priorities.html.

University of California at Los Angeles. (2006a). *Asia media.* Available: http://www.asiamedia.ucla.edu/ [accessed Dec. 2006].

University of California at Los Angeles. (2006b). *Asia Pacific arts.* Available: http://www.asiaarts.ucla.edu/ [accessed Dec. 2006].

University of California at Los Angeles. (2006c). *Outreach world: A resource for teaching kids about the world.* Available: http://www.outreachworld.org/index.asp [accessed Dec. 2006].

University of California at Los Angeles. (2006d). *UCLA language materials project.* Available: http://www.lmp.ucla.edu/ [accessed Nov. 2006].

University of Connecticut School of Business CIBER. (2005). *Securing our nation's future through international business education. 15 years of CIBER 1989-2004.* Available: http://ciberweb.msu.edu/NationalImpact/15YearReport.pdf [accessed Feb. 2007].

University of Hawaii. (2006). *Business college jumps in rankings of undergraduate international business programs.* Available: http://www.hawaii.edu/cgi-bin/uhnews?20060821110511 [accessed Feb. 2007].

University of Minnesota. (2006a). *CARLA summer institutes for language teachers.* Available: http://www.carla.umn.edu/institutes/ [accessed Nov. 2006].

University of Minnesota. (2006b). *Instructional materials.* Available: http://www.carla.umn.edu/lctl/materials/index.html [accessed Nov. 2006].

University of New Mexico. (2006). *Center for Latin American resources and outreach.* Available: http://laii.unm.edu/claro/index.php [accessed Dec. 2006].

University of North Carolina. (2006). *Welcome to the home page of the K-12 international outreach program evaluation toolkit.* Available: http://www.ucis.unc.edu/k12outreachevaluation/indes.html [accessed Dec. 2006].

University of Wisconsin. (2007). *Warung Sinema-Indonesian language project.* Available: http://warungsinema.wisc.edu/project.html [accessed Jan. 2006].

Valdés, G. (2000). The teaching of heritage languages: An introduction for Slavic-teaching professionals. In O. Kagan, B. Rifkin, and S. Bauckus (Eds.), *The learning and teaching of Slavic languages and cultures* (pp. 375-403). Columbus, OH: Slavica.

Valdés, G. (2001). Heritage language students: Profiles and possibilities. In J.K. Peyton, D. Ranard, and S. McGinnis (Eds.), *Heritage languages in America: Preserving a national resource* (pp. 37-77). McHenry, IL and Washington, DC: Delta Systems and Center for Applied Linguistics.

van Lier, L. (1989). Reeling, writhing, drawling, stretching, and fainting in coils: Oral proficiency interviews as conversation. *TESOL Quarterly, 23*, 489-508.

van Weeren, J., and Theunissen, T.J.J. (1987). Testing pronunciation: An application of generalizability theory. *Language Learning, 37*, 109-122.

Ver Bryck Block, K. (2006). *IEPS update.* Presentation, National Research Council Committee to Review Title VI and Fulbright-Hays International Education Programs. Oct. 5, Washington, DC.

Vestal, T.M. (1994). *International education: Its history and promise for today.* Westport, CT: Praeger.

Vollmer, H.J., and Sang, F. (1983). Competing hypotheses about second language ability: A plea for caution. In J.W. Oller (Ed.), *Issues in language testing research* (pp. 29-74). Rowley, MA: Newbury House.

Weiss, C.H. (1998). *Evaluation* (2nd ed.). Upper Saddle River, NJ: Prentice-Hall.

Welles, E.B. (2003). *Supply and demand for Ph.Ds in modern languages in higher education: Present circumstances and future directions.* Paper presented at Global Challenges Conference, Jan., Duke University, Durham, NC.

Welles, E.B. (2004). Foreign language enrollments in United States institutions of higher education, fall 2002. *ADFL Bulletin, 35*(2), 1-206. Also available: http://www.adfl.org/resources/enrollments.pdf [accessed Feb. 2007].

Whitehead, K.D. (2004). *Learning the language: Title VI is in need of reform.* Available: http://www.nationalreview.com/comment/whitehead200401140823.asp [accessed June 2006].

Wilds, C.P. (1975). The oral interview test. In R.L. Jones and B. Spolsky (Eds.), *Testing language proficiency.* Arlington, VA: Center for Applied Linguistics.

Wiley, D. (1997). *Conference rapporteur's synthesis of the findings of the national policy conference on Title VI of the Higher Education Act and Fulbright Hays programs.* Los Angeles: University of California International Studies and Overseas Programs. Also available: http://www.isop.ucla.edu/pacrim/title6/T6%20contents.htm [accessed Sept. 2006].

Wiley, D. (2001). Forty years of the Title VI and Fulbright-Hays programs. In P. O'Meara, H.D. Mehlinger, and R.M. Newman (Eds.), *Changing perspectives on international education* (pp. 11-29). Bloomington: Indiana University Press.

Wiley, D. (2006). *The importance of Title VI programs that develop research and teaching materials—The technological innovation and cooperation for foreign information access (TICFIA) program and international research and studies (IRS) program.* Presentation and written submission, Feb. 14, National Research Council Committee to Review the Title VI and Fulbright-Hays International Education Programs, Washington, DC.

Wiley, T.G. (1996). *Literacy and language diversity in the United States.* McHenry, IL and Washington, DC: Delta Systems and Center for Applied Linguistics.

Wiley, T.G., and Lukes, M. (1996). English-only and standard English ideologies in the United States. *TESOL Quarterly, 30*, 511-535.

Young, R.F. (2002). Discourse approaches to oral language assessment. *Annual Review of Applied Linguistics, 22*, 243-262.

Young, R.F., and He, A.W. (Eds.) (1998). *Talking and testing.* Amsterdam, Netherlands: John Benjamins.

APPENDIX

A

Legislative History*

The current array of Title VI and Fulbright-Hays (Title VI/FH) international education programs is the product of nearly 50 years of legislative accretion. The result is a dense and at times complicated legislative history. Title VI, for example, was conceived as a temporary emergency measure in the National Defense Education Act of 1958. Later it was extended and revised several times, then folded into the Higher Education Act in 1980 and reviewed every six years. Existing programs were amended or reorganized repeatedly, new programs created, and some programs introduced but later cancelled.

Despite nearly a half-century of legislative adjustments, the fundamental rationales for the programs have changed little since the decade after their inception. The original goals of providing linguistic and international expertise to serve the national interest and global understanding endure. So too does the original *mechanism* selected to serve that goal, that is, working with institutions of higher education.

Within that broader framework, however, several interesting changes have occurred. For example:

•   In the last 25 years, the original goals were supplemented with the aim of linking Title VI to the nation's economic competitiveness, producing two new programs.

---

*This appendix is based largely on a paper written for the committee by Joanna Slater, who was then a graduate student at Columbia University.

- The original requirements that beneficiaries of certain Title VI programs enter teaching or public service were later dropped.
- The relative emphasis placed on improving language skills versus increasing knowledge of area studies has shifted back and forth.
- Outreach efforts beyond higher education became a priority.

It is important to note that although the Title VI/FH 102(b)(6) programs have a common administrative home in the U.S. Department of Education, they have distinct legislative trajectories. Unlike the Title VI programs, which have been pushed and prodded regularly by Congress, the Fulbright-Hays 102(b)(6) programs entered the governmental bloodstream in 1961 and have stayed there, nearly undisturbed, ever since. The adjustments to these programs have been more administrative than legislative.

The legislative history outlined here therefore focuses on the Title VI program, which has been influenced by 10 major pieces of legislation since its inception. When it is possible to discern, we have highlighted the apparent congressional intent behind the various program changes to provide additional insight into the program's evolution.[1] Overall, the legislative history of the Title VI program reveals how something that started as "a planned response to a national emergency" gradually became a "focus of national resources for . . . understanding and managing interdependence, trade, security, and other international issues" (Ruther, 2002, p. 134). In that same time period, the programs grew to embrace all levels and categories in the higher education system. However, while Congress adjusted the program configuration over time—largely by adding programs to address specific needs, such as international education for business purposes and the training of minorities—it did not make significant changes to the original core legislation.

This evolution reflects shifting congressional priorities as well as efforts on the part of institutions of higher education and other constituencies to influence the future of the Title VI programs. In particular, the link between Title VI and foreign policy concerns has guided the programs since their inception in 1958. For example, the revision to Title VI that took place in 1998 provided a robust restatement of its goals for the post–cold war era.

The legislative history of Title VI programs can be viewed as following three rough periods of development: the early years (1958-1972), when the foundation of the programs was established, a middle period (1973-1991) of embedding and revising, and the current phase (1992 onward), during

---

[1] The programs that form Title VI have always represented a relatively small provision within a larger piece of legislation, first in the National Defense Education Act and later in the Higher Education Act. The result is that Title VI receives very little attention in congressional debates, which tend to be consumed by discussions of such topics as student loan programs.

which the scope of the programs has been broadened. See Attachment A for the complete current statute. (Attachment A is available online. Go to http://www.nap.edu and search for International Education and Foreign Languages.)

LAYING THE FOUNDATIONS (1958-1972)

Three pieces of legislation form the foundation for today's Title VI/FH programs: the National Defense Education Act of 1958, the Mutual Educational and Cultural Exchange Act of 1961, and the International Education Act of 1966. Although the latter was never funded, its programs, focus, and some of its language were later incorporated into Title VI.

National Defense Education Act of 1958 (P.L. 85-864)

The launch of the unmanned satellite Sputnik by the Soviet Union on October 4, 1957, provided the impetus for the legislation that was to become the National Defense Education Act (NDEA). The scientific coup by the country's cold war rival produced widespread alarm and, by December of the same year, the Eisenhower administration announced its legislative proposal to address the situation. Much of the administration's plan focused on improving scientific expertise, but it also included graduate fellowships and grants to universities for language study. After two different versions of the proposed legislation were introduced in Congress in 1958, six months of hearings followed. For the most part, however, the testimony demonstrated a "conspicuous silence" (Gumperz, 1970, p. 51) regarding the language title in the bill.

One exception was the testimony of Lawrence Derthick, the commissioner for education, who noted that the bill's "fundamental objective is to improve greatly the quality of foreign language instruction at all levels of our education system. . . . [A]s a first step, the urgent need is to improve the language competence of teachers and supervisors now in service and to seek to stimulate the whole field of language instruction."[2] Only two outside groups lent their support to the embryonic Title VI: the Modern Language Association (MLA) and the American Council of Learned Societies. Some of the provisions included in Title VI can be traced to the influence of the MLA and its executive director, William Parker, who wrote a book in 1954 entitled "The National Interest and Foreign Languages." Parker was a vocal advocate for greater government support of foreign language teaching in higher education and recommended integrating foreign language and area

---

[2]Senate Committee on Labor and Public Welfare, *Hearings on Science and Education for National Defense*, 85th Con., 2nd sess., February 1958, 343.

study. He later joined the U.S. Office of Education "to help administer the new structures [he] had done so much to create" (Gumperz, 1970, p. 59).

The overall aim of the NDEA was to correct "critical areas of shortage and neglect which now carry highest priority in the national interest"[3]—in particular, science, math, and foreign languages. In describing the purpose of the section that would become Title VI, the House committee report states that its primary objective is to extend and improve the *teaching* of foreign languages in the United States. It adds that the title will also "provide the means of preparing more Americans to conduct governmental, business, and cultural relations in an effective way." [4]

To create such language specialists and improve foreign language instruction, the act relied on four main tools:

• Language and area centers for instruction in modern foreign languages and other fields "needed to provide a full understanding" of the areas in which those languages are used. The centers would be operated by institutions of higher education under contract with the government, which would provide up to 50 percent of the funding. The foreign languages taught in the centers were limited to those for which "adequate instruction" was not already readily available in the United States (National Resource Centers).

• Stipends to individuals engaged in such language training, with the understanding that the recipients would be "available for teaching a modern foreign language in an institution of higher education or for [sic] other service of a public nature" (Foreign Language and Area Studies Fellowships).

• Studies and research on the need for foreign language instruction, improved teaching methods, and the development of specialized teaching materials (International Research and Studies).

• Summer and academic year language institutes for foreign language teachers in elementary or secondary schools. Like the language and area centers, the institutes would be operated by institutions of higher education under contract with the government (this part of Title VI was later repealed and transferred).

The congressional debate on the legislation featured discussions on the scarcity of scientists in the United States, the alarming Soviet advantage in technical fields, and the advisability of federal meddling in higher education.

---

[3]House Committee on Education and Labor, *Report No. 2157 to accompany H.R. 13247,* 85th Cong., 2nd sess., July 15, 1958, 4743.

[4]House Committee on Education and Labor, *Report No. 2157 to accompany H.R. 13247,* 85th Cong., 2nd sess., July 15, 1958, 4743.

At least one representative scoffed at the notion that the bill—intended as a temporary measure—would be short-lived: "There is nothing so permanent as a temporary Government agency. Nor is there anything more lingering than the emergency in which it was born," noted William Dawson (R-UT) in the House of Representatives debate on the bill on August 7, 1958.

Several representatives bemoaned the lack of language skills in the American diplomatic corps, especially when compared with their Soviet counterparts. The foreign language section of the bill inspired little controversy and at least one staunch defender, Representative James Roosevelt (D-CA):

> In all conscience there is probably no section of the bill which would be entitled to more universal support than this section. . . . [L]anguage instruction in our schools and colleges is so badly neglected that we do not even have enough people who are proficient in French, Spanish, and German to meet the requirements of our international affairs. . . . The fast-moving events of the last few years have dramatically—often, for us, tragically—revealed the emergence of the peoples of Africa and Asia into the centers of world power. Yet for the most part we know nothing of their languages and all too little of their cultures.[5]

Some parts of the discussion are surprisingly contemporary. One representative described his shock upon discovering that only five American diplomats working in Arabic-speaking countries were fluent in the language (the comparable figure for the Soviet Union, he claimed, was 300). Another representative shared this frustration but went on to note that "even though we train these individuals in foreign languages under this bill, there is nothing in the bill that can compel them to go to Lebanon or any other territory or country on the face of the earth after they have learned that foreign language."[6]

President Eisenhower signed the NDEA into law in September 1958. The law was authorized for an initial period of four years, but Congress repeatedly extended its life span at different points during the 1960s.

The 1958 statute left significant concepts open to interpretation—for example, what exactly constituted a "center." The center concept was not formally delineated in the act and it "in no way prescribed the directions of growth which a center was to take. . . . The doctrine of "local option"—the center's right to self-determination—prevailed from the beginning" (Axelrod and Bigelow, 1962, pp. 13-14).

The most enduring legacy of the act was the establishment of a federal role in stimulating certain programs in higher education. When once universities funded foreign language and international studies internally or

---

[5]*Congressional Record*, House, August 7, 1958, 16692-3.
[6]*Congressional Record*, House, August 7, 1958, 16568.

looked to private foundations for such support, the legislation introduced the option of federal funding. Although the amount of funding available was modest, it nevertheless represented a significant change in the academic landscape. As Ellen Gumperz has noted, once institutions of higher education are in "competition for federal funds, they must suffer the fortunes of the national market economy so created" (1970, p. 76).

Mutual Educational and Cultural Exchange Act of 1961 (P.L. 87-256)

Much like the NDEA three years earlier, the Mutual Educational and Cultural Exchange Act of 1961 was shaped by cold war concerns. Politicians and diplomats worried that the Soviet Union was bolstering its own educational and cultural exchanges and wanted to ensure that American programs remained effective. Brooks Hays, then the assistant secretary of state, wrote a letter in support of the legislation, arguing that it would allow the United States to maintain its advantage in this arena at a time when "competitive efforts by the adversaries of free society are continually increasing."[7]

The main goal of the legislation was to consolidate and simplify a host of existing governmental exchange programs in order to better serve American interests abroad. The House committee report, for example, remarks that, "in the current struggle for the minds of men, no other instrument of foreign policy has such great potential."[8] The legislation aimed not only to better coordinate visits by foreigners to the United States, but also to improve the flow of Americans abroad, whether they were students, teachers, artists, or athletes. In the service of this latter objective, legislators proposed a section on overseas study for teacher training. This was a new type of exchange, focusing on "language training and specialized studies of areas or countries [by] Americans who teach such subjects in schools, colleges, and universities."[9] The final wording of the statute aimed to support visits and study abroad by teachers and "prospective teachers." The House committee noted that it expected the administrators of the program to implement "rigid criteria"[10] to ensure that recipients enter teaching for a certain period of time following the program abroad.

In the congressional debate on the legislation, Senator J. William Ful-

---

[7]House Committee on Foreign Affairs, *Report No. 87-1094 to accompany H.R. 8666*, 87th Cong., 1st sess., August 31, 1961, 2775.

[8]House Committee on Foreign Affairs, *Report No. 87-1094 to accompany H.R. 8666*, 2759.

[9]House Committee on Foreign Affairs, *Report No. 87-1094 to accompany H.R. 8666*, 2765.

[10]House Committee on Foreign Affairs, *Report No. 87-1094 to accompany H.R. 8666*, 2765.

bright (D-AR) declared, "The activities of the [Soviet] bloc do serve as a reminder of the foreign policy significance of exchanges, and of the need to put our own house in order."[11] Representative John Lindsay (R-New York) described the prior approach to educational and cultural exchanges as "piecemeal and sporadic," despite the fact that such programs are "an essential part of our foreign relations. . . . Educational and cultural exchange is as fundamental—though far less costly—an instrument of foreign policy as our massive programs of defense and foreign aid."[12]

Thanks to the intervention of the U.S. Department of Health, Education, and Welfare, the act featured a provision that allowed the president to transfer authority for certain exchanges to different arms of the government—a move aimed squarely at the teacher exchanges created by Section 102(b)(5). In a letter to the Senate Committee on Foreign Relations, Abraham Ribicoff, the secretary of health, education, and welfare, wrote that the aim of such exchanges was "essentially the same" as the programs of Title VI—that is, to promote "modern foreign language training and area studies in U.S. schools, colleges, and universities."[13] He asked that the authority for these exchanges be vested in his department, and the president later agreed.

In later years these programs "were recast into more functional categories to ensure balanced coverage with available resources (for example, Faculty Research Abroad, Doctoral Dissertation Research Abroad, Group Projects Abroad, and Foreign Curriculum Consultants, now Seminars Abroad-Bilateral Projects)" (Vestal, 1994, p. 129). No further major legislative changes to these programs occurred.

International Education Act of 1966 (P.L. 89-698)

In a speech given in honor of the bicentennial of the Smithsonian Institution in fall 1965, President Lyndon Johnson announced the creation of a broad initiative in global health and education. "Ideas, not armaments, will shape our lasting prospects for peace," he told the assembled dignitaries. "The conduct of our foreign policy will advance no faster than the curriculum of our classrooms." In a speech to Congress in February 1966, he outlined a 20-point plan to bolster international education in the United States while also strengthening educational assistance and disease prevention efforts abroad. For some of the points mentioned, new legislation was required.

---

[11]*Congressional Record*, Senate, June 27, 1961, 11400.

[12]*Congressional Record*, House, September 6, 1961, 18273-4.

[13]Senate Committee on Foreign Relations, *Hearings on the Mutual Educational and Cultural Exchange Act*, 87th Cong., 1st sess., March and April 1961, 109.

During the hearings on the proposed legislation, John Gardner, the secretary of health, education, and welfare, testified that it was "based on a new premise—the premise that international education at home and educational relations with other nations are permanent and important aspects of our national interest. . . . [T]he reason becomes plain when we think about the enemy we seek to conquer. That enemy is ignorance, inadequate skills, parochialism, and lack of sensitivity as to why people from different cultures react and behave differently."[14]

Instead of instituting training mechanisms or educational exchanges to directly serve national security or foreign policy goals, the International Education Act (IEA) sought to improve international studies more broadly. The rationale provided in the act was that "a knowledge of other countries is of the utmost importance in promoting mutual understanding and cooperation between nations."

The goals of the legislation were twofold: to build a strong base at the graduate level for international research and studies and to allow students at the undergraduate level "a chance to learn more about the world and the cultures, customs, and values of other countries."[15] The latter program was included for substantive as well as political reasons: ever since the passage of the NDEA, smaller universities and colleges had agitated for their share of federal support for international studies and language programs (Gumperz, 1970, p. 68).

The act's two main sections established the following programs:

• Grants to institutions of higher education to operate graduate centers for research and training in international studies and the international aspects of professional and other fields of study; grants to nonprofit agencies and organizations were also authorized for the same objective; and

• Grants to institutions of higher education to assist them in strengthening undergraduate instruction in international studies, including such activities as curriculum development, expansion of language courses, and training of faculty members abroad.

A separate provision in the IEA also made three amendments to the NDEA that (1) revised the NDEA to allow area centers to focus on such languages as French, Spanish, and Italian, (2) removed the 50 percent ceiling on federal participation in centers, and (3) allowed the government to fund centers through grants as well as contracts.

Although the IEA was a White House initiative, the Johnson admin-

---

[14]*Congressional Record*, House, March 30, 1966, 7284.

[15]Senate Committee on Labor and Public Welfare, *Report No. 1715 to accompany H.R. 14643*, 89th Cong., 2nd sess., October 12, 1966, 3566.

istration provided little help to the House managers working to pass the bill. At the time, the administration was besieged with other issues, among them "urban rioting, civil rights and Black Power demonstrations, antiwar protests, and concerns about inflation" (Vestal, 1994, p. 67).

Opposition to the bill surfaced during the congressional debates on the new measure. Senator Strom Thurmond (D-SC), for example, questioned the wisdom of spending on a new domestic program while the country was at war in Vietnam. Senator Fulbright voiced the opposite view: "If there is any hope at all for a peaceful world," he declared, "It will result from the kind of activity for which this bill provides."[16]

Although the bill was eventually passed and later signed into law in October 1966, opposition from Congress continued to plague the IEA, which was never funded. Numerous factors contributed to its failure: the president was consumed with the war in Vietnam, while Congress was increasingly distrustful of presidential initiatives and wary of new spending. One scholar described the mood on Capitol Hill as one of "weariness and a feeling of having been overcommitted, at home at abroad, by an Administration that enters ventures without looking down the road to where they may lead" (Vestal, 1994, p. 94).

Theodore Vestal also believes that "the lack of political clout" (Vestal, 1994, p. 119) on the part of representatives of higher education contributed to the defeat of the IEA. Still, the unfunded IEA—like a "continuing stream of light from a dead but brilliant star" (Ruther, 2002, p. 119)—would provide the direction for several of the changes to Title VI over the following two decades. The IEA's supporters drew several lessons for future international education efforts from its demise: don't disregard the national security rationale for such programs, try to make sure the program isn't mistaken for foreign aid, and beware of a situation in which legislation is hostage to larger domestic and geopolitical forces.

Education Amendments of 1972 (P.L. 92-318)

Despite an attempt by the Nixon administration to eliminate Title VI, lobbying by representatives of higher education (combined with an intervention by national security adviser Henry Kissinger himself) managed to save the programs. Still, the Nixon and Ford administrations represented a difficult time for the advocates of Title VI, who found themselves engaged in a constant struggle against funding cuts. The Educational Amendments of 1972 once again extended and revised the programs. At the same time, the amendments enshrined a shift in federal higher education policy toward

---

[16]*Congressional Record*, Senate, October 13, 1966, 26562-3.

prioritizing student aid over support to institutions. This shift in turn contributed to the difficult funding environment for Title VI.

The amendments reflected both the goals of the IEA and arguments advanced by higher education advocates during the hearings on the proposed legislation. Two important new arguments for the programs surfaced in the testimony: the first was that the centers served as a national resource and therefore it was critical to maintain and expand them; the second was that the centers had a positive impact beyond their immediate university surroundings by disseminating expertise to other educational institutions and to society writ large. This line of argument presaged the role the centers would later play in outreach efforts.

The most significant change to Title VI stemming from the 1972 amendments was the creation of an undergraduate grant program similar to that envisioned by the IEA: the Undergraduate International Studies and Foreign Language Program. The purpose, according to the House committee report, was to reflect the conviction that "additional emphasis should now be placed on undergraduate education in language and area studies" and that "the center approach be modified to include a more program oriented concept of language and area studies."[17]

EMBEDDING AND REVISING (1973-1991)

Fifteen years after its inception, Title VI could be deemed a success: although originally a temporary program, it had been extended several times. Still, debates remained over the appropriate funding levels, how broadly the programs should extend across the higher education system, which languages warranted focus, and whether the programs were effective in addressing foreign policy concerns.

Especially in the early to mid-1970s, some of these debates would translate into a difficult period for Title VI. As Nancy Ruther has noted, during this time the programs were "consolidated and refined in the trenches of regulations rather than on the sunny playing fields of legislative initiatives and authorizations of earlier periods" (2002, p. 119).

Things began to look up during the Carter administration. In 1980, Title VI finally found a permanent statutory home within the Higher Education Act (HEA). It also began to incorporate a new rationale for international education efforts—economic competitiveness. The result was several new programs as well as minor amendments to existing programs.

---

[17]House Committee on Education and Labor, *Report No. 92-554 to accompany H.R. 7248*, 92nd Cong., 2nd sess., October 8, 1971, 2499.

Education Amendments of 1976 (P.L. 94-482)

The Education Amendments of 1976 did not make any major changes to the existing Title VI programs. However, they did institute a new program to deepen student understanding of "cultures and actions of other nations to better evaluate the international and domestic impact of major national policies." Unlike other Title VI programs, the grant recipients under the program were not limited to institutions of higher education. Ruther suggests that the program was a response to "increasing pressure from post-secondary education and school advocacy groups traditionally distant from core Title VI funding" (2002, p. 126). Four years later, the program was transferred to the Elementary and Secondary Education Act (Foreign Language Assistance Program). The program's short tenure in Title VI illustrates the scramble for resources among different constituencies in education and the focus of Title VI on higher education. It also demonstrates the fact that beyond the centerpiece programs of Title VI—the centers and their fellowships—there continued to be a good deal of flux in the program mix.

Education Amendments of 1980 (P.L. 96-374)

After weathering a hostile funding environment for much of the 1970s, the Title VI programs received a more positive form of attention under the Carter administration. President Carter created the Commission on Foreign Language and International Studies by executive order in 1978. A year later, it produced a report calling for $178 million in new funding for international education programs.[18]

More broadly, the late 1970s were a time of concern about the place of the United States in the world economy as the country appeared to lose ground to more nimble competitors. In 1979, for example, Congress passed major trade legislation. For Title VI, such concerns translated into an entirely new section, with the aim of promoting activities that "contribute to the ability of United States business to prosper in an international economy." In its report on the bill, the House Committee on Education and Labor emphasized the "interdependent nature of the world's economy" and the "vulnerability of the United States if it does not become more aware of the cultures and languages of other countries."

Representative Paul Simon (D-IL) initiated hearings in 1979 with the goal of finding Title VI a more permanent statutory home in HEA. Originally intended as a temporary measure, Title VI had become a permanent

---

[18]Ruther notes that due to the timing and focus of the report, these recommendations were not as effective as they might have been. It was not completed in time for the 1979 hearings on incorporating Title VI into the Higher Education Act.

fixture on the federal stage. It had undergone numerous revisions and carried with it the lingering aspirations of the failed IEA. In an effort to consolidate and clarify the government's international education efforts, Congress repealed Title VI of the NDEA and Title I of the IEA and replaced them with a new Title VI in the Higher Education Act entitled "International and Foreign Language Studies."

In its report on the bill, the Senate Committee on Labor and Human Resources described the shift as a way to "mainstream" the Title VI programs, "a matter of putting an existing program in a framework which has become more appropriate and offers greater impact." It also spoke approvingly of bringing a "reinvigorating international business perspective into juxtaposition with the old NDEA programs."

The new Title VI to be incorporated into the Higher Education Act articulated a clear basis for international education programs: that knowledge of other countries is important to promoting mutual understanding and cooperation between nations, and that acquiring such knowledge was critical to the economy and security of the United States. In other words, it combined the rationales expressed in the NDEA, the Mutual Educational and Cultural Exchange Act, and the IEA.

During the debate on the measure, Representative Simon made sure to highlight Title VI, which he described as "a part of this legislation which is not likely to receive much attention but which is significant to the nation."[19] He continued:

"What this legislation does is, for the first time, really coordinates [international studies programs]. What we have had up to this point is just kind of spasmodic programs. . . . I think we will now finally not only have an aid to higher education, but literally an aid to the Nation."[20]

The legislation made several important changes to the Title VI programs:

•   Grants to institutions of higher education were authorized to create centers to act as regional resources focused either on specific geographic areas or on particular international issues; in order to qualify for such grants, the centers would provide programs to strengthen international studies and foreign languages in the two-year and four-year colleges and universities in their region (in another example of programmatic flux, this program was replaced six years later).
•   The act dropped the requirement that recipients of stipends be available for teaching or public service. The report of the House Committee on Education and Labor explained that this requirement was too "restric-

---

[19]*Congressional Record*, House, October 29, 1979, 29844.
[20]*Congressional Record*, House, October 29, 1979, 29844.

tive" in light of the scarcity of teaching positions and its desire to encourage individuals seeking careers outside teaching—such as business—to participate in these programs.

• The act stipulated that excellence would be the primary criterion for the awarding of grants to the graduate and undergraduate centers, with equitable distribution in terms of geography a secondary consideration.

• Grants to institutions of higher education for programs designed to promote linkages with the U.S. business community were authorized, for example to internationalize the curriculum at business schools, to develop specialized materials and facilities for business-oriented students, or to establish student and faculty fellowships, among other activities (Business and International Education Program).

• An advisory board was created and directed to meet four times a year to review the Title VI programs. Members of the board would represent different government departments, the higher education community, the business community, and the public (this provision was later eliminated, presumably as a cost-cutting measure.)

• For the first time, the act provided definitions of such terms as "area studies," "international business," "export education," and "internationalization of curricula."

Higher Education Amendments of 1986 (P.L. 99-498)

During the next round of amendments to Title VI, only one major change occurred: the regional network of international studies centers established in 1980 was replaced with a program of language resource centers. The goal of the new program was to "develop research on teaching methods and materials for foreign languages, including developing language proficiency exams."[21] The change represents a swing of the statutory pendulum back toward a focus on language teaching in the Title VI programs.

Other changes tinkered with the way existing Title VI programs operated. The amendments introduced a second tier of fellowships for graduate students in their third year of training to be awarded on the basis of a national competition (this change was never implemented and later dropped). Legislators also directed the secretary of education to set separate criteria for the selection of graduate and undergraduate centers in the centerpiece program of Title VI. Perhaps not coincidentally, a definition of what constituted a "comprehensive" and "undergraduate" center finally appeared

---

[21]House Committee on Education and Labor, *Report No. 99-383 to accompany H.R. 3700*, 99th Cong., 2nd sess., November 20, 1985, 2686.

in the statute. Since some centers had already existed for nearly 30 years, however, the definition was probably more descriptive than prescriptive:

> [T]he term "comprehensive language and area center" means an administrative unit of a university that contributes significantly to the national interest in advanced research and scholarship, employs a critical mass of scholars in diverse disciplines related to a geographic concentration, offers intensive language training in languages of its area specialization, maintains important library collections related to the area, and makes training available in language and area studies to a graduate, postgraduate, and undergraduate clientele.

Omnibus Trade and Competitiveness Act of 1988 (P.L. 100-418)

As the 1980s drew to a close, there was renewed concern about U.S. competitiveness, as Asian economies continued their remarkable rise and Western Europe moved closer to an integrated market. The concern was paired with the realization that the United States would be competing in an increasingly globalized economy, a world for which traditional business curricula were little prepared. Embedded in the Omnibus Trade and Competitiveness Act of 1988 was a provision to create Centers for International Business Education to act as a focal point for internationalizing business education. The program was later transferred to Title VI, which, although it already had a program aimed at business education, did not have *centers* designated for the task.

BROADENING THE SCOPE (1992 ONWARD)

In the post–cold war environment beginning in the early 1990s, outreach efforts became increasingly important, as did attempts to promote diversity. Renewed concern surfaced about the quality of language instruction, together with moves to improve it. Funding also began to incrementally increase as the nation's need for global and language expertise expanded.

Higher Education Amendments of 1992 (P.L. 102-325)

The next opportunity to review the Title VI programs arrived at a momentous time in geopolitical terms. As legislators discussed and negotiated the higher education amendments, not even three years had passed since the fall of the Berlin Wall, and the Soviet Union was close to collapse. Meanwhile, the Persian Gulf war in early 1991 formed the backdrop for the hearings and committee reports on the amendments. The House report described the period as one of "unprecedented global challenges" and reaffirmed its support for the Title VI programs as "vital to the national interest." However, its goal with respect to the programs was modest—merely "to refine the title further."[22]

Indeed, there were no sweeping changes made to the Title VI programs in light of post–cold war realities, in terms of either language or programming. The most significant revision was the addition of a new program, the Institute for International Public Policy, which aimed to increase the number of underrepresented minorities entering the international career field. In its report, the Senate Committee on Labor and Human Resources noted with concern that only 13 percent of those serving in the U.S. Foreign Service were minorities, and only 6 percent were black.

One reason for the relative modesty of the changes to the Title VI programs at this juncture may be that, in 1991, Congress passed the David L. Boren National Security Education Act, the first major new piece of legislation targeting international education in nearly 30 years. The act authorized a new program of scholarships, fellowships, and grants for undergraduate and graduate students to be administered by the U.S. Department of Defense. Some scholars credit the act's creation to the stature enjoyed by its sponsor, Senator David Boren (D-OK) (Ruther, 2002). The noteworthy amendments to Title VI in 1992 were as follows:

- The creation of the Institute for International Public Policy, consisting of a competitive grants program in which a host institution leads a consortium of historically black colleges and other institutions with significant minority enrollment; the institute was directed to offer a program leading to a master's degree in international relations, to conduct an academic year abroad program, and to provide an academic year internship program for sophomores and juniors to work in an international voluntary or government agency.
- The amendments established a new type of grant in the center program to be used specifically for outreach purposes. The House committee noted that the Middle Eastern studies centers had played a role in providing expertise and background to the government, private organizations, and the media during the Persian Gulf war. As the world becomes "more complex and unpredictable," it noted, "the need for public outreach is also increasing." Although the department never awarded separate outreach grants, outreach was added as a core component of all existing National Resource Centers grants.
- A definition of the term "critical languages" was included in the statute for the first time via reference to the U.S. Department of Educa-

---

[22]House Committee on Education and Labor, *Report No. 102-447 to accompany H.R. 3553*, 102nd Cong., 2nd sess., February 27, 1992, 435.

tion's list posted in the *Federal Register* (the published lists includes 171 languages).

• Grants to American research centers situated overseas were permitted in order to enable such centers to promote postgraduate research, exchanges, and area studies, on the condition that they received more that 50 percent of their funding from public or private sources in the United States (American Overseas Research Centers).

• The Senate committee attempted to create a new section of Title VI to incorporate the Fulbright-Hays 102(b)(6) programs. Its logic was that "at a time of growth and evolution in international education . . . the two programs [should] not only be administered together but also reviewed together."[23] It also specified that the move should not be construed as a consolidation that invites a reduction in funding. In the end, however, the House conferees objected to the change and the Fulbright-Hays 102(b)(6) programs remained in their original statutory home.

Higher Education Amendments of 1998 (P.L. 105-244)

The main contribution of this round of amendments was to provide a robust restatement of the goals and purpose of Title VI in a unipolar world:

> The security, stability, and economic vitality of the United States in a complex global era depend upon American experts in and citizens knowledgeable about world regions, foreign languages, and international affairs. . . .

> Advances in communications technology and the growth of regional and global problems make knowledge of other countries and the ability to communicate in other languages more essential. . . .

> Dramatic post–cold war changes in the world's geopolitical and economic landscapes are creating needs for American expertise and knowledge about a greater diversity of less commonly taught foreign languages and nations of the world.

Another fresh development was the creation of a grant program (Technological Innovation and Cooperation for Foreign Information Access) to promote ways to use new electronic technologies to address teaching and research needs in international education and foreign languages.

---

[23]Senate Committee on Labor and Human Resources, *Report No. 102-204 to accompany S. 1150*, 102nd Cong., 1st sess., November 12, 1991.

CONCLUSION

The legislative history of the Title VI/FH programs charts the evolution of a temporary international education program into an enduring fixture on the federal stage. The program mix has shifted in response to foreign policy imperatives, economic concerns, lobbying by institutions of higher education, and perceived needs in language training and international studies. The programs have been broadened to embrace not only immediate national security concerns but also concerns related to global competitiveness and a more internationally aware citizenry.

Although there have been multiple changes in the program throughout its legislative history, core aspects of the program have remained unchanged. It acknowledges the importance of not only foreign language learning, but also an understanding of the cultural context in which the languages are spoken and the political, social, and economic issues in a range of nations of the world. It also supports the value of internationalization both in terms of producing experts needed to address national security, government, business and higher education needs and enriching the higher education curriculum.

Overall, the legislative history of the Title VI/FH programs suggests that significant shifts in direction are largely the result of three types of forces: a catalytic event, such as the Sputnik launch; a presidential initiative, such as the IEA or the Commission on Foreign Languages and International Studies; or the involvement of a dedicated and respected member of Congress.

Unlike the Fulbright-Hays programs, Title VI has a built-in six-year review process that provides regular opportunities for revision and change. That same process also provides an opening for a tussle over resources among various players in the higher education arena as well as a continuous target for both proponents and detractors of a greater federal role.

Attachment A-1, Current Title VI Statute, pages 284-308,
is not printed in this book but is available online.
Go to *http://www.nap.edu* and search for
International Education and Foreign Languages.

APPENDIX
B

The Committee's Approach to Its Review

This appendix describes the approach taken by the committee in fulfilling its charge to review the effectiveness of the foreign language, area, and international studies programs of the U.S. Department of Education (ED). It describes the activities we undertook and the conceptual model we developed to examine program effectiveness. The appendix includes a number of attachments: (B-1) a summary of studies evaluating the Title VI and Fulbright-Hays (Title VI/FH) programs, (B-2) a list of written comments submitted by people and organizations knowledgeable about the programs, (B-3) agendas of the public meetings held, and (B-4) the guides we developed for the site visit interviews held at eight universities.

To begin our study and ensure a complete understanding of the programs' statutory history and missions, including how their missions relate to those of other similar federal programs, the committee (1) reviewed descriptive information about the Title VI/FH programs and related federal foreign language and international education programs and (2) commissioned an analysis of the program's *legislative history*.

As a result of our review of congressional language and the statutes and the judgment of our individual members, the committee identified other questions in addition to the eight key areas specified by Congress, aimed at assessing the effectiveness of the programs at meeting their statutory missions. We asked:

- How responsive are the programs to changing national priorities? What is the role of Title VI programs in relation to other programs in addressing national needs?

- To what extent are the programs producing best practices that are used broadly in the international education arena? How are best practices identified and shared?
- To what extent does Title VI help channel other university resources toward national goals and fund programs or resources that they might not otherwise fund?
- How effective are the programs at coordinating with one another within programs, within universities, and across universities?
- How are the programs administered? What can and should be done to improve future monitoring of the programs?

To guide the review and provide a model for how the programs support the eight key questions and are expected to lead to particular results, we outlined a potential *conceptual model*. This model, which illustrates the interconnectedness of the programs, is discussed in more detail below.

To assess the degree to which the programs meet the combined set of questions, the committee undertook a series of activities:

- **Reviewed all extant evaluations.** The committee conducted a literature review, requested from ED copies of evaluations funded through its International Research and Studies (IRS) Program, and asked experts in the field about available evaluations. The committee reviewed all extant evaluations identified, although very few were available. (See Attachment B-1 for a summary of available evaluations.)
- **Reviewed program monitoring data, selected grant applications, historical financial data, and written comments from experts and officials.** The committee requested and received from ED all available program data, including historical funding[1] information and program monitoring data collected via the Evaluation of Exchange, Language, International and Area Studies (EELIAS) database. We had hoped that the EELIAS database would be a rich source of information about program performance. Instead, the problems we encountered using EELIAS and the comments from grantees on our site visits led us to make the database itself a focus of our review (see Box B-1 for a summary of database issues). In addition to the EELIAS data, we also reviewed the FY 2006 performance plan for international education and foreign language studies programs (domestic, overseas, and the Institute for International Public Policy, IIPP) and the Program Assessment

---

[1]Although committee staff worked with ED staff to clarify obvious errors or questions about the data provided, the data were accepted as accurate and not independently verified by the committee.

BOX B-1
Technical Issues with EELIAS Database

The committee encountered multiple technical issues with the EELIAS database that hampered our ability to use the data for analyses:

- **Lack of internal controls.** Although the text of data entry screens indicates that certain fields are required, the system does not always have internal controls that enforce that requirement before data are submitted.

- **Use of open-ended questions.** For questions that might require a large number of response options, responses are left as open-ended questions. One example is a recently added question asking whether a standardized proficiency test was given to Foreign Language and Area Studies (FLAS) recipients and, if so, the type of test. This resulted in responses such as "ACTFL," "ACTF Scale," "ACTFL OPI," "Oral Proficiency Interview," "ACTFL/ILR," and "ACCTF? I don't remember exactly," all of which were probably indicating the same test. More useful data might have been obtained by a series of predefined options for the most common measures, even if it necessitated an additional, "other" category. If the "other" option were supplemented by a question related to the language, it would have provided even more useful information.

- **Use of "other" category for key questions.** In several cases, EELIAS supplements a drop-down menu for key data with an "other" option; for example, languages offered and type of language instructor. In the case of languages, responses submitted in the other category included, among others, "Advanced Arabic," "Intensive Elementary Portuguese," and "Elementary Persian I," even though Arabic, Portuguese, and Persian were included in the drop-down menu.

- **Limited data validation/review.** The committee was told that reports are reviewed by individual project officers and that the information submitted is used to make continuation awards. It was clear, however, that project officers have limited time to review the consistency or reliability of data submitted from individual grantees. ED has begun efforts with its contractors to review the consistency of data across grantees and to address identified data issues.

- **Inconsistency across programs.** The data collected for individual programs vary. Although this might be expected to some extent given the variability in program missions, the differences do not always appear to be purposeful. For example, it is not clear why only the Technological Innovation and Cooperation for Foreign Information Access (TICFIA) Program is required to report on the use of technology despite its recognized importance. Similarly, not all programs are required to submit abstracts.

- **Contractor coding of some information.** The service area descriptor, a potentially useful analytic tool added by the department after it assumed management of the system, has been coded by the contractor based on the project abstract. Given the limited information available in the abstract, this approach has significant limitations. Project staff will be required to enter this information in the redesigned system.

Rating Tool (PART) performance measurements of the Office of Management and Budget (OMB) for international education domestic programs.[2]

The review of extant evaluations and monitoring data showed that there were insufficient current data available to provide meaningful insights on five of the eight original questions. Given the time constraints on the review, the committee decided to use commissioned targeted analyses, meetings with stakeholders and experts, public testimony, and site visits to selected universities to address the research questions.

• **Commissioned papers and targeted analyses.** The committee reviewed or commissioned targeted analyses on increasing representation of minorities,[3] technology and instructional materials,[4] oral proficiency assessment,[5] and implementation issues.[6] We conducted an analysis of Modern Language Association enrollment data to explore the possible role of National Resource Centers (NRC) in the teaching of less commonly taught languages, and we examined various definitions of "internationalization" of higher education. The committee also obtained preliminary data from ED generated by a contracted study by InfoUse entitled "Study of Graduate Fellowship Programs Participants," which includes a survey of all FLAS and Doctoral Dissertation Research Abroad (DDRA) Fellowships from 1997 to 1999.

• **Reviewed written comments and conducted public meetings to get input from experts, officials, and others and met with grantees in Washington and ED officials with responsibilities for these programs.** Written comments were submitted in response to a set of questions developed by the committee (see Attachment B-2), and public meetings included presen-

---

[2]PART reviews program evaluation and performance measurement information to assign program ratings. The international education domestic programs were reviewed by OMB in 2004 and assigned a rating of "results not demonstrated."

[3]Joyner, C.C. (2006). *Increasing representation of minorities in international service through international education programs.* Paper commissioned by the National Research Council Committee to Review the Title VI and Fulbright Hays International Education Programs, Washington, DC.

[4]Joyner, C., and Suarez, T. (2006). *Technology and instructional materials in Title VI and Fulbright-Hays international education programs.* Paper commissioned by the National Research Council Committee to Review the Title VI and Fulbright-Hays International Education Programs, Washington, DC.

[5]Malone, M.E. (2006). *The oral proficiency interview approach to foreign language assessment.* Paper commissioned by the National Research Council Committee to Review the Title VI and Fulbright-Hays International Education Programs, Washington, DC.

[6]Ruther, N.L. (2006). *Implementation issues and options for the HEA Title VI and Fulbright Hays programs.* Paper written for the National Research Council Committee to Review the Title VI and Fulbright-Hays International Education Programs, Washington, DC.

tations by grantees, federal agency staff, and outside experts (see Attachment B-3). We also met with NRC and Language Resource Centers (LRC) grantees when they were in Washington, DC, for an ED-sponsored grantee meeting and with ED officials with responsibilities for these programs.

•   **Conducted site visits to eight universities.** To become acquainted with Title VI center programs and gather illustrative examples, committee members and staff conducted site visits to eight universities (Georgetown University, George Washington University, Indiana University, New York University, Ohio State University, San Diego State University, the University of California, Los Angeles, and the University of Wisconsin-Madison) and reviewed selected grant applications from these universities. The universities were chosen to represent a variety of public and private institutions, Title VI funding levels, and geographic locations. Although the site visits do not represent a random sample, they were selected to provide a general picture of the diversity of NRC, Centers for International Business Education and Research (CIBER), and LRC grantees. At each location, we met with university administrators and staff, faculty, students, and librarians associated with the Title VI programs on their campuses. An interview guide based on the eight key areas specified by Congress guided the interviews at each location (see Attachment B-4).

Several factors limited our review. First, in the case of the large center programs (NRC, LRC, CIBER), Title VI typically represents a funding stream rather than a discrete program; that is, Title VI funds combine with other funding sources in order to achieve the desired outcomes, so that it is difficult to attribute specific outcomes to Title VI (U.S. General Accounting Office, June, 1998). Second, we did not have time to conduct a survey of all grantees, so some of our observations and findings are not generalizable; the illustrations based on the site visits, for example, may not be applicable to all grantees. In addition, extant data provided significant information for only three of the eight congressional questions, and the major data system (EELIAS), which theoretically could have provided answers to many questions, has significant problems.

CONCEPTUAL MODEL

Understanding how a program is expected to lead to particular results can be extremely useful in designing and implementing it and in planning its evaluation. A basic logic model provides a systematic and visual way to present and share an understanding of the relationships among the resources/inputs, activities, outputs, outcomes, and impact expected of

TABLE B-1 Categories of Performance Measures

Category	Definition	Examples
Impacts	The degree to which broad social objectives are achieved	Increased competitiveness, enhanced level of education, income of graduates, improved quality of educational institutions
Outcomes	Accomplishment of program objectives attributable to program outputs	Academic performance improvement, students accepted at next level of education, graduates certified as teachers, employer satisfaction
Outputs	The direct result of program activities	Number of students enrolled, targeted students completing training, students applying to next level of education
Activities	The work performed by the grantee that directly produces the core products and services	Amount of training given, counseling provided, conferences held, reports published
Inputs	Resources consumed by the organization	Generally limited to funds and grant years

SOURCE: U.S. Department of Education. (1998). *Demonstrating results: An introduction to the Government Performance and Results Act.* Washington, DC: Author, Office of Postsecondary Education.

the program.[7] Logic models can range from an activities approach model, which describes activities in great detail and is especially useful as a management tool, to a theory approach model, which emphasizes the theory of change that has influenced the design and plan for a program and is especially useful during program planning and design. A third kind of logic model is perhaps more relevant to the committee's work: *an outcome approach model*, which shows the causal linkages thought to exist among program components and is especially useful in designing effective evaluation and reporting strategies.

In considering the programs and the results expected from them, it will be useful to keep in mind the distinctions among several categories of measures established under the Government Performance and Results Act (GPRA) and used by ED in monitoring and reporting on its activities. Table B-1 shows one way of describing those categories.[8]

---

[7]W.K. Kellogg Foundation (2003). *Logic model development guide.* Battle Creek, MI: Author.

[8]Others might define categories in slightly different ways. In addition, assigning a measure to one or another category (for example, outcome or impact) is often a judgment call on which opinions might differ from one situation to another. Distinctions are sometimes made, as well, between short-term outcomes and longer-term outcomes.

In requesting this review, Congress asked the committee to address the performance of these programs in eight specific areas, which implies that these areas might be seen as program goals about which information is needed. Some of those eight areas reflect questions about activities, whereas others address outputs or outcomes. Table B-2 shows these eight areas with comments about the category of performance measure specified or implied.

Figures B-1 through B-5 represent a modified "outcome approach" logic model. That is, individual programs are grouped in ways that show how their activities in combination are expected to lead to certain short-term and longer term outcomes. While grouping programs provides a better appreciation for the ways in which they interact, it necessitates some loss of detail in describing the activities and their associated output measures. Figure B-1, which presents an overview of all 14 programs, has the least amount of detail.

The schematic in Figure B-1 shows all 14 programs along with their links to the goals identified in the congressional request, other short-term and longer term outcomes that can be inferred from that request, and the legislation and regulations addressing allowable activities in the programs. For the purpose of this report, the goal of "supporting research, education, and training" is represented at the level of three inferred subgoals: (1) increased research capacity, (2) enhanced body of knowledge about foreign languages and area studies, and (3) increased institutional capacity of education and training in K-12 and institutions of higher education (IHE). Reading from left to right, the relationship between short-term and longer term outcomes can be seen. For example, the schematic posits that improving instructional materials is important because of its contribution to improving the institutional capacity of education and training, which in turn contributes to a decrease in the shortage of experts as well as an increase in the global understanding of academics and U.S. educators. The figure also shows that nearly all of the programs are related to multiple outcomes.

In Figures B-2 through B-5, programs are grouped by similarity in the way they function or in their purpose. By reducing the number of programs in a single schematic, it is possible to include more detail about the activities that are expected to lead to the outcomes.

Figure B-2 shows the six programs that provide funds to individuals: the four Fulbright-Hays programs (DDRA, Faculty Research Abroad or FRA, Group Projects Abroad or GPA, and Seminars Abroad or SA) as well as FLAS and IIPP. Some of these programs could be expected to contribute to a reduction in the shortage of experts, including those who are minorities, while others should lead to an enhanced body of knowledge about foreign languages and area studies or improved global understanding. As

TABLE B-2 Program Areas to Be Addressed in Responding to Congress

Area	Comment
1. Supporting research, education and training in foreign language and international studies, including opportunities for such research, education, and training overseas	As stated, **output** measure would assess the extent to which research, education, and training occurred. One could plausibility link the question to **short-term** and **longer term outcomes** of (a) improved institutional research capacity, (b) improved institutional capacity to provide quality education and training in K-12 and institutions of higher education, and (c) improved body of knowledge about foreign language and area studies.
2. Reducing shortages of foreign language and area experts	**Outcome** measure would be decreased shortage of foreign language and area studies experts in public service and academia.
3. Infusing a foreign language and area studies dimension throughout the education system and across relevant disciplines, including professional education	**Short-term outcome** measure would be increased infusion of this dimension into elementary, secondary, and higher education, including professional education. One could make an expected causal link between this outcome and a **longer term outcome** of improved institutional capacity in K-12 and IHE.
4. Producing relevant instructional materials that meet accepted scholarly standards	**Short-term outcome** measure would be improved instructional materials. That is, one would go beyond the **output** measure of quantity of materials produced to assess that they are "improved" over what previously existed by virtue of meeting accepted scholarly standards. This measure, in turn, would lead to the **longer term outcome** of improved institutional capacity for education and training.
5. Advancing uses of new technology in foreign language and international studies	**Output** measure would describe the ways in which projects use technology. **Short-term outcome** measure would be improved technology to enhance foreign language and international studies and its use. This, in turn, would contribute to the **longer term outcome** of an improved institutional capacity for research, education, and training.
6. Addressing business needs for international knowledge and foreign language skills	A **short-term outcome** measure would be enhanced materials and activities to meet business needs.
7. Increasing the numbers of underrepresented minorities in international service	**Outcome** measure would be increased representation of minorities in international service. Lacking that information, **output** measure would describe program activities and participants.
8. Conducting public outreach/dissemination to K-12 and higher education, media, government, business, and the public	As stated, **output** measure would assess the extent to which these outreach and dissemination activities were conducted. One could plausibly link the question to the **short-term outcome** measure of improved outreach and dissemination of information about other cultures.

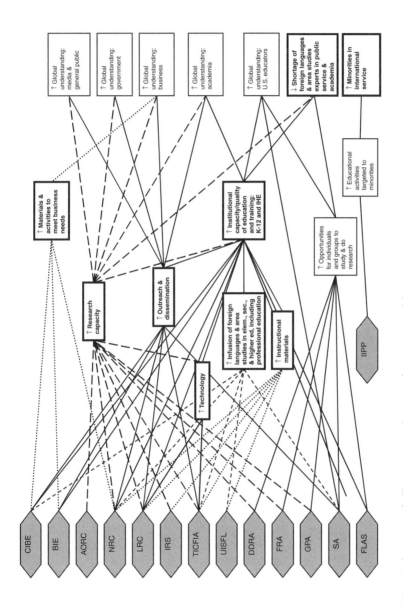

FIGURE B-1 Schematic of all programs, showing short-term and longer term outcomes.

NOTE: Boxes with solid shading show programs. Bold boxes show goals and inferred subgoals identified in the congressional request for the study.

318

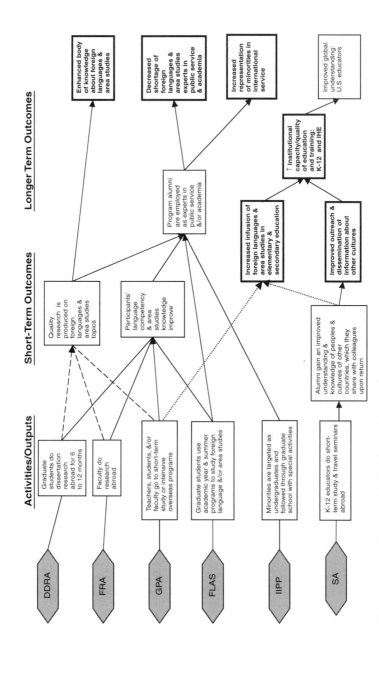

FIGURE B-2 Programs that provide funds to individuals.

NOTE: Boxes with solid shading show programs. Bold boxes show goals and inferred subgoals identified in the congressional request for the study.

interim outcomes, one would expect to see improvement in individuals' language competency, production of quality research, and an improved understanding of peoples and cultures of other countries on the part of nonspecialists.

In Figure B-3, the two programs specifically intended to support international business education (CIBER and Business and International Education or BIE) are shown. Meeting business needs is intended to lead to an improved global understanding in the business community, which in turn is expected to enhance U.S. leadership in the global economy.

The three programs that function through institutional centers (American Overseas Research Centers, AORC, NRCs, and LRCs) are shown in Figure B-4. In a variety of ways, these program activities are expected to improve institutional capacities for research and for education and training. In turn, these institutional changes should lead to an improved body of knowledge about foreign languages and area studies and to both an increase in experts and to enhanced general global understanding. Their activities are expected to focus especially on the less commonly taught languages (LCTLs).

The remaining three programs (IRS, Undergraduate International Studies and Foreign Language or UISFL, and Technological Innovation and Cooperation for Foreign Information Access or TICFIA) address the specialist and generalist outcomes through the intermediary outcome of improving the institutional capacity for education and training on foreign languages and area studies in K-12 and IHE. As Figure B-5 shows, their activities increase the infusion of these areas into higher education, improve instructional materials, improve outreach and dissemination, and improve technology, which in turn improves institutional capacities for research and education and training.

Not shown in the individual schematics is the overall impact expected of the set of programs and some of the theoretical assumptions that underlie their creation. For example, in its FY 2007 Performance Plan, ED describes the program goal being addressed by all these programs as "to meet the nation's security and economic needs through the development of a national capacity in foreign languages, and area and international studies." Given this goal, an impact assessment would attempt to determine whether the nation is more secure and economically sound as a result of the programs. An assessment of this sort is beyond the scope of the committee's charge. Indeed, although we endeavored to assess outcomes, the available data often restricted our analysis to assessment of inputs, activities, and outputs. In the report, the committee makes recommendations aimed at moving future program monitoring and evaluation efforts toward assessment of outcomes.

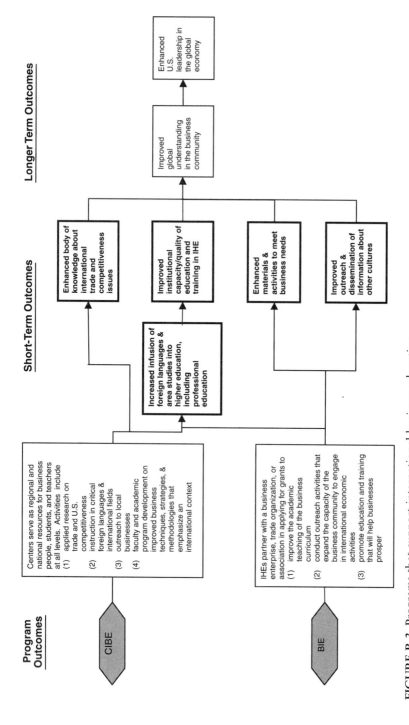

FIGURE B-3 Programs that support international business education.
NOTE: Boxes with solid shading show programs. Bold boxes show goals and inferred subgoals identified in the congressional request for the study.

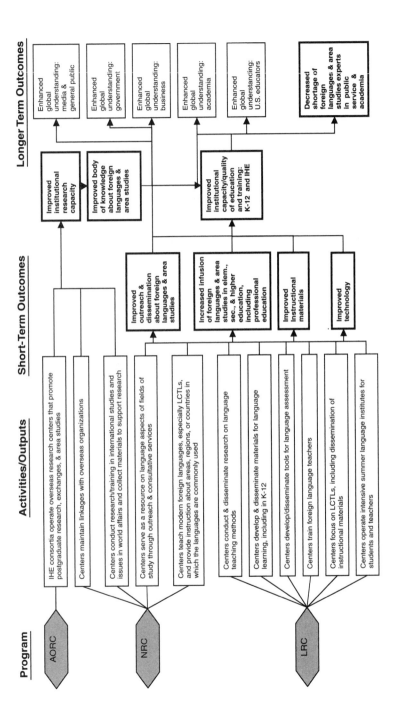

FIGURE B-4 Programs that support centers with a focus on foreign languages and area and international studies.
NOTE: Boxes with solid shading show programs. Bold boxes show goals and inferred subgoals identified in the congressional request for the study.

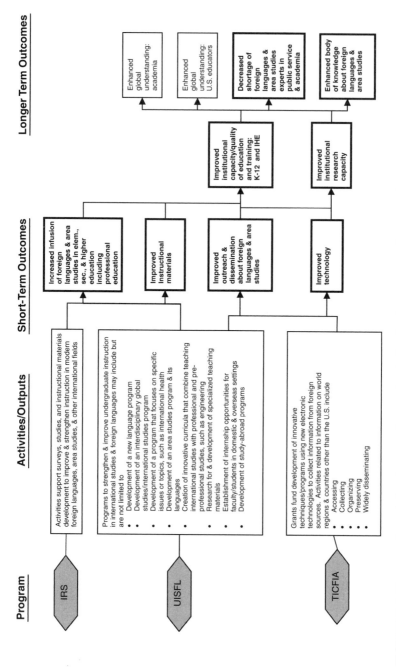

FIGURE B-5 Programs intended to improve instruction in foreign languages and area studies.
NOTE: Boxes with solid shading show programs. Bold boxes show goals and inferred subgoals identified in the congressional request for the study.

SUMMARY

The model outlined above illustrates the interconnectedness of the programs and the varied but complementary ways in which they contribute to the program goals and to the key areas specified in the committee's charge. We aimed to understand the synergies between the programs and the ways in which they complement or duplicate one another. Some programs (CIBER, BIE, TICFIA, IIPP) are by design focused on one or more of the key specific areas. Others (NRC, LRC) are broader in focus and will address a larger set of outcomes. The available data do not support an analysis of the individual program components in the Title VI/FH programs. Instead, the committee has approached the review as an assessment of the degree to which the 14 programs—as a synergistic set of complementary activities—respond to the eight key areas.

ATTACHMENT B-1

Summary of Title VI and Fulbright-Hays Evaluation Studies

Name of Study	Description	Main Findings
Increasing Representation of Minorities in International Service Through International Education Programs (Joyner, 2006a)	The study was commissioned by the committee. The evaluator reviewed grant applications and program descriptions to find Title VI-funded projects that involved efforts to reach out to minority students and encourage participation in programs which emphasize international study and employment in international fields. The evaluator also examined and built upon data on post-program employment for participants in the IIPP. **Shortcomings:** Lack of data, many programs and research studies not yet completed, evaluations of programs not yet completed.	**Criticisms:** IIPP reaching only a small number of students and data is lacking on what students do after they participate in the program. More potential is in grants to institutions that serve a larger number of students. IRS-funded studies will identify barriers to participation in international program for minority students, and how to overcome those barriers.

Name of Study	Description	Main Findings
Technology and Instructional Materials in Title VI and Fulbright-Hays International Education Programs (Joyner and Suarez, 2006)	The study was commissioned by the committee. The purpose was to gauge the extent to which Title VI/FH are using new technology to advance foreign language and international studies, and the extent to which the programs are producing quality instructional materials. The author reviewed 124 Title VI-funded projects, including all of those under TICFIA and IRS, and those in other programs that had a focus on use of new technology and/or development of new instructional materials and assessments. **Shortcomings:** No available criteria as to how much use of technology or production of instructional materials would represent a "high" or "admirable" extent and how much would represent a "low" or "unacceptable" extent. Lack of criteria made it impossible to judge the quality of the instructional materials produced. Missing data in ED's EELIAS database, and limited information on grantee's plans and progress.	Two-thirds of the reviewed projects (82 projects) used computer-based technology in the generation of instructional materials and assessments. Technology is frequently used as an important delivery tool to make information more broadly available to users, such as distance learning. Technology is also used to enhance the content being produced. This use was especially obvious in the TICFIA and IRS projects, where the use of technology included activities such as gathering information from diverse locations and modifying it to make it accessible to English-speaking users and using the interactive and multimedia capabilities of the Internet for instruction or assessment. The study describes efforts to provide materials for instruction and assessment for the study of various languages and cultures. Materials were produced for instruction in a wide range of languages, including many of the LCTLs. The materials included some resources for instructors, but most were products that would be used directly in instruction or by students. Projects produced assessment tools less often than other instructional materials. All the assessments reported were in projects funded by IRS or LRC. **Criticisms:** ED's current EELIAS database does not provide convenient access to reliable program information for use by Congress, agency managers, and the public.

continued

Name of Study	Description	Main Findings
Institute for International Public Policy Impact Assessment (United Negro College Fund Special Programs Corporation, August 2006)	This study is an internal review of the IIIPP program. It is based on surveys of program participants and two focus group sessions. **Shortcomings:** Low response rate, particularly for earlier cohorts. The survey also had inadequate response choices for program alumni career paths; therefore the percentage of alumni who go onto careers in international service cannot be established with any precision.	The program has positive effects in terms of its impact on participants, who report that the program has "increased intellectual capabilities" and "strengthened interpersonal communication skills" as well as other positive personal outcomes. Other relevant findings: • 40% of former participants found employment congruent with program goals. • Over half of participants speak another language for work-related reasons. • Much better data collection and tracking of participants is required. • Graduate school and career service advising programs should be improved.

Name of Study	Description	Main Findings
Language and Critical Area Studies After September 11: An Evaluation of the Contributions of Title VI/FH to the National Interest (Brecht et al., 2007)	This is an update of the Brecht and Rivers study. It examines outputs of career paths, dissertations, articles and academic awards in Middle Eastern and Slavic studies, comparing Title VI and non-Title VI institutions. It also attempts to isolate the programs' "criticality," i.e., the extent to which the programs would function as they do currently without federal support. **Shortcomings:** Lots of data on student placement in the EELIAS system is missing. The study only examines Middle East and Slavic studies, not all subject areas. In addition, measuring "criticality" is difficult. The programs have an impact, but value to society is a "societal question, best answered by the political process."	Title VI-funded NRCs and LRCs produce a disproportionate amount of expertise in language and area studies, compared to non-Title VI funded institutions, even the most prestigious ones. They are especially critical in research, teaching, and maintaining the capacity to teach LCTLs. **Criticisms:** Funding for the programs should be increased, and they should be well-integrated with the coming National Security Language Initiative. For this reason, the authors argue for the creation of a National Language Advisor.
E-LCTL Initiative (2005)	This was a collaborative effort among several Title VI-funded centers to assemble data on the teaching of LCTLs; the study itself was partially funded by ED. The project collected and analyzed data from applications for NRC and FLAS awards and compared with published data about language instruction in the Foreign Service Institute, Defense Language Institute (DLI), and all U.S. universities.	In centers funded by Title VI, more than 30,000 students were enrolled in 128 LCTLs in 55 universities in 27 states in 2001-2002. These centers enroll more than 60% of the students in the 10 languages deemed "critical" by the Department of Defense. During 2001-04, 226 LCTLs were available through Title VI centers while federal agencies offered 75 LCTLs. For the past decade, an estimated more than 80% of all instruction in LCTLs was in Title VI-supported centers.

continued

Name of Study	Description	Main Findings
Securing Our Nation's Future Through International Business Education: 15 Years of CIBER, 1989-2004 (University of Connecticut School of Business CIBER, 2005)	This study performed by staff at one CIBER sought to summarize the program's accomplishments over 15 years. It collected data from CIBERs nationwide on the number of doctorates awarded, courses taught, courses created or upgraded as the result of CIBER funding, number of students, and the number of new degree programs initiated or revised.	CIBER leveraged additional resources from universities, foundations and businesses. CIBER programs have had a "wide spillover effect" on other universities & colleges in "deepening the international expertise of US higher education." CIBERs are "building capacity and then collaborating to develop networks across the nation which are greatly enhancing the overall impact of programs."
Title VI BIE Funding: A Survey of Success (Gerber, 2002)	This study was based on a questionnaire sent to institutions receiving BIE grants. It surveyed the institutions on funded activities: faculty training and research; course development; curriculum development; business outreach; and academic outreach. **Shortcomings:** One drawback of the study was that the respondents (there was a 58% response rate) might have given a more positive outlook on the program than non-respondents.	BIE has been "highly successful" in meeting the intended program goals. Funded projects have "not only demonstrated high impact on targeted populations in education and business, but have proved to be highly sustainable." The receipt of BIE grants opened the door to funding from other sources. BIE programs helped to establish relationships with the business community and university administrators.
Producing International Expertise in MBA Programs (Folks, 2003)	The study compared 31 MBA programs at CIBER institutions with 35 MBA programs at non-CIBER institutions.	The study found CIBER-funded programs were more likely to have international business (IB) courses in core program of business schools, and offer more international business courses in general; integrate language instruction into the MBA curriculum and offer a greater variety of languages, especially LCTLs.

Name of Study	Description	Main Findings
Language and National Security in the 21st Century: The Role of Title VI/Fulbright-Hays in Supporting National Language Capacity (Brecht and Rivers, 2000)	This is a wide-ranging study that evaluated the Title VI/FH against the overall strategic goals of the programs and a set of language-specific objectives the authors believe follow from those goals. The analysis was conducted, to the extent possible, within the GPRA framework. It did not cover area studies. The authors attempted to address the "criticality" of the set of programs, through the question "what evidence exists that a language function critical to the nation would not be accomplished were it not for the programs funded under Title VI/FH?" **Shortcomings:** Focuses on language expertise, not area studies. Evaluates program as a whole, not component parts.	Most of Brecht and Rivers conclusions center around the value of Title VI/FH in supporting the study and teaching of LCTLs. The authors clearly indicate that much of the teaching of LCTLs would not exist were it not for Title VI/FH funding. Title VI/FH is less successful in other areas, and many aspects of its effectiveness are difficult to measure due to lack of data. Their conclusions: Title IV/FH has had a significant impact on basic research in LTCLs, the production of scholars and teachers in LCTLs, and in applied research in the form of learning and teaching materials. It has played a critical role in the development and maintenance of language capacity in its strengthening of flagship programs in LCTLs. It has also lead to greater levels of proficiency in these languages. Much of the teaching of LCTLs would not exist were it not for Title VI/FH funding. NRCs and LRCs contributed to about half of all published research on LCTLs. Its role in supporting the more commonly taught modern languages is less critical. The contribution of Title IV/FH to the national pool of practitioners is unclear, because of a lack of data, particularly on the career paths of students it supports. **Criticisms:** Should be refocused on languages rather than area studies. Goals of the program are very broad, and a debate over the programs is whether they should fund programs as a matter of general educational importance or to train specialists. Legislation suggests both but current funding levels make that impossible.

continued

Name of Study	Description	Main Findings
Federal Funding for International Studies: Does It Help? Does It Matter? Long-Term Impacts of Federal Funding on International Studies and Foreign Language Programs (Schneider and Burn, 1999)	The study was intended to inform ED about grantee performance. It took the form of a questionnaire sent to a sample of 107 institutions receiving UISFL funding in alternate years between 1982 and 1990 regarding campus environment, project focus, outcomes, and factors contributing to the project. There was a 75% response rate. There were also site visits to half of the institutions surveyed. **Shortcomings:** Some supplemental data could not be obtained from ED.	80% reported a high overall institutional impact of the project. Over 90% reported that the institution is currently supporting a program that received funding 5 or more years previously. The "program had a positive effect on many elements deemed critical to the development and strengthening of international education," such as requiring an "international" course as a general education graduation requirement and having a formally designated advisor for students doing international or area studies. Grantee institutions made considerable "matches" to UISFL grants. There were many instances of leveraging for additional funds and use of seed money for innovation that would not have taken place otherwise. Grants bestowed a great deal of prestige, which facilitated interdisciplinary activity. Grantees reported adding new courses and languages, and nearly all were still being offered with solid enrollments after the grant ended. Programs offered an average of 2.8 new and 2.9 revised courses. Enrollment in languages increased. **Criticisms:** There were no criticisms, but recommendations are meant to address some shortcomings, including: ED should keep better records of program outcomes and other basic information. ED should encourage applications from a wider array of institutions. Programs deserve more funding.

Name of Study	Description	Main Findings
Three Decades of Excellence 1965-1994: The Fulbright-Hays Doctoral Dissertation Research Abroad Fellowship Program and its Impact on the American Academy (Council of American Overseas Research Centers, 1998)	The study tried to determine the impact of receiving a DDRA Grant on a person's career. It collected information on recipients, such as the regions where their research was conducted, languages used, academic disciplines, the time it took to complete a Ph.D., future employment, etc. The survey was sent to 783 of 3,200 total recipients, and the response rate was 53%. **Shortcomings:** Length of questionnaire may have affected response rate among highest-achieving participants, thus understating effects of the program.	Analysis of changes across time showed an increase in fellowships awarded to women to 51% in 1990-1994. By 1995, fellows were teaching in nearly 400 academic institutions across the country. Almost all those responding (more than 99%) said that the program was a critical element in their success as professional area-studies and foreign language specialists. Respondents also described intangible and unquantifiable benefits such as a deeper understanding of other cultures, the experience of living in a foreign country, and the greater awareness of one's global identity.
Continuing and Emerging National Needs for the Internationalization of Undergraduate Education (McCarthy, 1998)	The purpose of the study was to gauge the impact of UISFL-funded programs. Administrators of all of the 195 UISFL projects funded 1990-1995 were sent surveys. The respondents were asked to rate UISFL project's impact on their home institution, unanticipated multiplier effects, and questions. **Shortcomings:** A methodological issue was the 44% response rate and self-reporting. A majority of administrators rated their own programs a "5" or "6" on a scale of 1 to 6.	Respondents had a high degree of satisfaction with their projects' impacts. Most felt they had been successful in maintaining gains made during the course of the projects. Vast majority of the projects focused on improving existing structure rather than making major changes. Specifically, developing skills and knowledge of existing faculty, acquiring library and teaching materials, revising existing courses, and revising or expanding foreign language curriculum. Respondents cited several institutional changes that went beyond specific project activities. **Criticisms:** None, but some recommendations for increased funding and sharing of best practices.

ATTACHMENT B-2

Written Comments Submitted to the Committee

The committee invited individuals and organizations knowledgeable about the Title VI and Fulbright-Hays programs to submit comments based on the following guiding questions:

- What do you view as the purpose of the Department of Education's Title VI and Fulbright-Hays program(s)? What are the program(s)' strengths, weaknesses, and criticisms?
- How would you define "success" for the program(s)? How would you determine if the program(s) are "successful" or "effective"? Would you measure effectiveness differently for the various Department of Education Title VI and Fulbright-Hays programs?
- What data/information do you use to measure the effectiveness of this program(s)?
- What data/information do you think is necessary or should be used to measure effectiveness?
- How would you use the results of an evaluation?
- How do you view the role of the Department of Education's Title VI and Fulbright-Hays programs as similar or different from the role of other related federal programs?

The following individuals or organizations submitted written comments:

Melissa H. Birch, *Director, Center for International Business Education and Research, University of Kansas,* Title VI Centers for International Business Education and Research Program

William Brustein, *Director, University Center for International Studies, University of Pittsburgh,* General Statement/Title VI and Fulbright-Hays

Mark Chichester, *Director, Institute for International Public Policy, The College Fund/UNCF,* Title VI Institute for International Public Policy

*Donna Christian, *President, Center for Applied Linguistics (CAL),* CAL's Perspective on the International Research and Studies Program

Dan E. Davidson, *President, American Council of Teachers of Russian,* Fulbright Group Projects and Seminars Abroad Programs

---

*These individuals did not present their comments to the committee in person.

*J. David Edwards, *Executive Director, JNCL-NCLIS*, The Joint National Committee for Languages and the National Council for Languages and International Studies Perspectives on Title VI

Uliana Gabara, *Dean of International Education, University of Richmond*, Title VI Undergraduate International Studies and Foreign Language Programs

*Interagency Language Roundtable (*ILR*), written comments submitted on May 9, 2006, by:
    Frederick H. Jackson, *Coordinator, ILR*
    Scott G. McGinnis, *Steering Committee, ILR*
    Glenn Nordin, *Office of the Secretary, U.S. Department of Defense*

Catharine Keatley, *Associate Director, The National Capital Language Resource Center*, Title VI Language Resource Center Program

*Stanley Kurtz, *Fellow, Hudson Institute*, six articles on Title VI:
    The Language Gap by Lee Smith
    Learning the Language by Kenneth Whitehead
    Title VI: Turn on the Defogger by Martin Kramer
    Boycott Exposure by Stanley Kurtz
    Scholars Revive Boycott of U.S. Grants to Promote Language Training by Anne Marie Borrego
    Who Will Defend the Defenders by Stanley Kurtz

Mary Ellen Lane, *Executive Director, Council of American Overseas Research Centers*, Title VI American Overseas Research Centers

Gilbert Merkx, *Vice Provost for International Affairs, Center for International Studies, Duke University*, Title VI NRC and FLAS; Fulbright DDRA and FRA Programs

Kelly Jett Murphrey, *Director, Center for Study of Western Hemispheric Trade, Center for International Business Studies, May Business School, Texas A&M University*, Title VI Business and International Education Program

Amy W. Newhall, *Executive Director, Middle East Studies Association, University of Arizona*, The Higher Education Act, Title VI, and the Mutual Educational and Cultural Exchange Act, Section 102(b)(6), International Education and Foreign Language

Tony Stewart, *Professor of South Asian Religions, North Carolina State University*, Title VI Programs

Vivien Stewart, *Vice President, Education, Asia Society,* K-12 International Education

David Wiley, *Director, African Studies Center, Michigan State University,* Title VI Research and Studies and TICFIA Programs

ATTACHMENT B-3

Open Committee Sessions

First Committee Meeting

February 14-15, 2006

OPEN SESSION AGENDA

500 Fifth Street, NW

Room 204

Washington, DC

Tuesday, February 14

10:45 a.m.   Welcome and Introductions
              Janet Norwood, *Committee Chair, Committee to Review
                  the Title VI and Fulbright-Hays International Education
                  Programs*

10:55 a.m.   Sponsor Perspective
              Susan Beaudoin, *Deputy Assistant Secretary, Higher
                  Education Programs, Department of Education*

11:15 a.m.   Department of Education Study of Graduate Fellowship
                  Programs Participants
              Lewis Kraus, *Vice President, InfoUse*

12:15 p.m.   Lunch (Room 213)

12:45 p.m.   Program Administration and Monitoring at the Department
                  of Education
              Ralph Hines, *Director, International Education Programs
                  Service (IEPS), Department of Education*
              Karla Ver Bryck Block, *Senior Program Specialist, IEPS*

1:45 p.m.   Public Forum: Part I (*8-9 Minutes per Speaker*)
              William Brustein, *Director, University Center for
                  International Studies, University of Pittsburgh*, General
                  Statement/Title VI and Fulbright-Hays

Dan E. Davidson, *President, American Councils for International Education and Professor of Russian, Bryn Mawr*, Fulbright-Hays Group Projects and Seminars Abroad Programs

Gilbert Merkx, *Vice Provost for International Affairs, Center for International Studies, Duke University*, Title VI NRC and FLAS, and Fulbright DDRA and FRA Programs

David Wiley, *Director, African Studies Center, Michigan State University*, Title VI Research and Studies, and TICFIA Programs

Catharine Keatley, *Associate Director, The National Capital Language Resource Center*, Title VI Language Resource Center Program

Uliana Gabara, *Dean of International Education, University of Richmond*, Title VI Undergraduate International Studies and Foreign Language Programs

Mary Ellen Lane, *Executive Director, Council of American Overseas Research Centers*, Title VI American Overseas Research Centers

3:15 p.m.   Break

3:30 p.m.   Public Forum: Part II (*8-9 Minutes per Speaker*)

Melissa H. Birch, *Director, Center for International Business Education and Research, University of Kansas*, Title VI Centers for International Business Education and Research Program

Kelly Jett Murphrey, *Director, Center for Study of Western Hemispheric Trade, Center for International Business Studies, May Business School, Texas A&M University*, Title VI Business and International Education Program

Mark Chichester, *Director, Institute for International Public Policy, The College Fund/UNCF*, Title VI Institute for International Public Policy

Vivien Stewart, *Vice President, Education, Asia Society*

Amy W. Newhall, *Executive Director, Middle East Studies Association, University of Arizona*

Tony Stewart, *Professor of South Asian Religions, North Carolina State University*

Ann Imlah Schneider, *International Education Consultant*

5:00 p.m.   Adjourn

Second Committee Meeting

May 18, 2006 Workshop

OPEN SESSION AGENDA

The Lecture Room—The National Academy of Sciences

2100 C Street, NW, Washington, DC

Thursday, May 18

8:00 a.m.   Continental Breakfast

8:30 a.m.   Welcome and Introductions
Martin Orland, *Director, Center for Education*
Janet Norwood, *Chair, Committee to Review the Title VI and Fulbright-Hays International Education Programs*

8:45 a.m.   Profiles of Two University International Education Programs

Moderator: **Fernando Reimers,** *Committee Member and Professor of International Education, Harvard Graduate School of Education*

University of Michigan:

- **Mark Tessler,** *Vice Provost for International Affairs, Director, University of Michigan International Institute*
- **Bradley Farnsworth,** *Director, Center for International Business Education*
- **Michael Kennedy,** *Director, Center for Russian and East European Studies, Center for European Studies and European Union Center of Excellence*
- **Linda Lim,** *Professor of Strategy, Stephen M. Ross School of Business, Director, Center for Southeast Asian Studies*
- **Barbara Metcalf,** *Director, Center for South Asian Studies*

Yale University:

- **Nancy Ruther,** *Associate Director, Yale Center for International and Area Studies*

- **William Foltz,** *Heinz Professor of African Studies and Political Science*
- **Sandra Sanneh,** *Director, Program in African Languages*

11:00 a.m.   Break

11:15 a.m.   Discussion of Profiles

Moderator: **Sheila Biddle,** *Committee Member and Independent Consultant*

12:30 p.m.   Lunch

1:30 p.m.   The Role of Universities in Addressing the Demand for Area Studies, International, and Foreign Language Expertise: A Moderated Panel Discussion of Demand Perspectives

Moderator: **Ambassador Michael Lemmon,** *Committee Member and Faculty Advisor, National Defense University*

Panelists:

- **Christine Brown,** *Assistant Superintendent, Glastonbury Public Schools*
- **Diane Castiglione,** *Director of Recruitment, U.S. Department of State*
- **Susan Kelly,** *Special Assistant to Deputy Undersecretary of Defense Policy Planning and Evaluation, Department of Defense*
- **Charles Kolb,** *President, Committee for Economic Development*
- **James Nye,** *Director, South Asia Language and Area Center, University of Chicago*

3:00 p.m.   Break

3:15 p.m.   The Role of Universities in Addressing the Demand for Area Studies, International, and Foreign Language Expertise: A Moderated Panel Discussion of University/Title VI Perspectives

Moderator: **Chris Cross,** *Committee Member and Chairman, Cross & Joftus, LLC*

Panelists:

- **Ben L. Kedia,** *Wang Professor of International Business, Director, Wang CIBER, The University of Memphis*

- Linda Lim, *Professor of Strategy, Stephen M. Ross School of Business, Director, Center for Southeast Asian Studies*
- Patrick O'Meara, *Professor and Dean, International Programs, Indiana University*
- Steven M. Poulos, *Director, South Asia Language Resource Center, The University of Chicago*
- Karla Ver Bryck Block, *Senior Program Specialist, IEPS, Department of Education*

5:00 p.m. Adjourn

Fourth Committee Meeting

October 5-6, 2006

OPEN SESSION AGENDA

The Beckman Center of the National Academies

The Board Room

Irvine, CA

(and via videoteleconference at The National Academy of Sciences

2100 C Street, NW, Room NAS 250, Washington, DC)

Thursday, October 5

8:00 a.m. PST Breakfast (for those in Irvine)
(11:00 a.m. EST)

8:30 a.m. PST Welcome
(11:30 a.m. EST) **Janet Norwood,** *Chair, Committee to Review the Title VI and Fulbright-Hays International Education Programs*

8:45 a.m. PST Panel Discussion of Title VI in the 21st Century
(11:45 a.m. EST) **Al Fishlow,** *Columbia University* (via videoteleconference from Columbia University)

Martin Kramer, *The Washington Institute for Near East Policy*
Robert Blake, *University of California Language Consortium*

10:15 a.m. PST **(1:15 p.m. EST)**	Break
10:30 a.m. PST **(1:30 p.m. EST)**	Recent Developments in IEPS Data Collection and Reporting **Karla VerBryck Block,** *International Education Programs Service*
11:15 a.m. PST **(2:15 p.m. EST)**	**The Honorable David S.C. Chu,** *Undersecretary of Defense for Personnel and Readiness* (via videoteleconference from the Department of Defense)
12:00 p.m. PST **(3:00 p.m. EST)**	Break (for lunch in Irvine)
1:00 p.m. PST **(4:00 p.m. EST)**	End of Open Session

NOTE FOR PUBLIC MEETINGS: This meeting is being held to gather information to help the committee conduct its study. This committee will examine the information and material obtained during this, and other public meetings, in an effort to inform its work. Although opinions may be stated and lively discussion may ensue, no conclusions are being drawn at this time; no recommendations will be made. In fact, the committee will deliberate thoroughly before writing its draft report. Moreover, once the draft report is written, it must go through a rigorous review by experts who are anonymous to the committee, and the committee then must respond to this review with appropriate revisions that adequately satisfy the Academy's Report Review Committee and the chair of the National Research Council before it is considered a National Research Council report. Therefore, observers who draw conclusions about the committee's work based on today's discussions will be doing so prematurely.

Furthermore, individual committee members often engage in discussion and questioning for the specific purpose of probing an issue and sharpening an argument. The comments of any given committee member may not necessarily reflect the position he or she may actually hold on the subject under discussion, to say nothing of that person's future position as it may evolve in the course of the project. Any inferences about an individual's position regarding findings or recommendations in the final report are therefore also premature.

ATTACHMENT B-4

Site Visit Interview Guide

8-03-06

Topics to be addressed in every interview:

- The 8 areas of review, including how they evaluate their own progress in these areas.
- Unique strengths/challenges of their programs.
- Impact of Title VI/FH funding (except student interviews).
- How can Title VI/FH be improved (except student interviews)?

Key to eight areas of review:

Q1. Supporting research, education, and training in foreign languages and international studies, including opportunities for such research, education, and training overseas;

Q2. Reducing shortages of foreign languages and area experts;

Q3. Infusing a foreign language and area studies dimension throughout the educational system and across relevant disciplines including professional education;

Q4. Producing relevant instructional materials that meet accepted scholarly standards;

Q5. Advancing uses of new technology in foreign language and international studies;

Q6. Addressing business needs for international knowledge and foreign language skills;

Q7. Increasing the numbers of underrepresented minorities in international service; and

Q8. Conducting public outreach/dissemination to K-12 and higher education, media, government, business, and the general public.

PROVOST/SENIOR INTERNATIONAL OFFICER

Questions related to the eight study areas:

1. Could you give us an overview of your international programs across the university, including among faculty, undergraduates, graduate students, and the professional schools? (Q1, Q3)

2. How do you monitor and evaluate the effectiveness of these programs? What sources of information do you use to assess outcomes and/or impacts?

Question about the unique aspects of their program:

3. What do you see as your university's greatest strength(s) in the field of international education? Its greatest challenge(s)?

Questions about the impact of Title VI/FH funding:

4. Please tell me about the impact of Federal Title VI/FH funding on the development and evolution of your university's international programs. Does the availability of Title VI/FH funding allow you to support programs or activities that you might not be able to otherwise? Can you provide some specific activities?

   (Probes): Languages that would not otherwise be offered?
   Interdisciplinary work that might not otherwise be carried out?
   Outreach or support to K-12 education?

5. What would happen at your university if Title VI funds were increased by 50%? If they were eliminated?

Question about how to improve Title VI/FH:

6. Are there ways in which Title VI/FH programs might be changed so that they were more effective?

   (Probes): More flexibility in the use of funds.
   Different allocation of funds among the program's several components and objectives.
   More funding for professional schools.

NATIONAL RESOURCE CENTERS (NRC) DIRECTORS AND DEPUTIES

Questions related to the eight study areas:

1. Give us an overview of your center and how it fits in the broader university context. What has been the role of Title VI/FH in the development and evolution of your center? (Q1, Q3)

2. How do you publicize your center and its offerings? How do you recruit students?

(Probes): Do you think the center is widely known on campus? Are your language classes fully subscribed, or could you accept more students into your classes or into the program as a whole?

3. How and how well are the center's instructional needs in language being met? (Q1)

(Probe): Through language and literature departments and/or other programs?
Through collaboration with the LRC?

4. What are the language requirements for the certificate and degree programs, for entering students and for completing students? What standard or standards do you use to measure language proficiency? (Q1)

5. What career paths do students who receive certificates and/or degrees follow? (Q2)

6. Tell us about your outreach activities. Who is your primary audience? Can you tell us about some of your most effective outreach activities and why you consider them effective? (Q6, Q8)

Question about the unique aspects of the program:

7. What do you see as your center's greatest strength(s)? Your greatest challenge(s)?

Questions about the impact of Title VI/FH funding:

8a. (For Centers with continuous funding) Please tell me about the impact of federal Title VI/FH funding on your center's programs. What activities are supported?

(Probes): Is it used to support core instruction?
Is it used to support specialized activities like teaching of LCTLs?
Does it allow you to support programs that you might otherwise not be able to offer, such as particular languages, interdisciplinary research, or support to the K-12 system?

8b. (For centers that lost funding and then regained it)[1]   Please tell me about how your center's programs were affected by the temporary loss of federal funding.

(Probes): What activities are you conducting or planning now that you were not able to carry out when you lost federal funding? Can you provide examples?
What sources of funding did you turn to when federal funds were gone?
What types of activities were you able to maintain?
What types of activities were you forced to eliminate?

9. (For centers with continuous funding—do not use for centers that temporarily lost funding) What would happen at your center if Title VI funds were increased by 50%? If they were eliminated?

Question about how to improve Title VI/FH:

10. Are there ways in which Title VI/FH programs might be changed so that they were more effective?

(Probes): More flexibility in the use of funds.
Different allocation of funds among the various programs and objectives.
More involvement of professional schools.

LANGUAGE RESOURCE CENTERS (LRC) DIRECTORS AND DEPUTIES

Questions related to the eight study areas:

1. In what specific ways is your center helping to support research, education, and training in foreign languages across the university (including in the professional schools)? (Q1,Q3)

2. Tell us about the instructional materials you produce. Who is the primary audience for these materials, and how do you ensure that they are of high quality and relevant to the audience? (Q4)

(Probe): Are the materials reviewed by other scholars who have

[1]San Diego State University: none; George Washington University: none; Georgetown University: none; Indiana University: East Asia and West Europe (lost funding 2000-2006); New York University: Latin America (lost funding 2003-2005) and Center for European Studies (lost funding 2000-2002); Ohio State University: East Asia (lost funding 2003-2005); University of California, Los Angeles: Latin American Center (lost funding 2000-2003) and Europe/Russian Center (lost funding 2003-2005).

language and area expertise? If so, what is the process by which the materials are reviewed?

3. How do you evaluate the use and impact of these instructional materials?

   (Probe):   What types of data do you maintain on the use of your materials?
              Among various audiences, such as K-12 education, higher education, professional schools, and business? (Q4, Q6, Q8)

4. Do you coordinate or collaborate with other LRCs or NRCs on campus? With other international-focused programs on campus? Do you collaborate with Title VI-funded programs at other universities? Please give examples.

Question about the unique aspects of the program:

5. What do you see as your center's greatest strength(s)? Your greatest challenge(s)?

Questions about the impact of Title VI/FH funding:

6. Please tell me about the impact of federal Title VI/FH funding on your LRC. What activities are supported that might not otherwise?

   (Probes): Is it used to support core language instruction?
              Is it used to support specialized activities related to LCTLs?
              Does it allow you to support programs that you might otherwise not be able to offer, such as particular languages, interdisciplinary research, or support to the K-12 system?

7. What would happen to your center if Title VI funds were increased by 50%? If they were eliminated?

Question about how to improve Title VI/FH:

8. Are there ways in which Title VI/FH programs might be changed so that they were more effective?

   (Probes): More flexibility in the use of funds.
              Different allocation of funds among the various programs and objectives.

CIBER DIRECTORS

Questions related to the eight study areas:

1. Can you provide some examples of the ways in which your programs address business needs for international knowledge and foreign language skills? (Q6)

2. Tell us about your outreach activities. Do you target outreach primarily to business or to several different audiences? Which of these efforts do you view as most effective and why? (Q3, Q6, Q8)

   (Probe): In addition to business, do you reach out to other audiences, such as K-12 education, other parts of your university, the general public, the media?

3. Do you coordinate or collaborate with other CIBERs at other universities? With other Title VI-funded programs on campus? Other international-focused programs on campus? Please give examples.

Questions about unique aspects of the program:

4. What do you see as your center's greatest strength(s)? Your greatest challenge?

Questions about the impact of Title VI/FH funding:

5. Please tell me about the impact of federal Title VI/FH funding on your CIBER. What activities are supported that might not otherwise?

6. What would happen to your center if Title VI funds were increased by 50%? If they were eliminated?

Question about how to improve Title VI/FH:

7. Are there ways in which Title VI/FH programs might be changed to be more effective?

   (Probes): More flexibility in the use of funds?
   Different allocation of funds among the various programs and objectives?

FACULTY

NOTE: Try to meet with faculty alone, without the presence of the NRC director, LRC director, or other administrator.

Questions related to the eight study areas:

General orientation

Ask faculty to identify their discipline, home department, particular field of expertise, and center they are associated with.

1. Would you describe the intellectual benefits you gain from participating in the center?

    (Probe): Do you gain insights from other disciplines?
    Does the center provide opportunities for interdisciplinary collaboration in research, teaching, and/or service?
    Do you learn about new scholarship?

2. How do you publicize your center and its offerings? How do you recruit students?

    (Probes): Do you think the center is widely known on campus?
    Are your language classes fully subscribed, or could you accept more students into your classes or into the program as a whole?

3. (For language instructors) How many levels of instruction are offered in the language(s) you teach? (Q1)

    (Probes): What levels of proficiency are required for students in certificate programs, M.A., Ph.D. programs? How is proficiency measured?

4. Are you or have you been an undergraduate or graduate student advisor? What are the motivations and goals of students pursuing certificate and degree programs in your field? In international/area studies in general? (Q2)

    (Probe): What career fields do graduates enter (government, business, and academia)?

Question about unique aspects of the program:

5. What do you see as your university's greatest strength(s) in the area of international education and foreign language instruction? Its greatest challenge?

Questions about the impact of Title VI/FH funding:

6. Please tell me about the impact of federal Title VI/FH funding on your teaching, research, and other activities. For what types of ac

tivities have you and/or your students received direct support from Title VI and/or Fulbright-Hays?

(Probe): Can you provide any examples of ways in which Title VI/FH funds helped to leverage additional university resources for your research and/or teaching?

7. What would happen to your research and teaching if Title VI funds were increased by 50%? If they were eliminated?

Question about how to improve Title VI/FH:

8. Are there ways in which Title VI/FH programs could be changed to be more effective?

(Probes): More flexibility in the use of funds?
Different allocation of funds among the program's several components and objectives?
More funding for professional schools?

STUDENTS

General orientation

Ask students to identify themselves based on their field of study, whether they are studying a language, and if so, what language, the NRC with which they are associated, and whether they have benefited from direct support from Title VI (i.e., FLAS or DDRA)

Questions related to the eight study areas:

1. What motivated you to enroll in language/area studies?

(Probes): What did you expect to get from the program (or courses) when you enrolled in it/them?
Did you have any ideas about a career in/related to this program? (Q2)

2. Where and how did you first hear about the area or language program you are enrolled in?

(Probes): Do you think other students are aware of these programs?
Do you feel your center is isolated from or connected to other departments, divisions, and schools? (Q3)

3. In what subjects or disciplines has your learning experience been the strongest? (Q1)

(Probe): Have you found that language instruction is integrated within courses in such fields as economics, political science, religion and culture?

4. (For those who have gone abroad) Was the preparation appropriate and adequate for your to take advantage of the cultural and linguistic immersion? What aspects of the learning facilities and/or living conditions enhanced or detracted from your study or research abroad? (Q1)

5. In what ways (if any) do you expect to use your training in area studies, international studies, or foreign languages after graduation or after completing your graduate degree? (Q2)

   (Probe): Are you considering a job in government, business, academia or a nonprofit?

6. (For graduate students): What aspects of the facilities, that is the library and the technological resources, support or detract from your research? (Q5)

7. In what ways does the faculty integrate technology into instruction in foreign language and area studies? (Q5)

8. Have your studies met or failed to meet your expectations?

   (Probe): In what ways? Which aspects of your studies?

Question about the unique aspects of their program:

9. What do you see as your university's greatest strength(s) in the field of international education? Its greatest challenge?

INTERNATIONAL STUDIES LIBRARIANS

From your perspective:

1. In what ways have Title VI funds enabled you to provide greater international studies and language resources to the university community?

2. Are these resources accessed by people outside the university? Who?

3. How do you measure the people who have accessed these resources?

APPENDIX
C

Selection Criteria and Priorities in Title VI and Fulbright-Hays Programs

Appendix C, Selection Criteria and Priorities in Title VI and
Fulbright-Hays Programs, pages 350-359,
is not printed in this book but is available online.
Go to *http://www.nap.edu* and search for
International Education and Foreign Languages.

A Brief History of
Foreign Language Assessment
in the United States

This appendix presents a brief history of the development of foreign language proficiency assessments in this country over the past half-century to provide context for the current status of foreign language assessment.

The dominant approach to language proficiency assessment in the United States is based on the Interagency Language Roundtable (ILR) (see http://www.utm.edu/staff/globeg/ilrhome.shtml) and the American Council on the Teaching of Foreign Languages (ACTFL) oral proficiency interview (OPI) (see http://www.sil.org/lingualinks/languagelearning/otherresources/actflproficiencyguidelines/ACTFLGuidelinesReadingIntermed.htm). This approach, which involves a face-to-face oral interview, was originally developed at the Foreign Service Institute (FSI) in the mid-1950s. The notion of a scale of language ability from zero to total mastery was the brainchild of the linguist Henry Lee Smith, who was dean of the FSI Language School at the time. The idea was translated into a scale based on mastery of specific criteria in consultation with John B. Carroll, a psychometrician at Harvard University. From these two ideas—the linguistic idea of a range of language proficiency and a psychometric formulation of a criterion-referenced scale—came the now-familiar five levels of the ILR scale (0-5) which were developed for speaking (S) and listening (L) (Sollenberger, 1978). By 1968, the Defense Language Institute and Central Intelligence Agency were using the approach (Wilds, 1975); in 1969, the Educational Testing Service began administering oral interview assessments for the Peace Corps (Clark, 1978); and in 1973 ILR, comprising representatives from government agencies concerned with language teaching and testing, assumed primary responsibility for the Oral Proficiency Rating Scale (Lowe and Stansfield, 1988). In the mid-1980s, several developments led to the adaptation of the rating scale for use with audiences outside the government. This involved a refinement of the distinctions at the lower end of the scale in recognition of a need to test individuals with lower levels of proficiency (Clark and Clifford, 1988, p. 132).

Table D-1 is a comparison of the two rating scales. The table presents only the labels for the different scale levels. In addition to labels, each scale level has associated with it a much more fully specified description of the kinds of language use situations in which individuals at a given level can be expected to participate. Table D-2 is a comparison of the intermediate-mid ACTFL guideline and level 1 on the ILR scale for speaking and reading.

The differences between the ACTFL and ILR scales are apparent in the specific wording of these scale descriptors, which reflect the adaptations made to the ILR scale to make it more appropriate to academic settings. Another, perhaps more significant difference between the ACTFL and ILR approaches is that, whereas government agencies use the same scale descriptors across all languages, ACTFL has developed different scale descriptors for different languages.

The ACTFL scale and the OPI testing procedure were adopted by ACTFL in the 1980s and have been widely disseminated to the foreign language teaching profession since that time. In addition to the scales for listening and speaking that are obtained from an oral interview, ACTFL has also developed rating scales for assessing reading and writing; the latter is the ACTFL Writing Proficiency Test (see http://www.actfl.org/i4a/pages/index.cfm?pageid=3642). These scales have also been adapted to specific languages so that there are now ACTFL scale descriptors for speaking in 48 different languages (see http://www.languagetesting.com/index.html). Furthermore, these scales are the basis for most current development of proficiency assessments, including those using computer and web technologies. This includes the range of foreign language assessments that have been developed and that are currently under development at the Center for Applied Linguistics (see http://www.cal.org/topics/ta/flassess.html) and various Title VI-funded efforts.

REFERENCES

Clark, J.L.D. (1978). Interview testing research at educational testing service. In J.L.D. Clark (Ed.), *Direct testing of speaking proficiency: Theory and application* (pp. 211-228). Princeton, NJ: Educational Testing Service.

Clark, J.L.D., and Clifford, R.T. (1988).The FSI/ILR/ACTFL proficiency scales and testing techniques: Development, current status and needed research. *Studies in Second Language Acquisition, 10*(2), 129-147.

Lowe, P., Jr., and Stansfield, C.W. (1988). Introduction. In P. Lowe, Jr., and C.W. Stansfield (Eds.), *Second language proficiency assessment: Current issues.* Englewood Cliffs, NJ: Prentice Hall Regents.

Malone, M.E. (2006). *The oral proficiency approaches to foreign language assessment.* Unpublished manuscript, Center for Applied Linguistics, Washington, DC.

Sollenberger, H.E. (1978). Development and current use of the FSI oral interview test. In J.L.D. Clark (Ed.), *Direct testing of speaking proficiency: Theory and application.* Princeton, NJ: Educational Testing Service.

Wilds, C.P. (1975). The oral interview test. In R.L. Jones and B. Spolsky (Eds.), *Testing language proficiency.* Washington, DC: Center for Applied Linguistics.

TABLE D-1 Comparisons Between the ACTFL Guidelines and ILR Scale

ACTFL	ILR
Superior	5 Native or bilingual proficiency
	4+
	4 Distinguished proficiency
	3+
	3 Professional working proficiency
Advanced high	2+
Advanced mid	
Advanced low	2 Limited working proficiency
Intermediate high	1+
Intermediate mid	1 Survival proficiency
Intermediate low	
Novice high	0+
Novice mid	0 No practical proficiency
Novice low	

SOURCE: Malone (2006).

TABLE D-2 Comparison Between the ACTFL and ILR Descriptors

	ACTFL: Intermediate-Mid	ILR 1: Elementary Proficiency
Speaking	Able to handle successfully a variety of uncomplicated, basic, and communicative tasks and social situations. Can talk simply about self and family members. Can ask and answer questions and participate in simple conversations on topics beyond the most immediate needs, e.g., personal history and leisure time activities. Utterance length increases slightly, but speech may continue to be characterized by frequent long pauses, since the smooth incorporation of even basic conversational strategies is often hindered as the speaker struggles to create appropriate language forms. Pronunciation may continue to be strongly influenced by first language and fluency may still be strained. Although misunderstandings still arise, the intermediate-mid speaker can generally be understood by sympathetic interlocutors.	Able to satisfy minimum courtesy requirements and maintain very simple face-to-face conversations on familiar topics. A native speaker must often use slowed speech, repetition, paraphrase, or a combination of these to be understood by this individual. Similarly, the native speaker must strain and employ real-world knowledge to understand even simple statements/questions from this individual. This speaker has a functional but limited proficiency. Misunderstandings are frequent, but the individual is able to ask for help and to verify comprehension of native speech in face-to-face interaction. The individual is unable to produce continuous discourse except with rehearsed material.

continued

TABLE D-2 Continued

	ACTFL: Intermediate-Mid	ILR 1: Elementary Proficiency
Reading	Able to read consistently with increased understanding simple, connected texts dealing with a variety of basic and social needs. Such texts are still linguistically noncomplex and have a clear underlying internal structure. They impart basic information about which the reader has to make minimal suppositions and to which the reader brings personal interest and/or knowledge. Examples may include short, straightforward descriptions of persons, places, and things written for a wide audience.	Sufficient comprehension to read very simple connected written material in a form equivalent to usual printing or typescript. Can read either representations of familiar formulaic verbal exchanges or simple language containing only the highest frequency structural patterns and vocabulary, including shared international vocabulary items and cognates (when appropriate). Able to read and understand known language elements that have been recombined in new ways to achieve different meanings at a similar level of simplicity. Texts may include simple narratives of routine behavior; highly predictable descriptions of persons, places, or things; and explanations of geography and government such as those simplified for tourists. Some misunderstandings possible on simple texts. Can get some main ideas and locate prominent items of professional significance in more complex texts. Can identify general subject matter in some authentic texts.

SOURCES: American Council on the Teaching of Foreign Languages, available: http://www.sil.org/lingualinks/languagelearning/OtherResources/ACTFLProficiencyGuidelines/ACTFLGuidelinesReadingIntermed.htm. [accessed April 2007] and Interagency Language Roundtable, available: http://www.utm.edu/staff/globeg/ilrhome.shtml [accessed April 2007].

APPENDIX
E

Appendix E, Summary of Federal Foreign Language and
Area Studies Programs, pages 365-371,
is not printed in this book but is available online.
Go to *http://www.nap.edu* and search for
International Education and Foreign Languages.

APPENDIX
F

Biographical Sketches of Committee Members and Staff

Janet L. Norwood *(Chair)* is a counselor and senior fellow at the Conference Board, where she chairs the Advisory Committee on the Leading Indicators. From 1979 to 1992 she served as U.S. commissioner of labor statistics and was then a senior fellow at the Urban Institute until 1999. She is a past member of the Committee on National Statistics (CNSTAT) and the Division of Engineering and Physical Sciences of the National Research Council. She currently serves on the Board of Scientific Counselors at the National Center for Health Statistics and was designated a national associate of the National Research Council in 2001. She is a fellow and past president of the American Statistical Association, a member and past vice president of the International Statistical Institute, an honorary fellow of the Royal Statistical Society, and a fellow of the National Academy of Public Administration and the National Association of Business Economists. She has a B.A. from Rutgers University and M.A. and Ph.D. degrees from the Fletcher School of Law and Diplomacy of Tufts University. She has received honorary LL.D. degrees from Carnegie Mellon, Florida International, Harvard, and Rutgers universities.

William M. Arnold is director of International Government Relations for Shell Oil Company, where his team provides strategic guidance and advice for projects in approximately 40 countries. Previously he was senior international advisor to the Coastal Capital Corporation with responsibilities that included preparing country analyses for executive use, liaising with export credit agencies and multilateral institutions for funding and risk mitigation. From 1983 to 1988 he was senior vice president of the Export Import Bank of the United States. His international banking experience includes positions in the Latin America Division of Texas Commerce Bancshares, Inc. (now JPMorganChase), COMIND International Banking Corporation, a subsidiary of Banco do Commercio e Industria de Sao Paulo, Brazil, and First City National Bank. He has a B.A. in economics from Cornell University as well as an M.A. in Latin American Studies and an M.B.A. from the University of Texas at Austin. He completed graduate studies on European economic integration at the Europa Instituut of the University of Amsterdam and the Graduate School of Banking at the University of Wisconsin.

Lyle F. Bachman is professor and chair of the Department of Applied Linguistics and Teaching English as a Second Language in the Humanities Division at the University of California, Los Angeles. He serves as a consultant in language assessment and language program design, evaluation, and research to government agencies and institutions in Hong Kong, Korea, the United States, and the United Kingdom and is currently co-editor of the Cambridge University Press series, *Language Assessment.* His international experience includes Peace Corps service in the Philippines, six years in Thailand as a project specialist for the Ford Foundation, three years at Tehran University in Iran, and two years at the Chinese University of Hong Kong. He is a past president of the American Association for Applied Linguistics and of the International Language Testing Association, was the first winner of the TESOL/Newbury House award for outstanding research, and has won the Modern Language Association of America's Kenneth Mildenberger award for outstanding research publication twice. In 2004, he received a lifetime achievement award by the International Language Testing Association. He is currently a member of the National Research Council's Board on Testing and Assessment. He has a Ph.D. from Indiana University.

Burt S. Barnow is an economist, associate director for research, and principal research scientist at the Institute for Policy Studies of the Johns Hopkins University. His work focuses on evaluating social programs, and he has conducted research and evaluations in the labor, welfare, and education fields. He also teaches program evaluation in the institute's graduate public policy program as well as labor economics in the Department of Economics. Before joining Johns Hopkins, he was vice president of a consulting firm in the Washington, DC, area. He served nine years in the Department of Labor, most recently as director of the Office of Research and Evaluation for the Employment and Training Administration. He is a member of the National Research Council's Board on Higher Education and the Workforce and recently cochaired the Committee on Workforce Needs in Information Technology. He has a B.S. in economics from the Massachusetts Institute of Technology and a Ph.D. in economics from the University of Wisconsin-Madison.

Sheila Biddle is an independent consultant in New York. The author of *Internationalization: Rhetoric or Reality*, a study of internationalization in U.S. universities published in 2003, she was a senior research scholar at Columbia University from 1996 to 2002, while she was completing the research and writing of the project. From 1982 to 1996, she was a program officer in the Ford Foundation's Education and Culture Program, working in the field of higher education. With the former director, she developed and launched the Foundation's Predissertation Fellowship Program, designed to encourage doctoral students in the social sciences to gain competence in an international or area studies field. She was also responsible for programming in African-American studies and for initiatives to increase the numbers of underrepresented minorities on college and universities faculties. She has served as a consultant on internationalization for a number of universities and organizations, including the Social Science Research Council, the Carnegie Corporation, and Franklin A. Thomas, former president of the Ford Foundation, for a project on South Africa. She has a Ph.D. from Columbia University and taught in its history department for 13 years.

Naomi Chudowsky (*Senior Program Officer*) is a senior program officer at the National Research Council, where she works on a variety of projects related to education and testing. She also conducts research on federal and state education policies for several national organizations. Her previous experience includes working on test development for President Clinton's Voluntary National Testing Initiative at the U.S. Department of Education. She also served as project manager for Connecticut's statewide high school assessment. She has a Ph.D. in educational psychology from Stanford University.

Christopher T. Cross is chairman of Cross & Joftus, LLC, an education consulting firm. He has served as a senior fellow with the Center for Education Policy and as a distinguished senior fellow with the Education Commission of the States. From 1994 to 2002 he served as president and chief executive officer of the Council for Basic Education (CBE). Before joining CBE, he served as director of the education initiative of The Business Roundtable and as assistant secretary for educational research and improvement in the U.S. Department of Education. He chaired the National Assessment of Title 1 Independent Review Panel on Evaluation for the U.S. Department of Education from 1995 to 2001 and the National Research Council Panel on Minority Representation in Special Education from 1997 to 2002. In 2001, he completed a six-year term on the Board of International Comparative Studies in Education of the National Research Council. He has lectured on American education issues in Hong Kong, Japan and the United Arab Emirates. He has a B.A. from Whittier College and an M.A. in government from California State University, Los Angeles.

Margaret Hilton (*Senior Program Officer*) is a senior program officer in the Center for Education (CFE) at the National Research Council. She is currently directing a workshop on future skill demands for work and previously directed a consensus study of the role of high school science laboratories in supporting science learning. She has made contributions to several workshop and committee reports on topics related to K-12 and higher education, workforce skill demands, and continuing education. In 2003, she was guest editor of a special issue of *Comparative Labor Law and Policy*. Prior to joining the National Academies in 1999, she was a consultant to the National Skill Standards Board. Earlier, she directed projects on workforce training, employee involvement, and competitiveness at the Congressional Office of Technology Assessment. She has a B.A. in geography (with high honors) from the University of Michigan and an M.R.P. (master of regional planning) from the University of North Carolina, Chapel Hill, and she is currently studying for an M.A. in human resource development at George Washington University.

Eleanor Liebman Johnson is a consultant on educational evaluation and policy analysis working with the Social Science Research Group and Cross & Joftus, LLC. She recently retired as an assistant director for education issues at the U.S. Government Accountability Office (GAO), where she led over 60 studies, including groundbreaking, high-visibility evaluations of school finance and school facilities, as well as reports on a wide range of elementary and secondary education issues. Recommendations and information from these reports redefined the model for school finance policy and the metrics of school finance equity nationwide and guided efforts to rebuild and modernize America's schools and the U.S. Department of Education. As senior methodologist, she supervised the design of nearly 50 other studies, primarily for justice and law enforcement issues. She has a B.A. from Brandeis University, an M.A. from Columbia University, and an Ed.D. from George Washington University.

Michael C. Lemmon is currently on detail from the U.S. Department of State to the National War College of the National Defense University as a faculty advisor teaching national security studies. Previously he served four years as dean of the School of Language Studies at the State Department's Foreign Service Institute, where he represented State in multiple interagency and public fora on language issues, including the intelligence community's

Foreign Language Executive Committee and the Interagency Language Roundtable. Since entering the Foreign Service in 1974, he has also served as U.S. ambassador to Armenia, deputy assistant secretary of state for political-military affairs, and in a range of State Department positions in Washington, Morocco, Tunisia, Pakistan, and Russia. He is the recipient of multiple honor awards and was selected as an international affairs fellow at the Council on Foreign Relations in New York. He served as a U.S. Army warrant officer helicopter pilot in the Republic of Vietnam and the Federal Republic of Germany. He did undergraduate and graduate studies in international relations and comparative government at the University of Virginia.

Mary Ellen O'Connell (*Study Director*) is a senior program officer in the Division of Behavioral and Social Sciences and Education (DBASSE) of the National Research Council. She has served as study director for three previous consensus studies: on ethical considerations for research on housing-related health hazards involving children, reducing underage drinking, and assessing and improving children's health. She also served as study director for the Committee on Standards of Evidence and the Quality of Behavioral and Social Science Research, a DBASSE-wide strategic planning effort; developed standalone workshops on welfare reform and children and gun violence; and facilitated meetings of the national coordinating committee of the Key National Indicators Initiative. She came to DBASSE from the U.S. Department of Health and Human Services, where she spent eight years in the Office of the Assistant Secretary for Planning and Evaluation, most recently as director of state and local initiatives. She has a B.A. (with distinction) from Cornell University and an M.A. in the management of human services from the Heller School at Brandeis University.

Kenneth Prewitt is the Carnegie professor of public affairs in the School of International and Public Affairs at Columbia University. His previous positions include director of the U.S. Census Bureau, president of the Social Science Research Council, senior vice president of the Rockefeller Foundation, and director of the National Opinion Research Center and professor at the University of Chicago. Among his awards are a Guggenheim fellowship, honorary degrees from Carnegie Mellon University and Southern Methodist University, and the Officer's Cross of the Order of Merit from the Federal Republic of Germany. He is a fellow of the American Academy of Arts and Sciences, the Center for Advanced Study in the Behavioral Sciences, the Academy of Political and Social Science, and the American Association for the Advancement of Science, as well as a member of other professional associations. He is currently a member of the National Research Council's CNSTAT, and chair of the Committee on Research and Evidentiary Standards. He has a Ph.D. from Stanford University.

Fernando M. Reimers is the Ford Foundation professor of international education and director of the international education policy and global education programs at the Harvard Graduate School of Education. He focuses his research and teaching on identifying education policies that support teachers in helping low-income children succeed academically. His current research focuses on the relationship between teacher quality, educational expansion, and social inequality in Mexico and on civic education in Latin America. He also advises governments, development agencies, and private groups involved in education reform in developing nations and has worked in Latin America, Egypt, Jordan, and Pakistan. Prior to joining the Harvard faculty, he served as senior education specialist at the World Bank, at the Harvard Institute for International Development, and on the faculty at the Universidad Central de Venezuela. He is also active in several organizations supporting the development of global skills in American schools. He is currently a member of the advisory board for the National Research Council's DBASSE. He has a Ph.D. in educational planning and social policy from Harvard University.

David M. Trubek is the Voss-Bascom professor of law emeritus and a lecturer at the University of Wisconsin-Madison. He is a senior fellow of the university's Center for World Affairs and the Global Economy and served as its director from 2001 to 2004. From 1990 to 2001, as dean of international studies, he coordinated the university's area and international studies, managed the International Institute, directed the Office of International Studies and Programs, oversaw relations with foreign universities, managed study abroad programs, and was responsible for campus-wide strategic planning in international education. He has published articles and books on the future of international studies, the role of law in development, human rights, European integration, and the impact of globalization on legal systems and social protection schemes. In 2001, he was appointed Chevalier des Palmes Académiques by the French Government for his work on globalization. He has an undergraduate degree from the University of Wisconsin-Madison and a J.D. from Yale Law School.

Monica Ulewicz (*Program Officer*) was, until March 2006, a program officer in CFE at the National Research Council. In her five years at CFE, she worked on a wide range of issues related to international education, including cross-national assessments, child labor, and education for development. She contributed to the reports *Monitoring International Labor Standards: Human Capital Investment* and *The Power of Video Technology in International Comparative Research in Education*. She served as a Peace Corps volunteer in Uganda. She has a B.A. (with honors) in biology from Earlham College and an M.A. in environmental management from Duke University.

Elizabeth B. Welles is an education consultant and former director of foreign language programs and the Association of Departments of Foreign Languages (ADFL) at the Modern Language Association (MLA). While at MLA, she developed and coordinated new and continuing foreign language studies projects, served as editor of the *ADFL Bulletin* (for which she wrote editorials and numerous articles), and was an officer in the Joint National Committee on Language. She was involved in the initial development of the MLA's web-based language map of the United States and recently completed a survey of foreign language enrollment among higher education students in the United States. From 1987 to 1993, she served as a program officer in the Division of Education Programs at the National Endowment for the Humanities. Currently, she is a member of the Washington International Education Group and participates in the Interagency Language Round Table. She has a Ph.D. from Yale University in Italian literature, which she taught for 15 years in several colleges and universities.

Lori Houghton Wright (*Program Officer*) is a program officer for the Board on Testing and Assessment at the National Research Council. She has worked with the Committee on Performance Levels in Adult Literacy and the Committee Evaluating the National Board for Professional Teaching Standards Certification, and was lead organizer for a workshop on the use of school-level assessment data for evaluation of federal education programs. Before joining the National Research Council, she oversaw mathematics assessment for the Massachusetts state tests and served as a visiting professor at the University of the Virgin Islands in St. Croix. She has a background in educational leadership, policy analysis, and mathematics. She has a Ph.D. from the University of Missouri, Columbia.

Yong Zhao is a university distinguished professor at Michigan State University, where he also serves as the founding director of the Center for Teaching and Technology as well as the US-China Center for Research on Educational Excellence. He joined the faculty at Michigan State University in 1996 after working at Willamette University, Hamilton College, and Colgate University as a specialist in technology and language education. Zhao's research interests include diffusion of innovations, teacher adoption of technology, computer-assisted language learning, globalization and education, and international and comparative education. He is a fellow of the International Academy of Education. He has a B.A. from Sichuan International Studies University and A.M. and Ph.D. degrees in education from the University of Illinois at Urbana-Champaign.

Index

A

Abraham Lincoln Study Abroad Fellowships, 369
Absolute priority, 73, 350
Academic freedom, 23
ACLS. *See* American Council of Learned Societies
ACTFL. *See* American Council on the Teaching of Foreign Languages
ACTFL scale, 360–364
Activities, performance measures based on, 213, 314
ADFL. *See* Association of Departments of Foreign Languages
ADFL Bulletin, 165
ADLP. *See* Center for the Advancement of Distinguished Language Proficiency
Advanced Overseas Intensive Language Projects, 99
African Studies Association, 106
Agency for International Development, 306
Agricultural Extension Service, 189
AIBER. *See* Association for International Business Education and Research
American Competitiveness Initiative, 66
American Council of Learned Societies (ACLS), 269
American Council on the Teaching of Foreign Languages (ACTFL), 45n. 1, 56, 97, 134–136, 159, 165–167, 235–239, 360
  guidelines, 361–364
  Writing Proficiency Test, 361
American Educational Research Association, 139, 234
American Overseas Research Centers (AORC), 17, 19, 64, 127, 141, 221–222, 282, 295–296, 319
  centers authorized, 295
  development of grants, 296
  limitation, 295–296
  planned performance measures, 215
  use of grants, 295
Application process, 73–74
  priorities in CIBER, 356
  priorities in IRS, 358
  priorities in LRCs, 355
  priorities in NRCs, 352–353
  recommendation concerning, 10, 111–112
Area studies programs
  awards in, 69
  infusion into the business curriculum, 191–194
  at Ohio State University, 96
  overlap in activities of, 65

programs intended to improve
    instruction in, 322
programs that support centers with a
    focus on, 321
shortage of experts in, 113
summary of, 365–371
Title VI/FH demand for expertise in,
    36–57
Asia Media, 108
Asia Pacific Arts, 108
Asia Studies Association, 222
Assembly of Collegiate Schools of Business,
    183
Assessment. *See* Foreign language
    assessment; Self-assessment
Association for International Business
    Education and Research (AIBER),
    185, 189, 221
Association of Departments of Foreign
    Languages (ADFL), 165
Auralog, 241
Authority, in creating new programs in
    undergraduate international studies,
    289
Award transparency, future needs,
    223–224, 226–227
    recommendation concerning, 11, 227

B

Berlitz, 58–59n. 1
BIE. *See* Business and International
    Education program
Bilingual Cross-Cultural Language and
    Academic Development Certificate
    Program, 107
Blackboard, 241
Boyer Commission on Educating
    Undergraduates in the Research
    University, 164–165
Brigham Young University, 136, 187
Bureau of Educational and Cultural
    Affairs, 28
Business and International Education (BIE)
    program, 19, 64, 76, 90–91, 109,
    117, 140, 182–183, 190–194, 197,
    201, 222, 296–303, 319, 328
    authorization of appropriations, 303
    course development, 192
    criteria and points, 357
    curriculum development, 193
    education and training programs,
        301–303
    faculty development, 192
    findings and purposes, 296–297
    implementation challenges, 194
    infusion of foreign languages and area
        studies into the business curriculum,
        191–194
    institutional capacity, 194
    outreach, 193
    planned performance measures, 215
    projects related to increasing
        representation of minorities, 202
Business for Diplomatic Action, 41
Business needs addressed, 182–195
    BIE program, 190–194
    CIBER program, 183–190
    conclusions, 195

C

CAL. *See* Center for Applied Linguistics
California Commission on Teacher
    Credentialing, 107
California Department of Education, 167
CAORC. *See* Council of American
    Overseas Research Centers
Carnegie classifications, 142
    percentage of grants by type of
        institution, 90
Carnegie Commission on Higher
    Education, 90
CASLS. *See* Center for Applied Second
    Language Studies
CAST. *See* Computer-assisted screening
    tool
CED. *See* Committee for Economic
    Development
Center for Advanced Research on
    Language Acquisition, 178
Center for Applied Linguistics (CAL), 56,
    98, 100, 136, 169, 177, 235–236,
    361
Center for Applied Second Language
    Studies (CASLS), 136
Center for Near Eastern Studies, 100, 131
Center for the Advancement of
    Distinguished Language Proficiency
    (ADLP), 131

Center for Transnational and Comparative Studies, 178
Center for World Languages, 132, 168
Center grants, and Title VI and Fulbright-Hays in the Department of Education, 74–76
Center on Reinventing Public Education, 56, 98
Centers for International Business Education and Research (CIBER, CIBE) program, 17, 19, 64, 70–76, 80–81, 86, 91, 102, 109–110, 114, 140–141, 175, 182–190, 197, 221–222, 297–301, 313, 319, 328, 356–357
  advisory council, 299–300
  application priorities, 356
  authorized activities, 298–299
  authorized expenditures, 297–298
  average grant amounts, 70
  competition results, 71
  criteria and weights, 357
  director questions asked during site visit interviews, 346
  enhanced body of knowledge, 187–189
  foreign languages in the business curriculum, 186–187
  grant conditions, 301
  grant duration, federal share, 300–301
  homeland security and U.S. international competitiveness, 186
  institutional capacity, 190
  and Ohio State University, 191
  planned performance measures, 214
  program highlights, 185–190
  projects related to increasing representation of minorities, 202
  recommendation concerning, 9, 11, 226
  and San Diego State University (SDSU), 191
  for undergraduate and graduate business training, 191
Central Intelligence Agency, 48–49, 64, 122, 360
Charles Rangel International Affairs Graduate Fellowship Program, 205, 207
CIBER, CIBE. See Centers for International Business Education and Research program

CIBER network, 184–185
  Association for International Business Education and Research (AIBER), 185
  legislative and administrative supports, 184–185
  network activities, 185
CIBERWeb, 176, 184, 195, 211
Civilian Linguist Reserve Corps (CLRC), 231
Coalition for International Education (CIE), 222
Cold War, 18
Collaborative approaches, to conducting outreach, 106
Commission on Foreign Languages and International Studies, 67n. 6, 283
Commission on Higher Education, 66, 223
Committee for Economic Development (CED), 39, 97
Committee on Science, Engineering, and Public Policy, 77
Committee About Teaching on Asia, 106
Committee to Review the Title VI and Fulbright-Hays International Education programs, 23–24
  approach to its review, 309–349
  commissioning papers and targeted analyses, 312
  conceptual model, 313–322
  conducting site visits, 92, 148, 190, 223, 313
  evaluation study summary, 324–331
  open committee sessions, 335–340
  site visit interview guide, 341–349
  summary, 323
  written comments submitted, 332–334
Common European Framework of Reference for Languages, 237n. 4
Competition results
  in LRCs, 71
  in NRCs, 71, 144
  recommendation concerning, 11, 227
Competitive grants, 294
Competitive priorities, 73, 350
Computer-assisted screening tool (CAST), 136, 180
Computer networks, 173
Computerized Oral Proficiency Instrument (COPI), 236

Conceptual model, in committee review, 24, 313–322
Congress. *See* Legislative history; U.S. Congress
Congressional Budget Office, 123
Congressional Research Service (CRS), 48, 63–64
Consortium for Language Learning and Teaching, 132
Consortium in Latin American Studies, 106
Continuing and Emerging National Needs for the Internationalization of Undergraduate Education, 331
Continuous improvement, future needs, 221–223, 226
    recommendation concerning, 9, 11, 226
COPI. *See* Computerized Oral Proficiency Instrument
Cornell University, 158–159, 179
Council of American Overseas Research Centers (CAORC), 221, 331
Council of Directors of National Foreign Language Resource Centers, 105, 221
Council of Middle East Outreach Directors, 101
Council of NRC Directors, 93, 221
Course development, in the BIE program, 192
Criteria and weights
    in BIE, 357
    in CIBER, 357
    in IRS, 359
    in LRCs, 355
    in NRCs, 354
Critical languages, 4–6, 22–23, 29, 43, 52–53, 127, 131
    priorities in, 30
    varying definitions of, 30, 281
Cross-cultural competence, 43
Cross-national communications, 174
CRS. *See* Congressional Research Service
Curriculum development, in the BIE program, 193

D

David L. Boren National Security Education Act, 62, 281

DDRA. *See* Doctoral Dissertation Research Abroad
Dearborn Public Schools, 132, 232
Defense Language Institute (DLI), 6, 25, 29, 59, 127, 136, 149–152, 327, 360, 370
    LCTLs offered, 152
Defense Language Transformation Roadmap, 53, 233
Demand
    overall, and Title VI and Fulbright-Hays in the Department of Education, 76
    in specific federal agencies, 50–53
Department of Education Organization Act, 243
Desert Storm, 62
Difficult languages, 154
Digital Media Archive, 92–93
Digital revolution, 172–173
Digital technology, 240
Dissemination, of an enhanced body of knowledge, 188–189
DLI. *See* Defense Language Institute
Doctoral Dissertation Research Abroad (DDRA), 18–19, 72, 120, 133–134, 141, 150, 153–154, 220, 225, 273, 312, 315, 331
    fellowships awarded, 153
    planned performance measures, 215
DoD. *See* U.S. Department of Defense
Duke University, 188

E

E-LCTL Initiative, 130, 327
ED. *See* U.S. Department of Education
Education Amendments of 1972, 275–276
Education Amendments of 1976, 277
Education Amendments of 1980, 277–279
Education for Economic Security Act, 307
Educational needs and teaching gaps, 96–98
Educational Testing Service, 360
EELIAS. *See* Evaluation of Exchange, Language, International and Area Studies database
Electronic outreach, 101
Elementary and Secondary Education Act, 277
Enhanced body of knowledge, 187–189
    dissemination, 188–189

graduate placements, 189
  research, 188
Enrollments. *See* Foreign language
  enrollments
Equitable distribution, of grants, 294
Evaluation
  in creating new programs in
    undergraduate international studies,
    292
  of a foreign language institute, 103
  K-12 outreach activities, 102
  recommendation concerning, 8–9, 11,
    225
  summary of studies in committee
    review, 324–331
Evaluation of Exchange, Language,
  International and Area Studies
  database (EELIAS), 74, 74n. 9,105,
  114–120, 134, 142, 145, 157, 176,
  197, 211–212, 216–221, 218n. 6,
  225, 310, 325
  data transparency in, 218–219
  evolution of, 217
  technical issues with, 217, 311
Export-Import Bank, 306

F

Faculty development
  in the BIE program, 192
  in teaching foreign languages for
    business purposes, 187
Faculty questions, during site visit
  interviews, 346–348
Faculty Research Abroad (FRA), 18, 20,
  62, 90, 134, 141, 153, 273, 315
  planned performance measures, 215
FAO. *See* U.S. Army Foreign Area Officer
  Program
Fastlane, 227
Federal Bureau of Investigation (FBI), 44,
  48–49, 50n. 2, 58–59n. 1, 124–125
  demand in, 50–51
Federal foreign language programs,
  summary of, 365–371
Federal funding, as a catalyst for outreach
  activities, 105
*Federal Funding for International Studies:
  Does It Help? Does It Matter?*, 330
Federal Register, 73, 218, 282

FH. *See* Fulbright-Hays International
  Education Act programs (formally
  known as the Mutual Educational
  and Cultural Exchange Act)
FIPSE. *See* Fund for the Improvement of
  Postsecondary Education
Fisher College of Business, 191
FLAP. *See* Foreign Language Assistance
  Program
FLAS. *See* Foreign Language and Area
  Studies Fellowships
Florida International University, 178, 183
Florida Network for Global Studies, 178
Ford Foundation, 222
Foreign Curriculum Consultants, 273
Foreign Language and Area Studies
  Fellowships (FLAS), 2, 7, 17, 19,
  34, 67–70, 73, 81, 94, 114–116,
  120–121, 127–128, 133–143, 151,
  154, 212, 217, 220, 225, 236, 245,
  311, 315
  disciplines of fellows, 95
  planned performance measures, 214
  recommendation concerning, 10, 138
Foreign language assessment, 246–247
  expanded needs, 234–235
  recommendation concerning, 7–8, 10,
    139
Foreign Language Assistance Program
  (FLAP), 6, 25–26, 61, 132, 208,
  230, 232, 232nn. 1, 2, 242, 277,
  367
Foreign language enrollments, in selected
  languages in U.S. institutions of
  higher education, 55, 56, 57, 130,
  150–151
Foreign languages in the business
  curriculum, 186–187
  development of language teaching and
    testing materials, 187
  faculty development in teaching foreign
    languages for business purposes,
    187
  research on business languages, 187
  teaching foreign languages for business
    purposes, 186–187
Foreign languages programs
  awards in, 69
  programs intended to improve
    instruction in, 322

programs that support centers with a focus on, 321
shortage of experts in, 113
Foreign Service, 204, 206, 235
Foreign Service Institute (FSI), 6, 25, 29, 45, 51–52, 59, 127, 149–152, 234–235, 246, 327, 360, 370
LCTLs offered, 152
FRA. *See* Faculty Research Abroad
Fulbright-Hays International Education Act (FH) programs, 2–3, 9, 16–18, 28–29, 64, 67–68, 72, 98, 101–102, 141, 143, 150–151, 230, 268, 282, 366
allocation history, 72
at the Departments of Education, 61–62
at the Department of State, 61, 65, 366
Fund for the Improvement of Postsecondary Education (FIPSE), 61, 367
Funding
allocations and Title VI and Fulbright-Hays in the Department of Education, 32–34, 68–73
history of, 32–34
sources for NRCs, 145
Future needs, 228–248
award transparency, 223–224, 226–227
conclusions and recommendations, 224–227, 242–248
continuous improvement, 221–223, 226
foreign language assessment, instruction, and technology, 246–248
new demands and opportunities, 233–242
new federal directions, 229–233
program evaluation, 219–220, 225
program monitoring, 212–219, 224–225

G

GAO. *See* Government Accountability Office (formerly known as General Accounting Office)
Garvin School of International Management, 187
General Accounting Office. *See* Government Accountability Office

George Washington University, 100, 177
Georgetown University, 100, 109, 148, 158, 177, 219
Gilman International Scholarship Program, 205–206, 231, 368
Global Business Breakfast Series, 188
Global Business Languages, 187
Global e-commerce training for business and educators, 178
Globalizing Business Schools project, 198
Government Accountability Office (GAO), 47–48, 121, 123, 212
Government demand, 47–53
demand in specific federal agencies, 50–53
Federal Bureau of Investigation, 50–51
federal employment of people with language and area expertise, 48–49
turnover, 49
U.S. Department of Defense, 52–53
U.S. Department of State, 51–52
Government Performance and Results Act (GPRA), 115–116, 192, 213, 217, 314, 329
GPA. *See* Group Projects Abroad
Graduate fellowships, 199
Graduate placements, and an enhanced body of knowledge, 189
Grand Valley State University, 222
Grant amounts
average in LRCs, 70
average in NRCs, 70
Grant conditions, in creating new programs in undergraduate international studies, 291
Grant monitoring process, and Title VI and Fulbright-Hays in the Department of Education, 74
Group Projects Abroad (GPA), 18, 20, 72, 98–99, 101, 133–134, 140, 151, 273, 315
planned performance measures, 215

H

Hawaii World Trade Center, 188
HBCUs. *See* Historically black colleges and universities
Heritage language speakers, 130–133
communities of, 100

Higher Education Act (HEA), 2, 23, 26, 32n. 4, 129, 197, 220n. 8, 221–222, 267, 276, 278
Higher Education Amendments of 1986, 279–280
Higher Education Amendments of 1992, 280–282, 308
Higher Education Amendments of 1998, 282
Historically black colleges and universities (HBCUs), 190, 201
History of foreign language assessment in the United States, 360–364
    comparison between ACTFL and ILR descriptors, 363–364
    comparison between ACTFL guidelines and ILR scale, 362
Homeland security, and U.S. international competitiveness, 186
Hot Potatoes, 241
Hotel Rwanda (motion picture), 108
House Committee on Education and Labor, 277–278
House Permanent Select Committee on Intelligence, 47

I

IB, IBE. *See* International Business Education
ICT. *See* Information and communication technologies
IEA. *See* International Education Act
IEPS. *See* International Education Programs Service
IIPP. *See* Institute for International Public Policy
IIPP fellowship program, 197–201
Illustrations of, 178
ILR. *See* Interagency Language Roundtable
ILR scale, 360–364
Impact, performance measures based on, 213, 314
Implementation challenges, in the BIE program, 194
Implementation Issues and Options for the HEA Title VI and Fulbright Hays Programs, 312n. 6

Incentives for the creation of new programs in undergraduate international studies and foreign language programs, 289–292
    application, 291–292
    authority, 289
    evaluation, 292
    grant conditions, 291
    non-federal share, 290–291
    priority, 291
    special rule, 291
    use of funds, 289–290
Inconsistency across programs, an issue with EELIAS database, 311
Increasing Representation of Minorities in International Service Through International Education Programs, 312n. 3, 324
Indiana University, 110, 162
    tracking Russia and East Europe Specialists at, 122, 180
Individuals, programs that provide funds to, 318
Information and communication technologies (ICT), 171–172, 177
    advances in, 172–174
    digital revolution, 172–173
    implications for Title VI/FH programs, 173–174
    mass communication, 172
    personalized publishing and broadcasting, 173
Informed citizenry
    cultural competencies, 40–41
    disciplines, 41–42
    foreign language, 42
    need for, 39–42
InfoUse, 120, 312
Infusion of foreign languages and area studies into the business curriculum, with the BIE program, 191–194
Inputs, performance measures based on, 213, 314
Institute for International Public Policy (IIPP), 17, 20, 32, 32n. 5, 34, 60n. 2, 67, 86n. 4, 141n. 1, 142, 196–200, 281, 303–306, 310, 315, 318, 324, 326
    authorization, 306
    gifts and donations, 306

internships, 305–306
junior year abroad program, 304–305
masters degree in international
    relations, 305
minority foreign service professional
    development program, 303–304
planned performance measures, 215
projects related to increasing
    representation of minorities, 202
recommendation concerning, 10, 207
report, 306
*Institute for International Public Policy
    Impact Assessment,* 326
Institutional capacity, 190
    in the BIE program, 194
Institutional Resource Development Grant
    Program, 198, 201
Instructional materials, 158–161
    approaches to ensuring relevance and
        quality, 163–169
    conclusions, 169–170
    contribution of Title VI programs
        to strengthening materials
        development, 166–169
    current efforts to ensure the quality of
        language instructional materials,
        164
    evaluating, 167–169
    examples, 158–159
    formats, 160
    intended uses, 158–159
    language focus, 160–161
    materials for instruction, 158
    materials for instructors, 158–159
    materials for students, 159
    producing relevant, 156–170
    scholarly standards, 163
    strengthening development of foreign
        language materials, 164–166
Interagency Language Roundtable (ILR),
    45, 50, 63, 67, 122, 128, 135, 150,
    154–156, 235, 238–239, 246, 360
Interdisciplinary Research on International
    Themes, 144
Internal controls, an issue with EELIAS
    database, 311
Internal Revenue Service, 295–296
International and foreign language studies,
    284–296
    American overseas research centers,
        295–296

authorization of appropriations, 296
equitable distribution of certain funds,
    294–295
findings and purposes, 284–285
graduate and undergraduate language
    and area centers and programs,
    285–287
grants to maintain library collections,
    286
national language and area centers and
    programs authorized, 285–287
outreach grants and summer institutes,
    286–287
special rule with respect to travel, 287
International business education (IB, IBE),
    programs that support, 320
International education, in the university
    environment, 78–79
International Education Act (IEA),
    273–275, 278
International Education Programs Service
    (IEPS), 16, 67, 74, 74n. 9, 110, 212,
    221, 225
    and Title VI and Fulbright-Hays in the
        Department of Education, 67–68
International Monetary Fund, 306
International Research and Studies (IRS)
    program, 2, 17–18, 18n. 2, 21, 64,
        85n. 2, 101, 128, 140–141, 156–
        157, 157n. 3, 160–163, 170, 176,
        218–219, 225, 310, 319, 358–359
    application priorities, 358
    criteria and weights, 359
    Darvazah, a door into Urdu, 180
    illustrations of technology as a content
        enhancer in projects funded by, 180
    language focus, 161
    online diagnostic tests and course
        materials for dialects of Arabic,
        Chinese, and Persian, 180
    planned performance measures, 214
    projects classified as research and
        evaluation, 141
    projects related to increasing
        representation of minorities, 203
    Uzbek-English/English-Uzbek
        Dictionary, 180
International Resource Information System
    (IRIS), 8, 74n. 9, 212n. 2, 217–218
    recommendation regarding, 8, 10, 225

International studies librarian questions, during site visit interviews, 349
Internationalizing higher education, 90–96
Internationalizing K-12 education, 96–104
  educational needs and teaching gaps, 96–98
  electronic outreach, 101
  evaluating K-12 outreach activities, 102
  Group Projects Abroad, 98–99
  National K-12 Foreign Language Resource Center, 100
  NRC and LRC outreach to K-12, 99–102
  outreach priorities, 99
  preparing teachers for international education, 103–104
  review, development, and dissemination of instructional materials, 101–102
  role of Title VI/FH programs in K-12 education, 98–99
  school site programs, 100–101
  Seminars Abroad, 99
  teacher training, 100
Internet, the, 172–173
  courses on, 178
Invitational priority, 73, 350
Iowa State University, 167
Iraq Study Group, 52
IRIS. See International Resource Information System
IRS. See International Research and Studies program

J

JNCL. See Joint National Committee for Languages
Job placements, 114–126
  addressing unmet needs in government, 121–126
  experience in the National Security Education Program, 125–126
  inadequate communication of government needs to the field, 123–124
  matching skills with openings, 125
  in NRCs, 118
  recruitment issues, 124–125
  tracking problems, 120–121
  where graduates are going, 116–120

Joint National Committee for Languages (JNCL), 222
Journal of Language for International Business, the, 187
Junior Summer Policy Institute, 199
Junior Year Study Abroad Program, 199, 306

K

K-12 education, 96–104, 136, 167
K-16 education, 103

L

Language Acquisition Resource Center, 131
Language Across the Curriculum program, 92
Language and Critical Area Studies After September 11, 327
Language and National Security in the 21st Century, 329
Language assessment, new approach needed, 235–237. See also Foreign language assessment
  recommendations concerning, 7, 8, 10, 11, 139, 247–248
Language Materials Project (LMP), 168
Language platforms, 240–242
  recommendation concerning, 8, 11, 247–248
Language proficiency, 128–136
  assessing in FLAS recipients, 134–136
  heritage language speakers, 130–133
  recommendations concerning, 7, 8, 10, 11, 139, 247–248
  and Study Abroad and Foreign Language and Area Studies fellowships, 133–134
Language Resource Centers (LRC), 17, 21, 34, 64, 69–76, 86, 89–93, 98, 101–102, 107, 128, 132, 135–136, 139–141, 145, 149, 156–157, 162, 167, 175, 178, 197, 221–222, 232–233, 288–289, 313, 319, 355–356
  application priorities, 355
  authorized activities, 288
  average grant amounts, 70
  competition results, 71
  conditions for grants, 288–289

criteria and weights, 355
director and deputy questions asked
    during site visit interviews, 344–345
planned performance measures, 214
projects related to increasing
    representation of minorities, 202
recommendations concerning, 9–11,
    111–112, 226
Languages. *See* Conversational language;
    Critical languages; Difficult
    languages; Heritage language
    speakers; Less commonly taught
    languages
Latin American Business Environment, 189
LCTLs. *See* Less commonly taught
    languages
Legislative history, 26–32, 267–308
    broadening the scope, 280–282
    conclusion, 283
    Education Amendments of 1972,
        275–276
    Education Amendments of 1976, 277
    Education Amendments of 1980,
        277–279
    embedding and revising, 276–280
    Higher Education Amendments of
        1986, 279–280
    Higher Education Amendments of
        1992, 280–282, 308
    Higher Education Amendments of
        1998, 282
    International Education Act (IEA),
        273–275
    laying the foundations, 269–276
    Mutual Educational and Cultural
        Exchange Act, 272–273, 278
    National Defense Education Act
        (NDEA), 269–272
    Omnibus Trade and Competitiveness
        Act, 280
Less commonly taught languages (LCTLs),
    7–8, 93, 126–127, 148, 155, 161,
    319, 327
    catalyzing instruction, 148
LMP. *See* Language Materials Project
Los Angeles Unified School District, 100
Lost (television program), 108
Louis Stokes Educational Scholarship
    Program, 205, 207
LRCs. *See* Language Resource Centers

M

Market disequilibrium, 37
Mass communication, 172
Master's and Ph.D. graduates, in NRCs,
    119
Master's "graduates" by discipline, in
    NRCs, 94
MESA. *See* Middle East Studies Association
Michigan State University, 101, 132, 158,
    176, 179, 184, 232
Middle East Centers, 100, 118
Middle East Outreach Council, 102, 106
Middle East Studies Association (MESA),
    55, 106, 129
Middlebury College, 199
Minorities in international service
    Charles Rangel International Affairs
        Graduate Fellowship Program, 205,
        207
    Gilman International Scholarship,
        205–206
    IIPP fellowship program, 197–201
    increasing the numbers of
        underrepresented, 196–208
    Louis Stokes Educational Scholarship
        Program, 205, 207
    other federal programs with similar
        goals, 204–206
    projects related to increase in LRCs,
        202
    projects related to increase in NRCs,
        202
    Public Policy and International Affairs
        Fellowship Program, 206
    recommendations concerning, 206–208
    Title VI-funded projects aimed at
        minority students, 201–203
Minority foreign service professional
    development program, 303–304
    application, 304
    definition of eligible recipient, 303–304
    duration, 304
    establishment, 303
    match required, 304
Mobile phone technology, 172
Modern Language Association (MLA), 55,
    78, 148–149, 165, 269, 312
Monitoring. *See* Program monitoring
Moodle, 241
Multimedia Annotator, 241

Multimedia Lesson Builder, 241
Mutual Educational and Cultural Exchange Act, 272–273, 278. *See also* Fulbright-Hays International Education Act programs

N

National Academies, 77, 222
National Capital Language Resource Center, 136, 158, 177
National Center for Education Statistics, 57, 98
National Commission on Asia in the Schools, 97
National Commission on Terrorist Attacks Upon the United States, 48
National Council of Area Studies Associations (NCASA), 55n. 6
National Council of Organizations of Less Commonly Taught Languages (NCOLCTL), 148
National Cryptologic School, 370
National Defense Education Act (NDEA), 18, 26, 28, 129, 171–172, 267–274, 278
National Flagship Language Program (NFLP), 57, 63, 132, 230–232, 242
National Foreign Language Assessment and Technology Project, recommendation concerning, 8, 11, 247–248
National Foreign Language Center, 217
National Geographic/Roper Survey, 97
National Heritage Language Center, 132
National K-12 Foreign Language Resource Center, 100, 136, 167
National Language Conference, 130
National Language Service Corps, 230
National Online Early Language Learning Assessment, 136
National Research Council, 2, 37, 92
National Resource Centers (NRC), 2–3, 9, 21–25, 34, 67, 71–76, 80, 85n. 1, 86, 89–95, 98, 101–106, 110, 114–116, 121–123, 128, 130, 133–156, 162, 175, 181, 197, 200, 212, 217, 221, 233, 312–313, 319, 352–354
    application priorities, 352–353
    average grant amounts, 70

    competition results, 71, 144
    criteria and weights, 354
    director and deputy questions during site visit interviews, 342–344
    funding sources, 145
    job placements of graduates, 118
    master's and Ph.D. graduates, 119
    master's "graduates" by discipline, 94
    numbers by world area and tier, 75
    planned performance measures, 214
    projects related to increasing representation of minorities, 202
    recommendations concerning, 9–11, 111–112, 226
    students in LCTLs enrolled at, 150–151
National Science Foundation (NSF), 163, 166, 174, 227, 305
National Security Agency (NSA), 44, 125, 205
National security considerations, 1, 4–5, 28–30, 129, 137
National Security Council, 306
National Security Education Act. *See* David L. Boren National Security Education Act
National Security Education Program (NSEP), 6–7, 23, 25, 57, 60–64, 81, 123, 125, 131, 137, 150, 230–232, 242, 245, 366
National Security Language Initiative (NSLI), 4, 6, 23, 29, 64n. 4, 66, 187, 228, 231–232, 242–244
    components of proposed, 230–231
    future role, 231–232
National Virtual Translation Center, 58–59n. 1
NCASA. *See* National Council of Area Studies Association
NCOLCTL. *See* National Council of Organizations of Less Commonly Taught Languages
NDEA. *See* National Defense Education Act
New Visions in Action, 167
New York University, 92, 131
NFLP. *See* National Flagship Language Program
9/11 Commission, 18, 48, 124
No Child Left Behind Act, 112, 235
North Carolina State University, 180
NRCs. *See* National Resource Centers
NSA. *See* National Security Agency

NSEP. *See* National Security Education
    Program
NSF. *See* National Science Foundation
NSLI. *See* National Security Language
    Initiative

O

Office of International Affairs, 66, 96
Office of International Education, 96
Office of Language Services, 58–59n. 1
Office of Management and Budget (OMB),
    9, 66, 213, 213n. 3, 217, 312
Office of Personnel Management, 124
Office of Planning, Evaluation and Policy
    Development (OPEPD), 120, 220,
    225
Office of Postsecondary Education (OPE),
    16, 61, 66–67, 233
Office of the Director of National
    Intelligence, 5
    recommendation concerning, 7, 11,
        244–246
Office of the United States Trade
    Representative, 306
Ohio State University, 95, 100–101, 144,
    148, 158
    infusion of foreign languages and area
        studies, 96
Oklahoma State Department of Education,
    167
OMB. *See* Office of Management and
    Budget
Omnibus Trade and Competitiveness Act,
    280
Online collaboration, 174
OPE. *See* Office of Postsecondary Education
Open committee sessions, in committee
    review, 335–340
Open-ended questions, an issue with
    EELIAS database, 311
OPEPD. *See* Office of Planning, Evaluation
    and Policy Development
OPI. *See* Oral proficiency interview
*Oral Proficiency Interview Approach to
    Foreign Language Assessment, The,*
    312n. 5
Oral proficiency interview (OPI), 136, 139,
    235, 237–239, 360
    comparability in ratings, 239

conversational language, 238
developmental scale, 239
expense and limited availability, 239
issues with, 238–239
nature of language ability, 239
reliability, 238
validity, 238
Oral Proficiency Rating Scale, 361
Organization of American States, 306
"Other" category used for key questions,
    an issue with EELIAS database, 311
"Outcome approach" logic model, 315
Outcomes
    performance measures based on, 213,
        314
    schematic of all programs showing
        short-term and longer-term, 36, 317
Outputs, performance measures based on,
    213, 314
Outreach Council of the African Studies
    Centers, 106
Outreach to other audiences, 107–110
    activities, 105–106
    in the BIE program, 193
    business, 109–110
    challenges, 104–105
    collaborative approaches, 106
    conducted, 104–106
    federal funding as a catalyst for
        outreach activities, 105
    government, 109
    heritage communities, 107–108
    media, 108–109
    priorities, 99
    public, the, 110
Outreach World, 102, 162, 176
Overlap in activities, of three federal
    foreign language and area studies
    programs, 65
Overseas Private Investment Corporation,
    306
Overseas study, 133–134
    recommendation concerning, 10, 138
    support for research, education and
        training, 150–153

P

Pacific Basin Economic Council, 188
PART. *See* Program Assessment Rating
    Tool

Partnership for Public Service, 124–125
Pat Roberts Intelligence Scholars Program,
    60, 369
Peace Corps, 126, 360, 367
Pennsylvania State University, 159
Performance measures, 213–216, 226
    categories of, 213, 314
    planned measures, 214
    recommendation concerning, 226
Personalized publishing and broadcasting,
    173
Pickering Program. *See* Thomas Pickering
    Foreign Affairs Fellowship Program
Pittsburgh Science of Learning Center, 174
Portland Public Schools, 232
PPIA. *See* Public Policy and International
    Affairs Fellowship Program
President's Commission on Foreign
    Language and International Studies,
    212
Priorities
    absolute, 73, 350
    in CIBER application process, 356
    competitive, 73, 350
    in critical languages, 30
    invitational, 73, 350
    in IRS application process, 358
    in LRC application process, 355
    in NRC application process, 352–353
*Producing International Expertise in MBA
    Programs,* 328
Proficiency. *See* Foreign language
    assessment; Language proficiency;
    Oral proficiency interview;
    Simulated oral proficiency interview
Program Assessment Rating Tool (PART),
    213, 213n. 3, 220, 220n. 8, 310, 312
Program evaluation, future needs,
    219–220, 225
Program monitoring, 212–219, 224–225
    EELIAS database, 216–219
    future needs, 212–219, 224–225
    IRIS, 8, 74n. 9, 212n. 2, 217–218
    performance measures, 213–216
    recommendations concerning, 6–8,
        10–11, 225, 243–244
Provost/senior international officer
    questions, during site visit
    interviews, 341–342
Public Policy and International Affairs
    Fellowship Program (PPIA), 206–207
Purdue University, 184–185, 187

R

REEI. *See* Russian and East European
    Institute
Report to Congress, recommendation
    concerning, 7, 11, 244–246
Request for applications (RFA), 73,
    350–351
Research
    into an enhanced body of knowledge,
        188
    on business languages, 187
Reserve Officers' Training Corps, 131
Review, committee's approach to, 309–349
RFA. *See* Request for applications
Ribicoff, Abraham, 273
*Rising Above the Gathering Storm:
    Energizing and Employing America
    for a Brighter Future,* 38
Russian, East European, and Eurasian
    Studies (REEES) Consortium, 178
Russian and East European Institute
    (REEI), 122, 162

S

SA. *See* Seminars Abroad
San Diego State University, 92, 107, 131,
    136, 180
    developing and disseminating
        curriculum, 93
School site programs, 100–101
Schools and Staffing Survey, 57, 98
Science and Mathematics Access to Retain
    Talent (SMART), 66
*Securing Our Nation's Future Through
    International Business Education,*
    328
Security. *See* National security considerations
Selection criteria and priorities in Title
    VI and Fulbright-Hays programs,
    350–359
    absolute priority, 73, 350
    CIBER, 356–357
    competitive priority, 73, 350
    invitational priority, 73, 350
    IRS, 358–359
    LRC, 355–356
    NRC, 352–354
Selection of certain grant recipients, 294
    competitive grants, 294

equitable distribution of grants, 294
selection criteria, 294
Self-assessment, recommendation
    concerning, 7–8, 10, 139
Seminars Abroad (SA), 18, 20, 62, 99, 101,
    140, 156, 273, 315
    planned performance measures, 215
Senate Committee on Foreign Relations,
    273
Senate Committee on Labor and Human
    Resources, 196, 278, 281
September 11, 2001, 1, 22, 29, 47, 50,
    100–101, 186, 222. *See also* 9/11
    Commission
Simulated oral proficiency interview
    (SOPI), 235–236
Site visit interview guide, 341–349
    CIBER director questions, 346
    in Committee review, 341–349
    faculty questions, 346–348
    international studies librarian questions,
        349
    key to eight areas of review, 341
    LRC director and deputy questions,
        344–345
    NRC director and deputy questions,
        342–344
    provost/senior international officer
        questions, 341–342
    student questions, 348–349
    topics addressed in every interview, 341
Site visits, 92, 148, 190, 223, 313
Slavic Review, 147
SMART. *See* Science and Mathematics
    Access to Retain Talent
"Social demand," 37
Social Science Research Council (SSRC),
    85n. 2, 218
Sophomore Summer Policy Institute, 199
SOPI. *See* Simulated oral proficiency
    interview
Special Operations Forces Language Office,
    371
Sputnik satellite, 26
SSRC. *See* Social Science Research Council
Stokes Educational Scholarship Program,
    60, 81, 204, 207, 368
Student questions, during site visit
    interviews, 348–349
Study Abroad and Foreign Language and
    Area Studies fellowships, 133–134

Summary of federal foreign language
    and area studies programs, 323,
    365–371
    Abraham Lincoln Study Abroad
        Fellowships, 369
    Defense Language Institute, 370
    Foreign Language Assistance Program,
        367
    Foreign Service Institute, 370
    Fulbright Program, 366
    Fund for the Improvement of Post-
        secondary Education, 367
    Gilman International Scholarship
        Program, 368
    National Cryptologic School, 370
    National Security Education Program,
        366
    Pat Roberts Intelligence Scholars
        Program, 369
    Peace Corps, 367
    Special Operations Forces Language
        Office, 371
    Stokes Educational Scholarship
        Program, 368
    Title VI/Fulbright-Hays, 369
    Title VIII Program, 368
Summer Language Institute, 199
Support for research, education and
    training, 140–155
    conclusions, 153–155
    dissemination of knowledge, 146–147
    enhancing the body of knowledge in
        FLAS, 142–147
    leverage, 144–146
    overseas study, 150–153
    research capacity and prestige, 142–144
    support for less commonly taught
        languages, 148–150

T

Teacher training, 100
Technical issues with EELIAS database,
    217, 311
Technological Innovation and Cooperation
    for Foreign Information Access
    (TICFIA), 17, 21, 64, 76, 156, 159,
    168, 175–181, 282, 293–294, 311,
    319, 325
    application, 294

authority, 293
authorized activities, 293–294
match required, 294
planned performance measures, 215
Technology
in the Center for Advanced Research on
Language Acquisition, 178
as a content enhancer, 177
as a delivery tool, 176–177
in the Florida Network for Global
Studies, 178
global e-commerce training for business
and educators, 178
illustrations of, 178
and instruction, 237–240, 247–248
language platforms, 240–242
recommendation concerning, 8, 11,
247–248
in the Russian, East European,
and Eurasian Studies (REEES)
Consortium, 178
*Technology and Instructional Materials
in Title VI and Fulbright-Hays
International Education Programs,*
312n. 4, 325
Terrorism, threat of, 186, 222
Texas A&M University, 191
Thomas Pickering Foreign Affairs
Fellowship Program, 60, 204, 207
Three Decades of Excellence 1965-1994,
331
Thunderbird Center for International
Business, 187
TICFIA. *See* Technological Innovation
and Cooperation for Foreign
Information Access
Title VI and Fulbright-Hays (Title VI/FH)
programs, 1–6, 13–81, 22–25, 32–
37, 32n. 5, 54, 57–61, 64, 81–86,
89–91, 104, 110–116, 123–130,
133, 136–141, 144–146, 149–150,
153–161, 164, 166, 169, 171, 184,
196–197, 203, 209, 211–212, 217,
228–229, 245–248, 267–269, 329,
369
appropriations for, 33
brief history and federal context, 26–34
charge to the committee, 23–26
conclusion, 81
current controversies, 22–23

demand for foreign language, area, and
international expertise, 36–57
in the Department of Education, 66–76
evaluation study summary, 324–331
implementation, 58–81
legislative time line of current, 27
list of, 19–21
meeting national needs, 18–23
planned performance measures, 214–215
recommendation concerning, 9–11,
208, 226
in relation to other federal programs,
58–65
selection criteria and priorities in,
350–359
and the university context, 76–81
Title VI BIE Funding: A Survey of
Success, 328
Title VI of the Higher Education Act (Title
VI) institutions
cumulative placements of Slavic and
Middle Eastern Studies students,
116–117
dissertations in Slavic and Middle
Eastern Studies, 129
expanding Arabic instruction, 131
graduate and undergraduate
enrollments in most popular
language courses, 130
projects related to increasing
representation of minorities,
202–203
Title VI of the Higher Education Act (Title
VI) programs, 2–3, 9, 16–17, 24–25,
29, 61, 68, 70, 92, 95–96, 105, 109,
112, 116, 119, 127, 129, 133, 137,
143–154, 169, 171, 268, 325, 327
aimed at minority students, 201–203
allocation history for, 68
benefits and complexities of funding,
79–81
LCTLs offered, 152
and the National Security Education
Program, 62–64
proportion of applications funded, 77
unique components of, 64–65
Title VIII Program, 368
Tomsk State University, 96, 144
Transparency, in the EELIAS database,
218–219

Tribally Controlled Community College
Assistance Act, 304–305
Turnover concerns, 49

U

Undergraduate International Studies and
Foreign Language (UISFL) Program,
17, 21, 32n. 4, 64, 76, 90–92, 140,
146, 154, 178, 194, 276, 289–292,
319, 330–331
funding support, 292
incentives for the creation of new
programs in undergraduate
international studies and foreign
language programs, 289–292
planned performance measures, 214
programs of national significance, 292
United Nations, 306
United Negro College Fund, 86n. 4,
197–198, 200–201, 326
United States Information Agency, 306
University context of Title VI and Fulbright-
Hays implementation, 76–81
benefits and complexities of Title VI
funding, 79–81
challenges for international education,
78–79
University of Arizona, 158
University of California, Los Angeles, 91,
100–101, 108–110, 131–132, 158,
162, 168, 176, 179
University of Chicago, 179
University of Connecticut, 185–186,
188–189
University of Florida, 178, 188
University of Hawaii, 167, 183, 188
University of Iowa, 103, 178
University of Kansas, 179
University of Maryland, 199
University of Minnesota, 166, 178
University of New Mexico, 127
University of North Carolina, 102
University of Oregon, 136, 232
University of Pennsylvania, 101
University of Richmond, 146
University of South Carolina, 183
University of Texas, 187
University of the Incarnate Word, 201
University of Virginia, 179
University of Washington, 56, 98, 188, 201

University of Wisconsin, 159, 179, 241
University officials, recommendation
concerning, 9, 11, 226
U.S. Army Foreign Area Officer (FAO)
Program, 127
U.S. Congress, 2, 7, 23–24, 26, 89, 114,
268, 309
program areas to be addressed in
responding to, 316
recommendation concerning, 7, 11,
244–246
U.S. Department of Agriculture, 189
U.S. Department of Commerce, 16, 48, 193
U.S. Department of Defense (DoD), 5–6,
22, 44, 52, 57, 62–63, 121, 123,
125–126, 132, 137, 168, 232–233,
243
demand in, 52–53
recommendation concerning, 7, 11,
244–246
U.S. Department of Education (ED), 2–9,
15–17, 64, 73–74, 81, 84, 98, 103,
112, 115–116, 115n. 3, 119–120,
128, 132–145, 151n. 5, 156, 162,
166, 168, 182, 197n. 1, 211, 217,
223–224, 228–229, 233, 242–244,
270, 281–282, 330, 350
FH programs at, 61–62
future role, 232–233
recommendations concerning, 6–11,
111–112, 138–139, 208, 225–227,
243–244
U.S. Department of Education (ED)
and Title VI and Fulbright-Hays
implementation, 66–76
application process, 73–74
center grants, 74–76
funding allocations, 68–73
grant monitoring process, 74
International Education Programs
Service, 67–68
overall demand, 76
U.S. Department of Health, Education, and
Welfare, 273
U.S. Department of State, 5–6, 22, 25,
28n. 3, 41, 48–49, 51n. 3, 58–59n.
1, 60–62, 123, 125–127, 196, 200,
204–205, 243, 306
demand in, 51–52
FH programs at, 61–62
recommendation concerning, 7, 11,
244–246

U.S. Export Assistance Centers, 189, 193
U.S. Freedom Support Act, 123
U.S. Information Agency, 29
U.S. military, 48–49, 118
U.S. News & World Report, 147, 183, 191

V

Virtual conferences, 174

W

Wall Street Journal, the, 41
Washington Institute for Near East Policy,
    219
WebCT, 241
Weighting. *See* Criteria and weights
What Works Clearinghouse, 112
Wisconsin International Outreach
    Consortium, 106

Woodrow Wilson Fellowships in Public
    Policy and International Affairs.
    See Public Policy and International
    Affairs Fellowship Program
WordChamp.com, 241
World Affairs Council, 188
World Bank, the, 306
"World languages," 15n. 1
World Trade Center attacks. *See*
    September 11, 2001
World War II, 31
Written comments submitted, in committee
    review, 332–334

Y

Yale University, 179
Young Americans, 41–42